Away

Away

The Indian Writer
as an Expatriate

Edited by
Amitava Kumar

Routledge
New York

Published in 2004 by
Routledge
29 West 35th Street
New York, NY 10001
www.routledge-ny.com

Published in Great Britain by
Routledge
11 New Fetter Lane
London EC4P 4EE
www.routledge.co.uk

Library of Congress Cataloging-in-Publication Data

Away : the Indian writer as an expatriate / edited by Amitava Kumar.
  p. cm.
  ISBN 0-415-96896-8 (acid-free paper) — ISBN 0-415-96897-6 (pbk. : acid-free paper)
  1. Indic literature (English)—Foreign countries—History and criticism. 2. East Indians—Foreign countries—Intellectual life. 3. Emigration and immigration in literature.
4. Expatriation in literature. I. Kumar, Amitava, 1963–
PR9485.45 .A93 2004
823.009'954—dc22   2003019121

For my parents

CONTENTS

PART II

ACKNOWLEDGEMENTS

My thanks to Kamini Mahadevan at Penguin India who, along with Kai Friese, came up with the idea for this book; my editor at Routledge, Bill Germano, who supported the project from the moment it was first brought to him; several of the writers included in these pages, some of whom are my friends, who helped with the process of getting permission for publication; Poulomi Chatterjee at Penguin India who painstakingly went over each detail at every step of the production process; my sister Divya, and her daughter, Mishu, who have often asked me to name books by Indian writers describing their lives abroad; and in Patna, my parents, Ishwar Chandra Kumar and Lakshmi Nidhi Singh, to whom this anthology is dedicated, for having borne without complaint the costs of my going away.

Longing and Belonging

You meet Indian writers in the strangest places.

I was once in the Mojave Desert in California with friends who were spending their winter vacation in a wooden cabin. There were Joshua trees all around us, thick cacti standing solidly in the sand. It was New Year's Eve and my American friends had lit a bonfire outside. We were asked to write down our wishes for the New Year on slips of paper and then throw the scraps into the fire.

A middle-aged man in a tracksuit flung on the flames what looked like a letter; a woman bent down and placed on the fire a navy-blue kite; my hosts had fashioned elaborate wish lists bound together with many-coloured threads. What was I going to do?

From my car I took out the Rand McNally road map of the United States. I found the page that had the map of the state of Indiana; I cut out only the part that said INDIA. This was what I would throw in the fire: I wanted to go back home. It was my only wish for the New Year.

Another guest, an older woman I had met at that party, saw what I was doing to my road map. She laughed. 'I so very much want to go to India,' she said. 'Our book club has been reading Vikram Seth's *A Suitable Boy* …'

Indian writers are ubiquitous in the West. But, now, as I think back on that night in the desert, I am reminded of something else. I had wanted to return to India so that I could begin work on a book. I wanted to write about the landless labourers in Bihar, the men from my ancestral village who migrated each summer to the rock quarries and wheat fields of Punjab. I had decided that *they* were the real migrants, not I. What did I know about the pains of leaving home to work? After all, I had a Rand McNally road map with me. Also, unlike the workers who left the village to board a train that took them to the western plains over several days, I had in my possession a rented Honda. On its hood, while I slowly cut out a section of a page from the atlas, rested my gleaming glass of Chianti. And besides, I was warm with the dream of becoming a writer.

As I recall that night, I am struck once again by how often Indian—or desi—writers in the West return to India in what they write. This is not simply a case of nostalgia. Distance produces a shift in perspective, and the immigrant writers find that they are discovering not only the new country, but also the place that they have left behind. A new India is explored and mapped in the imagination of the writer abroad.

However, there is another reason why Indian writers, through their writing, repeatedly make their way back to the Indian subcontinent. What the writers miss, I suspect, is the 'authentic Indian', which they fear they themselves are not. I include myself in this group, and recognize that this is a different kind of nostalgia.

On occasion, a writer of Indian origin based in the West is himself confused for the typical, representative Indian. At such moments, especially if there is very little space for developing distinctions, the nervous writer throws the eight arms of the narrative around the toiling poor and holds up the 'real India' for everyone else to see. A few good writers escape this problem. Most others in the diaspora, many of whom are celebrated as good writers, don't. They produce sentimental fiction from a great distance.

In the 1930s, expatriate Indians like Sajjad Zaheer and Mulk Raj Anand had founded the Progressive Writers' Association in London. Anand, for example, in novels like *Coolie*, made an attempt to represent the Indian underclass in English fiction. Closer to the end of the twentieth century, we have witnessed the emergence of a new brand of diasporic Indian writing with its similar evocation of the 'real India', magical or otherwise. This has won our writers many readers but has also raised a number of questions.

A silly question whose answer is often assumed in advance is whether the desi writer settled abroad can ever write well about India. An earlier, more moth-ridden variant is whether it is possible to write well about India in English. And the answer to both is assumed to be no. Anyone who has read any good literature, and not necessarily by Indian writers, wouldn't pose such questions.

However, there are more thoughtful inquiries that can be addressed to the new Indian writing from abroad.

In the seventies, Adil Jussawalla wrote in his introduction to *New Writing in India* that the literature around him reflected 'the Indian petty bourgeoisie's present inability to find a dynamic role for itself in a society which is slowly transforming itself from the semi-feudal to the capitalist'. At the same time, for Jussawalla, the members of this writing class, caught between their employers and the broad masses beneath them, were also capable of 'a bold experimenting with forms, a sincere desire to expose social evils and a conscious attempt to rework traditional myths and symbols in a modern context'.

Today, even if we regard only those writers who live in India, there has been a dramatic shift in fortunes. A part of this shift can be understood in a vulgar way as a better integration of the Indian market with world capitalism. The Indian writers, certainly those who write in English, are perched, however precariously, on the ladder of bourgeois upward-mobility. But, there have been more complex changes. The failures of the Indian State in the years after Independence have, paradoxically enough, freed the writer from carrying the twin burdens of idealism and impotence. New promises and new contradictions now demand the writer's attention. The subjects that are taken up do not inevitably have a national or reformist cast to them. Most Indian writers in English are members of that rather elastic stratum called the middle class; more and more, these writers give attention in their stories to the problems of their own class instead of to the imagined woes of the underclass. I do not see this as self-indulgent or solipsistic, I see in it signs of the emergence of the writer's confidence as well as an attempt to exercise his or her will.

This new complexity, as well as the comfort of respectability, opens new spaces of exploration. In a few writers who have earned just recognition, this altered context provides the backdrop for the most striking, and subtle, engagement with the English language; and, in the case of writers like Amit Chaudhuri, a carefully refined language unlocks the whole universe of the bourgeois Indian sensibility as it negotiates a transition from the old to the new.

If we can agree on what I am saying about this changed landscape, we can go on to ask the following question: How does the writer of Indian origin living abroad, which in most cases means living in the West, negotiate longing and belonging?

For a long while—beginning with Rushdie's *Midnight's Children* and all his other novels about India that followed, Seth's *A Suitable Boy*, and Rohinton Mistry's *Such a Long Journey* and *A Fine Balance*—it had begun to appear that Indian writing needed to have the capaciousness that was generally granted to the Indian nation itself. It had seemed to me at least that the heft of novels was an index of anxiety, and an indication that the expatriate Indian writer had been beset by the need to produce a monumental national narrative. While in the years following Independence, it had been the short story, more than anything else, that had served as the vehicle for newly independent India's literary expression, in the diaspora, the novel had emerged in recent times as the form of choice. Isn't it telling that just when India erupted in a series of separatist struggles, and Indians migrated abroad in large numbers, our writers in the West revived the genre of the omnibus novel? This choice would appear an affectation, if not also the result of arrogance, but we can more sympathetically also easily grasp its pathos.

What makes this pathos ironic is that the diasporic writers have crafted for themselves a script which allows them to be seen as more Indian than the Indians they have left behind. The recent onslaught of books and films around the theme of ABCDs—American Born Confused Desis—does not so much present mixed-up lives. Rather, this hybrid or masala self is held up as an essentially Indian trait, a trait which the Indian abroad is able to embody, and which the rest of the Indians on the subcontinent are supposed to emulate.

However, not all such writers have embraced this role. A few have even sought to depart from the mandatory presentation of Indianness and eschew all marks of easy ethnicity demanded by the Western literary establishment. The best examples are Seth's *The Golden Gate* and *An Equal Music*. In this case, the traveller does not go back to his roots, but branches out to new places where he or she acquires new identities.

The writers in the diaspora are a product of movement. They embody travel. The kind of language that these writers use, especially if one thinks of the manic energy of Rushdie's imagistic prose, conveys the variety of their translated lives. And in their writing they record the enormous richness, and pain, of displacement and loss.

In the closing lines on the last page of Jhumpa Lahiri's *The Interpreter of Maladies*, we come across a touching tribute to that experience. Lahiri has given those lines to an Indian man, her father, who had arrived in America on the day that two Americans had landed on the moon. Recalling that day, the man in the story says,

> While the astronauts, heroes forever, spent mere hours on the moon, I have remained in this new world for nearly thirty years. I know that my achievement is quite ordinary. I am not the only man to seek his fortune far away from home, and certainly I am not the first. Still there are times I am bewildered by each mile I have travelled, each meal I have eaten, each person I have known, each room in which I have slept. As ordinary as it all appears, there are times when it is beyond my imagination.

In some measure, this anthology of essays pays homage to the ordinary experience of migration which can be at once modest and magnificent.

Often, more than their writing about India, it is the portraits of the lands in which they now live, portraits drawn by discerning outsiders, which represent the greatest achievement of the desi writer. This is even truer of those writers who are of Indian origin and have been brought up in the suburbs and cities of the West.

A good example of the genre is Hanif Kureishi's debut novel *The Buddha of Suburbia*, which famously begins with the declaration, 'My name is Karim Amir, and I am an Englishman born and bred, almost.' This present anthology is also a tribute to that voice and its creativity.

One can only hope that as the years pass, desi writers will feel confident to write about the extraordinary complexity that surrounds their new lives. Perhaps I am speaking of a time when the new lives will no longer be new. What will be new about them will not be their ethnicity, but their relationship to other aspects of their social being. They will, then, no longer be the diasporic writers.

Then, I will miss the desi writer, but I will also feel excited, I think, about the change. I believe that the change will rescue us from the stereotypical fare, which I have described elsewhere as 'the mistress of spices, the heat and dust, sweating men and women in lisping saris, brought together in arranged marriages, yes, the honking traffic, and the whole hullabaloo in the guava orchard'.

As I write this, my mind goes back to the woman I met in the desert, the one who wanted to travel to India because she had loved *A Suitable Boy*. It strikes me that if she were to undertake her trip today, she would encounter travelogues written by Indian writers living in India. It is not the glossy travel magazines—a sign of the expansion of India's homegrown affluent middle class—that I have in mind. Rather, our traveller would find books that announced new discoveries of India. I am thinking of a book like Arundhati Roy's *The Algebra of Infinite Justice*. Most of Roy's essays are, in a sense, travelogues, accounts of a writer discovering the cost of living in her own country. In writers like Roy one will find that it is not the person in Wembley or New Jersey who is in exile from home, but the Dalit tribal displaced by a large dam that has drowned whole villages.

In those books, our visitor would discover how the Indian writer, at home in English, has made English the home for the remaining part of our lives. The bits and pieces. The engraved lines from the Constitution where the policeman leans his *danda*; the fragments that never made it to the evening news; even the ordinary details of unnoticed lives that were too ordinary, or just too intractable, to find entry in the pages of fiction celebrated abroad.

'There's no place like home.' That particular formulation is an ambiguous one. It suggests that there can be no other place like home, a sentiment often espoused by those who are seen as having gone away; alternatively, it can also mean that the idea of home is a delusion, it never existed in its safely pure form.

The latter meaning appeals to me. It means that India was a place which was never closed to such migration before though it has experienced this movement in a new, aggressive form in recent years, and that writers in India, those who have written in English as also others who write in the so-called vernacular, have understood this very well and always expressed this condition in their work.

This is the reason why this book begins with imaginary journeys. The experience of going away—the journey and its consequences—sometimes get played out only in the imagination of the writer. The pieces that have been selected for the prologue speak to that reality. Nirad C. Chaudhuri writes of the deep preoccupation with England when he was a student in a small town in India. Salman Rushdie's marvellous story about a beautiful young woman's attempt to get a British visa to travel to 'Bradford, London' from India lays out the fears as well as the fantasies that lurk behind whatever it is that compels people, particularly those who are poor, to leave their homes. In the extract from his novel *Shadow Lines*, Amitav Ghosh presents a boy who, while living in Calcutta, has memorized the map of London. A poem by Nissim Ezekiel, describing a farewell to an office worker who is leaving for an unnamed foreign locale, captures in a flawed, idiomatic English both desire and regret, a nostalgia for an escape which, because denied, is not in the future but in the past.

This book ends with a similar insistence on a more complex understanding of home. The epilogue is not a piece of prose about an Indian's life abroad, but a writer's memoir about the noisy world of transnational capital coming to a small town in northern India. It is written by Pankaj Mishra who, coincidentally, has also written a novel about a provincial youth in Benaras, in eastern India, discovering Flaubert and the writings of Edmund Wilson.

Such discoveries of the further world with which the writer is in conversation inaugurate another meaning of the phrase 'there is no place like home'. And the clearest articulation of this meaning comes to us by way of the poet and editor Arvind Krishna Mehrotra who, in his introduction to *An Illustrated History of Indian Literature in English*, writes: 'In 1964, the year Nehru died, the year V.S. Naipaul's *An Area of Darkness* was published, I was sitting in darkness's heart, in a bungalow in Allahabad, in a railway waiting room in Bilaspur, and as scores of Indian poets—from Henry Derozio to Srinivas Rayapol—had done before me, I was taking my bearings from distant stars. The two I took mine from were e.e. cummings and Kahlil Gibran.' More than anything else, *Away* was conceived as a tribute to the wonderful and amazing centrifugal passions, including curiosity, that turn our hearts and our eyes away from home.

May this volume serve only as a point of departure.

A NOTE ON THE SELECTION

I am writing this note in Riverside, California, very close to that cabin in the Mojave Desert where I had met the woman who wanted to go to India because she had been reading *A Suitable Boy*. And here, now, once again, I can say that one meets Indian writers in the strangest places. I have just been given a book by an Indian published in 1889. The book is *A Visit to Europe* and its author is T.N. Mukharji.

Mukharji's book was given to me by my friend Joe Childers, a cultural historian here at the University of California. My friend is studying accounts of nineteenth-century travellers to the heart of whiteness, and in a note on the book's author, he writes: 'The world, at least the Western world, does not remember much about T.N. Mukharji. A Bengali civil servant of the late nineteenth and early twentieth centuries, his mark on the history of empire is now only barely legible, requiring a very particular sort of knowledge even to recognize let alone to decipher it.'

The distance that is suggested in those words hints at what we might call the pre-history of Indian writing abroad. Part I of *Away* presents the writings of a wide variety of individuals, a few of whom are not what one conventionally thinks of as Indian writers. But their published pieces have been chosen because they serve as a record of earlier travels that were undertaken by Indians to the West. Dean Mahomed, for example, was born in Patna and travelled to eighteenth-century Ireland, and then to England. He opened a bath in Brighton and introduced a novel method of shampooing to the British. His advertisements open this section primarily because he has been described as 'the first Indian author in English'.

Sunity Devee, the Maharani of Cooch Behar, offers an account of her visit to England, including her candid display of loyalty to Queen Victoria. Her travelogue presents perhaps the earliest report of an

Indian woman's journey abroad. Rabindranath Tagore, who was later to be awarded the Nobel Prize for literature, describes his first journey on an aeroplane. Tagore was using the newly invented 'flying machine' to make his way to Persia. The other travel pieces and letters that have been selected include Tagore's enthusiastic account of a visit to Bolshevik Russia and his version of the process through which a Bengali makes himself a citizen of London.

The excerpts from Mahatma Gandhi's *Autobiography* narrate two different phases of his travels abroad: his trip to England to study law, and the journey to South Africa and his life-changing encounter with indentureship and racism. Such narratives foreshadow the theme of nationalism, or more properly, the discovery of nationalism, that was soon to emerge in Indian writing in English (as in Raja Rao, for instance).

Sarojini Naidu's letters to her husband and also to Edmund Gosse, written from London, represent a young Indian woman's delight in poetry as also her loneliness away from home. In more mature ways, Subhas Bose and Mulk Raj Anand, also new to life in England, offer in their letters and reminiscences an encounter with the West that is filled with excitement and unease. Bose and Anand were in England as students, but they could not merely be students. The nationalist movement gaining force in India could not leave them untouched. Their writings convey an ambivalence about the West, but often, it is more than that, it is a bold rejection that they are also able to embody. Today, this ambivalence finds its echo in new forms in contemporary Indian writing; the gesture of rejection, however, is not by itself considered desirable or even viable in such writing. I regard this as a part of the strength and maturity of writers in post-Independence India.

The letters written by Jawaharlal Nehru to his sister are different from Bose's because they are from a later period, the late thirties, and they represent a leader in pre-Independence India who is already speaking with great confidence to audiences in very different parts of the world. This is a writer who is burdened not with an inhibiting self-consciousness—except in the letter from Hanoi where he writes that the drawstring of his pyjama has snapped, and he has had to hold on to his garment during a press conference—but with an urgency to communicate India's needs to the people with whom he is meeting.

A bit of this excitement, and also the difficulties of negotiating the challenges that the prospect of independence is bringing, is given vivid form in the extract from Qurratulain Hyder's *River of Fire*. This extract details the debates of the 'red Indians' in England who talk about art and revolution in their home country and who try, with varying success, to make those changes mesh with the shifts in the smaller spaces of their own personal lives.

R.K. Narayan's writing opens Part II. Narayan's stories of his visit to America, his first visit, when he was already fifty, are not as exuberant as his contemporary G.V. Desani's. But Narayan, through his difference from later Indian writers, offers a valuable record of a sensibility that preserved its limits. This contrast between an insular and a more outward-looking attitude is illustrated in the different outlooks and styles of Narayan and Dom Moraes. Moraes had no special affection for India, and was happy to leave. In the brief memoir published in this volume, Moraes describes his arrival in England as a teenager and his other global travels. The story of Moraes's return to India is tinged not so much with failure as with a sense that the West can be cruel even to those who have made their homes in its cities. India, as the place of origin, has no choice but to play the role of home.

Farrukh Dhondy's memoir about reading Naipaul in India and wanting to be a writer, and his transformations in the England of the sixties and the seventies, offers an instructive lesson about writing. Dhondy learns that he cannot go on seeking his audience in the ghetto of the diaspora: 'Winning sympathy for oneself through writing defeats the ironical object of writing. Gaining the reader's sympathy for one's characters, good ones and bad ones, as perhaps Dickens does, and George Eliot, Tolstoy, D.H. Lawrence and Joseph Conrad do, is a better way to write.'

Ved Mehta and A.K. Ramanujan were two of the most important post-Independence Indian writers in the US. In his article which was originally published in the *New Yorker*, Mehta reports on the experience of applying for citizenship in America. Ramanujan's poem, which is made up of several parts, puts Indian travellers in different places and different times in history. Sharp and ironical, Ramanujan's images tell a story of India and Indian commodities: in a few lines, the poet sketches a history of Indian travel, ancient as well as modern, which is full of unexpected turns and discoveries.

These older lines of travel that Ramanujan sketches between places and dates, lines which we had encountered also in Gandhi's writings on South Africa, come alive most forcefully in the writings of V.S. Naipaul, especially when he addresses the history of Indian indentureds in Trinidad. The selected excerpt from Naipaul's *The Enigma of Arrival* is a moving account of the writer's journey to Trinidad to attend his sister's funeral; the narrative is also about the way in which rituals, especially among immigrant communities, travel across time and place. Naipaul's meditation is profound because it captures so well the pain of sustaining faith in a past that might have become attenuated in a diasporic space away from the place of origin.

Salman Rushdie's most famous traveller is arguably Gibreel Farishta who transforms London into a tropical city by divine decree. Farishta's transformative decree from on high mirrors the secular changes that Indian migrants have already introduced in the English lifestyle, and through him the writer pays homage to the enormous energies of the ordinary people. For the purposes of this collection, however, I have chosen from Rushdie's writings a portion about a visit to Sandinista-ruled Nicaragua. Here we are shown an image of the Indian writer as a traveller not to the West but to other areas of the so-called Third World, and we are lucky to get an account that is lyrical as well as defiant. In his more recent writings, especially after the attacks on the Twin Towers, Rushdie has turned his back on his earlier criticism of America. His celebratory view of America was anticipated in some ways by another Indian writer, slightly older than Rushdie, who had travelled to the US as a student. This is Bharati Mukherjee and she, more than any other desi writer, has served as the model, whether for good or bad, of the Indian immigrant's invention of America as a site of newness and liberation. Her essay in this volume, which was first published in the *New York Times*, pays homage to the narrow ideal of assimilation. But Mukherjee's piece also provides a powerful reminder that the two emotions—the impulse to assimilate, and the desire to resist—are often found very close to each other, between two sisters for instance, and perhaps even within one single self.

This section ends with two pieces that, among other things, capture the sexual anxieties as well as ambitions of Indian immigrants. Hanif Kureishi's 'Wild Women, Wild Men', originally published in *Granta*, is a remarkable, disturbing, account of a lesbian double-act at a party in Southall. All the participants are Asians from India and Pakistan. The narrative is not without humour but it is shot through with emotional, and also physical, violence. This is followed by Abraham Verghese's 'The Cowpath to America' which has the charm of an adolescent dream, although it concerns grown men, mostly medical interns, and their ambitions of making it to America. Laced with comedy and despair, Verghese's essay is a fine account of the hunger for an American visa among Indian professionals.

In Part III, an extract from Amit Chaudhuri's novel *Afternoon Raga* introduces the reader to Indian migrants in England. The extracts are about the lives of Indian students at Oxford and the ways in which their distinct, but shared, destinies are entangled. Chaudhuri writes: 'Strange place, Oxford, and strange discoveries one makes within it! . . . Oxford is such a lonely place, such a small place, so few its streets and its landmarks, that those who have felt some affection for each other come together again and again.'

Meera Syal, who like Hanif Kureishi was born in England, has been successful in presenting the experiences of both the first generation of migrants from India and the lives of their children in the new country. In Syal's *Anita and Me*, we hear the narrator's Punjabi father dreamily singing songs from Hindi films in a small British town. While the father sings 'Sajan re jhooth mat bolo', his daughter is at the fair picking up phrases like 'shagging the arse off her'. In *Life Isn't All Ha Ha Hee Hee*, Syal produces a rich narrative of travels into the heart of whiteness: a wedding *baraat* arrives in a part of East London, and the sight of the bridegroom makes an old white man wonder why the Indians have put a Christmas tree on a horse.

In the same section, I have also included brief excerpts from writings about Indians in America. Anurag Mathur's story about a young man who stumbles his way through school in America has been found funny by some; the selected section from the opening pages of Mathur's book is a letter, self-consciously gauche, written by the protagonist to his relatives in India. Anita Desai's *Fasting, Feasting* provides the reader with an ethnographic trip through American suburbia. In the selection, her character, Arun, is taken by his host family to the American supermarket, and he is repulsed by the display of clean, bright, gleaming food, wrapped in plastic. Several preconceptions about the place fall away in this paradoxical response, and, like Arun, the reader discovers those real details that give continuity to the experiences of people who step across the line dividing fasting from feasting, the East and the West. The next piece in the volume is a poem, by the Indian American poet Agha Shahid Ali, about a sign on Route 80 in Ohio that says 'Calcutta'. India, the poet writes, exists off the turnpikes of America. Rohinton Mistry's 'Swimming Lessons' is set in Canada and engagingly addresses not only life in Toronto but its connection to the lives of the narrator's parents in Bombay. Unlike much of Mistry's later writing, this work most overtly comments on the distance between Toronto and Bombay.

The last two pieces in Part III serve as dramatic enactments not only of Indian travels in the West but of our encounter with the paradox of modernity. Amitav Ghosh's tale of his argument with a village imam while Ghosh was in rural Egypt working as a student-researcher, is a record of a meeting between 'delegates from two superseded civilizations, vying with each other to establish a prior claim to the technology of modern violence'. The West, Ghosh writes, 'meant only this—science and tanks and guns and bombs'. This tale of 'a loss of a world of accommodations' is also repeated in the narratives that have begun to come out in the West. In Hanif Kureishi's 'My Son the Fanatic', for example, we find the opposition, not finally between the East and the West, but between the two contrasting notions that a father and a son have about what it means to be human. Like Ghosh's account of the meeting in Egypt, Kureishi's story is also replete with irony, with disappointment, and with a search for solidarity in surprising places. With the appearance of Islamic as well as Hindu fundamentalism among the diasporic desi communities, it is evident that Indian writers are finding imaginative ways of posing questions about what it means to be an Indian abroad. The event of 11 September 2001 presented the world with a shocking vision of travellers in airplanes—all of them migrants—as fanatical killers. But, as always, there are many other smaller stories that a dominant narrative elides. For example, will the hijackings of that fateful September morning erase from public consciousness the presence of other illegal passengers, the humble stowaways from countries like India and Pakistan, whose frozen corpses tumble out of airplanes near the cities of the West? I have taken the liberty of including in this volume my own essay 'Flight' at the close of Part III, in order to emphasize that 'not everyone crosses borders alive, despite the cheerful acceptance of globalization by many governments of the world.'

There were at least a dozen other writers—starting with the incomparable G.V. Desani—that I wanted to include in this volume, but it was not possible to do so because of financial as well as space constraints. I also regret that I was not able to include younger writers of Indian origin whom I have seen reading from their work at desi festivals in places like Toronto and New York City. I am pleased, however, that we have here a collection spanning a wide historical period and also bringing together, for the first time, a record of Indian voices away from India.

Amitava Kumar

PROLOGUE

Nirad C. Chaudhuri

England

What I have written about Shillong leads me naturally to speak of the intangible and exotic element in the ecology of our lives. To us it was absent and yet real, as Shillong was, but its power was immensely greater, for while our conception of Shillong soon reached the perimeter which bounded it, our idea of this other thing never struck against barriers from which it had to recoil. In the end this came to be very much like the sky above our head, without, however, the sky's frightening attribute of vast and eternal silence, for it was always speaking to us in a friendly language in the knowledge of which we were improving from day to day. Perhaps I need not formally proclaim that this was England as we defined and understood it, that is to say, with Scotland, Ireland, and Wales merged in it, and Europe conceived of as its corona.

The story of our preoccupation with England may justifiably give rise to scepticism. I have described the three places which constituted our boyhood's actual environment. If these descriptions have served their purpose, then with the sensation of that environment fresh in mind, one could question the presence in it, not only of any knowledge of England, but also of all means of knowledge. I too shall most readily admit that our means of knowing was as casual as our knowledge was extraordinarily uneven. If I may put it that way, the chiaroscuro of our knowledge of England was extremely sensational. It had intense

This extract is taken from *The Autobiography of an Unknown Indian*, published by Jaico Publishing House, New Delhi, 1963.

highlights in certain places and deep unrelieved shadows in others, so that what we knew gripped us with immeasurably greater power than it would have done had we seen it in more diffused and, consequently, more realistic light. On the other hand, what we did not know was so dark that we could easily people the void with phantasms evoked of our ignorance. In this chapter I shall give some specimens of both kinds, of what was thrown on our mind and what was thrown out by it.

I shall begin with our knowledge of English and personalities. I cannot remember the time when I learned, just as I cannot remember any time when I did not know, the names of Queen Victoria, Prince Albert, Napoleon, Shakespeare, and Raphael. The next series comprising Milton, Burke, Warren Hastings, Wellington, King Edward VII, and Queen Alexandra is almost as nebulous in origin. Lord Roberts, Lord Kitchener, General Buller, Lord Methuen, Botha, and Cronjé entered early, thanks to the Boer war. Next in order came Mr Gladstone, Lord Rosebery, Martin Luther, Julius Caesar, and Osman Pasha (the defender of Plevna in the Russo-Turkish War of 1877–8)—these too belonging to the proto-memoric age. The beginnings of true memory in my case were marked by the names of Fox and Pitt, and Mirabeau, Robespierre, Danton, Marat, Junot (Napoleon's marshal), and also perhaps George Washington. On the literary side, in addition to the names of Shakespeare and Milton which we imbibed unconsciously, we came to know of Homer as soon as we began to read the *Ramayana* and the *Mahabharata*, which was fairly early.

Of course, these names were not just names to us. They possess some meaning and much more of associations. These ideas and associations constituted what I may describe as the original capital of our intellectual and spiritual traffic with the West. As years went by the names acquired ever greater precision and ever greater significance for us, but the process never lost its incompleteness. It has not done so even to this day.

Queen Victoria we thought of as everybody else in England and India thought of her after the Diamond Jubilee, and about the Prince

Consort our ideas were identical with those of the queen herself: he was the paragon of every virtue. But King Edward VII—he was already king before we had acquired the faculty of thinking—we regarded only as an elderly boy. The story we had heard that he was never taken seriously by his mother clung to our memory and prevented our acquiring till many years later even the popular notion of him as an astute diplomatist who had brought about the Anglo-French Entente. On the contrary, we thought of Queen Alexandra as a very gentle, gracious, and beautiful princess. Personally, I formed a notion that she had not been very well treated by the old queen. The origin of this idea is most curious to trace. Very early in life I had read an account in Bengali that soon after her marriage the princess had been distressed over the Prussian invasion of Schleswig and Holstein and had expected her mother-in-law to intervene on the side of Denmark, which of course the queen did not. Combining this detail with the general state of the mother-in-law daughter-in-law relationship in Bengal, my child's mind entertained no doubt that the imperious old queen was something of what we in Bengal called a daughter-in-law-baiting mother-in-law.

Coming to the literary and artistic group, the initial explanation I have to give is that although we had heard the story of King Lear from our mother and knew who it was by, our first notion of Shakespeare was of a man whose writings all grown-up persons were expected to discuss and, what was even more important, to recite. It did not take us long, however, to pass from the rank of spectators to that of participants in the Shakespearean procession. By the time we had learnt a second story by Shakespeare—and that was the *Merchant of Venice*—we were almost ready ourselves to recite both the *Merchant of Venice* and *Julius Caesar.* Our familiarity with the name of Julius Caesar was only a by-product of our knowledge of Shakespeare, and the first idea we formed of the great Roman was in the image of Mr Rames Roy, a top-form boy of Kishorganj High School, who in a black English suit had taken the part of Caesar in a performance of Act III, Scene I, given by the senior students.

Of Homer we had a fuller but less correct notion. We were not so narrowly patriotic as to deny his claim to be the father of poetry, but we made him its joint father with Valmiki, the legendary author of the

Sanskrit *Ramayana*. We knew the name and the story of the *Iliad* and regarded it as the Greek counterpart of our *Ramayana*. It was the obvious parallelisms which deceived us. In both cases there was an abducted woman, Sita in the *Ramayana* and Helen in the *Iliad*. In both cases there were two rescuing brothers, Rama and Lakshmana in the Indian epic and Menelaus and Agamemnon in the Greek. In either case there was a magic car which could pass through the upper air. And last of all, in both instances there was a long struggle round a fortified city before the woman could be recovered and brought back. All the similarities made us think of the spirit of the *Ramayana* and of the *Iliad* as comparable, and this misconception was natural because of the fact that we were told the outlines of the story from a Bengali version which gave no idea of the quality of the original.

Raphael's name we came to know as the painter of the picture above our front door, which we always called by its original Italian name of 'Madonna della Sedia'. We had taken over the word 'Madonna' as equivalent of the mother of Jesus and never translated it into Bengali. 'Raphael's Madonna' had passed into our language as a phrase of almost everyday use, the first part of which was inseparable from the second, for, strange to say, even educated people thought that Raphael was a painter of Madonnas and of nothing else and that all the extant Madonna pictures were by him. But we, even at that early age, were somewhat wiser. Certainly we also spoke of Raphael's Madonnas, of which we had seen a number of monochrome half-tone reproductions in a Bengali magazine. So far as I can remember, they seem to have been reproductions of the 'Madonna della Granduca', 'Madonna della Colonna', 'Madonna in the Meadow', and one or two others, but we also knew that he had painted other kinds of pictures as well, because in the same magazine we had seen reproductions of his 'Knight's Dream' and a self-portrait. This last we took as a final and decisive proof of Raphael's greatness, for we placed a painter's capacity to paint his own portrait on a par with a surgeon's capacity to operate on himself. We knew nothing, however, of the 'Sistine Madonna' or of Raphael's great frescoes; nor did we know the name of any other painter either of Italy or of any other country. Raphael reigned supreme over us, but when after the theft of the 'Mona Lisa' from the Louvre we for the first time learned the name of Leonardo and a few other

Italians, we also picked up with that information the fashionable disparagement of Raphael.

Milton stood before us in solitary and somewhat awe-inspiring grandeur. His claims upon us were manifold. In the first place, he was the author of the bright volume in the glass-fronted cupboard. Secondly, he was the model of Michael Madhusudhan Dutt. Thirdly, he was the writer of a most striking line which my father was fond of repeating and which ran as follows: 'Better to reign in hell than serve in heaven!' Lastly, it appeared he had something to do with the execution of Charles I, who had tried to deprive the English people of their liberties. The idea of Milton as a stern, unbending and powerful champion of liberty was confirmed in our mind by a picture of him we saw in an edition of Macaulay's essay on Milton, which was in the cupboard. It showed him as an old man, with long hair and a deeply lined face, in severely simple puritanical clothes. We knew that the old poet was blind and this added a touch of compassion to our awe of him.

From our admiration of Milton to our admiration of Napoleon there must appear to be a long and difficult passage. We made it with the greatest ease and did not perceive any chasm. If any whole-hearted Bonapartists were to be found anywhere in the world at the end of the nineteenth century and the beginning of the twentieth they were to be found in Bengal. All educated Bengalis literally adored Napoleon and, not satisfied with mere worship, tried to understand his military campaigns. In one of the historical novels by our greatest novelist, Bankim Chandra Chatterji, a not very necessary allusion occurs to the Austerlitz campaign and to Wellington's Salamanca campaign. My father, without having any occasion at all to make a study of the life or the campaigns of Napoleon, had read one or two biographies and the memoirs of some of his marshals. I got from him quite a businesslike summary of the alternative theories of Napoleon's defeat at Waterloo, including the theory of his mental degeneration. Amidst all the wealth of Napoleonic literature it was quite a surprise to discover in one of our cupboards a torn copy of Sir Neil Campbell's *Napoleon at Fontainebleau and Elba*. In the public library of a small place like Kishorganj was to be found even the memoirs of Napoleon's valet, Constant.

As in France, so amongst us too, Louis Napoleon reaped the harvest of our Bonapartism. I made this discovery in the volume of secular songs entitled *Pearl Necklace of Song*, previously referred to. I found in it two songs devoted to the younger Bonaparte family, one purporting to be the speech of Napoleon III to General Wimpffen pointing out the futility of further resistance at Sedan, and the other the dying soliloquy of the Prince Imperial, mortally wounded in a skirmish in the Zulu War. I have forgotten the words of the soliloquy and only remember that it was addressed to his mother, Empress Eugénie, and expressed the Prince's regret that he was dying so far away in a strange land without being able to see her face once again. But I have still got by heart the first two lines of the speech of Napoleon III and give below a French translation, because I find that I can reproduce the metre and the alliterativeness of the original better in that language than in English:

'En vain, Wimpffen! vous voulez
Livrer bataille dans Sedan!'

I would implore the reader not to set down the effect these lines produce on him solely to my inadequate French.

Thanks to this prevalence of Bonapartism amongst us we began to hear of Napoleon quite early in life, and the first picture of him that became fixed in my mind was that of a young artillery commander bending over his guns and laying them. For the siege of Toulon was the point at which my father began our Napoleoniad, initially skipping Corsica, Brienne, and the *Souper de Beaucaire*. I heard of Junot as part of the same story. I was told that during the siege Junot was engaged in writing near a battery and when a shell burst close to him and scattered some sand he coolly remarked that the sand was welcome as a blotter; and that that was the beginning of his friendship with Napoleon.

I have now to disclose a paradox. Although we regarded Napoleon almost as a god, and as invincible and unconquerable by straight-forward methods of warfare, sometimes ascribing his defeat at Waterloo to the bribing of Grouchy, we still came to think of Wellington as the greatest general that ever lived. There are two possible theories on which I can explain this curious self-contradiction. Either we were thinking unconsciously of England only, which, while considering the outer world, we often did, totally forgetting the other European countries, or we were thinking of Napoleon and Wellington on quite different planes. That is to say, when we were thinking of Napoleon we had in mind only transcendental and supra-rational military genius whereas we judged Wellington as the best rational and human general. It is a far-fetched explanation, and perhaps childish self-contradiction calls for no explanation at all.

From Wellington we made an easy descent to Lord Roberts, whom we regarded as the greatest living soldier, with only Lord Kitchener as a second. The Bullers, the Whites, and the Methuens, we sympathized with, but they were defeated generals. The prestige of Lord Roberts and Lord Kitchener with us was immense. Both were victors of the Boer War. In addition, Lord Roberts was the hero of the Afghan War and Kitchener of Omdurman. Kitchener was Commander-in-Chief in India and Roberts in England, fitly dividing between them the military responsibility for the British Empire. With unspeakable disgust we heard from our father that the post of Commander-in-Chief had been abolished in England and an Inspector-General installed in his place. Without knowing anything about Cardwell we were wholly Cardwellian in our military conceptions and thought of the military might of Great Britain as equally distributed between England and India. By the abolition of the post of Commander-in-Chief the English half was to our mind thoroughly disgraced, for a Commander-in-Chief was a man next only to the Viceroy, while an Inspector was only a police inspector and even the highest inspector was no higher than the Inspector of Schools.

The military glory of the two men, however, remained unaffected, and the two panoramic pictures of the Boer War in our West Hut always served to remind us of it. Every few days I asked my brother to climb on the trunks and read out to me the names of the regiments and officers provided in the key below. I listened mechanically to the names of the regiments, which conveyed very little to me, but as soon as my brother came to the commanders I pricked my ears. Standing in front of the Pretoria picture he would say: 'General Roberts, General Kitchener, General Staff, General Staff, General Staff. . . .' 'All General Staff?' I would ask perplexed. 'Yes,' my brother would confirm. Then

I would ask him to explain the other picture, which was more exciting, for it showed the bend of the Modder River, the Boer laager formed by carts in the background, and, filling up the whole foreground, a long line of British guns, not simply flashing, but literally blazing away and bombarding the Boer positions. At the left-hand corner, on a small hillock, was a group of high officers on horseback. 'Who are they?' I enquired of my brother. 'General Kitchener,' he replied. 'And who else?' Again the reply was, 'General Staff.' It appeared to both of us that Staff was a very common surname among British generals.

The Boer War was very frequently in our thoughts and not less frequently on our lips. Its hold was reinforced by a magic-lantern show with brightly coloured slides to which we went. We thought of the Boers as a heroic people and of their leaders, particularly of Cronjé and Botha, as men of superhuman valour. Our reaction to the Boer War, as to every war in which England was involved, was curiously mixed. One-half of us automatically shared in the English triumph while the other and the patriotic half wanted the enemies of England to win. When our patriotic half was in the ascendant, as it usually was after an English victory, we went so far as to believe that the victory had been won by bribing one of the opponent's generals. We were told that General French's successful dash to Kimberley was made possible by the treachery of a Boer commander who had been bribed. An Indian's faith in bribes is infinite and unshakable. Not only is bribing believed to be an infallible remedy for all workaday inconveniences— a belief justified by experience—it is also regarded as an equally effective means of managing high affairs of state; but in this instance without the same warranty. We heard that the English had won the battle of Waterloo by bribing Grouchy, that they had won the Sikh War by bribing Lal Singh and Tej Singh. These suggestions are so commonplace that they have worked their way into history books. I, however, can cite an example which is far more striking and which has not received the publicity it deserves. During the late war it was believed by many Indians, and quite sincerely, that the help of the United States to begin with, and finally its participation, were secured by Mr Churchill by bribing President Roosevelt.

Besides the Boer War we also heard of the Graeco-Turkish War, the Russo-Turkish War, and the Franco-Prussian War. All this knowledge was gained by us from a systematic enumeration given for our benefit of the more important European wars of the previous fifty years. It was in connexion with the Russo-Turkish War that we heard of Osman Pasha and of his heroic defence of Plevna. My father was something of a pro-Turk. After the Italian attack on Tripoli in 1911 he surprised us by making the observation, as we were seated at a meal discussing the latest news, that it was downright robbery. We were shocked by this exhibition of pro-Turkish partisanship, for we had in the meanwhile acquired a violent prejudice against Muslims and wanted them to get a licking everywhere. But at the time we first heard of Osman Pasha we had no such feeling and we thought of him as a very heroic man.

It is curious that the Russo-Japanese War was not followed by us from day to day, although it was fought when we were old enough to take notice of public affairs. Of course, we heard a good deal of the heroism of the Japanese, of the retreats of Kuropatkin, who came to be known to us as the 'Retreating General', and also about Port Arthur. Our attention was drawn to change that had come over the character of wars so that Marshal Oyama could now direct the Japanese armies from Tokyo. We heard too that the surrender of Port Arthur might have been due to the treachery of the Russian commander, General Stoessel—another instance of our nose for treachery—but we were conscious neither of the concrete military results nor of the far-reaching political significance of this war. But that holds good perhaps only for the conscious part of our being. There was not the least doubt that something had reached the subconscious. After the Japanese victory we felt an immense elation, a sort of reassurance in the face of Europeans, and an immense sense of gratitude and hero-worship for the Japanese.

I have still to explain our familiarity with the other twelve names: Luther, Burke, Fox, Pitt, Washington, Warren Hastings, Mirabeau, Danton, Marat, Robespierre, Gladstone, and Rosebery. But I cannot do so without going into a short digression about the religious and political ideas of our family. My father and mother believed in a form of Hinduism whose basis was furnished by a special interpretation of the historical evolution of the Hindu religion. According to this interpretation the history of Hinduism could be divided into three stages: a first age of pure faith, in essence monotheistic, with its foundations in the Vedas and the Upanishads; secondly, a phase of eclipse during the predominance of Buddhism; and thirdly, the later phase of gross and corrupt polytheism. The adherents of this school further held that all the grosser polytheistic accretions with which popular Hinduism was disfigured had crept in at the time of the revival of Hinduism after the decline of Buddhism in the seventh and eighth centuries of the Christian era, and that they were due primarily to the influence of Mahayana or polytheistic northern Buddhism and the Tantric cults. This degenerate form of Hinduism was given the name of Puranic Hinduism in order to distinguish it from the earlier and purer Upanishadic form of Hinduism. The reformists claimed that they were trying only to restore the original purity of the Hindu religion.

The very simplicity of the interpretation should serve to put historical students on their guard against it. But the reformers implicitly believed in it, and since they believed, their belief gave shape to and coloured their attitude to the other religious movements of the world; they failed to detect the true filiation of their theory, to see that it was only an echo and duplication of the theory of the Protestant Reformation. Although their claim to be restoring the pure faith of the Upanishads by ridding it of Puranic excrescences was certainly inspired by an unconscious absorption of the idea of the Protestants that they were reviving the pure faith of the Scriptures, the Apostles, and the early Fathers, the Hindu reformers looked upon Protestantism as the product of a parallel religious movement and were deeply sympathetic to it. They were correspondingly prejudiced against Romanism. As faithful followers of this school, we were little Hindu Protestants and No-Popery fanatics. Consequently we looked upon Luther as a reformer possessing as great importance and merit as our Rammohun Roy or Keshub Chunder Sen, and regarded the Pope as the European version, and a very magnified and therefore all the more condemnable version, of our worldly and luxurious *mohunts*, or heads of religious orders and monastic establishments.

With such views on religion our parents could not but be liberals in their social and political opinions, and from their casual talk rather than any deliberate instruction we imbibed the notion that European history was a series of struggles for freedom, as a result of which the ambit of a beneficent and fertilizing freedom had been enlarged in ever widening circles in the course of modern history. The more important and epoch-making of these struggles, to our thinking, were the Reformation, the Puritan Rebellion in England, the American War of Independence, and the French Revolution. The heroes of these movements were also our heroes, although about the heroes of Ninety-three our feelings were a little mixed. Not that we had much moral condemnation for them, for we thought it very exhilarating to be able to chop off heads as easily as Danton and Robespierre, incited by Marat, were reported to us to have done. But pondering over the guillotine's indiscrimination in its personal implication we were somewhat awed by it. Of mob violence too we were afraid. We had seen one highly realistic woodcut showing the head of Princesse de Lamballe carried aloft on a pike. The effect of this picture was, however, somewhat tempered by another woodcut printed in ultramarine blue depicting Theroigne de Méricourt on a prancing steed waving a sabre. The beginnings of the Revolution appeared to us as a more generous phase, free from excesses, and matinal in its promise, and of this phase we took Mirabeau to be the intrepid fighter as well as wise counsellor.

Towards Burke we felt nothing but whole-hearted reverence. We had heard that not only had he supported the American colonists but that he had also impeached Warren Hastings for his oppression of the Indian people. The two bulky grey-blue volumes of his impeachment speeches in the cupboard were in our eyes the impressively concrete evidence of his championship of the down-trodden. The names of Fox, Warren Hastings, Washington, and of the two Pitts were to us the names of actors in a very big, many-sided, and slowly unfolding drama, which in our conception of it was nevertheless very closely knit. We seemed never to have lost the sense of the underlying unity of the whole historical epoch beginning with the Seven Years' War and ending with Waterloo. The two Pitts constituted for us the visible symbol of this unity, although apart from this we also recognized their intrinsic greatness. In addition, we saw in them the marvel so rare in the sequence of human generations of a father and a son being equally great.

After all that has been said so far I need not make the explicit declaration that in our attitude towards current English politics we were unapologetic liberal partisans. In fact, we saw no reason for any apology. We had been told that English politics were run by two parties, but we hated the Conservatives, because we gave the same appellation to the orthodox Hindus whom we looked down upon as the upholders and adherents of superstition, by which we understood belief in ghosts, evil spirits, magic, witchcraft, and the like. We could think of no worse insult than to be called a Conservative, and with me this persisted up to the age of adolescence. When I was about seventeen I was having an argument one day with a cousin of my mother about the way to stage a play. We had staged it once before and I insisted that the second performance must be exactly like the first, while my uncle observed good-humouredly that it hardly mattered if there were small departures, particularly as we were going to give the repeat at very short notice. I still stuck to my point, and my obstinacy perhaps annoyed my uncle and he remarked in English, 'You are very conservative.' I felt hot and angry. I could not have felt more outraged if he had called me a liar. He understood my feelings and said with a reassuring smile, 'Don't be so upset. Burke was a Conservative.' I was astonished. Burke a Conservative! I had never heard of such a thing, never thought it possible. That remark became the starting point of a new understanding of Burke on my part.

From this it followed that we had a natural bias in favour of Liberal statesmen. Since we were carefully taught the names of the English Prime Ministers, it is quite impossible that we should not have been told the names of Lord Salisbury and Mr Balfour, but I remembered nothing about them. Our idea was that Lord Rosebery was the last Prime Minister and the coming Prime Minister and we were passing through a sort of interregnum. Disraeli we had heard of, but thought of him only as a clever adventurer, not worthy to bear the shoes of his great rival, Mr Gladstone. That was why we felt so interested in Lord Rosebery when we looked at the picture of the coronation of Edward VII at Banagram. But after the Liberal return in 1906 we seemed to have got very easily reconciled to Sir Henry Campbell-Bannerman although we thought his a very funny name. I still remember the day we heard of his death at Kishorganj. My father had gone to the court but he came back at about twelve o'clock. I asked him why he had returned so early. He replied that Sir Henry Campbell-Bannerman, the Prime Minister, was dead, and the courts had closed as a mark of respect. When I asked who was the new Prime Minister my father said, 'Mr Asquith.' He did not explain that Mr Asquith had been Prime Minister already for some days. That brought our knowledge of the English Liberal Prime Ministers up to date for the time being.

However scrappy and simple ideas of English life and society might have been, they could not exist at all without the accompaniment of some visual suggestion. Everything we read about the British Isles or in English evoked pictures of the external appearance of the country even when not avowedly descriptive. But we had plenty of verbal descriptions, and in addition to these we had pictures to go upon. Taken together, these gave us the impression of a country of great reality of aspect, a country which possessed not only beautiful spots but also place-names which sounded beautiful. Isle of Wight, Osborne House, Windsor, Grasmere, Balmoral, Holyrood Palace, Arthur's Seat, Firth of Forth, Belfast were some of the names which attracted us. I seemed, speaking of my personal preferences, to like Osborne House and Holyrood Palace best. Their beauty of appearance produced a vivid effect on me, and Holyrood Palace especially gathered intensely romantic associations from the allusions to Mary Stuart, Darnley and Bothwell contained in an article written by a Bengali student of Edinburgh University and published in a Bengali magazine.

Two coloured pictures seen in a school text-book printed in England made a profound impression on me. One of them was the picture of a cricket match, showing not only the batsman, the wicket-keeper, and some of the fielders, but also the pavilions in the background. Cricket was our favourite game, and in Bengal at that time it had not been ousted in public affection by football. Football also we played, but we regarded it as a game on a rather plebeian level, while there was not the least room for doubt about the refinement and aristocratic attributes of cricket. An extra reason which inclined us to cricket was that one of its early pioneers in Bengal was a man from our district, who came of a wealthy family whose seat was a village only six or seven miles from Banagram. His full name was Sarada Ranjan Roy, but he was known in Calcutta and all over Bengal as Professor S. Roy, for he was a university teacher and ultimately rose to be the Principal of his college. He taught mathematics, but was a greater Sanskrit scholar, and in the department of sport he was a keen angler and a competent cricketer. It was from the shop run by him in Calcutta that we got our sports goods.

Years later, when I was at college in Calcutta and staying in a hostel run by the Oxford Mission, Father Prior (a descendant of the poet Prior), who was in charge of us, asked me one day if I had ever played any games. He had noticed that it was very difficult to make me play even badminton without dragging me out by main force, and that was the reason for his question. 'Yes,' I replied, 'I used to play cricket when I was a boy.' 'You call that cricket, do you?' observed Father Prior very justly. But whatever might have been the quality of our cricket there was no dross in our enthusiasm. Our school team, composed of the teachers and the boys, was not quite despicable. We had some good players, and all the accessories—bats, balls, leg pads, gloves, stumps were by the best English makers. Some of the more fashionable boys even went into flannels. But our show, proud as we were of it, seemed to be reduced to total drabness by the side of the cricket work revealed in that coloured picture. The game was transformed, it was cricket suffused with the colours of the rainbow.

The other picture was of a battleship which, so far as I can recall its outlines, seems to have been a ship of the 1895 *Majestic* class, or might have been even of the 1901 *Formidable* class. Under this picture was the caption: 'Hearts of Oak are our Ships, Hearts of Oak are Men.' The coloured illustration fascinated me not only because I had an inborn liking for ships, but also because it gave me an impression of the seas being an appanage and projection of England. I could never think of England, as I thought of Bengal and of India, as a stretch of land alone. Combined visions of land and sea were always fleeting through my mind and before my eyes whenever I tried to think of England. Of only one other country in the world did I ever think in that way when I was a boy, and that was ancient Greece.

This characteristic vision of the physical aspect of England as half land and half sea was confirmed in me by my reading of English poetry. The first piece of real English poetry which I heard was Colley

Cibber's 'O say what is that thing call'd light', read out to me by my brother from his text-book. But it was illustrated with a picture showing a blind Indian boy and therefore called up no associations in English life. English life proper struck me with the full force of its romance when about a year later I saw in my brother's new text-book a woodcut showing a high cliff, at its foot the sea, at the edge of the narrow beach a boat, near the boat a boy and a girl, and above and below the picture the following eight lines:

'Break, break, break,
On thy cold gray stones, O Sea!
And I would that my tongue could utter
The thoughts that arise in me.

'O well for the fisherman's boy,
That he shouts with his sister at play!
O well for the sailor lad,
That he sings in his boat on the bay!'

I did not understand half of it, but to me the lines distilled a yearning to which not even the magic casement of Keats about which I read three or four years later could stir me.

I had a serious grievance against my brother. He was always having more interesting text-books than I had, and that was due to the fact that in my time a change had come over the theory of teaching English to Indian boys. Formerly, Indian boys were being taught English mostly from text-books meant for use in England, or from the English classics. But when I was young the educational authorities had had a sudden inspiration that it was too much of a burden for young Indian boys to have to cope with English ideas in an English background in addition to having to master the intricacies of a foreign language. In pursuance of this theory our English text-books were being Indianized as the administration of India was Indianized later. Thus it happened that while my brother read things like:

'O Brignall banks are wild and fair,
And Greta woods are green . . .'

'Why weep ye by the tide, ladie?
Why weep ye by the tide?

I'll wed ye to my youngest son,
And ye shall be his bride . . .'

and also read fine stories from books like Andrew Lang's *Animal Story Book* and Kipling's *Jungle Book*, I was being forced to repeat:

'The fox sat on the mat'
'The dog is in the well'

—and at the next higher stage to read about three Mussalmans eating chilly and rice. I, however, tried to make amends by reading all my brother's text-books two years in advance of him, for in the school and by age he was two years my senior. I am still unconvinced that inflicting 'fat cats sitting on mats' on little Indian boys is the best method of making them learn English.

English poetry was to me and to my brother, even before we could understand it fully, the most wonderful reading in the world. We read the usual things, Wordsworth's 'Lucy Gray', 'We are Seven', and 'Daffodils', for example. We liked them, but we were too young to understand all their subtlety. The poem by Wordsworth which moved me most strongly at the time was 'Upon Westminster Bridge'. As I read:

'Earth has not anything to show more fair . . .
This City now doth, like a garment, wear
The beauty of the morning; silent, bare,
Ships, towers, domes, theatres, and temples lie
Open unto the fields, and to the sky;
All bright and glittering in the smokeless air.'

—the heavenly light of dawn with its purity and peace seemed to descend on us.

There were two other poems which made an even greater impression on us and they were placed one above the other in Palgrave's *Children's Treasury*, which was one of my brother's text-books. The first of them was Shakespeare's 'Full fathom five . . .' and the second Webster's 'Call for the robin-redbreast and the wren. . .' Again that juxtaposition of land and sea. The combination, as well as the contrast, was heightened in our mind by Palgrave's note in which Lamb was quoted, which we read very carefully without, however, taking it much beyond its general drift. But it was not necessary to understand more for the poems to set our imagination bestirring. What a magic country it was where the drowned were transformed into pearl and coral and where the robin and the wren covered the friendless bodies of unburied men with leaves and flowers, and the ant, the fieldmouse and the mole reared hillocks over them. Reading these lines of Webster, our hearts warmed up with a faith that could be described as the inverse of Rupert Brooke's. He was happy in the conviction that if he died in a distant land some part of that foreign soil would become for ever England. We had a feeling that if we died in England what would become for ever England would be a little foreign flesh, and with that faith there was happiness in perishing in an English glade, with the robin and the wren twittering overhead. But when we read the last two lines: 'But keep the wolf far thence, that's foe to men, For with his snails he'll dig them up again,' our boyish animalism got the better of us. Going on all fours on our earthen floor and stretching and spreading out our fingers as a cat stretches out and spreads its claws, we fell to scratching the ground.

If Webster's lines brought to us a very subtle realization of the quality of English land life, Campbell's 'Ye Mariners of England' gave us a wholly straightforward initiation into the spirit of British maritime enterprise. We recited the simple lines, not with the half-perplexed, half-intuitive appreciation we had for the two poems by Shakespeare and Webster, but with great gusto and complete understanding. The climax of my own initiation into English seafaring life was reached when as a boy of eleven I read about the battle of Trafalgar and saw a coloured picture of Nelson standing on the deck of the *Victory* with Hardy. Nelson's signal kept ringing within me and I shouted out time and again, 'England expects every man to do his duty' (that was the form in which I first learned the signal). On one of those days I was coming up from the river towards the road in front of our house, shouting at the top of my voice. 'England expects every man to do his duty', when I saw some gentlemen passing along the road on an elephant. The most elderly gentleman had the elephant stopped and, leaning out, asked me who I was. I replied that I was Upendra Babu's son. Then he asked me if I knew what those words were about. I said that they were Nelson's signal at Trafalgar. He seemed to be satisfied and went away on his elephant. I came to know later that he had spoken to my father about this meeting. It was my father who told me this.

It must on no account be imagined that in regard to English life and the English spirit we were always floating in the empyrean. In actual fact, we were as ready to walk on earth, and more often descend to the underworld, as to soar up to heaven. Our ideas of the Englishman in the flesh were very different from our ideas of his civilization. To be quite frank, our ignorance of the one remained quite unrelieved by our knowledge of the other, and it is this difference which I am now going to illustrate.

The normal reaction of the unsophisticated Indian villager in the face of an Englishman is headlong flight. I and my elder brother, as young boys, jumped into a roadside ditch. We did not do so, however, from any ignoble motive of self-preservation, but to save a precious cargo which we were carrying and which we believed to be in danger from the Englishman. The plain story is this. I and my brother had been sent to buy some bananas from the bazaar and were returning with a bunch when we saw an Englishman coming up the road from the opposite direction. I have no clear recollection who exactly he was, but he may have been Mr Stapleton, the Inspector of Schools whom I met with greater self-confidence some years later. As soon as we caught sight of him we hid ourselves in the ditch, because we had been told that Englishmen were as fond of bananas as any monkey could be and that they swooped on the fruit wherever and whenever they saw it. So we crouched in the ditch among the nettles until the Englishman had passed. This incident took place when my brother was only learning his English alphabet and when his sole source of knowledge about Englishmen was oral tradition. I was guided wholly by his example. Thus our behaviour on that occasion may be called behaviour appropriate to a state of innocence untinctured by any taste of the fruit of knowledge.

But this monkey analogy had deeper and less innocent antecedents. In our time it was trotted out rather jocosely. None the less I heard an old teacher of ours asserting it in the class with accents, not only of conviction, but of passion, and declaring that the English race were of a she-monkey by a demon born. The prevalent attitude towards Englishmen of our people was one of irrational and ineradicable cringing and equally irrational and unconquerable hatred. Grown-ups reserved the first for the Englishman present before them and the second for the absent Englishman. Our great moral and intellectual leaders in the nineteenth century were perfectly aware of this weakness in their parishioners and tried to cure them of it. Bankim Chandra Chatterji has written a satirical piece on Englishmen whose most sardonic and barbed point is reserved for his countrymen. A meeting of Englishmen is represented as a meeting of tigers, but the indigenes are shown as monkeys discreetly hiding themselves among the branches and leaves. When the tigers disperse, the monkeys swagger out and declare that they will now hold their meeting and abuse the tigers, and they do so. Finally, the meeting is closed with the observation from monkeys that after getting such a fusillade of bad language all the tigers must be dead in their lairs.

The remarkable similarity between the spirit of this satirical piece and the spirit of the passages about the *bandar log* in Kipling's story of Kaa's hunting has always intrigued me. Yet I can think of no explanation for it. Any possibility of borrowing on either side appears to be out of the question, for Bankim Chandra Chatterji died in the year in which *The Jungle Book* was published, and he had written the piece some years before his death, while Kipling could not have known anything about the Bengali skit since to my knowledge it has never been translated into English.

But the efforts of these manly and clear-sighted teachers of ours have been in vain. The servility and malice ingrained in every fibre of our being which made us indulge in grotesque antics of alternating genuflexion and defiance before the Englishman persist to this day, and a most striking proof of this persistence was furnished by Mahatma Gandhi himself only one day before the announcement of the final British Plan for transferring power to Indians, that is to say, on 2nd June 1947. After bestowing fulsome praise on Pandit Jawaharlal Nehru as the uncrowned king of India and emphasizing with what appeared like a licking of lips that he was a 'Harrow boy', 'Cambridge graduate', and 'Barrister', Mahatma Gandhi went on to declare that 'our future presidents will not be required to know English.' The disappearance of the Englishman from the Indian political scene has not seen the end of this combination of servility and malice. Rather, as Mahatma Gandhi's pronouncement foreshadowed, the two-fold manifestation of homage and hatred has been transferred from the real to the imitation Englishman. I am thankful to my parents that they inculcated a saner outlook in their children and taught them, Indian gentlemen to be, to treat Englishmen as English gentlemen, no less, no more. But we could not help coming in contact with the debasing tradition.

The next time we saw Englishmen at close quarters was when Mr Nathan, the Divisional Commissioner, arrived at Kishorganj with his wife. That was early in 1907. We had heard that he and his party were expected to arrive from the eastern side of the town at a particular time and waited for them to pass, perched on the top rail of the fence before our house. At last they drove past in a trap. The District Magistrate who was accompanying Mr and Mrs Nathan, was for want of room seated on the footboard at the back, and this fact was later made the text of copious moralizing to us. That a District Magistrate could travel in a syce's seat was held up to us as an example of the Englishman's sense of discipline. But for the moment we were far more vividly interested in Mrs Nathan, who gave us—the brothers—our first sight of an Englishwoman after we had become old enough to remember things. The resultant excitement was indescribable. We hardly talked about anything else but her blue eyes, her flaxen hair, her dress, and her hat for the whole day.

The next day the Commissioner was to distribute prizes to us in the school hall, and as both my brother and I were on the list of prize-winners we went to the prize-giving very neatly dressed and behaved with perfect propriety. As my brother went up solemnly to the Commissioner he clapped his hands and said, 'A clever little boy!' And when I went up a short while after he remarked without knowing the relationship, 'Here comes another little boy.' But our later conduct was not on the same plane of impeccable decorum. As we had put on silk coats and shoes for the prize-giving we made up for the artificiality the next morning by showing ourselves to Mrs Nathan in our unvarnished naturalness. While she was having her round of sight-seeing on foot, at least twenty scions of the best families of the town, bare-bodied, bare-footed, open-mouthed, round-eyed, and, at times absent-mindedly chewing the ends of their *dhotis*, formed her train. It was, I believe, out of respect for her that the local officials did not chase us away. Her flaxen hair, blue eyes, high-heeled shoes, Edwardian skirt, plate-like hat, and the hat-pin running through the hat were all pointed at and discussed in undertones. It was many years before I had a second opportunity of seeing an Englishwoman at the same close range. But the thorough examination I had made at the very first opportunity carried me well through the barren intervening years.

Within a few months, however, something happened which gave me confidence in dealing with Englishmen. Mr Stapleton had come to inspect our class and had asked the boy next to me, the best boy of our class and a particular friend of mine, to read a passage from our English text-book. The boy became a little nervous and began to trip and so I tried to help him in energetic whispers. Noticing this Mr Stapleton asked me to read the passage, which I did passably, except that I could not pronounce the word 'early' correctly. We always pronounced it as 'ahrlee', and the more Mr Stapleton said 'airly' the farther I got away from the right pronunciation. Then, giving it up, he asked me who I was, and how many brothers I had and a few similar questions. I answered in such tolerable English that that evening he sent his Bengali assistant to tell my father that he was very pleased with me. I was made much of and treated to some sweets, but from the next day a new torture began for me. My reputation as an English conversationalist got abroad and the senior boys took to asking me in English, 'Where do you lodge?'; 'Who is your father?'; 'What is your name?' which from them were meaningless and irritating questions. But on the whole I felt confident, and when next year Mr (later Sir Henry) Sharp, who was then the Director of Public Instruction in Bengal, came to inspect our school, I felt that I should be equal to the task if he asked me any questions. He did not. On that occasion the honours went to a senior student of the school, not for English, though, but for drawing. This boy, whose name was Sashi Bagchi, had made a very good drawing of a tiger and this pleased the Director so much that he gave the boy some money to buy a colour-box with.

Speaking of the visits of these high officials to Kishorganj I am reminded of a fresh count of our ignorance of English ways. We knew something about the everyday clothes of Englishmen, but were completely uninstructed about their formal attire. Accordingly, on this score, we were given to making grotesque mistakes. Our drillmaster, Mr Hem Chakravarty, seemed to have picked up some knowledge of these matters and on inspection days he came correctly apparelled in morning dress. But we, as soon as we caught sight of him in that dress, felt like going into roaring fits of laughter and were restrained only by the fear of getting a thrashing, which we knew would surely follow as retribution. This mirth, I discovered, had reached higher quarters. One day my father said to me, 'I hear your drill-master came dressed like a bandsman.' That was the word, and in private we began to call our drill-master band-master. Poor dears! We did not know that the civilized world had already adjudged between us and drill-master, and that while we believed that the joke was on him, it was really on us.

I have been furnished with very recent proof that this ignorance about the English morning dress and other formal costumes persists in my district even today. Early in the year 1947 a young nephew of mine (sister's son), who lived with his parents in a small town of east Mymensingh, came to visit us at Delhi. One day he was shown a picture of Mr Churchill in the uniform of the Lord Warden and Admiral of the Cinque Ports (the picture which appeared in the *Illustrated London News* for 24th August 1946) and asked to say who it was. Without a moment's hesitation he replied, 'A band-master, Uncle.' I could not help laughing out, because I had put him the question precisely with the object of testing whether our one-time ignorance was still surviving in Mymensingh. The little fellow was very much put out by my merriment and wanted to know the reason for it, and when I told him the story of our drill-master, instead of picking himself up, he appeared to fall into yet greater confusion. He did not like the idea of being held up as a vestigial specimen from the distant days of avuncular childhood.

I have now to tell the story of another and a more serious misconception, which is entwined with the central problem of our relationship with Englishmen, or, to be more exact, with all Europeans—the problem of colour. Their fair complexion was a matter of great curiosity and still greater perplexity with us, and we wanted to know why they were fair and we were dark. One theory was that we had been darkened by the sun whereas they had been bleached by the cold, both of us travelling in opposite directions from a golden or rather brownish mean. It is believed by some of our demonologists that the ghosts of cold countries are grey in complexion. So we argued that if pitch-black could become grey, brown could become pink. But one day a very close friend of mine told me a more sensational story. He was the son of a wealthy landowner who was also one of the leading lawyers of the town. All the sons of this gentleman bore different names of the god Siva. The eldest was called Lord of the Word, the second Trident Holder, the third Primeval Lord, the fourth Master of Serpents, and so on. The third, Primeval Lord, was my friend. I regarded him as particularly well-informed about the wider world, because he often went to Calcutta and had an uncle there who was one of the foremost lawyers of the High Court.

Now, one day Primeval Lord told me in great confidence that all English babies were actually born dark, even as dark as we were but that immediately after birth they were thrown into a tub filled with wine and it was the wine which bleached their skin white. Primeval Lord added that the English fathers sat by the tub holding in their hand the pronged instrument with which the English ate and watched if the babies were turning white within the expected time, and if they did not the fathers instantly thrust the pronged instrument down the throats of the babies and killed them. Primeval Lord did not improve on the story by pointing out its moral in so many words, but the hint was that if the English were fair they were so only because they were vicious. It was only through their alcoholism and cruelty that they got their fair complexion, while we were condemned to remain dark-skinned because we were not given to these vices.

I cannot say that I wholly believed the story, but I pondered long over it. As was always the case when we received some particularly esoteric truth from our friends regarding the deep mysteries of life and death, I kept back this bit of information also from the elders and put it in an imperceptible mental drawer with a secret spring. There it has lain all my life, and what interested me in later years was its affiliation with a general system of ideas, for this apparently crack-brained tale was only a freakish, and a very slightly freakish, product of an old and well-organized emotional predisposition amounting to a complex.

As I grew older I felt ever more intensely the implacable hatred of my countrymen for the fair complexion of Europeans. I shall give one or two instances. When I was a student of the higher school classes a university student whom I knew told me that another university student he knew had written in his examination paper of the 'leprous white Englishwomen' and had been punished with rustication for that offence. The way the student narrated the story left no room for doubt that he considered the writing an act of great moral courage and the student who wrote it as a martyr to patriotism.

Again, in 1928, I was present at a social gathering of journalists in Calcutta, where a popular Hindi poet sang a patriotic song of his own composition in a stentorian voice to the accompaniment of the harmonium. The lines which called forth the most effusive appreciation contained the following idea: 'One knee of Mother India is adorned by Tilak, the other by Das, but the White are spread all over her body as a disfiguring skin-disease.'

It is possible to trace this skin-disease symbolism far back into history. In the latter part of the nineteenth century there was discovered a Sanskrit poem which purported to be an authentic contemporary biography of Prithviraj of the Chauhan clan, King of Ajmere, Delhi and the adjoining regions, whose defeat at the hands of Mu'izzud-ud-din Muhammad bin Sam of Ghur (popularly known as Muhammad Ghuri) at the second battle of Taraori in 1192 finally established Muslim rule in India. There is no doubt that this work, which has only recently been published from the single manuscript known to exist, is contemporary. Internal evidence shows that it was substantially composed shortly before the final defeat of Prithviraj and was meant to celebrate his victory over Muhammad of Ghur at the first battle of Taraori in the winter of 1190–91. But the manuscript is incomplete and breaks off abruptly at the end of the twelfth canto. It is impossible to say whether the finished work contained more matter or whether the composition of the poem was interrupted by the defeat and death of Prithviraj. The prologue, which contains a lamentation over the Muslim occupation of Ajmere, suggests, however, that the poem was given the shape in which we have it after the Muslim victory. Now, this poem contains a description of the arrival of a Muslim envoy at the court of Prithviraj and of the physical appearance of this envoy, and in this account occurs the telltale aspersion that the envoy bore a paleness comparable to that given by the *unmentionable disease (avadya-roga-kalpam: Canto X, verse 46).*

Here then we have an emotional symbolism which dates from long before British rule, and which was only extended to the English rulers of India. What is the explanation? The obvious one is that it is an expression of the resentment of the autochthons against the colour prejudice or colour pride of their fair-complexioned foreign conquerors. This no doubt is partly true and needs no restatement at all. But what I want to say here is that there is another and a more fundamental element in this Hindu attitude which has not been noticed and which a Hindu would not disclose even if he were aware of it. It is this element, this locked-up secret, which I want to lay bare.

When not thinking of his foreign conquerors and taking up a self-pitying attitude in consequence, a Hindu is unsurpassed in his exaltation of colour and proneness to make a fetish of it. This comes out most blatantly in connexion with marriages, which certainly provide the most reliable test of the existence of colour feeling or colour prejudice among a people. An intense artificial selection in favour of fair complexion is going on throughout our country, and if we are not all as fair as the Nordics are it is certainly due to no fault of ours. I have seen many matrimonial advertisements laying down unreasonably un-Indian standards of complexion, and among them one, in one of the most important English dailies of Calcutta, asking for a bride of 'Jewish complexion'. At the time of the inspection of the girls for marriage their claim to fair complexion is scrutinized very rigorously. In West Bengal until recently it was not uncommon to rub apparently fair-looking girls with a wet towel to find out whether their complexion was natural or made up. On account of this insistence on fair complexion the fathers of marriageable dark girls sometimes substituted a fairer sister at the time of the inspection, with dire results for the dark girl after marriage. I have heard of such cases and personally know of one which occurred in a house next to ours in Calcutta with all the scandal of detection at the time of the wedding.

The life of a dark marriageable girl in Bengal used to be one of unending private and public humiliation. Her mother would be perpetually reproaching her that she would never get married and remain an eternal millstone round her father's neck, and the prospective bridegroom's people coming to inspect her would be looking significantly at her. In this atmosphere of disgrace the dark girls hid themselves or kept in the background even when ordinary visitors came, while the fair ones strutted about like vain peacocks. This torture did not end even with marriage. The mother-in-law would give a scream if the bride on her arrival was found to be dark. When I accompanied my sister after her marriage to the village of her father-in-law a pack of rustic women who were going to have a look at her at first scrutinized me. 'The brother of the bride,' they said, 'is dark', and went in with the greatest misgivings about the bride herself. Sometimes real tragedies happened. One of my uncles, a fair man himself, found after the wedding that his bride was dark and never saw her face again, and this aunt of mine was forced to live a widow's life. I shall give two more anecdotes from my personal experience.

In the late 'twenties I was requested by a friend of mine to accompany him for the inspection of a girl from whose father a proposal for marriage for him had been received. I am making repeated use of this word 'inspection' deliberately, for the mission that is fulfilled on these occasions, the mission on which I also was being asked to go, cannot be described as anything but a searching and exhaustive examination of all the data presented by the girl, among which the gynaecological are not included only because bare and elementary decencies stand in the way. The convention is that if the young man who is going to marry forms part of the inspecting delegation, as he sometimes but not invariably does, he is expected all the time to remain decorously silent but very indecorously staring at the girl, and have all his questions put through a confidant. In my life till now I have six times formed part of such delegations, thrice for three of my brothers and thrice for the single friend of mine.

Now it happened at this particular inspection that the girl (about four feet and a half in height and four stone in weight) was not actually dark, but she was very tanned and very freckled. My friend was glaring all the while and looking meaningly at me. The relations of the girls usually have keen eyes in these matters, and, as we were coming away, the father of the girl stepped up to us and said with a large gesture, 'Gentlemen, if you have any doubts on the score of complexion I am ready to give you a guarantee that my daughter will become fifty per cent fairer within three months of her marriage.' We replied politely that we had no complaints to make on the score of complexion, but as soon as we were out of hearing my friend, who had been boiling with rage, burst out, 'Oh, his guarantee! What should I do with the guarantee if she does not become fair once she is married off to me?' He went on harping on this grievance for some weeks for he could not forgive the craftiness of a man who had tried to palm off a tanned girl on him with nothing better than his verbal guarantee.

The other anecdote concerns my own marriage. After it had been settled, an old friend of our family caught hold of me and gave me what he considered a timely and necessary warning. He said that after having given up Government service and turned myself into a poor and struggling journalist in the first instance, I was going to commit the second folly of marrying a dark girl. The consequence of the union, he continued, could only be that a number of girls would be born who would inherit the poverty of the father and the complexion of the mother and who, in consequence again, would be quite unmarriageable. After enunciating this proposition he asked me whether I had seriously considered this aspect of the matter. At first I felt inclined to be amused at the long view he was taking of the outcome of my marriage, but soon my anger at his impertinence overcame my sense of humour and I went up to my father to tell him that if that gentleman were asked to my wedding there would be another person away and that would be myself. My father heard the story and was distressed. He fully sympathized with me but was embarrassed, for the family was under some obligation to this gentleman. At the moment I insisted on his exclusion, but in the end, not wishing to be unreasonably touchy, kept quiet. I maintained this self-restraint even when during the wedding I noticed the daughter of my well-wisher bustling about and did not give a public exhibition of my annoyance. For this act of forbearance Providence has rewarded me by giving me only sons, all three of whom have, for boys, the passably brown complexion of teak and not the impossible brown of mahogany. Thus have I been released from worry over the colour bar to marriages.

The adoration of colour in the Hindu has a profound historical basis. The Hindu civilization was created by a people who were acutely conscious of their fair complexion in contrast to the dark skin of the autochthons, and their greatest preoccupation was how to maintain the pristine purity of the blood-stream which carried this colour. *Varna* or colour was the central principle round which Hindu society organized itself, and the orthodox Hindu scriptures know of no greater crime than miscegenation, or, as they call it, *Varna-sankara,* the mixing of colours. The *Gita* declares with burning and resounding conviction

> 'Samkaro narakayai 'va
> Kulaghnanam kulasya ca . . .'
> (Chapter I, verse 42)
> 'Mixture (of caste) leads to naught but hell
> For the destroyers of the family and for the family . . .'
> (Edgerton's translation in the Harvard edition, 1944)

This faith in the sanctity of *Varna,* colour, or caste endures and abides in Hindu society, and the fact—from the point of view of doctrine, the adventitious fact—that the inevitable intermixture with the indigenous element has made many Hindus dark-skinned, makes no difference to the hold and fascination of the ideal of colour. The Hindu regards himself as heir to the oldest conscious tradition of superior colour and as the carrier of the purest and most exclusive stream of blood which created that colour, by whose side the Nazi was a mere parvenu. When with this consciousness and pride he encounters a despised *Mlechchha,* an unclean foreigner, with a complexion fairer than his, his whole being is outraged. His deep-seated xenophobia is roused. He is intolerably humiliated, and in his unforgiving envy and hatred he seeks to obliterate the foreigner's superiority by casting on it the shame of the most loathsome disease which can afflict a man. The demented creature tries to console himself with the illusion that if in this world there is a foreigner fairer than he, it is only because that foreigner is a leper.

SALMAN RUSHDIE

Good Advice is Rarer Than Rubies

On the last Tuesday of the month, the dawn bus, its headlamps still shining, brought Miss Rehana to the gates of the British Consulate. It arrived pushing a cloud of dust, veiling her beauty from the eyes of strangers until she descended. The bus was brightly painted in multicoloured arabesques, and on the front it said 'MOVE OVER DARLING' in green and gold letters; on the back it added 'TATA-BATA' and also 'O.K. GOOD-LIFE'. Miss Rehana told the driver it was a beautiful bus, and he jumped down and held the door open for her, bowing theatrically as she descended.

Miss Rehana's eyes were large and black and bright enough not to need the help of antimony, and when the advice expert Muhammad Ali saw them he felt himself becoming young again. He watched her approaching the Consulate gates as the light strengthened, and asking the bearded lala who guarded them in a gold-buttoned khaki uniform with a cockaded turban when they would open. The lala, usually so rude to the Consulate's Tuesday women, answered Miss Rehana with something like courtesy.

'Half an hour,' he said gruffly. 'Maybe two hours. Who knows? The sahibs are eating their breakfast.'

The dusty compound between the bus stop and the Consulate was already full of Tuesday women, some veiled, a few barefaced like Miss Rehana. They all looked frightened, and leaned heavily on the arms of

---

This story is taken from *East, West: Stories*, published by Pantheon Books, New York, 1994.

uncles or brothers, who were trying to look confident. But Miss Rehana had come on her own, and did not seem at all alarmed.

Muhammad Ali, who specialised in advising the most vulnerable-looking of these weekly supplicants, found his feet leading him towards the strange, big-eyed, independent girl.

'Miss,' he began. 'You have come for permit to London, I think so?'

She was standing at a hot-snack stall in the little shanty-town by the edge of the compound, munching chilli-pakoras contentedly. She turned to look at him, and at close range those eyes did bad things to his digestive tract.

'Yes, I have.'

'Then, please, you allow me to give some advice? Small cost only.'

Miss Rehana smiled. 'Good advice is rarer than rubies,' she said. 'But alas, I cannot pay. I am an orphan, not one of your wealthy ladies.'

'Trust my grey hairs,' Muhammad Ali urged her. 'My advice is well tempered by experience. You will certainly find it good.'

She shook her head. 'I tell you I am a poor potato. There are women here with male family members, all earning good wages. Go to them. Good advice should find good money.'

I am going crazy, Muhammad Ali thought, because he heard his voice telling her of its own volition, 'Miss, I have been drawn to you by Fate. What to do? Our meeting was written. I also am a poor man only, but for you my advice comes free.'

She smiled again. 'Then I must surely listen. When Fate sends a gift, one receives good fortune.'

He led her to the low wooden desk in his own special corner of the shanty-town. She followed, continuing to eat pakoras from a little newspaper packet. She did not offer him any.

Muhammad Ali put a cushion on the dusty ground. 'Please to sit.' She did as he asked. He sat cross-legged across the desk from her, conscious that two or three dozen pairs of male eyes were watching him enviously, that all the other shanty-town men were ogling the latest young lovely to be charmed by the old grey-hair fraud. He took a deep breath to settle himself.

'Name, please.'

'Miss Rehana,' she told him. 'Fiancée of Mustafa Dar of Bradford, London.'

'Bradford, England,' he corrected her gently. 'London is a town only, like Multan or Bahawalpur. England is a great nation full of the coldest fish in the world.'

'I see. Thank you,' she responded gravely, so that he was unsure if she was making fun of him.

'You have filled application form? Then let me see, please.'

She passed him a neatly folded document in a brown envelope.

'Is it OK?' For the first time there was a note of anxiety in her voice.

He patted the desk quite near the place where her hand rested. 'I am certain,' he said. 'Wait on and I will check.'

She finished the pakoras while he scanned her papers.

'Tip-top,' he pronounced at length. 'All in order.'

'Thank you for your advice,' she said, making as if to rise. 'I'll go now and wait by the gate.'

'What are you thinking?' he cried loudly, smiting his forehead. 'You consider this is easy business? Just give the form and poof, with a big smile they hand over the permit? Miss Rehana, I tell you, you are entering a worse place than any police station.'

'Is it so, truly?' His oratory had done the trick. She was a captive audience now, and he would be able to look at her for a few moments longer.

Drawing another calming breath, he launched into his set speech. He told her that the sahibs thought that all the women who came on Tuesdays, claiming to be dependents of bus drivers in Luton or chartered accountants in Manchester, were crooks and liars and cheats.

She protested, 'But then I will simply tell them that I, for one, am no such thing!'

Her innocence made him shiver with fear for her. She was a sparrow, he told her, and they were men with hooded eyes, like hawks. He explained that they would ask her questions, personal questions, questions such as a lady's own brother would be too shy to ask. They would ask if she was virgin, and, if not, what her fiancé's love-making habits were, and what secret nicknames they had invented for one another.

Muhammad Ali spoke brutally, on purpose, to lessen the shock she would feel when it, or something like it, actually happened. Her eyes remained steady, but her hands began to flutter at the edges of the desk.

He went on:

'They will ask you how many rooms are in your family home, and what colour are the walls, and what days do you empty the rubbish. They will ask your man's mother's third cousin's aunt's step-daughter's middle name. And all these things they have already asked your Mustafa Dar in his Bradford. And if you make one mistake, you are finished.'

'Yes,' she said, and he could hear her disciplining her voice. 'And what is your advice, old man?'

It was at this point that Muhammad Ali usually began to whisper urgently, to mention that he knew a man, a very good type, who worked in the Consulate, and through him, for a fee, the necessary papers could be delivered, with all the proper authenticating seals. Business was good, because the women would often pay him five hundred rupees or give him a gold bracelet for his pains, and go away happy.

They came from hundreds of miles away—he normally made sure of this before beginning to trick them—so even when they discovered they had been swindled they were unlikely to return. They went away to Sargodha or Lalukhet and began to pack, and who knows at what point they found out they had been gulled, but it was at a too-late point, anyway.

Life is hard, and an old man must live by his wits. It was not up to Muhammad Ali to have compassion for these Tuesday women.

But once again his voice betrayed him, and instead of starting his customary speech it began to reveal to her his greatest secret.

'Miss Rehana,' his voice said, and he listened to it in amazement, 'you are a rare person, a jewel, and for you I will do what I would not do for my own daughter, perhaps. One document has come into my possession that can solve all your worries at one stroke.'

'And what is this sorcerer's paper?' she asked, her eyes unquestionably laughing at him now.

His voice fell low-as-low.

'Miss Rehana, it is a British passport. Completely genuine and pukka goods. I have a good friend who will put your name and photo, and then, hey-presto, England there you come!'

He had said it!

Anything was possible now, on this day of his insanity. Probably he would give her the thing free-gratis, and then kick himself for a year afterwards.

Old fool, he berated himself. *The oldest fools are bewitched by the youngest girls.*

'Let me understand you,' she was saying. 'You are proposing I should commit a crime . . .'

'Not crime,' he interposed. 'Facilitation.'

'. . . and go to Bradford, London, illegally, and therefore justify the low opinion the Consulate sahibs have of us all. Old babuji, this is not good advice.'

'Bradford, *England*,' he corrected her mournfully. 'You should not take my gift in such a spirit.'

'Then how?'

'Bibi, I am a poor fellow, and I have offered this prize because you are so beautiful. Do not spit on my generosity. Take the thing. Or else don't take, go home, forget England, only do not go into that building and lose your dignity.'

But she was on her feet, turning away from him, walking towards the gates, where the women had begun to cluster and the lala was swearing at them to be patient or none of them would be admitted at all.

'So be a fool,' Muhammad Ali shouted after her. 'What goes of my father's if you are?' (Meaning, what was it to him.)

She did not turn.

'It is the curse of our people,' he yelled. 'We are poor, we are ignorant, and we completely refuse to learn.'

'Hey, Muhammad Ali,' the woman at the betel-nut stall called across to him. 'Too bad, she likes them young.'

That day Muhammad Ali did nothing but stand around near the Consulate gates. Many times he scolded himself, *Go from here, old goof, lady does not desire to speak with you any further.* But when she came out, she found him waiting.

'Salaam, advice wallah,' she greeted him.

She seemed calm, and at peace with him again, and he thought, *My God, ya Allah, she has pulled it off. The British sahibs also have been drowning in her eyes and she has got her passage to England.*

He smiled at her hopefully. She smiled back with no trouble at all.

'Miss Rehana Begum,' he said, 'felicitations, daughter, on what is obviously your hour of triumph.'

Impulsively, she took his forearm in her hand.

'Come,' she said. 'Let me buy you a pakora to thank you for your advice and to apologise for my rudeness, too.'

They stood in the dust of the afternoon compound near the bus, which was getting ready to leave. Coolies were tying bedding rolls to the roof. A hawker shouted at the passengers, trying to sell them love stories and green medicines, both of which cured unhappiness. Miss Rehana and a happy Muhammad Ali ate their pakoras sitting on the bus's 'front mud-guard', that is, the bumper. The old advice expert began softly to hum a tune from a movie soundtrack. The day's heat was gone.

'It was an arranged engagement,' Miss Rehana said all at once. 'I was nine years old when my parents fixed it. Mustafa Dar was already thirty at that time, but my father wanted someone who could look after me as he had done himself and Mustafa was a man known to Daddyji as a solid type. Then my parents died and Mustafa Dar went to England and said he would send for me. That was many years ago. I have his photo, but he is like a stranger to me. Even his voice, I do not recognise it on the phone.'

The confession took Muhammad Ali by surprise, but he nodded with what he hoped looked like wisdom.

'Still and after all,' he said, 'one's parents act in one's best interests. They found you a good and honest man who has kept his word and sent for you. And now you have a lifetime to get to know him, and to love.'

He was puzzled, now, by the bitterness that had infected her smile.

'But, old man,' she asked him, 'why have you already packed me and posted me off to England?'

He stood up, shocked.

'You looked happy—so I just assumed . . . excuse me, but they turned you down or what?'

'I got all their questions wrong,' she replied. 'Distinguishing marks I put on the wrong cheeks, bathroom decor I completely redecorated, all absolutely topsy-turvy, you see.'

'But what to do? How will you go?'

'Now I will go back to Lahore and my job. I work in a great house, as ayah to three good boys. They would have been sad to see me leave.'

'But this is tragedy!' Muhammad Ali lamented. 'Oh, how I pray that you had taken up my offer! Now, but, it is not possible, I regret to inform. Now they have your form on file, cross-check can be made, even the passport will not suffice.

'It is spoilt, all spoilt, and it could have been so easy if advice had been accepted in good time.'

'I do not think,' she told him, 'I truly do not think you should be sad.'

Her last smile, which he watched from the compound until the bus concealed it in a dust-cloud, was the happiest thing he had ever seen in his long, hot, hard, unloving life.

Amitav Ghosh

A to Z Street Atlas

We drove away soon. I sat between Nityananda and Tridib in the front seat, while Ila, her mother and Lizzie-missy dozed at the back. It took us much longer than usual to drive through the city: cars have no privilege on the roads at that time of the year; the streets are overwhelmed by the festivities. We had to inch forward near Gariahat, with Nityananda and Tridib hanging out of the windows, begging shoppers to make way. Near Sealdah it took us almost half an hour to skirt around a pandal that was jutting out from the pavement, right into the middle of the street. The car got hotter and hotter and Tridib began to shout curses at everything that crossed our path, his wire-rimmed glasses glinting in the sunlight, dwarfing his waspish, angular face. The traffic came to a virtual standstill again near Dakshineshwar. We crawled along till we reached the bridge, and then looked down in awe, from our height, at the vast crowds circulating in the courtyard of the temple below, like floodwaters sweeping through a garden. But once we had crossed the bridge the traffic grew thinner and soon we were speeding along the Grand Trunk Road. Then Tridib relaxed a little and leant back, smelling as he always did of fresh cigarette smoke and soap. I asked him a few questions but he seemed abstracted and wouldn't say much, so soon I dozed off too.

When I woke up, Nityananda was shaking my arm excitedly, crying: Wake up, wake up, there it is, there's the house, look, look.

This extract is taken from *The Shadow Lines*, published by Ravi Dayal Publisher, New Delhi, 1988.

It appeared suddenly on the edge of the windscreen: a bright yellow patch on a gentle knoll, rising like a cake out of that table-like plain. In a few minutes we reached an arched gateway that had outhouses on either side of it. The cars slowed down a little, and as we were overtaken by the cloud dust that had been following us, children swarmed out of the outhouses and ran along with the car, waving and shouting. The house had vanished behind a forest that stretched all the way up the knoll, the trees growing so thick and close together that they hid the house like a curtain. Tridib, grinning, told me to take a good look, for I wouldn't see trees like those again for a long time: his grandfather had wanted to live in a tropical rain-forest so he'd imported those trees from Brazil and the Congo.

Then Nityananda nudged me, pointing to the left, and turning, I saw a troop of monkeys hanging on the vines, staring down at us, somersaulting in alarm. The car turned a corner, still climbing steeply, and suddenly the house was in front of us: newly whitewashed and plastered, shining golden in the mid-morning sunlight, a festoon of flapping saris hanging wetly from the roof, a row of columns stretching across the portico in a broad, gap-toothed smile.

The paved terrace in front of the house was already buzzing when the cars drew up. The durwans who looked after the house had lit two fires from which thin feathers of smoke were now rising into the sky. Their wives had settled down in the shade of the portico, surrounded by mounds of vegetables. In readiness for Nityananda, huge brass pots had been set out on the terrace.

We were surrounded as soon as we got out of the car. Ila vanished into a knot of people, all eager to examine and exclaim over the only grandchild of the house. She let them fuss over her for a while then suddenly she broke free of them, snatched at my hand and dragged me across the paved terrace. Come on, she whispered urgently, let's hide.

I shot a glance back, over my shoulder. They're running after us, I shouted. What'll we do now?

Just follow me, she panted, vaulting up the plinth of the portico. We dodged through the columns into a vast, musty hall. Stumbling into it, blinded by the gloom, we bumped into each other, and then tripped and fell on a flight of cold marble stairs. Narrowing my eyes, I tried to see where they led. But I could only see a few feet ahead, and beyond that the stairs vanished into darkness. I could hear the durwans and the children racing across the courtyard now, shouting to each other.

It's too dark up there, I whispered to Ila. Where shall we hide? They're almost here.

She gestured at me impatiently to be quiet. She was looking around the hall, hesitating as though she had forgotten her way around the house. I pushed her, urging her on, my belly churning with a breathless hide-and-seek excitement.

Shut up, she snapped, pushing me back. And just when I was about to make a dash for a dim, high door on the far side of the hall, she cried: Come on, I remember now! and began to feel her way around the staircase. I followed her until we came to a low wooden door, hidden away behind the stairs. She found a knob and gave it a tug. The door creaked but showed no sign of coming open.

Come on pull, she said to me breathlessly. Aren't you good for *anything*?

I could hear feet thudding on the portico now. I caught hold of the knob and we pulled together, as hard as we could. The door creaked and a gust of musty air blew into our faces. We pulled harder still and the door opened, no more than a few inches wide, but enough for us to squeeze through. We slipped in and managed to push the door shut. A moment later we heard them pouring into the hall.

We tumbled down a couple of steps to a stone floor and lay there panting. We could hear them scattering in the hall now, some running up the staircase, some looking in the corners, shouting excitedly to each other. Ila smiled gleefully and squeezed my hand.

You watch, she said, none of them will think of looking in here.

For a while all I could see was a pale green glow filtering in through a window, set so high up in the wall that it seemed like a skylight. Its small rectangle of glass was mildewed over on the outside by grass and moss.

Look! I said to Ila. There's grass growing on that window.

Yes, she said. The window's on the ground. If you want to look in here you have to lie flat on your stomach.

But then, I said in amazement, this room must be under the ground.

Yes, of course, she said. You fool: couldn't you tell?

I shivered. I had never been underground before: as far as I knew only the underworld lay below the ground. I looked around and the cavernous room seemed suddenly full of indistinct shapes, murky green in that strangely acquatic light, like the looming heads of rock in a picture that Tridib had once shown me, of the cave of a moray eel.

We could hear Lizzie-missy shouting for Ila in the hall.

Let's go back, I said. We've been here long enough.

Ila clapped a hand over my mouth. Shut up, she whispered angrily; you can't go, now that I've brought you here.

Queen Victoria was shouting too, scolding Lizzie-missy: Why you let her running-running? Tridib was arguing with her: Let them be, they're just playing somewhere. . . . Their voices drew away slowly and we knew that they had gone outside, back to the terrace.

I don't like this place, I whispered to Ila. I don't want to stay here.

Coward, she said. Aren't you meant to be a boy? Look at me: I'm not scared. It's just some old furniture covered up with sheets. That's all.

But what are we going to do in here? I said. It's so dark. . . .

I know what we can do, she said, clapping her hands together. We can play a game,

A game! I cried, peering at the grey-green shapes rising out of the darkness. What kind of game can we play in a place like this?

I'll show you, she said. It's a nice game, many boys like it.

But there's no room in here, I protested. And I can't see very far.

She sprang up. I know where we can play, she said. I just hope it's still there.

I followed her as she picked her way through the looming shrouded shapes, stumbling in the darkness, raising little storms of dust. She led me to the far end of the room where it was so dark I could hardly tell where she was.

Yes, she cried in triumph, pointing at a vast, sheet-covered mound. It *is* still here. Help me pull off the sheet, come on.

I caught hold of one end of the sheet and she of another. We tugged, but instead of coming off, the sheet seemed to atomise in our hands, and for a moment everything vanished into a cyclone of dust.

I can still see it, taking shape slowly within that cloud of dust.

Like a magician's rabbit, laughed Ila.

Nothing as simple as that, said Robi wryly. No, at least a castle on a misty mountaintop.

But in my memory I see it emerging out of that storm of dust like a plateau in a desert.

It was a table, the largest I had ever seen; it seemed to stretch on and on. I used to wonder later whether this was merely a legacy of a child's foreshortened vision: an effect of that difference in perspective which causes all objects recalled from childhood to undergo an illusory enlargement of scale. But three years later, when I took May, a fully-grown twenty-four-year old adult, into that room and showed her the table, even she gasped.

Heavens! she said. It's huge: what could it possibly have been used for?

Tridib once told me all about it. My grandfather bought it on his first visit to London, he said, some time in the 1890s. He saw it at an exhibition in the Crystal Palace and couldn't resist it. He had it shipped to Calcutta in sections, but when it arrived he didn't know what to do with it so he had it put away here. And so, it was forgotten until you rediscovered it.

May walked around it, frowning. I wonder how much he paid for it, she said, running her thumb along the grain of the dark, heavy wood.

I wonder how much it cost to have it shipped here, she said loudly, her voice echoing in the shadows of the room. I wonder how many proper roofs that money would have bought for those huts we saw on our way here.

The indignation in her voice stabbed accusingly at me. I don't know, I said, lowering my head.

She tapped on the wood with her knuckles. Why did he bring *this* back for God's sake? she cried. Why this worthless bit of England; why something so utterly useless?

She was biting her lip in bewilderment now, shaking her head.

I could think of no answer to give her: it seemed impossible to me to think of that table as an object like any other, with a price and a provenance, for I had seen it taking shape with my own eyes, within a cloud of dust, in that very room.

All right, said Ila, let's go under it.

Under it? Aghast, I tugged at the back of her smock and asked her what kind of game we could possibly play under it.

Come on, she said; she was already on her knees crawling through the dust. Come on, I'll show you. It's the game I play with Nick.

Nick? I said, suddenly alert. Who's Nick?

Don't you know Nick? she said, and turning to look back at me, over her shoulder she said: Nick's Mrs Price's son, May's brother. We live in their house in London. He and I walk to school together in the morning and come back together in the afternoon, and then afterwards, every evening, we go down together to play in the cellar.

She reached for my hand and tried to pull me down. Come on, she said. I'll show you: it's a game called Houses.

No, I said, shaking my head, confused by the questions that were now stirring in my head.

This Nick, I found myself asking her. How big is he?

Oh he's big, she said, perching on the foot rest. He's very big. Much bigger than you: much stronger too. He's twelve, three years older than us.

I squatted beside her on the dusty floor, thinking.

What does he look like? I asked presently.

She screwed up her face and thought hard. He has yellow hair, she said after a while. It always falls over his eyes.

Why? I said. Doesn't he comb it?

He does comb it, she said. But it still falls over his eyes.

It must be long like a girl's.

No, it's not a bit like a girl's.

Then why is it so long?

It is not so long, she said. It's just very straight, and when he runs or something it falls over his eyes. He can even touch it with his tongue sometimes.

I spat on the floor in disgust. We watched the spit turning into a tiny pool of foaming mud.

He must be filthy, I said. Eating his own hair.

You're just jealous, Ila said grinning, because your own hair is so short. Nick looks sweet when his hair falls over his eyes: everyone says so.

After that day Nick Price, whom I had never seen, and would, as far as I knew, never see, became a spectral presence beside me in my looking glass; growing with me, but always bigger and better, and in some way more desirable—I did not know what, except that it was so in Ila's eyes and therefore true. I would look into the glass and there he would be, growing, always faster, always a head taller than me, with hair on his arms and chest and crotch while mine were still pitifully bare. And yet if I tried to look into the face of that ghostly presence, to see its nose, its teeth, its ears, there was never anything there, it had no features, no form; I would shut my eyes and try to see its face, but all I would see was a shock of yellow hair tumbling over a pair of bright blue eyes. And as for what he did, what he said, what he thought about, in the three years between the moment when Ila first told me about him, and that day when I took May down to that underground room, I knew nothing at all about him except one little snippet of a story that my father told me about him once, soon after returning from a business trip to England.

My father had telephoned Mrs Price soon after he arrived in London, just in case Ila and Queen Victoria were still there. It turned out that they had left long ago, but Mrs Price insisted that he come to tea with her anyway. He went, and when Mrs Price led him into her drawing room, he found Nick there too, dressed in his school uniform but with his tie hanging loose around his neck. He shook hands with my father and sat down quietly in an armchair in a corner. My father could not help being impressed: he had never seen such a definite air of self-possession in a child of thirteen.

For a while my father and Mrs Price chatted about Mayadebi and the Shaheb (who were in Rumania and had invited her to visit them there), about May, who was away at the festival in Bayreuth, and Tridib. Mrs Price remembered, laughing, that Tridib had once decided that he wanted to be an Air Raid Warden when he grew up. So then my father turned to Nick, for he hadn't said a word yet, and asked him whether *he* knew what he wanted to be when he grew up.

Nick tipped back his head, with a little smile, as though he were surprised that anyone should ask, and said, yes, of course he knew, he'd known for years; he wanted to be like his grandfather, grandfather Tresawsen, whose picture was hanging over there, above the mantelpiece.

To my intense disappointment, my father could tell me nothing about Nick's grandfather, except that in the picture he had had a square face, white hair, and a walrus moustache.

So, as always, it fell to Tridib to tell me, sitting on the grass in the Gole Park roundabout one evening, how Mrs Price's father, Lionel Tresawsen, had left the farm where he'd been born—in a village called Mabe, in southern Cornwall—and gone off to a nearby town to work in a tin mine; how he'd gone on from there—for no matter that he had very little education, he had deft hands, a quick mind and a great deal of ambition—to become the overseer of a tin mine in Malaysia; and then further and further on, all around the world—Fiji, Bolivia, the Guinea Coast, Ceylon—working in mines or warehouses or plantations or whatever came his way; how finally he had surfaced in Calcutta, making his living by working as an agent in a company which dealt in steel tubes, and then, later, gone on to make, if not exactly a fortune, certainly a respectable sum of money, by starting a small factory of his own, in Barrackpore. It was then, prosperous at last, in his middle age, that he married. His wife was the widow of a Welsh missionary doctor, and she bore him two children, Elisabeth and Alan. When Elisabeth was twelve and Alan ten, she made her husband sell his factory, and move back to England: she was determined that her children would have all the advantages of a proper education, university and all. And so they went back and settled in the bucolic tranquillity of a small Buckinghamshire village.

But in fact there was much more to Lionel Tresawsen than money, steel tubes and children. In his youth, for example, he had been a prolific inventor. After he died, his wife discovered that in the period of five years when he was living in Malaysia he had taken out no less than twenty-five patents—for gadgets ranging from mechanical shoe-horns to stirrup-pumps for draining water out of flooded mines.

He had given up inventing in disgust when manufacturers had proved strangely indifferent to his inventions.

And then there was the Lionel Tresawsen of middle-age, who had tried to set up a homeopathic hospital in a village near Calcutta; and the almost-old Lionel, who had developed an interest in spiritualism and begun to attend the meetings of the Theosophical Society in Calcutta, where he met and earned the trust and friendship of a number of leading nationalists. This had, of course, estranged him and his wife from most circles of British society in the city and led to innumerable colourful slights and insults at clubs and tea parties, but that had made very little difference to Lionel Tresawsen since those people had never been particularly pleasant to him anyway. He had also begun to attend séances conducted by a Russian medium, a large lady who had married an Italian who ran a restaurant in Chowringhee. It was at those séances that he met Tridib's grandfather, Mr Justice Chandrashekhar Datta-Chaudhuri, who liked indulging in matters spiritual when the High Court was not in session: their friendship was sealed across innumerable planchette tables while waiting for the large lady to summon her favourite spirit, the all-seeing astral body of Ivan the Terrible.

Listening to Tridib that evening, I thought I understood what Nick had meant when he had said to my father, with such untroubled certainty, that yes, of course he knew what he wanted to do, he wanted to travel around the world like Lionel Tresawsen, to live in faraway places halfway around the globe, to walk through the streets of La Paz and Cairo. At that moment, looking up at the smoggy night sky above Gole Park, wondering how the stars looked in London, I thought I had found at last the kindred spirit whom I had never been able to discover among my friends.

I couldn't hold my questions back any more after I had shown May the footrest under that immense table, where Ila had been sitting when she first introduced me to Nick Price. Is his hair really yellow? I cried. And does it really fall over his eyes?

May gave this a bit of thought and said, no, yellow was not quite the word she would use, it was sort of straw-coloured hair, but yes, it did fall over his eyes.

And what was he like? I found myself asking her. Did he like school, and what was he going to do afterwards?

I was being clever. I didn't want her to know that I already knew.

She found an upturned chair, righted it, and sat down. Oh he's a very grown-up little boy, she said. He knows exactly what he's going to do after school.

What?

He's going to join a firm of chartered accountants and once they've trained him, he's going to get a nice job with a huge salary—preferably abroad, not in England. England's gone down the drain, he says. It can't afford to pay anyone properly except old age pensioners.

What's a chartered accountant? I said.

She smiled and wiped the back of her hand across her face, leaving a dark smudge on her cheek.

I don't know, she said, with a snort of laughter. I think they have big books full of numbers on which they make little marks with red pencils.

I steadied myself against her chair. But May, I said, doesn't he want to travel—like your grandfather. . . ?

Oh, travel doesn't mean the same thing to everyone, she said. She gave me a long speculative look, narrowing her eyes, and said: I wonder whether you'd like him.

Of course I'd like him, I cried. I like him already.

You don't know him, she said. He's not at all like us, you know.

What do you mean 'us'? I said.

Not much like me, she said. Nor like our parents, or Tridib, or you, or anyone. . . .

She stood up, dusted her shirt and said, under her breath, to herself, as though in reproof: But all the same he's a dear old chap.

I hope I'll meet him some day, I said.

I'm sure you will, she said, smiling. I wonder what you'll have to say to him when you do.

I met him seventeen years later, in London.

The day before Robi was to leave for Boston, Ila arranged to take the two of us to meet Mrs Price. I was delighted: I had been planning to visit her ever since I arrived in London, four weeks before, but somehow I had not quite picked up the courage to go on my own.

Ila and Robi met me at the Indian Students' Hostel in Bloomsbury where I was staying temporarily. They arrived late in the afternoon when I was in the dining hall, drinking tea and eating dum aloo and puris, while listening to a bearded student leader from Allahabad who was campaigning to be elected president of the hostel union.

The moment I saw Ila coming through the door, I could tell from her pursed lips and shining eyes that she was nursing a secret. But when I asked her what it was, on the way to the Goodge Street tube station, she shook her head and hurried on ahead of us.

It was not till the red sign of the Mornington Crescent tube station had flashed past my window like a palmed card that Ila sprang her surprise.

Do you know who's going to be waiting for us at the station when we get there? she said.

May? said Robi.

No, not May, said Ila. May's away touring with her orchestra.

Then who? Go on, tell us.

Nick, she said, her eyes shining. Nick Price. I haven't seen him in, it must be all of ten years. He was a pimply youth of nineteen then, and I was a buck-toothed belle with braces.

But I thought he was away in Kuwait, said Robi. Getting rich, doing chartered accountancy or whatever.

He was, said Ila. He's been away for a very long time. But he came back unexpectedly a couple of weeks ago—I don't know why. Mrs Price didn't talk about it much.

She looked out at the black walls of the tunnel, smiling to herself.

I'll tell you what, she said presently. After we've been to see Mrs Price, I'll treat you two to dinner at my favourite Indian restaurant—it's a small Bangladeshi place in Clapham. You'll like it. We can ask Nick too—maybe he'd like to come.

I knew him the moment I saw him. He was at the far end of the platform, standing under a 'Way Out' sign. He was wearing a blue suit, a striped institutional tie and a dark overcoat. He looked very tall and broad to me at first, just as I had imagined him. But when he and Robi met halfway and shook hands, I saw that I was wrong, that my eyes had been deceived by the distorted perspectives of the long, straight lines of the platform: I saw that most of his breadth lay in the thickness of his overcoat and that his head reached no higher up Robi's shoulder than did mine.

When he turned to Ila, and stuck out his hand, I wondered whether he looked older than he ought because his face had been burnt and coarsened by the desert sun. But it wasn't that: it was because of a premature, slightly suspicious, gravity that made him wrinkle up his eyes appraisingly when he talked, like a banker who has seen too many good debts turn bad.

Ila laughed, looking at his outstretched hand, and raising herself on tiptoe, she flung her arms around his neck and kissed him, full on the mouth. The blood rushed to his face and he laughed too, awkwardly, and his face suddenly unwrinkled and throwing his arms around her he hugged her to his chest, and then, when he was kissing her, I saw that his hair had fallen over his eyes, in exactly the way Ila had described on that long ago October morning.

So, when he walked up to me, flicking his straw-coloured hair back, and said: How nice to meet you, I've heard so much about you from my mother and May and everyone. . . . What could I say? I said: I'm not meeting you for the first time; I've grown up with you.

He was taken aback.

That must have taken some doing, he said drily, since I grew up right here, in boring suburban old West Hampstead.

I've known the streets around here for a long time too, I said.

And then I began to show off.

When we came out of the tube station I stopped them and pointed down the road. Since this is West End Lane, I said, that must be Sumatra Road over there. So that corner must be where the air raid shelter was, the same one that Robi's mother and your mother and your uncle Alan ducked into on their way back from Mill Lane, when one of those huge high-calibre bombs exploded on Solent Road, around the corner, blowing up most of the houses there. And that house, that one, just down the road, over there, on the corner of Lymington Road, I know what it's called: it's called Lymington Mansions, and an incendiary bomb fell on it, and burned down two floors. That was on the 1st of October 1940, two days before your uncle died.

Nick Price inclined his head at me, in polite incredulity. He turned to Ila and they walked on ahead, cutting me short.

Robi fell into step beside me, and jabbing me in the ribs, told me not to bullshit; didn't I know that the Germans hadn't developed high-calibre bombs till much later in the war? In 1940 they simply hadn't possessed a bomb that was powerful enough to knock down a whole street.

But that's what happened, I said.

How do you know? Robi said.

Because Tridib told me.

How was *he* to know? He was just a kid, nine years old. Every little bomb probably seemed like an earthquake to him.

Look, I said, that's what happened.

O.K., Robi said. Since you're so sure, let's go and take a look at that road of yours and see what it's like now.

All right, I said. I called out to Nick and Ila: We're going over there to take a look at Solent Road, where the bomb fell.

Ila made an impatient face. You and your silly bombs, she said. We're late already; hurry up. We'll wait for you at the corner.

Solent Road's over there, said Nick, laughing. Do tell us if you find it all bombed out.

He did not have to tell me where it was. I knew already, for the map was in my head: down Sumatra Road, fourth turning to the right.

Here we are, said Robi, when we got there. That's your bombed-out road.

It was a short road, lined with trees and hedges on either side. The trees were a pale honey-green—the colour of English greenery—but gentler still now, gilded by the steep afternoon sunlight. The red brick houses were all exactly the same, on both sides of the road: with sharply pointed tiled roofs and white window frames and doorways, each with its own patch of garden hidden behind a hedge. There were rows of small cars parked on either side of the road. Right beside us was a small blue Citroën with a sticker on the windshield which said: Save the Whales. On the back seat there was a pile of oddly-shaped green bottles and next to them a kind of plastic bucket strapped to the seat.

I found myself suddenly absorbed in the trappings of the lives that went with that car.

Are those wine bottles? I asked Robi.

No, you fool, he laughed. Those are mineral water bottles.

And that; what's that? I asked, pointing to the plastic bucket.

That's a seat for a baby, he said impatiently. Haven't you seen one before? It's to keep a baby safe inside a car.

I could not take my eyes off the Citroën.

Enough of that bloody car, said Robi. Take a look at your bombed-out Solent Road now.

I looked up at the quiet, pretty houses on that tranquil road. I caught his eye and we both burst into laughter.

Not exactly what you had expected, Robi said.

I did not tell him then, but he was wrong.

I had not expected to see what Tridib had seen. Of course not. I had not expected to see rubble sloping down from burnt-out houses like scree in a mountain quarry, with a miraculously undamaged bathtub balanced precariously at the top; nor had I expected to find the road barricaded by policemen while the men from the Heavy Rescue Service tried to dig beneath the rubble for the lost pensioner. I had known that I would not see uprooted trees or splintered windows or buckled flagstones: I had expected nothing of all that, knowing it to be lost in a forty-year old past.

But despite that, I could not still believe in the truth of what I did see: the gold-green trees, the old lady walking her Pekinese, the children who darted out of a house and ran to the postbox at the corner, their cries hanging like thistles in the autumn air. I could see all of that, and yet, despite the clear testimony of my eyes, it seemed to me still that Tridib had shown me something truer about Solent Road a long time ago in Calcutta, something I could not have seen had I waited at that corner for years—just as one may watch a tree for months and yet know nothing at all about it if one happens to miss that one week when it bursts into bloom.

I wanted to know England not as *I* saw her, but in her finest hour— every place chooses its own and to me it did not seem an accident that England had chosen hers in a war.

Nick and Ila were waiting for us where we had left them, at the corner where Sumatra Road joined West End Lane. Nick was talking and he did not notice us.

One can't really *like* Kuwait, we heard him say. There's nothing to do there except drink and watch video films. I'm quite relieved to be back.

So have you got yourself a new job? Ila asked.

Oh I'll start looking around soon, he said. It shouldn't be a problem; I have a lot of experience.

He stopped to run his fingers through his hair.

You may say what you like about Kuwait, he said. But there's serious money to be made out there. Really serious money. Nothing like the chickenfeed I'd get working for some tupenny company in the Midlands.

Then he saw us and exclaimed: Ah, there you are. So did you find your bombed-out road?

He found it all right, said Robi. But instead of the remains of some dreadful battlefield, all he got to see was a little old lady with a blue rinse, out walking her Pekinese.

But still, said Nick, you did find your way there. Now would you like to have a go at finding your way to 44 Lymington Road?

I could try, I said.

Go ahead then.

It was easy enough on the A to Z Street Atlas of London that my father had brought me. I knew page 43, square 2 F by heart: Lymington Road ought to have been right across the road from where we were. But now that we had reached the place I knew best, I was suddenly uncertain. The road opposite us was lined with terraces of cheerfully grimy, red-brick houses, stretching all the way down the length of the road. The houses were not as high or as angular as I had expected.

But still, as far as I could tell that was where Lymington Road should have been, so I pointed to it and asked whether that was it.

Yes! said Nick. Good boy: got it first time.

We crossed West End Lane at a zebra crossing and I went ahead of the others, absorbed in taking in the details of the woodwork over the doorways, the angles of the bow windows that jutted out into the little patches of garden, the patterns of the wrought-iron gates. Then I caught a glimpse of a cricket field in the distance and at once I knew where number 44 was. I shouted to the others pointing at the house. They smiled to see me so excited and when they caught up with me Nick burst into laughter.

Well, he said, following my pointing finger, you're positively a mystic from the east. You've done it again.

When we reached the house I leaned over the hedge to look into the garden before Nick could unlatch the little gate. The cherry tree in the garden was much taller than I had expected.

The front door opened when we were halfway down the path that led through the little patch of garden. Mrs Price had seen us coming; she stood framed in the doorway. She was a small woman, very thin and stooped with age. Her face was small too, but she had large, prominent eyes, like May's. She had a tight wreath of silver curls, and a short-sighted, slightly worried frown was etched into the lines of her forehead. She was wearing a severe military-green skirt, a white blouse and a grey cardigan. I had seen many pictures of her, but they had not prepared me for the transparent, almost translucent quality of her complexion: even at a distance, I could see an intricate circuitry of veins filigreed on her skin.

She met us halfway up the path and kissed Ila, and shook hands with Robi and me. She was so glad, she said to me, that we had met at last, it was such a pity May was away, she would very much have liked to meet me, she spoke so often of the kindness my family had shown her in Calcutta . . .

Nick, hugely amused, told her how I had shown them the way to the house, and how I had known that they had a cherry tree.

I've heard so much about it you see, I said awkwardly. I was embarrassed now.

Well, said Mrs Price, smiling, we must give you a guided tour, but come and have a glass of sherry first.

She led us into the hall, showed me where to hang my coat, and ushered us into a large, sunny room.

Well here we are, she said, turning to a tray that had a decanter and several glasses on it. And what will you have to drink?

She had to repeat herself twice before I heard her; I was absorbed in looking around the room.

NISSIM EZEKIEL

Goodbye Party for Miss Pushpa T.S.

Friends,
our dear sister
is departing for foreign
in two three days,
and
we are meeting today
to wish her bon voyage.

You are all knowing, friends,
what sweetness is in Miss Pushpa.
I don't mean only external sweetness
but internal sweetness.
Miss Pushpa is smiling and smiling
even for no reason
but simply because she is feeling.

Miss Pushpa is coming
from very high family.
Her father was renowned advocate
in Bulsar or Surat,
I am not remembering now which place.

Surat? Ah, yes,
once only I stayed in Surat

This poem is taken from *Ten Twentieth-Century Indian Poets*, edited by R. Parthasarathy, published by Oxford University Press India, New Delhi, 1975.

with family members
of my uncle's very old friend—
his wife was cooking nicely . . .
that was long time ago.

Coming back to Miss Pushpa
she is most popular lady
with men also and ladies also.

Whenever I asked her to do anything,
she was saying, 'Just now only
I will do it.' That is showing
good spirit. I am always
appreciating the good spirit.

Pushpa Miss is never saying no.
Whatever I or anybody is asking
she is always saying yes,
and today she is going
to improve her prospects
and we are wishing her bon voyage.

Now I ask other speakers to speak
and afterwards Miss Pushpa
will do the summing up.

PART I

Advertisements in Brighton 1822–38

This extract is from Michael H. Fisher's *The First Indian Author in English*. Fisher's account, which has been put in parantheses, is eloquent on one very important point: it shows the first published Indian writer in English as someone who was ceaselessly inventing himself and his world. As a 'shampooing surgeon'—but also, no less, as a writer—Mahomed constructed a new and changing identity as an Indian in the West. His advertisements for the self are not the least of his legacies to the Indian world of letters.

—Ed.

[Following the opening of his grand Mahomed's Baths, Dean Mahomed's fame and popularity grew dramatically. He enhanced this growth through frequent self-promotional publicity, projecting himself and his method as the latest in medical science and exotic fashion. In addition to his continuing newspaper advertisements, he expanded his book: *Cases Cured by Sake Deen Mahomed* (1820) into a full medical case book. Dean Mahomed followed this popular case book genre by organizing his book around a quasi-scientific analysis of diseases, symptoms, methods, cures, and testimonials. He named it:]

This extract is taken from Michael H. Fisher's *The First Indian Author in English*, published by Oxford University Press India, New Delhi, 1996.

Shampooing, or, Benefits Resulting From the use of The Indian
Medicated Vapour Bath, As introduced into this country by S.D.
Mahomed (A Native of India); containing a brief but
comprehensive view of the effects produced by the use of The
Warm Bath, in comparison with Steam Or Vapour Bathing. Also
A detailed account of the various Cases to which this healing
remedy may be applied; its general efficacy in peculiar diseases,
and its success in innumerable instances, when all other remedies
have been ineffectual. To which is subjoined An Alphabetical
List Of Names (Many of the very first consequence,) Subscribed
in testimony of the important use and general approval of The
Indian Method of Shampooing.

[In all, Dean Mahomed published three editions of this book: in 1822,
1826, 1838. Each edition expanded the previous one, adding another
layer to his identity to reflect the self-image he wished to project at
that time. This work received serious attention in at least one leading
literary journal.

In the first edition of *Shampooing* (1822), Dean Mahomed created
formal medical credentials for himself. In an age when each medical
faculty (Physicians, Surgeons, and Apothecaries) was gradually
organizing itself into a Royal College, with standards of formal training
required for admission, Dean Mahomed clearly felt the need to
qualify himself. In the 1820s, the standards for such medical
qualifications were still in the process of formulation; decisive
legislation to regulate the medical profession did not pass in Parliament
until 1858. In this entrepreneurial environment of the early nineteenth
century, a range of self-proclaimed experts made fortunes selling
medicine and medical treatments to the public. Dean Mahomed,
therefore, remained well within the bounds of medical and advertising
ethics of the day.

In *Shampooing*, Dean Mahomed modified his autobiography
considerably from that in *Travels*. As we have already seen, he had
lopped off his thirty years in Ireland and London, at first by tacit
omission and later by explicit statement. In *Shampooing,* he provided
himself with ten years of medical training in India, prior to his entry
into the Company's Army:]

The humble author of these sheets, is a native of India; and was born in the year 1749, at Patna, the capital of Bihar, in Hindoostan, about 290 miles N.W. of Calcutta. I was educated to the profession of, and served in the Company's Service, as a Surgeon, which capacity I afterwards relinquished, and acted in a military character, exclusively for nearly fifteen years. In the year 1780, I was appointed to a company under General, then Major Popham; and the commencement of the year 1784, left the service and came to Europe, where I have resided ever since.

[Thus in Brighton, Dean Mahomed increased his official age by a decade.

Later family traditions among Dean Mahomed's descendants attributed to him medical training in the Calcutta Hospital and such medical success that he received his promotion to Subedar as a result of them: 'Of Mahomed's early life in India it is definitely known that he was a medical student at the hospital in Calcutta. He had much success in treating cholera in the 27th Regiment of Native Infantry; in grateful recognition of this the Colonel appointed him Soobahdar of the Regiment.' This family tradition, including that Dean Mahomed served in the 27th Native Infantry, is not supported either by East India Company records or *Travels*. Rather, Captain Hugh Cossart Baker, with whom Dean Mahomed lived for a time in Cork, was an officer in the 27th Regiment of the Royal Army. Other descendants of Dean Mahomed explained the decade-wide discrepancy in the date he gave for his birth as due to the 'difficulty' of conversion from the Muslim Hijri calendar to the Christian calendar. While Dean Mahomed may have given this implausible explanation to the curious and his descendants, the 1759 date of birth he stated in *Travels* accords perfectly with existing records and the chronology of the events of his life, while the 1749 date he asserted in *Shampooing* does not.

In the next edition of *Shampooing* (1826), Dean Mahomed further enhanced the amount of scientific medical development that had gone into his 'invention'. He repeated how he developed his 'hypothesis' about the properties of his vapour and shampooing. Echoing a scientific paper, he continued: '[I] sedulously applied myself, when I arrived here, in trying such preliminary experiments' on a range of medical conditions. He deduced that this process 'which in India is used as a restorative luxury, would, with certain improvements, operate in this country also, as a most surprising and powerful remedy for many cases of disease. I felt justified in publishing to the world the discovery I had made, a discovery supported by proof the most flattering and convincing'. He further recounted the empirical evaluation by impartial (and initially sceptical) men of science who tested and proved his method:]

Since the publication of the first edition of this work [*Shampooing*], public attention has been excited; medical men of the first professional reputation did not think it beneath their dignity, to investigate the merits of my discovery, to apply the power of reasoning to account for causes and effects; and soon were convinced of the salutary and invigorating power of the Indian Vapour Baths combined with Shampooing, if judiciously applied. Upwards of a hundred medical gentlemen have since tried the experiment on themselves; most of them were invalids, but many were merely prompted by an honourable desire to ascertain truth. By those means the Faculty in general, even on the Continent, have had their attention drawn towards my humble discovery. I feel this flattering distinction, and am in return most grateful and happy—I might add proud—when names like the following have thought proper to send patients to me.

[He then named twenty-one physicians and surgeons who had referred patients to him, and continued:]

I have had recommendations from two of the first Physicians at Paris; several German Physicians have visited my establishment and honoured it with their approbation. Under such auspices, it is not to be wondered at, when I assert that I could easily swell this edition with many hundreds of additional cases: but I shall only select a few which are peculiar and important. To the Public in general, and to the Faculty in particular, who with a candour worthy of their enlightened pursuits, not only appreciated the value of the invention, but at once grasped at the full capability of it, by pointing out diseases, the cure of which had not been contemplated, such as incipient pleurisy, putrid sore throat, etc. where the curative process depends principally on inhaling the warm steam;—to all I return my most grateful thanks, and I shall, by perseverance, prove myself worthy of such signal patronage.

[Thus, by this time, Dean Mahomed had located his medical discoveries within the European scientific discourse.

In addition to 'modern' medicine, Dean Mahomed also drew upon the European classical tradition to support his method. He pointed (albeit vaguely) to laudatory references to medical bathing in Greek literature:]

BATHING is coevil with the remotest periods of antiquity. Homer mentions the use of private baths, which baths possessed medicinal properties, and were enriched by the most fragrant perfumes. In the eastern part of the world, it has ever been known and esteemed, and is continued in a variety of forms, to the present period. It is not distinctly stated by any author, I believe, that the Romans directed their attention in particular to the actual cure of disease by impregnated waters, nor did they, that I can collect, imagine any virtue to result from steam immersions, or any thing beyond the simple application of water.

[This passage contrasted strikingly with the more specific, and scathing, classical references to it by Martial and Seneca that Dean Mahomed published in *Travels* (XXV).

Dean Mahomed further took authority for his method from ancient Hindu practice: 'To the Hindoos, who are the cleanest and finest people in the East, we are principally indebted for the Medicated Bath, in cases of disease and bodily infirmity. Many complaints to which we are subject, arise from languid circulation, and for an inactive state of the animal functions, and which in many instances resist the use of medicine, and beget consequences the most protracted and fatal; the native practitioners of India are aware of this, and Shampooing has always proved a most salutary and effective remedy with them.' Dean Mahomed thus presented himself as building on Hindu traditions, somewhat broadening his personal identification from that which he

advanced in *Travels*. Many among the British public never understood
the distinction between Hindu and Muslim, or Dean Mahomed's
relationship to either religious community, even after he had lived in
Britain for well over half a century.

Dean Mahomed also selectively appropriated European descriptions
of the 'oriental' practice of shampooing. For example, in the course of
showing the extent of the practice, he republished an account by the
illustrious British traveller, Sir R.K. Porter, about shampooing in
Persia. Dean Mahomed, however, made no effort to link himself to the
Muslim practitioners whom Porter described, nor to Islamic Persia.
His inclusion of this westerner's description appeared as just another
justification for the practice.

Nowhere, indeed, did Dean Mahomed specify his own training
in his methods, or any family tradition, that would have prepared
him for this career. His very self-identification as a 'native' of India
thus would seem to have qualified him as a master of 'eastern'
knowledge generally. Familiar as we now are with his earlier years,
we can understand how, although he came to this career in his mid-
fifties, he sought to indicate to his patients and potential patients a
far longer commitment to the profession.

As Dean Mahomed retrospectively (1826) represented his start in
Brighton, he revealed his image of the difficulties which he initially
faced. He described himself as an innovative, but doubted, medical
practitioner whose empirically derived method eventually triumphed
over prejudice. This prejudice, however, appeared in his words to the
British public not so much against him on racial grounds, but rather
against him as an innovator with a better method, a challenge and rival
to more established and conventional medical practitioners:]

> On my arrival in Brighton, I was not immediately enabled to
> promulgate the decided advantages which my method had over
> the common Warm-bathing; I was fortunate however, in several
> gratuitous cures, after every other attempt had been made and
> failed; cures which soon gained circulation among those who
> were ignorant of the virtues of my Bath, and adducing the most
> positive and convincing evidence of the great superiority of
> Shampooing over every other description of treatment, in peculiar

cases. It is not in the power of any individual to give unqualified satisfaction, or attempt to establish a new opinion without the risk of incurring the ridicule, as well as censure, of some portion of mankind. So it was with me: in the face of indisputable evidence, I had to struggle with doubts and objections raised and circulated against my Bath, which, but for the repeated and numerous cures effected by it, would long since have shared the common fate of most innovations in science. Fortunately, however, I have lived to see my Bath survive the vituperations of the weak and the aspersions of the [in]credulous.

[Here he explained clearly how the value and virtues of his methods ultimately vindicated him.

DEAN MAHOMED'S PROPRIETARY CLAIM TO THE INDIAN METHOD

Through the rest of his career, Dean Mahomed increasingly wove together the identities of his method and himself, since each went to legitimize the other. Alone among his rival bath house keepers, he could point to his identity as an Indian and therefore to his proprietary right to his India-derived method. Nevertheless, as Dean Mahomed's fame grew, various competitors sought to appropriate the terms and methods of 'Indian Medicated Bath' and 'Shampooing' for themselves. By the 1820s, both these terms had become generic labels for a variety of methods found in many baths. Dean Mahomed himself broadened Indian to mean Asian generally. Further, Dean Mahomed also enhanced his stress on the primacy of his practice as the 'original', drawing upon seniority as well as ethnicity to legitimize his status.

As his success led to imitation by rivals, Dean Mahomed increasingly attributed to himself exclusive links and access to India. One of his most competitive rivals, John Molineux, opened a bath house similar to Mahomed's Baths (but somewhat smaller and less elegant), two doors down on East Cliff in 1821. In clear imitation of Mahomed's shampooing and Indian medicated vapour baths, Molineux offered first 'affriction' and then, in an effort to shift the origin of this method away from Dean Mahomed's area of expertise: 'TURKISH

MEDICATED SEA-WATER, VAPOUR, AND SHAMPOOING BATHS . . . the soothing mode of pressing the muscles and joints, which process is performed whilst in the vapour, and is called in TURKEY, and other parts, SHAMPOOING.' Much to Dean Mahomed's disgust, many patrons and guidebooks conflated the two baths, so similar were they in advertisement, location, and operation.

In response to this situation, from June 1821 onward, Dean Mahomed ran a series of front-page newspaper advertisements warning the public not to be fooled by such false imitators:]

> In consequence of the many IMITATIONS of and the repeated attempts to rival his celebrated Indian Bath, [Dean Mahomed] thinks it necessary to assure the public that the art of SHAMPOOING, as practiced in India, is exclusively confined to himself in Brighton. The well known efficacy of HIS Bath, and the numerous cures performed by him (a book of which may be had at his house) will, he feels confident, save from reproach this invaluable remedy, should error result from a SPURIOUS and IMITATIVE process, or the application be attended with less favourable effects than have been witnessed in most cases where the GENUINE INDIAN method of SHAMPOOING has been administered. HIS BATH is well known to the faculty, and is recommended in all cases of Gout, Rheumatism, Paralysis, old Sprains, Colds, Hurts of various kinds, and many other diseases to which the human frame is subject. It is simple in its operation and therefore more easily imitated, but though the outward appearance may be copied, the EFFICACY of it defies competition. To avoid mistake the public are particularly requested to enquire for MAHOMED'S BATHS, No. 39, EAST CLIFF.

SUNITY DEVEE

My First Visit to England

The year 1887 was expected to be a memorable one for India, as our late beloved Queen-Empress would celebrate her Jubilee. India was anxious to show her loyalty to the Sovereign whose high ideals and humanity endeared her to all her people. Many of our princes therefore decided to render their homage in person. My husband made his plans for this eventful year long beforehand, but he cleverly kept all of us in the dark as to his intention that I should accompany him to England. It must be remembered that the conditions of life among Indian ladies were very different in 1887 from what they are today. The Maharani of Baroda, I believe, had once gone to Switzerland, but for the wife of a ruler to visit England with her husband caused quite a sensation. I think I am right in saying that I was the first Maharani to do such a thing, and I may as well confess that I was very apprehensive of what the visit would hold for me. I knew absolutely nothing about the journey. I was going to be a stranger in a strange land, and I was sensitive enough to dread being ogled at, for I well knew that this must be my fate in London.

We sailed on the P. and O. boat—Ganges or Ballarat—I forget which. I remember the Captain of the boat took great pains to ensure our comfort on board. Our entourage consisted of my two brothers, Nirmal and Profulla, two ADCs, J. Raikut and S. Singh, our English private secretary, the late Mr Bignell and his family, and our English

This extract is taken from *The Autobiography of an Indian Princess*, published by John Murray, London, 1921.

nurse, besides our two selves and our three little children. We also had some Indian servants. I cannot describe my feelings when I realized that I had actually left the shores of my native land, India, had passed another milestone on the road of life; but I little dreamed that the far-off country for which I was bound was destined to be a land of sorrow for me in the distant future.

The glory of the sea enchanted me. When the boat was out on the ocean and no land could be seen, all Nature seemed to speak of the infinite God, and I felt so small. In the dark evenings when the water gleamed with phosphorescence, it looked as though there were thousands of stars under the sea responding to the stars above. It really was grand; a grandeur that no one could describe unless he had actually experienced it. Before we embarked, I tasted meat for the first time in my life, and I disliked the flavour so much that for the first few days of the voyage I ate nothing but a few vegetables. I often had fits of depression and sometimes left the dinner table to relieve my feelings with a good cry.

The Maharajah parted from us at Port Said, as it was decided that it would be easier and less fatiguing for me with my little ones to go by sea instead of taking the shorter route across Europe. I was delighted when I first saw Malta and Gibraltar. Mr Bignell met us at Tilbury Docks. Just as we were seated in the train, I was handed a message from Queen Victoria that she wished to see me at Court in my national dress. It was May, but very cold for the time of year, and my first sight of London on a Sunday did nothing to lift my spirits. I saw half-deserted streets swept with a bitter wind which had already chapped my face, and I was heartily glad when at last we reached the Grosvenor Hotel. There all was brightness and animation. My husband was pleased to see me and the children and to show me the grand suite of rooms which had been reserved for us. The housekeeper at the Grosvenor had thought of everything that would make us comfortable, and my memory of her is of a pleasant woman with plenty of common sense. One thing I did not like. Our luxurious suite of rooms had no bathroom. I was told I was to have a bath in my room, but this I would not do. I was shown to a big bath, but was horrified when I was told that I must pass all those corridors each time I wanted a bath. I refused point-blank, and they finally prepared a small room as a bathroom for me.

Kind invitations poured in, and I was happy to see many old friends. I shall never forget the question Sir Ashley Eden put to me: 'What do you think of our London fog?' for although it was May, I had experienced a yellow fog. I answered:

'Not much, Sir Ashley; I do not think I shall ever care for the London fog.'

We dined at Sir Ashley's, and there I first met the present Lord Crewe. We had a large drawing-room at the hotel which I could never make cosy or comfortable; on rainy days especially, it felt damp and gloomy. When I went out for drives I used to see little children with their toy boats in Hyde Park, and I soon got a nice little sailing yacht for my Rajey, and both mother and son enjoyed floating this vessel on the Serpentine. Rajey's little face beamed with delight when he saw his boat cruising along. The late Lady Rosebery was most kind to my little ones; Rajey and Girlie spent some happy afternoons at her house. The present Lady Crewe was a little girl then, and her brother, Lord Dalmeny, made a great friend of dear Rajey and always remained the same.

Soon after we arrived in London, I was alarmed to find my baby, Jit, develop bronchitis. Both my husband and I were most anxious about the child, and two Royal ladies—one of whom was Her Royal Highness the Princess of Wales, now Queen Alexandra—offered the services of their own doctors. When Jit got better the nursery was often honoured by two Royal visitors, Her Royal Highness the late Duchess of Teck and our present Queen, then Princess May. These two charming ladies graciously came and played with my children. It was lovely to see little Jit in Princess May's arms. I have seldom met so sweet a personality as the Duchess of Teck. She simply radiated kindness and good nature. One glance at her happy, handsome face inspired confidence. I was greatly honoured when she said she would chaperone me during the Jubilee festivities. The present Queen was then a tall graceful girl, with a wild-rose freshness and fairness, and gifted with the same simple, unaffected charming manners as her mother, which had already endeared her to me.

It had been intimated to me that Queen Victoria wished to see me privately before the Court, and it was arranged that I should go to Buckingham Palace for an audience. The question of what I was to wear had to be settled. The Maharajah, who always displayed the greatest interest in my wardrobe toilets, selected and ordered my gown for this great occasion. I was extremely nervous, and as I saw my reflection in the mirror in the pale grey dress I felt more terrified than ever. My maid, seeing me look so pale and shaken, brought me a glass of port. I never touch wine, except when it is absolutely necessary. My hand trembled so that I spilt half of the wine over my gown. Instantly a chorus of 'How lucky' arose. But I gazed rather ruefully at the stains.

'Well, Sunity, it is time for us to start' said my husband, and I followed him to the carriage. Lord Cross, who was then Secretary of State for India, received us, and his wife whispered a few reassuring words to me before the officials escorted us down the corridors to the small room where Her Majesty was.

I cannot describe my feelings when I found myself in the presence of the Queen. To us Indians she was more or less a legendary figure endowed with wonderful attributes, an ideal ruler, and an ideal woman, linked to our hearts across 'the black waters' by silken chains of love and loyalty. I looked at Her Majesty anxiously, and my first impression instantly dispelled my nervousness: a short, stout lady dressed in mourning who came forward and kissed me twice. I made a deep curtsy, and stepped back, and then my husband came forward and bent low over the Queen's hand. I experienced a feeling, as did everyone with whom Her late Majesty came in contact, that she possessed great personal magnetism, and she certainly was the embodiment of dignity. Her conversation was simple and kindly, and every word revealed her as a queen, woman and mother. I was delighted to find that I had not been disappointed in my ideal, and felt eager to go back to India that I might tell my country-women about our wonderful Empress. The audience occupied only a few minutes, but nothing could have exceeded Her Majesty's graciousness, and I came away proud and glad, and laughed at myself for my earlier apprehensions at being received by one so gracious. The Maharajah was very pleased at our reception and told me how proud he was of me.

The next day we attended the Drawing-room. I wore a white and gold brocade gown and a Crepe de Chine sari. I waited with the other ladies, and as it was a cold afternoon I was very glad to find a little cosy corner to sit down. I looked around me, and was admiring the pretty dresses and faces when I suddenly saw what I thought was a gentleman wearing a diamond tiara. I gazed at the face and then discovered it belonged to a lady who had a thick moustache. I went into the throne-room, and as I was told by Lady Cross that I need not kiss her Majesty when I made my curtsy, as I had already been received privately, when Her Majesty wanted to kiss me I avoided her! But later I distinctly heard the Queen say to the Princess of Wales: 'Why would not the Maharani kiss me?' This made me so nervous that I thought I would drop on the floor.

After I had finished making all my curtsies I went and stood near kind Lady Salisbury and watched the other ladies pass. One of the duchesses, an elderly woman in a very low-cut dress trimmed with old lace and wearing magnificient jewels, to my mind looked extremely miserable. I can still see her trembling as she curtsied; whether it was the cold or her aged body was tired I cannot say. I was greatly interested in all I saw; but shocked at the low-cut gowns worn by the ladies present. The cold was most trying to complexions and shoulders, the prevailing tints of which were either brick-red or a chilly reddish-blue. Now that the Courts are held in the evenings women's beauty is seen to greater advantage, but I shall never forget that May afternoon and the inartistic exposure of necks and arms.

We received an invitation for the State ball. My husband chose a gown of blue and silver brocade for me for this important occasion. Just before we left the hotel for the palace, the Maharajah said: 'Sunity, if the Prince of Wales asks you to dance with him, you must; it would be a very great honour.'

'I can't,' I faltered, 'I simply can't; you know I do not dance.'

'Never mind, you cannot refuse your future king.'

'Well,' I said, 'I don't think I will go; let me send a letter of apology.'

'Impossible! We are bound to attend; it is a command.'

I said no more, but prayed and hoped that I might be overlooked by the Prince. Not so, however. Soon after we entered the ballroom a message was sent by His Royal Highness asking me to dance with him. I returned the answer that, although I greatly appreciated the honour, I must refuse as I never danced. Then came another message: It was only the Lancers, and His Royal Highness would show me the steps.

Again I refused; then, to my great surprise, the late King George of Greece came up to where I was sitting. 'Do come and dance, Maharani,' he said, 'I assure you there is nothing in it.'

'Please forgive me, Your Majesty,' I stammered, 'but I cannot dance.' The late King of Denmark, then Crown Prince, also graciously asked me to dance. By this time I was too nervous for words, and I heard a sweet voice say: 'Oh, look! Hasn't the Maharani tiny little feet?' I glanced in an agony of shyness at the dais from whence the tones proceeded, quite close to where I was sitting, and saw that the speaker was none other than the Prince of Wales! I did not know what to do, and felt for the moment as if I were all feet. My skirt was rather short, and I could not tuck my shoes out of sight. I was very glad and relieved when supper-time came. I went in with the Royal family to supper. Everyone was most gracious, and the Prince of Wales teased me about my not accepting him as a partner.

'What do you think of the ball?' asked one of the Princesses.

'It is a grand sight, ma'am; I think the jewels are wonderful.' I was introduced to several foreign royalties, and one girl I loved directly I saw her. She was the Grand Duchess Sergius of Russia with whom I afterwards became very friendly.

On the morning of the Jubilee I was astir early. I wore a pale orange-coloured gown with a sari to match. We left the hotel at a quarter-past nine. As we drove to the Abbey I was struck by the perfect behaviour of the crowd.

It was a hot, dusty drive, and I was glad of the shade of my parasol. Suddenly a shout arose. 'Put down that sunshade, please, and let's have a look at you.'

'Don't,' whispered the Maharajah, 'you'll get sunstroke.' I hesitated. 'Come now, put it down.' I closed my parasol, and as I did so was heartily cheered. 'That's right,' roared the good-humoured crowd, 'thank you very much.'

On entering the Abbey we were escorted to our seats.

It was an impressive ceremony, and the Queen looked inspired when she came back from the altar. After the service was over, as Her Majesty walked down the aisle, her eyes met mine, and she smiled. I was the only Maharani present, and I like to remember this signal honour.

RABINDRANATH TAGORE

Letters and Notes

LONDON (?), 1879

By and by the ship arrives and docks at Southampton. The Bengali passengers have reached the shores of England. They set off for London. As they disembark from the train an English porter approaches them. Politely he enquires if he can be of service. As he takes down their luggage and ushers them into a carriage, the Bengali thinks to himself, How extraordinary! How polite the English are! That Englishmen could be so polite, he had no idea. He presses a whole shilling into the porter's hand. Never mind the cost, the newly arrived Bengali youth tells himself, the salaam of a white man was worth every penny of that shilling . . .

Before the Bengalis arrive in England, their friends who are already here have arranged rooms for them. As the Bengali enters his room, he sees a carpet on the floor, pictures hanging on the walls, a large mirror in its proper place, a sofa, stools and chairs, one or two glass flower vases, and to one side a baby piano. Good heavens! The Bengalis summon their friends: 'We aren't here as rich men, you know! My dear fellows, we haven't much cash on us, we can't afford to stay in rooms like these.' Their friends are highly amused, having completely forgotten their own precisely similar behaviour when *they* first arrived. Treating the new arrivals as thoroughgoing rice-eating rustics they tell them in voices full

This extract is taken from *Rabindranath Tagore, An Anthology*, edited by Krishna Dutta and Andrew Robinson, published by St. Martin's Press, New York, 1997.

of experience, 'All rooms are like this over here.' This reminds the newcoming Bengalis of the rooms in our own country: damp, with a wooden cot covered by a wicker mat, here and there people puffing on hookahs, others lounging around a board game, their bodies bare to the waist, their shoes cast casually aside, while a cow lies tethered in the courtyard that has walls plastered in cow-dung cakes, and wet washing hangs drying over a veranda. For the first few days the Bengalis find themselves terribly embarrassed to sit on a chair or stool, lie on a bed, eat off a table or walk about a carpet. They sit very awkwardly on the sofas, fearful lest they make them dirty or damage them in any way. They imagine that the sofas have been put there for decoration, the owners surely cannot have intended them to be spoilt by use. But if that is their first impression of their rooms, there follows another impression, almost as immediate and even more significant.

In some smaller types of accommodation in England the figure called the 'landlord' still exists; but most Bengali logders must deal with a 'landlady'. Settling the rent, sorting out various problems, arranging food, is all down to the landlady. When my Bengali friends first stepped into their rooms, she quickly appeared, an Englishwoman waiting to greet them with the politest of 'good morning's. Hurriedly they returned the greeting in the most proper manner, and then stood struck dumb. And when they saw their various England-worshipping friends strike up an easy conversation with the lady in question, their awkwardness turned to absolute awe. To think of it: they were talking to a real live memsahib, complete in shoes, hat and dress! Here was a sight to stir real respect in a Bengali heart. Would they ever acquire this courage shown by their England-worshipping friends? Surely it was beyond the bounds of possibility.

Afterwards, having installed the newcomers, the England-worshipping friends went off to their respective residences and spent the next few days making fun of Bengali ignorance—while the aforementioned landlady came each day to enquire, most politely, what my newly arrived friends liked to have, and what they did not like to have. My friends soon came to regard these occasions with real pleasure. One of them even told me that when he first ticked off this Englishwoman—ever so slightly—he felt thrilled with himself for the rest of the day. Notwithstanding, the sun did not rise in the West, mountains did not move and fire did not freeze that day . . .

To know the *ingabanga*—the England-worshipping Bengali[1] —truly, one must observe him in three situations. One must see how he behaves with Englishmen; how he behaves with ordinary Bengalis; and how he behaves with fellow *ingabangas*. To see an *ingabanga* face to face with an Englishman is really a sight to gladden your eyes. The weight of courtesy in his words is like a burden making his shoulders droop; in debate he is the meekest and mildest of men; and if he is compelled to disagree, he will do so with an expression of extreme regret and with a thousand apologies. An *ingabanga* sitting with an Englishman, whether he be talking or listening, will appear in his every gesture and facial movement to be the acme of humility. But catch him with his own countrymen in his own sphere, and he will display genuine temper. One who has lived three years in England will regard himself as infinitely superior to one who has spent a mere one year here. Should the former type of resident happen to argue with the latter type, one may observe the 'three-year' man exert his prowess. Each word he utters, and each inflection he gives it, sounds like a dictum personally dictated to him by the lips of goddess Saraswati.[2] Anyone who dares to contradict him he will bluntly label 'mistaken', or even 'ignorant'—to his face . . .

Had you seen for yourself the thorough research these people put into which way up a knife or fork should be held when dining, your respect would surely be still further increased. What the currently fashionable cut of a jacket is, whether today's gentleman wears his trousers tight or loose, whether one should dance the waltz, the polka or the mazurka, and whether meat should follow fish or vice versa—these people know all these things with unerring accuracy. Their preoccupation with trivia—what is and is not 'done'—is far greater than that of the natives of this country. If you happen to use the wrong knife to eat fish, an Englishman would not think much of it; he would put it down to your being a foreigner. But if an *ingabanga* Bengali saw you, he would probably have to take smelling salts. Were you to drink champagne out of a sherry glass, he would stare at you aghast, as if your ignorant blunder had totally upset the world's tranquillity. And were

---

[1] Or anglomaniac.
[2] Goddess of learning.

you, God forbid, to wear a morning coat in the evening, had he a magistrate's power he would condemn you to solitary confinement . . .

There is one other special feature of the *ingabanga* I must tell you about. The majority of those who come here do not confess if they are married—because married men naturally command less attention from unmarried ladies. By pretending to be bachelors they can mix much more freely in society and have much more fun, otherwise their unmarried companions would never permit such goings on. There is a lot to be gained by declaring oneself unattached.

No doubt there are many England-worshipping Bengalis who do not fit my description. I have written only of the general characteristics of the species as I have spotted them.

MOSCOW, SEPTEMBER 1930

In Russia at last! Everything I see amazes me. This country is unlike any other. It is radically different. From top to bottom here they are rousing up everybody equally.

Through the ages, civilized communities have contained a body of common people. They form the majority—these beasts of burden, who have no time to become human beings. They grow up on the leftovers of a country's wealth, having the least food, the least clothes and the least education; and they serve the rest. They toil the most, yet receive the largest ration of indignity. At the least excuse they starve and are humiliated by their superiors. They are deprived of everything that makes life worth living. They are like a lampstand bearing the lamp of civilization on their heads: those above them receive light, while they are smeared with trickles of oil.

I had often thought about such people, but had come to the conclusion that there was no help for them. For if no one was down below, no one could be up above. People do not see beyond their immediate needs, unless they are above mere subsistence level. The earning of his livelihood cannot be the destiny of man. Human civilization consists of more than mere subsistence. The most cherished products of civilization have flourished in the field of leisure. Civilization must preserve a corner for leisure. So I used to think that for those fitted to labour at the bottom of the heap by their poor mental and physical constitution or by force of circumstances, the best that could be done was to make strenuous efforts to improve their education, health and comfort.

But the trouble is that nothing permanent can be built on charity; efforts to do good imposed from outside are vitiated at every step. Without equality, no real help can be rendered. I have not been able to think all this through satisfactorily—but whatever the case, the notion that the advance of civilization depends on keeping down the bulk of humanity and denying it its human rights, is a reproach to the human mind.

Consider how foodless India has fed England. Many English people think it natural that the fulfilment of India should lie eternally in the nourishing of England. To these people it is not wrong to keep a nation enslaved for ever, in order that England may become great and do great things for mankind—what does it matter if the nation has little to eat or wear? While other English people, out of sheer pity, sometimes feel they must help us to improve our conditions slightly. And yet, over the past hundred years we have acquired neither education nor health nor wealth.

At the level of the individual in all societies, the same truth applies: men cannot do good to those whom they do not respect. At the very least, one can say that whenever there is self-interest at stake, a clash ensues. Here in Russia they are seeking a root-and-branch solution to this problem. It is not yet time to consider the final results of the attempt, but for now I can say that whatever I see astonishes me. Education is the ideal path to solving all our problems. Everywhere the majority of people have been deprived of full opportunities for education—in India it is the vast majority. The extraordinary vigour with which education has taken hold of Russian society is amazing to witness. The measure is not merely the numbers being educated, but the thoroughness, the intensity of the education. What dedication and application to ensure that no one remains helpless or idle! Not only in European Russia, but among the semi-civilized races of Central Asia too, the floodgates of education have been opened. Tireless efforts are being made to bring the latest fruits of science to the people. The theatres and the fine opera houses are crowded, but those coming to them are peasants and workers. Nowhere are they humiliated. In the few institutions I have so far visited, I have seen the awakening of these people's spirit and the joy of their self-respect. The difference between them and the working class in England, leave alone our masses, is colossal. What we have been attempting to do at our Shriniketan, they are doing here at a superior level all over the land. How splendid it would be if our workers could come here for training. Every day I compare conditions here with those in India: what is, and what might have been! Doctor Harry Timbres, my American companion, is studying the health service of this country: its excellence is astonishing. But where does that leave diseased, hungry, hapless India! A few years ago, the condition of the Russian masses was fully comparable with that of the Indian masses. Over that short period things have rapidly changed here, whereas we Indians are still up to our necks in stagnation.

I do not say all is perfect here; there are grave defects, which will bring them trouble some day. Briefly, the problem is that they have made a mould for their education system—and human beings cannot endure being cast in a mould. If an educational theory does not correspond with the law of living minds, either the mould will shatter or the minds will be paralysed and men will become automata.

I notice that the boys here have been divided into groups and charged with different responsibilities. In running their dormitories, they have all sorts of duties: some look after health, others after the stores, over which they have sole control. They have only a single supervisor. I have long tried to do the same at our Shantiniketan, but little has happened beyond framing some rules. One reason is that the prime object of our school is seen as getting the boys through their examinations: everything else is considered secondary; in other words, if something extra can be achieved without bother, well and good, if not, let things be. Our lazy minds are loath to tackle tasks that lie beyond what is compulsory. Moreover, from childhood we have been used to cramming books. But of what use are rules, unless the rule-makers are sincere about them; otherwise, the rules are bound to be ignored. There is little happening here that goes beyond my own thinking on rural development and education—the difference is that here the ideas are backed by the power, enthusiasm and administrative ability of the authorities. Much of this derives from their greater physical strength: our malaria-struck, under-nourished bodies do not work at full vigour. Progress here is easy because in a cold climate people have strong bones. The strength of our workers cannot be reckoned by counting heads; for they are not whole men.

PERSIA, 13 APRIL 1932

Yesterday we got up at three-thirty in the morning, and left at four o'clock. The aeroplane reached Bushire at half-past eight. The governor himself is acting as our host, and there is no end to his solicitude for our comfort.

Let me set down various thoughts on how I, this son of earth, first became intimate with the sky.

The thing about flying creatures that has struck me from my earliest years is the effortlessness of their motion. Their wings and the air have all the sweetness of friendship. How well I remember that at noontime, as I gazed endlessly from the top of the stairs to our roof at the kites soaring above us, it seemed to me they were flying for the sheer joy of unimpeded buoyancy, rather than to serve any purpose; a joy that was manifest not only in the grace of their movement but in the beauty of their physical form. Sails look beautiful because they are nicely adjusted to the wind. The wings of a bird, likewise, acquire their graceful proportions through being poised in harmony with the air currents, to say nothing of their play of colours . . . Earthly motion always seems to require effort; gravity reigns supreme, and there is no getting rid of its burden. The aspect of the aerial regions that has long captivated me is the freedom they allow to the play of beauty, the freedom from weight.

Now comes an age in which man has lifted the burdens of earth into the air. His power is the aspect of himself he displays in flying. His progress is not in harmony with the wind, but in opposition to it, importing the spirit of conflict from the mundane world into the empyrean. Its sound is not that of a bird singing, but of a raging beast: the earth, having conquered the air, bellows its victory. . .

The herald of the modern age, the flying machine, is an unfeeling creature, which elbows aside whatever does not serve its purpose. Whether there is a rosy dawn suffusing the eastern sky or a pearl-lustre of departing day lingering over the soft blue of the western horizon, this upstart machine drones on hideously, without shame, like a monstrous beetle.

As it goes higher and higher, it reduces the play of our sense to that of one sense alone—sight—and even that does not fully remain. The signs that tell us the earth is real are gradually obliterated, and a three-dimensional picture is flattened into two-dimensional lines. . . Thus deprived of its substantiality, the earth's hold on our mind and heart is loosened. And it is borne in on me how such aloofness can become terrible, when man finds it expedient to rain destruction on the vagueness below. Who is the slayer and who the slain? Who is kin and who is stranger? This travesty of the teaching of the *Bhagavad Gita*—raised on high by the flying machine.

A British air force is stationed at Baghdad. Its Christian chaplain informs me that they are engaged in bombing operations on some Sheikh villages. The men, women and children done to death there meet their fate by a decree from the stratosphere of British imperialism—which finds it easy to shower death because of its distance from its individual victims. So dim and insignificant do those unskilled in the modern arts of killing appear to those who glory in such skill! Christ acknowledged all mankind to be the children of his Father; but for the modern Christians both Father and children have receded into shadows, un-recognizable from the elevation of his bombarding plane— for which reason these blows are dealt at the very heart of Christ himself.

The official priest of the Iraqi air force asked, on their behalf, for a message from me. I copy here what I gave them:

> From the beginning of our days man has imagined the seat of divinity to be in the upper air, from which comes light, and blows the breath of life, for all the creatures on this earth. The peace of its dawn, the splendour of its sunset, the voice of eternity in its starry silence, have inspired countless generations of men with a sense of the ineffable presence of the infinite, urging their minds away from the sordid interests of daily life. Man is content with this dust-laden earth for his dwelling place, for the acting of the drama of his tangled life, ever waiting for a call to perfection from the boundless depth of purity in the

translucent atmosphere surrounding him. If, in an evil moment, man's cruel history should spread its black wings to invade that realm of divine dreams with its cannibalistic greed and fratricidal ferocity, then God's curse will certainly descend upon us for such hideous desecration, and the curtain will finally be rung down upon the world of man, for whom God feels ashamed.

On the other hand, I should also mention the feeling of inferiority brought upon me by the aeroplane . . . The air-chariot of old, of which we read, belonged to the realm of Lord Indra—mortals like King Dushyanta occasionally had a ride in it by special invitation. This was exactly my situation. The inventors of the aeroplane belong to a different race. Had this achievement of theirs been merely a matter of superior skill, it would not have so affected me, but it denotes superior force of character: indomitable perseverance, unflagging courage, things to be really proud of. For this I offer them my salutation.

Look at our four Dutch pilots—immensely built, the personification of energy. Their country of birth has not drained them of life, but kept them fresh. Their rude, overflowing health, bequeathed by generations brought up on nourishing food, does not permit them to remain tied down by dull routine. But the millions of India have not enough to eat and, moreover, they have been exhausted by the toll paid to internal and external enemies. Any worthwhile achievement depends on the collaboration of man's physical and mental forces. We may have the mind, but where is our vitality?

TO CHARLES FREER ANDREWS

Andrews, an English missionary who became a close associate of both Tagore and Gandhi, was left in charge of Tagore's Shantiniketan school when Tagore visited the West in 1920–21. During this period, Gandhi launched his movement of non-cooperation with the Government.

2970 Ellis Avenue, Chicago
5 March 1921

Dear friend, lately I have been receiving more and more news and newspaper cuttings from India giving rise in my mind to a painful struggle that presages a period of suffering which is waiting for me.

I am striving with all my power to tune my mood of mind to be in accord with the great feeling of excitement sweeping across my country. But deep in my being why is there this spirit of resistance maintaining its place in spite of my strong desire to remove it? I fail to find a clear answer and through my gloom of dejection breaks out a smile and voice saying, 'Your place is on the seashore of worlds, with children; there is your truth, your peace, and I am with you there.' And this is why lately I have been playing with metres, with merest nothings. These are whims that are content to be borne away by the current of time, dancing in the sun and laughing as they disappear. But while I play, the whole creation is amused, for are not flowers and leaves never-ending experiments in metre, is not my God an eternal waster of time? He flings stars and planets in the whirlwind of changes, he floats paper boats of ages filled with his fancies on the rushing stream of appearance. When I tease him and beg him to allow me to remain his little follower and accept a few trifles of mine as the cargo of his paper boat, he smiles and I trot behind him catching the hem of his robe. But where am I among the crowd, pushed from behind, pressed from all sides? And what is this noise about me? If it is a song then my own *sitar* can catch the tune and I can join in the chorus, for I am a singer. But if it is a shout then my voice is wrecked and I am lost in bewilderment. I have been trying all these days to find a melody, straining my ear, but the idea of non-cooperation, with its mighty volume of sound does not sing to me, its congregated menace of negation shouts. And I say to myself, 'If you cannot keep step with your countrymen at this great crisis of their history, never say that you are right and rest of them wrong; only give up your role as a soldier, go back to your corner as a poet, be ready to accept popular derision and disgrace.'

Rathi,[3] in support of the present movement, has often said to me that the passion for rejection is a stronger power in the beginning than the acceptance of an ideal. Though I know it to be a fact, I cannot accept it as a truth. We must choose our allies once and for all, for they stick to us even when we might be glad to be rid of them. If we once claim strength from intoxication, then in the time of reaction our

---

[3] Son of Rabindranath Tagore.

normal strength is bankrupt, and we go back again and again to the demon that lends us resources in a vessel whose bottom it takes away.

Brahma-vidya[4] in India has for its object *mukti*, emancipation, while Buddhism has *nirvana*, extinction. It may be argued that both have the same idea [under] different names. But names represent attitudes of mind, emphasize particular aspects of truth. *Mukti* draws our attention to the positive, and *nirvana* to the negative side of truth. Buddha kept silence all through his teachings about the truth of the *Om*, the *everlasting yes*, his implication being that by the negative path of destroying the self we naturally reach that truth. Therefore he emphasized the fact *of dukkha,* misery, which had to be avoided and the *Brahma-vidya* emphasized the fact of *anandam*[5] which had to be attained. The latter cult also needs for its fulfilment the discipline of self-abnegation, but it holds before its view the idea of Brahma, not only at the end but all through the process of realization. Therefore the idea of life's training was different in the Vedic period from that of the Buddhistic. In the former it was the purification of life's joy, in the latter it was the eradicating of it. The abnormal type of asceticism to which Buddhism gave rise in India revelled in celibacy and mutilation of life in all different forms. But the forest life of the *Brahmanas* was not antagonistic to the social life of man, but harmonious with it. It was like our musical instrument *tanpura* whose duty is to supply the fundamental notes to the music to save it from going astray into discordance. It believed in *anandam,* the music of the soul, and its own simplicity was not to kill it but to guide it.

The idea of non-cooperation is political asceticism. Our students are bringing their offering of sacrifices to what? Not to a fuller education but to non-education. It has at its back a fierce joy of annihilation which in its best form is asceticism and in its worst form is that orgy of frightfulness in which human nature, losing faith in the basic reality of normal life, finds a disinterested delight in unmeaning devastation, as has been shown in the late war and on other occasions which came nearer home to us. *No* in its passive moral form is asceticism and in its active moral form is violence. The desert is as

---

[4] Branch of learning imparting knowledge of God.
[5] Bliss.

much a form of *himsa* as is the raging sea in storm, they both are against life.

I remember the day, during the Swadeshi Movement[6] in Bengal, when a crowd of young students came to see me in the first floor of our Vichitra house. They said to me that if I ordered them to leave their schools and colleges they would instantly obey me. I was emphatic in my refusal to do so, and they went away angry, doubting the sincerity of my love for my motherland. Long before this ebullition of excitement, I myself had given a thousand rupees, when I had not five rupees to call my own, to open a *swadeshi* store and courted banter and bankruptcy. The reason for my refusing to advise those students to leave their schools was because the anarchy of a mere emptiness never tempts me, even when it is resorted to as a temporary shelter. I am frightened of an abstraction which is ready to ignore living reality. These students were no mere phantoms to me; their life was a great fact to them and to the All. I could not lightly take upon myself the tremendous responsibility of a mere negative programme for them which would uproot them from their soil, however thin and poor that soil might be. The great injury and injustice which had been done to those boys who were tempted away from their career before any real provision was made, could never be made good to them. Of course that is nothing from the point of view of an abstraction which can ignore the infinite value even of the smallest fraction of reality. But the throb of life in the heart of the most insignificant of men beats in the unison of love with the heart-throb of the infinite. I wish I were the little creature Jack whose one mission was to kill the giant abstraction which is claiming the sacrifice of individuals all over the world under highly painted masks of delusion.

I say again and again that I am a poet, that I am not a fighter by nature. I would give everything to be one with my surroundings. I love my fellow beings and I prize their love. Yet I have been chosen by destiny to ply my boat there where the current is against me. What irony of fate is this, that I should be preaching cooperation of cultures between East and West on this side of the sea just at the moment when

---

[6] Nationalist movement in Bengal, started in 1905, akin to Ireland's Sinn Fein; Swadeshi means 'of our Country', i.e. indigenous.

the doctrine of non-cooperation is preached on the other side? You know that I do not believe in the material civilization of the West, just as I do not believe the physical body to be the highest truth in man. But I still less believe in the destruction of the physical body. What is needed is the establishment of harmony between the physical and the spiritual nature of man, maintaining of balance between the foundation and superstructure. I believe in the true meeting of the East and the West. Love is the ultimate truth of soul; we should do all we can not to outrage that truth, to carry its banner against all opposition. The idea of non-cooperation unnecessarily hurts that truth. It is not our hearth fire, but the fire that burns out our hearth.

While I have been considering the non-cooperation idea one thought has come to me over and over again which I must tell you. *Bara Dada*[7] and myself are zamindars, which means collectors of revenue under British Government. Until the time comes when we give up paying revenue and allow our lands to be sold we have not the right to ask students or anybody else to make any sacrifice which may be all they have. My father was about to give up all his property for the sake of truth and honesty. And likewise we may come to that point when we have to give up our means of livelihood. If we do not feel that that point has been reached by us then at least we should at once make ample provision out of our competency for others who are ready to risk their all. When I put to myself this problem the answer which I find is that by temperament and training all the good I am now capable of doing presupposes a certain amount of wealth. If I am to begin to earn my living, possibly I shall be able to support myself but nothing better than that. Which will mean not merely sacrificing my money but my mind. I know that my God may claim even that, and by the very reclaiming repay me. Utter privation and death may have to be my ultimate sacrifice for the sake of some ideals which represent immortality. But so long as I do not feel the call or respond to it myself how can I urge others to follow the path which may prove to be the path of utter renunciation? Let the individuals choose their own responsibility of sacrifice, but are we ready to accept that responsibility for them? Do we fully realize what it may mean in

---

[7] Rabindranath's eldest brother, a keen supporter of Gandhi.

suffering or in evil? or is it a mere abstraction for us which leaves us untouched [by] all the concrete possibilities of misery [for] individuals? Let us first of all try to think [of] them as the nearest and dearest to us and then ask them to choose danger and poverty for their share [in] life.

    With love,
      Ever yours
        Rabindranath Tagore

M.K. Gandhi

In England and South Africa

ENGLAND

With my mother's permission and blessings, I set off exultantly for
Bombay, leaving my wife with a baby of a few months. But on arrival
there friends told my brother that the Indian Ocean was rough in June
and July, and as this was my first voyage, I should not be allowed to
sail until November. Someone also reported that a steamer had just
been sunk in a gale. This made my brother uneasy, and he refused to
take the risk of allowing me to sail immediately. Leaving me with a
friend in Bombay, he returned to Rajkot to resume his duty. He put
the money for my travelling expenses in the keeping of a brother-in-
law, and left word with some friends to give me whatever help I might
need.

Time hung heavily on my hands in Bombay. I dreamt continually
of going to England.

Meanwhile my caste-people were agitated over my going abroad.
No Modh Bania had been to England up to now, and if I dared to do
so, I ought to be brought to book! A general meeting of the caste was
called and I was summoned to appear before it. I went. How I
suddenly managed to muster up courage I do not know. Nothing
daunted, and without the slightest hesitation, I came before the meeting.
The Sheth—the headman of the community—who was distantly related

This extract is taken from *An Autobiography or The Story of my Experiments
with Truth*, published by Navjivan Publishing, Ahmedabad, 1927.

to me and had been on very good terms with my father, thus accosted me:

'In the opinion of the caste, your proposal to go to England is not proper. Our religion forbids voyages abroad. We have also heard that it is not possible to live there without compromising our religion. One is obliged to eat and drink with Europeans!'

To which I replied: 'I do not think it is at all against our religion to go to England. I intend going there for further studies. And I have already solemnly promised to my mother to abstain from three things you fear most. I am sure the vow will keep me safe.'

'But we tell you,' rejoined the Sheth, 'that it is *not* possible to keep our religion there. You know my relations with your father and you ought to listen to my advice.'

'I know those relations,' said I. 'And you are as an elder to me. But I am helpless in this matter. I cannot alter my resolve to go to England. My father's friend and adviser, who is a learned Brahman, sees no objection to my going to England, and my mother and brother have also given me their permission.'

We entered the Bay of Biscay, but I did not begin to feel the need either of meat or liquor. I had been advised to collect certificates of my having abstained from meat, and I asked the English friend to give me one. He gladly gave it and I treasured it for some time. But when I saw later that one could get such a certificate in spite of being a meat-eater, it lost all its charm for me. If my word was not to be trusted, where was the use of possessing a certificate in the matter?

However, we reached Southampton, as far as I remember, on a Saturday. On the boat I had worn a black suit, the white flannel one, which my friends had got me, having been kept especially for wearing when I landed. I had thought that white clothes would suit me better when I stepped ashore, and therefore I did so in white flannels. Those were the last days of September, and I found I was the only person wearing such clothes. I left in charge of an agent of Grindlay and Co. all my kit, including the keys, seeing that many others had done the same and I must follow suit.

I had four notes of introduction: to Dr P.J. Mehta, to Sjt. Dalpatram Shukla, to Prince Ranjitsinhji and to Dadabhai Naoroji. Someone on board had advised us to put up at the Victoria Hotel in London. Sjt.

Mazmudar and I accordingly went there. The shame of being the only person in white clothes was already too much for me. And when at the Hotel I was told that I should not get my things from Grindlay's the next day, it being a Sunday, I was exasperated.

Dr Mehta, to whom I had wired from Southampton, called at about eight o'clock the same evening. He gave me a hearty greeting. He smiled at my being in flannels. As we were talking, I casually picked up his top-hat, and trying to see how smooth it was, passed my hand over it the wrong way and disturbed the fur. Dr Mehta looked somewhat angrily at what I was doing and stopped me. But the mischief had been done. The incident was a warning for the future. This was my first lesson in European etiquette, into the details of which Dr Mehta humorously initiated me. 'Do not touch other people's things,' he said. 'Do not ask questions as we usually do in India on first acquaintance; do not talk loudly; never address people 'sir' whilst speaking to them as we do in India; only servants and subordinates address their masters that way.' And so on and so forth. He also told me that it was very expensive to live in a hotel and recommended that I should live with a private family. We deferred consideration of the matter until Monday.

Sjt. Mazmudar and I found the hotel to be a trying affair. It was also very expensive. There was, however, a Sindhi fellow-passenger from Malta who had become friends with Sjt. Mazmudar, and as he was not a stranger to London, he offered to find rooms for us. We agreed, and on Monday, as soon as we got our baggage, we paid up our bills and went to the rooms rented for us by the Sindhi friend. I remember my hotel bill came to £3, an amount which shocked me. And I had practically starved in spite of this heavy bill! For I could relish nothing. When I did not like one thing, I asked for another, but had to pay for both just the same. The fact is that all this while I had depended on the provisions which I had brought with me from Bombay.

I was very uneasy even in the new rooms. I would continually think of my home and country. My mother's love always haunted me. At night the tears would stream down my cheeks, and home memories of all sorts made sleep out of the question. It was impossible to share my misery with anyone. And even if I could have done so, where was the use? I knew of nothing that would soothe me. Everything was strange—the people, their ways, and even their dwellings. I was a complete novice in the matter of English etiquette and continually had to be on my guard. There was the additional inconvenience of the vegetarian vow. Even the dishes that I could eat were tasteless and insipid. I thus found myself between Scylla and Charybdis. England I could not bear, but to return to India was not to be thought of. Now that I had come, I must finish the three years, said the inner voice.

Dr Mehta went on Monday to the Victoria Hotel expecting to find me there. He discovered that we had left, got our new address, and met me at our rooms. Through sheer folly I had managed to get ringworm on the boat. For washing and bathing we used to have seawater, in which soap is not soluble. I, however, used soap, taking its use to be a sign of civilization, with the result that instead of cleaning the skin it made it greasy. This gave me ringworm. I showed it to Dr Mehta, who told me to apply acetic acid. I remember how the burning acid made me cry. Dr Mehta inspected my room and its appointments and shook his head in disapproval. 'This place won't do,' he said. 'We come to England not so much for the purpose of studies as for gaining experience of English life and customs. And for this you need to live with a family. But before you do so, I think you had better serve a period of apprenticeship with—. I will take you there.'

I gratefully accepted the suggestion and removed to the friend's rooms. He was all kindness and attention. He treated me as his own brother, initiated me into English ways and manners and accustomed me to talking the language. My food, however, became a serious question. I could not relish boiled vegetables cooked without salt or condiments. The landlady was at a loss to know what to prepare for me. We had oatmeal porridge for breakfast, which was fairly filling, but I always starved at lunch and dinner. The friend continually reasoned with me to eat meat, but I always pleaded my vow and then remained silent. Both for luncheon and dinner we had spinach and bread and jam too. I was a good eater and had a capacious stomach; but I was ashamed to ask for more than two or three slices of bread, as it did not seem correct to do so. Added to this, there was no milk either for lunch or dinner. The friend once got disgusted with this state of things, and said: 'Had you been my own brother, I would have sent you packing. What is the value of a vow made before an illiterate mother, and in ignorance of conditions here? It is no vow at all. It would not be regarded as a vow in law. It is pure superstition to stick to such a promise. And I tell you this persistence will not help you to gain anything here. You confess to have eaten and relished meat. You took it where it was absolutely unnecessary, and will not where it is quite essential. What a pity!'

But I was adamant.

Day in and day out the friend would argue, but I had an eternal negative to face him with. The more he argued, the more uncompromising I became. Daily I would pray for God's protection and get it. Not that I had any idea of God. It was faith that was at work—faith of which the seed had been sown by the good nurse Rambha.

One day the friend began to read to me Bentham's *Theory of Utility*. I was at my wits' end. The language was too difficult for me to understand. He began to expound it. I said: 'Pray excuse me. These abstruse things are beyond me. I admit it is necessary to eat meat. But I cannot break my vow. I cannot argue about it. I am sure I cannot meet you in argument. But please give me up as foolish or obstinate. I appreciate your love for me and I know you to be my well-wisher. I also know that you are telling me again and again about this because you feel for me. But I am helpless. A vow is a vow. It cannot be broken.'

The friend looked at me in surprise. He closed the book and said: 'All right. I will not argue any more.' I was glad. He never discussed the subject again. But he did not cease to worry about me. He smoked and drank, but he never asked me to do so. In face he asked me to remain away from both. His one anxiety was lest I should become very weak without meat, and thus be unable to feel at home in England.

That is how I served my apprenticeship for a month. The friend's house was in Richmond, and it was not possible to go to London more than once or twice a week. Dr Mehta and Sjt. Dalpatram

Shukla therefore decided that I should be put with some family. Sjt. Shukla hit upon an Anglo-Indian's house in West Kensington and placed me there. The landlady was a widow. I told her about my vow. The old lady promised to look after me properly, and I took up my residence in her house. Here too I practically had to starve. I had sent for sweets and other eatables from home, but nothing had yet come. Everything was insipid. Every day the old lady asked me whether I liked the food, but what could she do? I was still as shy as ever and dared not ask for more than what was put before me. She had two daughters. They insisted on serving me with an extra slice or two of bread. But little did they know that nothing less than a loaf would have filled me.

But I had found my feet now. I had not yet started upon my regular studies. I had just begun reading newspapers, thanks to Sjt. Shukla. In India I had never read a newspaper. But here I succeeded in cultivating a liking for them by regular reading. I always glanced over *The Daily News, The Daily Telegraph* and *The Pall Mall Gazette.* This took me hardly an hour. I therefore began to wander about. I launched out in search of a vegetarian restaurant. The landlady had told me that there were such places in the city. I would trot ten or twelve miles each day, go into a cheap restaurant and eat my fill of bread, but would never be satisfied. During these wanderings I once hit on a vegetarian restaurant in Farringdon Street. The sight of it filled me with the same joy that a child feels on getting a thing after its own heart. Before I entered I noticed books for sale exhibited under a glass window near the door. I saw among them Salt's *Plea for Vegetarianism.* This I purchased for a shilling and went straight to the dining room. This was my first hearty meal since my arrival in England. God had come to my aid.

I read Salt's book from cover to cover and was very much impressed by it. From the date of reading this book, I may claim to have become a vegetarian by choice. I blessed the day on which I had taken the vow before my mother. I had all along abstained from meat in the interests of truth and of the vow I had taken, but had wished at the same time that every Indian should be a meat-eater, and had looked forward to being one myself freely and openly some day, and to enlisting others in the cause. The choice was now made in favour of vegetarianism, the spread of which henceforward became my mission.

My faith in vegetarianism grew on me from day to day. Salt's book whetted my appetite for dietetic studies. I went in for all books available on vegetarianism and read them. One of these, Howard Williams' *The Ethics of Diet*, was a 'biographical history of the literature of humane dietetics from the earliest period to the present day.' It tried to make out, that all philosophers and prophets from Pythagoras and Jesus down to those of the present age were vegetarians. Dr Anna Kingsford's *The Perfect Way in Diet* was also an attractive book. Dr Allinson's writings on health and hygiene were likewise very helpful. He advocated a curative system based on regulation of the dietary of patients. Himself a vegetarian, he prescribed for his patients also a strictly vegetarian diet. The result of reading all this literature was that dietetic experiments came to take an important place in my life. Health was the principal consideration of these experiments to begin with. But later on religion became the supreme motive.

Meanwhile my friend had not ceased to worry about me. His love for me led him to think that, if I persisted in my objections to meat-eating, I should not only develop a weak constitution, but should remain a duffer, because I should never feel at home in English society. When he came to know that I had begun to interest myself in books on vegetarianism, he was afraid lest these studies should muddle my head; that I should fritter my life away in experiments, forgetting my own work, and become a crank. He therefore made one last effort to reform me. He one day invited me to go to the theatre. Before the play we were to dine together at the Holborn Restaurant, to me a palatial place and the first big restaurant I had been to since leaving the Victoria Hotel. The stay at that hotel had scarcely been a helpful experience. For I had not lived there with my wits about me. The friend had planned to take me to this restaurant evidently imagining that modesty would forbid any questions. And it was a very big company of diners in the midst of which my friend and I sat sharing a table between us. The first course was soup. I wondered what it might be made of, but durst not ask the friend abut it. I therefore summoned the waiter. My friend saw the movement and sternly asked across the table what was the matter. With considerable hesitation I told him that I wanted to inquire if the soup was a vegetable soup. 'You are too clumsy for decent society,' he passionately exclaimed. 'If you cannot behave yourself, you had better go. Feed at some other restaurant and await me outside.' This delighted me. Out I went. There was a vegetarian restaurant close by, but it was closed. So I went without food that night. I accompanied my friend to the theatre, but he never said a word about the scene I had created. On my part of course there was nothing to say.

That was the last friendly tussle we had. It did not affect our relations in the least. I could see and appreciate the love by which all my friend's efforts were actuated, and my respect for him was all the greater on account of our differences in thought and action.

But I decided that I should put him at ease, that I should assure him that I would be clumsy no more, but try to become polished and make up for the vegetarianism by cultivating other accomplishments which fitted one for polite society. And for this purpose I undertook the all too impossible task of becoming an English gentleman.

The clothes after the Bombay cut that I was wearing were, I thought, unsuitable for English society, and I got new ones at the Army and Navy Stores. I also went in for a chimney-pot hat costing nineteen shillings—an excessive price in those days. Not content with this, I wasted ten pounds on an evening suit made in Bond Street, the centre of fashionable life in London; and got my good and noble-hearted brother to send me a double watch-chain of gold. It was not correct to wear a ready-made tie and I learnt the art of tying one for myself. While in India, the mirror had been a luxury permitted on the days when the family barber gave me a shave. Here I wasted ten minutes every day before a huge mirror, watching myself arranging my tie and parting my hair in the correct fashion. My hair was by no means soft, and every day it meant a regular struggle with the brush to keep it in position. Each time the hat was put on and off, the hand would automatically move towards the head to adjust the hair, not to mention the other civilized habit of the hand every now and then operating for the same purpose when sitting in polished society.

As if all this were not enough to make me look the thing, I directed my attention to other details that were supposed to go towards the making of an English gentleman. I was told it was necessary for me to take the lessons in dancing, French and elocution. French was not only the language of neighbouring France, but it was the *lingua franca* of the Continent over which I had a desire to travel. I decided to take dancing lessons at a class and paid down £ 3 as fees for a term. I must have taken about six lessons in three weeks. But it was beyond me to achieve anything like rhythmic motion. I could not follow the piano and hence found it impossible to keep time. What then was I to do? The recluse in the fable kept a cat to keep off the rats, and then a cow to feed the cat with milk, and a man to keep the cow and so on. My ambitions also grew like the family of the recluse. I thought I should learn to play the violin in order to cultivate an ear for Western music. So I invested £3 in a violin and something more in fees. I sought a third teacher to give me lessons in elocution and paid him a preliminary fee of a guinea. He recommended Bell's *Standard Elocutionist* as the text-book, which I purchased. And I began with a speech of Pitt's.

But Mr Bell rang the bell of alarm in my ear and I awoke.

I had not to spend a lifetime in England, I said to myself. What then was the use of learning elocution? And how could dancing make a gentleman of me? The violin I could learn even in India. I was a student and ought to go on with my studies. I should qualify to join the Inns of Court. If my character made a gentleman of me, so much the better. Otherwise I should forego the ambition.

These and similar thoughts possessed me, and I expressed them in a letter which I addressed to the elocution teacher, requesting him to excuse me from further lessons. I had taken only two or three. I wrote a similar letter to the dancing teacher, and went personally to the violin teacher with a request to dispose of the violin for any price it might fetch. She was rather friendly to me, so I told her how I had discovered that I was pursuing a false idea. She encouraged me in the determination to make a complete change.

This infatuation must have lasted about three months. The punctiliousness in dress persisted for years. But henceforward I became a student.

❦

There were comparatively few Indian students in England forty years ago. It was a practice with them to affect the bachelor even though they might be married. School or college students in England are all bachelors, studies being regarded as incompatible with married life. We had that tradition in the good old days, a student then being invariably known as a *brahmachari*[1]. But in these days we have child-marriages, a thing practically unknown in England. Indian youths in England, therefore, felt ashamed to confess that they were married. There was also another reason for dissembling, namely, that in the event of the fact being known it would be impossible for the young men to go about or flirt with the young girls of the family in which they lived. The flirting was more or less innocent. Parents even encouraged it; and that sort of association between young men and young women may even be a necessity there, in view of the fact that every young man has to choose his mate. If, however, Indian youths on arrival in England indulge in these relations, quite natural to English youths, the result is likely to be disastrous, as has often been found. I saw that our youths had succumbed to the temptation and chosen a life of untruth for the sake of companionships which, however innocent in the case of English youths, were for them undesirable. I too caught the contagion. I did not hesitate to pass myself off as a bachelor though I was married and the father of a son. But I was none the happier for being a dissembler. Only my reserve and my reticence saved me from going into deeper waters. If I did not talk, no girl would think it worth her while to enter into conversation with me or to go out with me.

My cowardice was on a par with my reserve. It was customary in families like the one in which I was staying at Ventnor for the daughter of the land-lady to take out guests for a walk. My land-lady's daughter took me one day to the lovely hills round Ventnor. I was no slow walker, but my companion walked even faster, dragging me after her and chattering away all the while. I responded to her chatter sometimes

---

[1] One who observes *brahmacharya*, i.e. complete self-restraint.

with a whispered 'yes' or 'no', or at the most 'yes, how beautiful!' She was flying like a bird whilst I was wondering when I should get back home. We thus reached the top of a hill. How to get down again was the question. In spite of her high-heeled boots this sprightly young lady of twenty-five darted down the hill like an arrow. I was shamefacedly struggling to get down. She stood at the foot smiling and cheering me and offering to come and drag me. How could I be so chicken-hearted? With the greatest difficulty, and crawling at intervals, I somehow managed to scramble to the bottom. She loudly laughed 'bravo' and shamed me all the more, as well she might.

But I could not escape scatheless everywhere. For God wanted to rid me of the canker of untruth. I once went to Brighton, another watering-place like Ventnor. This was before the Ventnor visit. I met there at a hotel an old widow of moderate means. This was my first year in England. The courses on the *menu* were all described in French, which I did not understand. I sat at the same table as the old lady. She saw that I was a stranger and puzzled, and immediately came to my aid. 'You seem to be a stranger,' she said, 'and look perplexed. Why have you not ordered anything?' I was spelling though the *menu* and preparing to ascertain the ingredients of the courses from the waiter, when the good lady thus intervened. I thanked her, and explaining my difficulty told her that I was at a loss to know which of the courses were vegetarian as I did not understand French.

'Let me help you,' she said. 'I shall explain the card to you and show you what you may eat.' I gratefully availed myself of her help. This was the beginning of an acquaintance that ripened into friendship and was kept up all through my stay in England and long after. She gave me her London address and invited me to dine at her house every Sunday. On special occasions also she would invite me, help me to conquer my bashfulness and introduce me to young ladies and draw me into conversation with them. Particularly marked out for these conversations was a young lady who stayed with her, and often we would be left entirely alone together.

I found all this very trying at first. I could not start a conversation nor could I indulge in any jokes. But she put me in the way. I began to learn; and in course of time looked forward to every Sunday and came to like the conversations with the young friend.

The old lady went on spreading her net wider every day. She felt interested in our meetings. Possibly she had her own plans about us.

I was in a quandary. 'How I wished I had told the good lady that I was married!' I said to myself. 'She would then have not thought of an engagement between us. It is, however, never too late to mend. If I declare the truth, I might yet be saved more misery.' With these thoughts in my mind, I wrote a letter to her somewhat to this effect:

'Ever since we met at Brighton you have been kind to me. You have taken care of me even as a mother of her son. You also think that I should get married and with that view you have been introducing me to young ladies. Rather than allow matters to go further, I must confess to you that I have been unworthy of your affection. I should have told you when I began my visits to you that I was married. I knew that Indian students in England dissembled the fact of their marriage and I followed suit. I now see that I should not have done so. I must also add that I was married while yet a boy, and am the father of a son. I am pained that I should have kept this knowledge from you so long. But I am glad God has now given me the courage to speak out the truth. Will you forgive me? I assure you I have taken no improper liabilities with the young lady you were good enough to introduce to me. I knew my limits. You, not knowing that I was married, naturally desired that we should be engaged. In order that things should not go beyond the present stage, I must tell the truth.

'If on receipt of this, you feel that I have been unworthy of your hospitality, I assure you I shall not take it amiss. You have laid me under an everlasting debt of gratitude by your kindness and solicitude. If, after this, you do not reject me but continue to regard me as worthy of your hospitality, which I will spare no pain to deserve, I shall naturally be happy and count it a further token of your kindness.'

Let the reader know that I could not have written such a letter in a moment. I must have drafted and redrafted it many times over. But it lifted a burden that was weighing me down. Almost by return post came her reply somewhat as follows:

'I have your frank letter. We were both very glad and had a hearty laugh over it. The untruth you say you have been guilty of is pardonable. But it is well that you have acquainted us with the real state of things. My invitation still stands and we shall certainly expect you next

Sunday and look forward to hearing all about your child-marriage and to the pleasure of laughing at your expense. Need I assure you that our friendship is not in the least affected by this incident?'

I thus purged myself of the canker of untruth, and I never thenceforward hesitated to talk of my married state wherever necessary.

SOUTH AFRICA

The port of Natal is Durban, also known as Port Natal. Abdulla Sheth was there to receive me. As the ship arrived at the quay and I watched the people coming on board to meet their friends, I observed that the Indians were not held in much respect. I could not fail to notice a sort of snobbishness about the manner in which those who knew Abdulla Sheth behaved towards him, and it stung me. Abdulla Sheth had got used to it. Those who looked at me did so with a certain amount of curiosity. My dress marked me out from other Indians. I had a frock-coat and a turban, an imitation of the Bengal *pugree*.

I was taken to the firm's quarters and shown into the room set apart for me, next to Abdulla Sheth's. He did not understand me. I could not understand him. He read the papers his brother had sent through me, and felt more puzzled. He thought his brother had sent him a white elephant. My style of dress and living struck him as being expensive like that of the Europeans. There was no particular work then which could be given me. Their case was going on in the Transvaal. There was no meaning in sending me there immediately. And how far could he trust my ability and honesty? He would not be in Pretoria to watch me. The defendants were in Pretoria, and for aught he knew they might bring undue influence to bear on me. And if work in connection with the case in question was not to be entrusted to me, what work would I be given to do, as all other work could be done much better by his clerks? The clerks could be brought to book, if they did wrong. Could I be, if I also happened to err? So if no work in connection with the case could be given me, I should have to be kept for nothing.

Abdulla Sheth was practically unlettered, but he had a rich fund of experience. He had an acute intellect and was conscious of it. By practice he had picked up just sufficient English for conversational purposes, but that served him for carrying on all his business, whether it was dealing with Bank Managers and European merchants or explaining his case to his counsel. The Indians held him in very high esteem. His firm was then the biggest, or at any rate one of the biggest, of the Indian firms. With all these advantages he had one disadvantage— he was by nature suspicious.

He was proud of Islam and loved to discourse on Islamic philosophy. Though he did not know Arabic, his acquaintance with the Holy Koran and Islamic literature in general was fairly good. Illustrations he had in plenty, always ready at hand. Contact with him gave me a fair amount of practical knowledge of Islam. When we came closer to each other, we had long discussions on religious topics.

On the second or third day of my arrival, he took me to see the Durban court. There he introduced me to several people and seated me next to his attorney. The Magistrate kept staring at me and finally asked me to take off my turban. This I refused to do and left the court.

So here too there was fighting in store for me.

Abdulla Sheth explained to me why some Indians were required to take off their turbans. Those wearing the Musalman costume might, he said, keep their turbans on, but the other Indians on entering a court had to take theirs off as a rule.

I must enter into some details to make this nice distinction intelligible. In the course of these two or three days I could see that the Indians were divided into different groups. One was that of Musalman merchants, who would call themselves 'Arabs'. Another was that of Hindu, and yet another of Parsi, clerks. The Hindu clerks were neither here nor there, unless they cast in their lot with the 'Arabs'. The Parsi clerks would call themselves Persians. These three classes had some social relations with one another. But by far the largest class was that composed of Tamil, Telugu and North Indian indentured and freed labourers. The indentured labourers were those who went to Natal on an agreement to serve for five years, and came to be known there as *girmitiyas* from *girmit*, which was the corrupt form of the English word 'agreement'. The other three classes had none but business relations with this class. Englishmen called them 'coolies', and as the majority of Indians belonged to the labouring class, all Indians were called 'coolies', or '*samis*'. '*Sami*' is a Tamil suffix occurring after many Tamil names, and it is nothing else than the Samskrit *Swami*, meaning a master. Whenever, therefore, an Indian resented being addressed as a '*sami*' and had enough wit in him, he would try to return the compliment in this wise: 'You may call me *sami*, but you forget that *sami* means a master. I am not your master!' Some Englishmen would wince at this, while others would get angry, swear at the Indian and, if there was a chance, would even belabour him; for '*sami*' to him was nothing better than a term of contempt. To interpret it to mean a master amounted to an insult!

I was hence known as a 'coolie barrister'. The merchants were known as 'coolie merchants'. The original meaning of the word 'coolie' was thus forgotten, and it became a common appellation for all Indians. The Musalman merchant would resent this and say: 'I am not a coolie, I am an Arab,' or 'I am a merchant,' and the Englishman, if courteous, would apologize to him.

The question of wearing the turban had a great importance in this state of things. Being obliged to take off one's Indian turban would be pocketing an insult. So I thought I had better bid goodbye to the Indian turban and begin wearing an English hat, which would save me from the insult and the unpleasant controversy.

But Abdulla Sheth disapproved of the idea. He said, 'If you do anything of the kind, it will have a very bad effect. You will compromise those insisting on wearing Indian turbans. And an Indian turban sits well on your head. If you wear an English hat, you will pass for a waiter.'

There was practical wisdom, patriotism and a little bit of narrowness in this advice. The wisdom was apparent, and he would not have insisted on the Indian turban except out of patriotism; the slighting reference to the waiter betrayed a kind of narrowness. Amongst the indentured Indians there were three classes—Hindus, Musalmans and Christians. The last were the children of indentured Indians who became converts to Christianity. Even in 1893 their number was large. They wore the English costume, and the majority of them earned their living by service as waiters in hotels. Abdulla Sheth's criticism of the English hat was with reference to this class. It was considered degrading to serve as a waiter in a hotel. The belief persists even today among many.

On the whole I liked Abdulla Sheth's advice. I wrote to the press about the incident and defended the wearing of my turban in the court. The question was very much discussed in the papers, which described me as an 'unwelcome visitor'. Thus the incident gave me an unexpected advertisement in South Africa within a few days of my arrival there. Some supported me, while others severely criticized my temerity.

My turban stayed with me practically until the end of my stay in South Africa. When and why I left off wearing any head-dress at all in South Africa, we shall see later.

I soon came in contact with the Christian Indians living in Durban. The Court Interpreter, Mr Paul, was a Roman Catholic. I made his acquaintance, as also that of the late Mr Subhan Godfrey, then a teacher under the Protestant Mission, and father of Mr James Godfrey, who as a member of the South African Deputation, visited India in 1924. I likewise met the late Parsi Rustomiji and the late Adamji Miyakhan about the same time. All these friends, who up to then had never met one another except on business, came ultimately into close contact, as we shall see later.

Whilst I was thus widening the circle of my acquaintance, the firm received a letter from their lawyer saying that preparations should be made for the case, and that Abdulla Sheth should go to Pretoria himself or send a representative.

Abdulla Sheth gave me this letter to read, and asked me if I would go to Pretoria. 'I can only say after I have understood the case from you,' said I. 'At present I am at a loss to know what I have to do there.' He thereupon asked his clerks to explain the case to me.

As I began to study the case, I felt as though I ought to begin from the ABC of the subject. During the few days I had had at Zanzibar, I had been to the court to see the work there. A Parsi lawyer was examining a witness and asking him questions regarding credit and debit entries in account books. It was all Greek to me. Book-keeping I had learnt neither at school nor during my stay in England. And the case for which I had come to South Africa was mainly about accounts. Only one who knew accounts could understand and explain it. The clerk went on talking about this debited and that credited, and I felt more and more confused. I did not know what a P. Note meant. I failed to find the word in the dictionary. I revealed my ignorance to the clerk, and learnt from him that a P. Note meant a promissory note. I purchased a book on book-keeping and studied it. That gave me some confidence. I understood the case. I saw that Abdulla Sheth, who did not know how to keep accounts, had so much practical knowledge that he could quickly solve intricacies of book-keeping. I told him that I was prepared to go to Pretoria.

'Where will you put up?' asked the Sheth.

'Wherever you want me to,' said I.

'Then I shall write to our lawyer. He will arrange for your lodgings. I shall also write to my Meman friends there, but I would not advise you to stay with them. The other party has great influence in Pretoria. Should any one of them manage to read our private correspondence, it might do us much harm. The more you avoid familiarity with them, the better for us.'

'I shall stay where your lawyer puts me up, or I shall find out independent lodgings. Pray don't worry. Not a soul shall know anything that is confidential between us. But I do intend cultivating the acquaintance of the other party. I should like to be friends with them. I would try, if possible, to settle the case out of court. After all Tyeb Sheth is a relative of yours'.

Sheth Tyeb Haji Khan Muhammad was a near relative of Abdulla Sheth.

The mention of a probable settlement somewhat startled the Sheth, I could see. But I had already been six or seven days in Durban, and we now knew and understood each other. I was no longer a 'white elephant'. So he said:

'Y . . . . es, I see. There would be nothing better than a settlement out of court. But we are all relatives and know one another very well indeed. Tyeb Sheth is not a man to consent to a settlement easily. With the slightest unwariness on our part, he would screw all sorts of things out of us, and do us down in the end. So please think twice before you do anything.'

'Don't be anxious about that,' said I. 'I need not talk to Tyeb Sheth, or for that matter to anyone else, about the case. I would only suggest to him to come to an understanding, and so save a lot of unnecessary litigation.'

On the seventh or eighth day after my arrival, I left Durban. A first class seat was booked for me. It was usual there to pay five shillings extra, if one needed a bedding. Abdulla Sheth insisted that I should book one bedding but, out of obstinacy and pride and with a view to saving five shillings, I declined. Abdulla Sheth warned me. 'Look, now,' said he, 'this is a different country from India. Thank God, we have enough and to spare. Please do not stint yourself in anything that you may need.'

I thanked him and asked him not to be anxious.

The train reached Maritzburg, the capital of Natal, at about 9 p.m. Beddings used to be provided at this station. A railway servant came and asked me if I wanted one. 'No,' said I, 'I have one with me.' He went away. But a passenger came next, and looked me up and down. He saw that I was a 'coloured' man. This disturbed him. Out he went and came in again with one or two officials. They all kept quiet, when another official came to me and said, 'Come along, you must go to the van compartment.'

'But I have a first class ticket,' said I.

'That doesn't matter,' rejoined the other. 'I tell you, you must go to the van compartment.'

'I tell you, I was permitted to travel in this compartment at Durban, and I insist on going on in it.'

'No, you won't,' said the official. 'You must leave this compartment, or else I shall have to call a police constable to push you out.'

'Yes, you may. I refuse to get out voluntarily.'

The constable came. He took me by the hand and pushed me out. My luggage was also taken out. I refused to go to the other compartment and the train steamed away. I went and sat in the waiting room, keeping my hand-bag with me, and leaving the other luggage where it was. The railway authorities had taken charge of it.

It was winter, and winter in the higher regions of South Africa is severely cold. Maritzburg being at a high altitude, the cold was extremely bitter. My over-coat was in my luggage, but I did not dare to ask for it lest I should be insulted again, so I sat and shivered. There was no light in the room. A passenger came in at about midnight and possibly wanted to talk to me. But I was in no mood to talk.

I began to think of my duty. Should I fight for my rights or go back to India, or should I go on to Pretoria without minding the insults, and return to India after finishing the case? It would be cowardice to run back to India without fulfilling my obligation. The hardship to which I was subjected was superficial—only a symptom of the deep disease of colour prejudice. I should try, if possible, to root out the disease and suffer hardships in the process. Redress for wrongs I should seek only to the extent that would be necessary for the removal of the colour prejudice.

So I decided to take the next available train to Pretoria.

The following morning I sent a long telegram to the General Manager of the Railway and also informed Abdulla Sheth, who immediately met the General Manager. The Manager justified the conduct of the railway authorities, but informed him that he had already instructed the Station Master to see that I reached my destination safely. Abdulla Sheth wired to the Indian merchants in Maritzburg and to friends in other places to meet me and look after me. The merchants came to see me at the station and tried to comfort me by narrating their own hardships and explaining that what had happened to me was nothing unusual. They also said that Indians travelling first or second class had to expect trouble from railway officials and white passengers. The day was thus spent in listening to these tales of woe. The evening train arrived. There was a reserved berth for me. I now purchased at Maritzburg the bedding ticket I had refused to book at Durban.

The train took me to Charlestown.

The train reached Charlestown in the morning. There was no railway, in those days, between Charlestown and Johannesburg, but only a stage-coach, which halted at Standerton for the night *en route*. I possessed a ticket for the coach, which was not cancelled by the break of the journey at Maritzburg for a day; besides, Abdulla Sheth had sent a wire to the coach agent at Charlestown.

But the agent only needed a pretext for putting me off, and so, when he discovered me to be a stranger, he said, 'Your ticket is cancelled.' I gave him the proper reply. The reason at the back of his mind was not want of accommodation, but quite another. Passengers had to be accommodated inside the coach, but as I was regarded as a 'coolie' and looked a stranger, it would be proper, thought the 'leader', as the white man in charge of the coach was called, not to seat me with the white passengers. There were seats on either side of the coach box. The leader sat on one of these as a rule. Today he sat inside and gave me his seat. I knew it was sheer injustice and an insult, but I thought it better to pocket it. I could not have forced myself inside, and if I had raised a protest, the coach would have gone off without me. This would have meant the loss of another day, and Heaven only knows what would have happened the next day. So, much as I fretted within myself, I prudently sat next the coachman.

At about three o'clock the coach reached Pardekoph. Now the leader desired to sit where I was seated, as he wanted to smoke and possibly to have some fresh air. So he took a piece of dirty sack-cloth from the driver, spread it on the footboard and, addressing me said, '*Sami*, you sit on this, I want to sit near the driver.' The insult was more than I could bear. In fear and trembling I said to him, 'It was you who seated me here, though I should have been accommodated inside. I put up with the insult. Now that you want to sit outside and smoke, you would have me sit at your feet. I will not do so, but I am prepared to sit inside.'

As I was struggling through these sentences, the man came down upon me and began heavily to box my ears. He seized me by the arm and tried to drag me down. I clung to the brass rails of the coach box and was determined to keep my hold even at the risk of breaking my wristbones. The passengers were witnessing the scene—the man swearing at me, dragging and belabouring me, and I remaining still. He was strong and I was weak. Some of the passengers were moved to pity and exclaimed: 'Man, let him alone. Don't beat him. He is not to blame. He is right. If he can't stay there, let him come and sit with us.' 'No fear', cried the man, but he seemed somewhat crestfallen and stopped beating me. He let go my arm, swore at me a little more, and asking the Hottentot servant who was sitting on the other side of the coach box to sit on the footboard, took the seat so vacated.

The passengers took their seats and, the whistle given, the coach rattled away. My heart was beating fast within my breast, and I was wondering whether I should ever reach my destination alive. The man cast an angry look at me now and then and, pointing his finger at me, growled: 'Take care, let me once get to Standerton and I shall show you what I do.' I sat speechless and prayed to God to help me.

After dark we reached Standerton and I heaved a sigh of relief on seeing some Indian faces. As soon as I got down, these friends said: 'We are here to receive you and take you to Isa Sheth's shop. We have had a telegram from Dada Abdulla.' I was very glad, and we went to Sheth Isa Haji Summar's shop. The Sheth and his clerks gathered around me. I told them all that I had gone through. They were very sorry to hear it and comforted me by relating to me their own bitter experiences.

I wanted to inform the agent of the Coach Company of the whole affair. So I wrote him a letter, narrating everything that had happened, and drawing his attention to the threat his man had held out. I also asked for an assurance that he would accommodate me with the other passengers inside the coach when we started the next morning. To which the agent replied to this effect: 'From Standerton we have a bigger coach with different men in charge. The man complained of will not be there tomorrow, and you will have a seat with the other passengers.' This somewhat relieved me. I had, of course, no intention of proceeding against the man who had assaulted me, and so the chapter of the assault closed there.

In the morning Isa Sheth's man took me to the coach, I got a good seat and reached Johannesburg quite safely that night.

Standerton is a small village and Johannesburg a big city. Abdulla Sheth had wired to Johannesburg also, and given me the name and address of Muhammad Kasam Kamruddin's firm there. Their man had come to receive me. So I decided to go to a hotel. I knew the names of several. Taking a cab I asked to be driven to the Grand National Hotel. I saw the Manager and asked for a room. He eyed me for a moment, and politely saying, 'I am very sorry, we are full up', bade me good-bye. So I asked the cabman to drive to Muhammad Kasam Kamruddin's shop. Here I found Abdul Gani Sheth expecting me, and he gave me a cordial greeting. He had a hearty laugh over the story of my experience at the hotel. 'How ever did you expect to be admitted to a hotel?' he said.

'Why not?' I asked.

'You will come to know after you have stayed here a few days', said he. 'Only *we* can live in a land like this, because, for making money, we do not mind pocketing insults, and here we are.' With this he narrated to me the story of the hardships of Indians in South Africa.

Of Sheth Abdul Gani we shall know more as we proceed.

He said: 'This country is not for men like you. Look now, you have to go to Pretoria tomorrow. You will *have* to travel third class. Conditions in the Transvaal are worse than in Natal. First and second class tickets are never issued to Indians.'

'You cannot have made persistent efforts in this direction.'

'We have sent representations, but I confess our own men too do not want as a rule to travel first or second.'

I sent for the railway regulations and read them. There was a loophole. The language of the old Transvaal enactments was not very exact or precise; that of the railway regulations was even less so.

I said to the Sheth: 'I wish to go first class, and if I cannot, I shall prefer to take a cab to Pretoria, a matter of only thirty-seven miles.'

Sheth Abdul Gani drew my attention to the extra time and money this would mean, but agreed to my proposal to travel first, and accordingly we sent a note to the Station Master. I mentioned in my note that I was a barrister and that I always travelled first. I also stated in the letter that I needed to reach Pretoria as early as possible, that as there was no time to await his reply I would receive it in person at the station, and that I should expect to get a first class ticket. There was of course a purpose behind asking for the reply in person. I thought that, if the Station Master gave a written reply, he would certainly say 'no', especially because he would have his own notion of a 'coolie' barrister. I would therefore appear before him in faultless English dress, talk to him and possibly persuade him to issue a first class ticket. So I went to the station in a frock-coat and necktie, placed a sovereign for my fare on the counter and asked for a first class ticket.

'You sent me that note?' he asked.

'That is so. I shall be much obliged if you will give me a ticket. I must reach Pretoria today.'

He smiled, and moved to pity, said: 'I am not a Transvaaler. I am a Hollander. I appreciate your feelings, and you have my sympathy. I do want to give you a ticket—on one condition, however, that, if the guard should ask you to shift to the third class, you will not involve me in the affair, by which I mean that you should not proceed against the Railway Company. I wish you a safe journey. I can see you are a gentleman.'

With these words he booked the ticket. I thanked him and gave him the necessary assurance.

Sheth Abdul Gani had come to see me off at the station. The incident gave him an agreeable surprise, but he warned me saying: 'I shall be thankful if you reach Pretoria all right. I am afraid the guard will not leave you in peace in the first class, and even if he does, the passengers will not.'

I took my seat in a first class compartment and the train started. At Germiston the guard came to examine the tickets. He was angry to find me there, and signalled to me with his finger to go to the third class. I showed him my first class ticket. 'That doesn't matter,' said he, 'remove to the third class.'

There was only one English passenger in the compartment. He took the guard to task. 'What do you mean by troubling the gentleman?' he said. 'Don't you see he has a first class ticket? I do not mind in the least his travelling with me.' Addressing me, he said, 'You should make yourself comfortable where you are.'

The guard muttered: 'If you want to travel with a coolie, what do I care?' and went away.

At abut 8 o'clock in the evening the train reached Pretoria.

I had expected someone on behalf of Dada Abdulla's attorney to meet me at Pretoria Station. I knew that no Indian would be there to receive me, since I had particularly promised not to put up at an Indian house. But the attorney had sent no one. I understood later that, as I had arrived on a Sunday, he could not have sent anyone without inconvenience. I was perplexed, and wondered where to go, as I feared that no hotel would accept me.

Pretoria station in 1893 was quite different from what it was in 1914. The lights were burning dimly. The travellers were few. I let all other passengers go and thought that, as soon as the ticket collector was fairly free, I would hand him my ticket and ask him if he could direct me to some small hotel or any other such place where I might go; otherwise I would spend the night at the station. I must confess I shrank from asking him even this, for I was afraid of being insulted.

The station became clear of all passengers. I gave my ticket to the ticket collector and began my inquiries. He replied to me courteously, but I saw that he could not be of any considerable help. But an American Negro who was standing nearby broke into the conversation.

'I see,' said he, 'that you are an utter stranger here, without any friends. If you will come with me, I will take you to a small hotel, of which the proprietor is an American who is very well known to me. I think he will accept you.'

I had my own doubts about the offer, but I thanked him and accepted his suggestion. He took me to Johnston's Family Hotel. He drew Mr Johnston aside to speak to him, and the latter agreed to accommodate me for the night, on condition that I should have my dinner served in my room.

'I assure you,' said he, 'that I have no colour prejudice. But I have only European custom, and, if I allowed you to eat in the dining room, my guests might be offended and even go away.'

'Thank you,' said I, 'even for accommodating me for the night. I am now more or less acquainted with the conditions here, and I understand your difficulty. I do not mind your serving the dinner in my room. I hope to be able to make some other arrangement tomorrow.'

I was shown into a room, where I now sat waiting for the dinner and musing, as I was quite alone. There were not many guests in the hotel, and I had expected the waiter to come very shortly with the dinner. Instead Mr Johnston appeared. He said: 'I was ashamed of having asked you to have your dinner here. So I spoke to the other guests about you, and asked them if they would mind your having your dinner in the dining-room. They said they had no objection and that they did not mind your staying here as long as you like. Please, therefore, come to the dining-room, if you will, and stay here as long as you wish.'

I thanked him again, went to the dining-room and had a hearty dinner. Next morning I called on the attorney, Mr A.W. Baker. Abdulla

Sheth had given me some description of him, so his cordial reception did not surprise me. He received me very warmly and made kind inquiries. I explained all about myself. Thereupon he said: 'We have no work for you here as barrister, for we have engaged the best counsel. The case is a prolonged and complicated one, so I shall take your assistance only to the extent of getting necessary information. And of course you will make communication with my client easy for me, as I shall now ask for all the information I want from him through you. That is certainly an advantage. I have not yet found rooms for you. I thought I had better do so after having seen you. There is a fearful amount of colour prejudice here, and therefore it is not easy to find lodgings for such as you. But I know a poor woman. She is the wife of a baker. I think she will take you and thus add to her income at the same time. Come, let us go to her place.'

So he took me to her house. He spoke with her privately about me, and she agreed to accept me as a boarder at 35 shillings a week.

Mr Baker, besides being an attorney, was a staunch lay preacher. He is still alive and now engaged purely in missionary work, having given up the legal profession. He is quite well-to-do. He still corresponds with me. In his letters he always dwells on the same theme. He upholds the excellence of Christianity from various points of view, and contends that it is impossible to find eternal peace, unless one accepts Jesus as the only son of God and the Saviour of mankind.

During the very first interview Mr Baker ascertained my religious views. I said to him: 'I am a Hindu by birth. And yet I do not know much of Hinduism, and I know less of other religions. In fact I do not know where I am, and what is and what should be my belief. I intend to make a careful study of my own religion and, as far as I can, of other religions as well.'

Mr Baker was glad to hear all this, and said: 'I am one of the Directors of the South Africa General Mission. I have built a church at my own expense, and deliver sermons in it regularly. I am free from colour prejudice. I have some co-workers, and we meet at one o'clock every day for a few minutes and pray for peace and light. I shall be glad if you will join us there. I shall introduce you to my co-workers who will be happy to meet you, and I dare say you will also like their company. I shall give you, besides, some religious books to read, though of course the book of books is the Holy Bible, which I would specially recommend to you.'

I thanked Mr Baker and agreed to attend the one o'clock prayers as regularly as possible.

'So I shall expect you here tomorrow at one o'clock, and we shall go together to pray', added Mr Baker, and we said good-bye.

I had little time for reflection just yet.

I went to Mr Johnston, paid the bill and removed to the new lodgings, where I had my lunch. The landlady was a good woman. She had cooked a vegetarian meal for me. It was not long before I made myself quite at home with the family.

I next went to see the friend to whom Dada Abdulla had given me a note. From him I learnt more about the hardships of Indians in South Africa. He insisted that I should stay with him. I thanked him, and told him that I had already made arrangements. He urged me not to hesitate to ask for anything I needed.

It was now dark. I returned home, had my dinner, went to my room and lay there absorbed in deep thought. There was not any immediate work for me. I informed Abdulla Sheth of it. What, I thought, can be the meaning of Mr Baker's interest in me? What shall I gain from his religious co-workers? How far should I undertake the study of Christianity? How was I to obtain literature about Hinduism? And how was I to understand Christianity in its proper perspective without thoroughly knowing my own religion? I could come to only one conclusion: I should make a dispassionate study of all that came to me, and deal with Mr Baker's group as God might guide me; I should not think of embracing another religion before I had fully understood my own.

Thus musing I fell asleep.

Sheth Tyeb Haji Khan Muhammad had in Pretoria the same position as was enjoyed by Dada Abdulla in Natal. There was no public movement that could be conducted without him. I made his acquaintance the very first week and told of my intention to get in touch with every Indian in Pretoria. I expressed a desire to study the conditions of Indians there, and asked for this help in my work, which he gladly agreed to give.

My first step was to call a meeting of all the Indians in Pretoria and to present to them a picture of their condition in the Transvaal. The meeting was held at the house of Sheth Haji Muhammad Haji Joosab, to whom I had a letter of introduction. It was principally attended by Meman merchants, though there was a sprinkling of Hindus as well. The Hindu population in Pretoria was, as a matter of fact, very small.

My speech at this meeting may be said to have been the first public speech in my life. I went fairly prepared with my subject, which was about observing truthfulness in business. I had always heard the merchants say that truth was not possible in business. I did not think so then, nor do I now. Even today there are merchant friends who contend that truth is inconsistent with business. Business, they say, is a very practical affair, and truth a matter of religion; and they argue that practical affairs are one thing, while religion is quite another. Pure truth, they hold, is out of the question in business, one can speak it only so far as is suitable. I strongly contested the position in my speech and awakened the merchants to a sense of their duty, which was twofold. Their responsibility to be truthful was all the greater in a foreign land, because the conduct of a few Indians was the measure of that of the millions of their fellow-countrymen.

I had found our people's habits to be insanitary, as compared with those of the Englishmen around them, and drew their attention to it. I laid stress on the necessity of forgetting all distinctions such as Hindus, Musalmans, Parsis, Christians, Gujaratis, Madrasis, Punjabis, Sindhis, Kachchhis, Surtis and so on.

I suggested, in conclusion, the formation of an association to make representations to the authorities concerned in respect of the hardships of the Indian settlers, and offered to place at its disposal as much of my time and service as was possible.

I saw that I made a considerable impression on the meeting.

My speech was followed by discussion. Some offered to supply me with facts. I felt encouraged. I saw that very few amongst my audience knew English. As I felt that knowledge of English would be useful in that country, I advised those who had leisure to learn English. I told them that it was possible to learn a language even at an advanced age, and cited cases of people who had done so. I undertook, besides, to teach a class, if one was started, or personally to instruct individuals desiring to learn the language.

The class was not started, but three young men expressed their readiness to learn at their convenience, and on condition that I went to their places to teach them. Of these, two were Musalmans—one of them a barber and the other a clerk—and the third was a Hindu, a petty shopkeeper. I agreed to suit them all. I had no misgivings regarding my capacity to teach. My pupils might become tired, but not I. Sometimes it happened that I would go to their places only to find them engaged in their business. But I did not lose patience. None of the three desired a deep study of English, but two may be said to have made fairly good progress in about eight months. Two learnt enough to keep accounts and write ordinary business letters. The barber's ambition was confined to acquiring just enough English for dealing with his customers. As a result of their studies, two of the pupils were equipped for making a fair income.

I was satisfied with the result of the meeting. It was decided to hold such meetings, as far as I remember, once a week or, may be, once a These were held more or less regularly, and on these occasions there was a free exchange of ideas. The result was that there was now in Pretoria no Indian I did not know, or whose condition I was not acquainted with. This prompted me in turn to make the acquaintance of the British Agent in Pretoria, Mr Jacobus de Wet. He had sympathy for the Indians, but he had very little influence. However, he agreed to help us as best he could, and invited me to meet him whenever I wished.

I now communicated with the railway authorities and told them that, even under their own regulations, the disabilities about travelling under which the Indians laboured could not be justified. I got a letter in reply to the effect that first and second class tickets would be issued to Indians who were properly dressed. This was far from giving adequate relief, as it rested with the Station Master to decide who was 'properly dressed'.

The British Agent showed me some papers dealing with Indian affairs. Tyeb Sheth had also given me similar papers. I learnt from them how cruelly the Indians were hounded out from the Orange Free State.

In short, my stay in Pretoria enabled me to make a deep study of the social, economic and political condition of the Indians in the Transvaal and the Orange Free State. I had no idea that this study was to be of invaluable service to me in the future. For I had thought of returning home by the end of the year, or even earlier if the case was finished before the year was out.

But God disposed otherwise.

It would be out of place here to describe fully the condition of Indians in the Transvaal and the Orange Free State. I would suggest that those who wish to have a full idea of it may turn to my *History of Satyagraha in South Africa.* It is, however, necessary to give here a brief outline.

In the Orange Free State the Indians were deprived of all their rights by a special law enacted in 1888 or even earlier. If they chose to stay there, they could do so only to serve as waiters in hotels or to pursue some other such menial calling. The traders were driven away with nominal compensation. They made representations and petitions, but in vain.

A very stringent enactment was passed in the Transvaal in 1885. It was slightly amended in 1886, and it was provided under the amended law that all Indians should pay a poll tax of £3 as fee for entry into the Transvaal. They might not own land except in locations set apart for them, and in practice even that was not to be ownership. They had no franchise. All this was under the special law for Asiatics, to whom the laws for the coloured people were also applied. Under these latter, Indians might not walk on public footpaths, and might not move out of doors after 9 p.m. without a permit. The enforcement of this last regulation was elastic so far as the Indians were concerned. Those who passed as 'Arabs' were, as a matter of favour, exempted from it. The exemption thus naturally depended on the sweet will of the police.

I had to experience the effect of both these regulations. I often went out at night for a walk with Mr Coates, and we rarely got back home much before ten o'clock. What if the police arrested me? Mr Coates was more concerned about this than I. He had to issue passes to his

Negro servants. But how could he give one to me ? Only a master might issue a permit to a servant. If I had wanted one, and even if Mr Coates had been ready to give it, he could not have done so, for it would have been fraud.

So Mr Coates or some friend of his took me to the State Attorney, Dr Krause. We turned out to be barristers of the same Inn. The fact that I needed a pass to enable me to be out of doors after 9 p.m. was too much for him. He expressed sympathy for me. Instead of ordering for me a pass, he gave me a letter authorizing me to be out of doors at all hours without police interference. I always kept this letter on me whenever I went out. The fact that I never had to make use of it was a mere accident.

Dr Krause invited me to his place, and we may be said to have become friends. I occasionally called on him, and it was through him that I was introduced to his more famous brother, who was public Prosecutor in Johannesburg. During the Boer War he was court-martialled for conspiring to murder an English officer, and was sentenced to imprisonment for seven years. He was also disbarred by the Benchers. On the termination of hostilities he was released and, being honourably readmitted to the Taransvaal bar, resumed practice.

These connections were useful to me later on in my public life, and simplified much of my work.

The consequences of the regulation regarding the use of footpaths were rather serious for me. I always went out for a walk through President Street to an open plain. President Kruger's house was in this street—a very modest, unostentatious building, without a garden, and not distinguishable from other houses in its neighbourhood. The houses of many of the millionaires in Pretoria were far more pretentious, and were surrounded by gardens. Indeed President Kruger's simplicity was proverbial. Only the presence of a police patrol before the house indicated that it belonged to some official. I nearly always went along the footpaths past this patrol without the slightest hitch or hindrance.

Now the man on duty used to be changed from time to time. Once one of these men, without giving me the slightest warning, without even asking me to leave the footpath, pushed and kicked me into the street. I was dismayed. Before I could question him as to his behaviour,

Mr Coates, who happened to be passing the spot on horseback, hailed me and said:

'Gandhi, I have seen everything. I shall gladly be your witness in court if you proceed against the man. I am very sorry you have been so rudely assaulted.'

'You need not be sorry,' I said. 'What does the poor man know? All coloured people are the same to him. He no doubt treats Negroes just as he has treated me. I have made it a rule not to go to court in respect of any personal grievance. So I do not intend to proceed against him.'

'That is just like you,' said Mr Coates, 'but do think it over again. We must teach such men a lesson.' He then spoke to the policeman and reprimanded him. I could not follow their talk, as it was in Dutch, the policeman being a Boer. But he apologized to me, for which there was no need. I had already forgiven him.

But I never again went through this street. There would be other men coming in this man's place and, ignorant of the incident, they would behave likewise. Why should I unnecessarily court another kick? I therefore selected a different walk.

The incident deepened my feeling for the Indian settlers. I discussed with them the advisability of making a test case, if it were found necessary to do so, after having seen the British Agent in the matter of these regulations.

I thus made an intimate study of the hard condition of the Indian settlers, not only by reading and hearing about it, but by personal experience. I saw that South Africa was no country for a self-respecting Indian, and my mind became more and more occupied with the question as to how this state of things might be improved.

SAROJINI NAIDU

Letters

To M. Govindarajulu Naidu[1]

London
24 April 1895

My Darling:

I am so tired—so tired—why are you not near to take me to your heart and kiss away my weariness? I have been out the greater part of the day—went for a walk all over Whitelip shops—and in the afternoon went, partly on foot, and partly in those disgusting 'buses to Norfolk Street to the Artists' Studio to see his pictures—some of which were very nice.[2] I saw a great deal today—the whole of London I thought—

These letters are taken from *Sarojini Naidu: Selected Letters 1890s to 1940s*, edited by Makarand Paranjape, published by Kali for Women, New Delhi, 1996.

[1] SN's lover and later husband. Naidu, a medical doctor by profession, trained in Edinburgh, was an officer in the Nizam's army. SN fell in love with him in 1894, when she was barely fourteen. There is evidence that her father, Aghorenath Chattopadhyaya, tried to separate them, first by sending SN to Sholapur, and then arranging a scholarship for her to go to England. PS 27 argues that it was not primarily on account of caste that Aghorenath objected to the relationship but on account of the disparity in their ages. At any rate, both SN and GRN proved loyal to each other and were married in December 1898 in Madras after SN's return to India.

[2] The artist's name is untraceable. SN was only fifteen when she wrote this letter; moreover this was her first month in England. There is a certain

Trafalgar Square, Regent Street, Tower Bridge, Cleopatra's Needle, and I don't know what not. I am duly impressed now with the grandeur of old London—but, yet, I want to go home. Darling, my Darling! I can't write more tonight—I want you so much, so much—that, if I write more I shall simply break down[3]—O stretch your arms across the seas and draw me to your heart—my love, goodnight, goodnight!

A sweet goodnight.

To M. Govindarajulu Naidu

London

25 April 1895

It is a big, heavy budget this mail is taking for you, my own dear Govindu—Ah!, I wonder, will the coming mail bring a volume of love and tender messages from you? It is cold and foggy and gray this morning—and ever and anon, the rain comes down pattering—such changeable, fickle weather! But, yesterday, it was exquisitely fine—for England—warm and sunny and between the billowy silver clouds gleamed bits of the most delicious blur. Govindu, dear Govindu, it seems so long since I saw you—so long Darling, that I begin to think it is time for me to return—back to your heart. Do you want me, Govindu, do you want me back my Darling—Ah! don't answer—for I shall surely return!

I have a little message for you, a little short message which was born in the silence of the night—born of love and longing and darkness—surely, your soul will hide its love.

[Encloses a poem 'Around my path the dark night-shadows fall']

Goodbye, Darling—stretch your arms across the wide blue seas to draw to your heart—in twilight dreams—your own,

Sarojini

---

kind of breathlessness and neglect of specific details which characterise these letters.

[3] SN's health was always delicate. Throughout her life she suffered from a variety of ailments.

To M. Govindarajulu Naidu

London

13 January 1896

[Opening portions are missing.]

Nevertheless, the poetry of the latter quarter of this century, has been exceedingly brilliant and original—Shelley and Byron, Moore and Scott, Keats and Campbell and Wordsworth were a brilliant starry coterie, but even as brilliant as their coterie, though rather differently are the new poets. Fancy the young, passionate, beautiful, gifted poets gathered together in a radiant galaxy . . . William Watson with his sublime, starry genius, Davidson with his wild, riotous, dazzling superabundant brilliance, Thompson with his rich, gorgeous, spiritual ecstasy of poesy, Yeats with his exquisite dreams and music, Norman Gale, redolent of springtime in the meadows and autumn in the orchard, Arthur Symons, the marvelous boy, with his passionate nature and fiery eyes, all gathered together in the friendly house of that dearest and lovingest of friends and rarest and most gifted of geniuses, Edmund Gosse. Take too the older men, with their beautiful gifts. . . Swinburne, with his marvelous spirit, his voluptuous ecstasy of word music . . . take that grand old Socialist William Morris, hammering with golden thunders . . . take that lovely singer Edwin Arnold and that graceful writer, the laureate of the English, Alfred Austin . . . Who says we have no rare geniuses and true poets in these days . . .? Of course, the younger men are the more gifted, and William Watson is the greatest and noblest of them all—[4]

---

[4] The 'new poets' are those whose work achieved a brief spell of fame in the 1890s. Except A.C. Swinburne (1837–1909) and W.B. Yeats (1856–1939), none of them is considered a significant poet today. Edmund Gosse (1849–1929) was a major literary figure in Victorian England, famous as a critic, biographer and poet. William Morris (1834–1896) was a painter, furniture designer (hence the Morris chair) and poet in addition to being an avowed socialist. Edwin Arnold (1832–1904) was a poet and journalist but was better known in India for his book *The Light of Asia*, on the Buddha and his teachings. Arthur Symons (1865–1945) was an influential critic in addition to being a poet. William Watson (1858–1935), Francis Thompson (1859–1907), Alfred Austin (1835–1913), who was also the

Now, now I have been rambling off, haven't I? To come back to my day, after lunch, the soft sunshine tempted me out again, so donning my 'velvet disguise', I went across the road to a stationer's to buy me some exquisitely tinted notepaper and then further, to borrow a book from the library, and returned to devour it. . . . It was Edmund Gosse's *The Scent of Narcissi*. I don't think Edmund Gosse has ever written a romance before, but of course, the master hand that, with such loving insight and sympathy united to grace and strength, has written critiques on other writers can never fail in a novel. There is in it a perfect finish of style, a deep, impressive strength—a quiet, polished beauty. . . . It does not excite you, it does not make your heart turn and your eyes glow, but it carries you along with it. The story is very simple, but full of lovely pathos—the secret of it is that the writer has a great command over himself. . . .

After finishing the book, I wrote one or two notes and cheques, then had a very long, and difficult music lesson, with some tea. At dinner time your letter came, your sweet loving letter. Govindu... what a dear, true, faithful lover you are! God bless you! Govind, God bless Afsin [?] Jung[5] for his kind sympathy. May I venture—wouldn't it be proper, do you think, to thank him very, very much for his great kindness to us? If you think it right, tell him—if not—why, no good wish or desire is ever unfulfilled is it?

Look here, dear one, no more news of fevers and headaches for me. You must take care of yourself, Govindu. I am trying to take care of myself, dear, really, but, then, mine is such a peculiar case. . . .[6] You

---

Poet Laureate, and John Davidson (1857–1909), were all associated, one way or the other, with the Decadents, a group of French and English writers of the late 19th century, whose work is characterized by over-refinement of style, and artificiality of content. Some of these poets were also associated with the Rhymer's Club, a group of poets who met at the Cheshire Cheese in Fleet Street between 1891–1894.

[5] Probably one of the large number of friends that SN and MGN shared. It is very likely that this correspondence between the two lovers was clandestine, certainly not known to Aghorenath. Afsin Jung may have helped SN and MGN in some matter concerning their affair.

[6] Another reference to her delicate health. SN was quite highly strung emotionally in addition to being physically fragile. When she grew older

ought really to be very careful of yourself, sweetheart, now that you don't have your little wife to look after you—Will you promise?— Now, goodnight with a loving kiss on your lips, and one long sweet one where my head has lain so often, on your heart. God bless you, beloved, O beloved—and if God blesses you, I am blessed indeed, for in your happiness lies mine!. . . .

To Edmund Gosse

33 Blomfiéld Road, Maida Hill, London
6 October 1896

Dear Mr Gosse:

I did not dare to trust myself to thank you for what you said on Sunday. You cannot know what those words meant to me, how they will always colour my life, how, when I am in the very depths of self-disgust and despair—as I so often am—they will give me new hope and new courage—no you cannot know! Poetry is the one thing I love so passionately, so intensely, so absolutely, that is my very life of life— and now you have told me that *I am a poet*—I am a poet! I keep repeating it to myself to try to realize it. Will you let me tell you a little about myself, because I want you to know how you have been an influence in my life—ever since I was eleven years old!

Beautiful and romantic and remarkable as were the circumstances amidst which I was brought up, there was nothing to directly encourage poetry—indeed, the strongest influences that were brought to bear upon us were scientific and mathematical. I always loved poetry but nothing could be further from my mind than trying to write verses myself, it never once occurred to me why, till one day, when I was about eleven, while I was trying to do a dull problem—Algebra it was I think—quite suddenly three verses came into my head and I wrote them down—of course they were worthless, but that day marked a new era in my life: I was going to be a poet! I did not tell any one about my new 'adventures', but went on writing—things began to come with great ease and rapidity—weak and childish no doubt—I have no records

---

she developed hypertension, heart disease, rheumatism, malaria, obesity and other maladies. None of these, however, could daunt her zest for life.

left to tell tales!—and somehow my father got hold of them and soon everybody got to know and I was of course the most marvellous thing in creation and everything I did henceforth was wonderful, divine, etc.—I was fully on the way to have my head turned with all that flood of sincere but remarkably blind and injudicious praise and flattery. About this time, I don't know how or why the name of Edmund Gosse began to be a sort of magical legend to me—legends were more real than realities then—and in a dim, vague kind of way I began to feel that somehow this magical name was to be one of the strongest and most inevitable influence[s] on my life. I went on writing, and Hyderabad began to get more and more mad about what I did—indeed I think nearly all over India I began to be looked on as a phenomenon—but the more they praised the more disgusted I got with myself, and longed, O how passionately—for somebody who could really criticize. I knew my verses were very poor, but I wanted to know whether they had even a grain of promise of better things to come. At last in despair I wrote you a letter—(it must have been very childish I suppose—this was when I was about 14 or 15)—but I burnt it the next day!

Then I had a long and terrible illness[7] which nearly killed me and I believe for a time half-paralysed my faculties—everything seemed gone—except the love of poetry and the longing to do better. Then I came to England—I was about sixteen then—I must have been singularly ignorant for sixteen, because I knew that England to me meant Shelley and Keats, who were dead—and Edmund Gosse who was alive and certainly made up by far the greater part of England!—(I think Westminster Abbey and the Thames made up the rest![)] Well, I made up my mind that I must know Edmund Gosse! For the first six months I did not, could not write a single line or indeed do anything, and then suddenly the fountains were unsealed and I began to write, write, write! In the three months I wrote I think nearly *45* pieces— horrible! But the verses had I thought less strength than some of my earlier ones—the first batch I sent you were in selections from this extraordinary outburst of bad verse!

---

[7] A nervous breakdown, probably in 1894, as a result of the discovery of her liaison with MGN and her father's order to end it. She was sent to Sholapur to recover.

Well, in January I first saw you: the magical legend had become a reality—and I was not disappointed—indeed I shall never forget that day—because with one great bound I seemed to wake into a new, large life—the life I had always longed for and so long in vain. From that day I seemed an altered being. I seemed to have put off childish things and put on the garments of a new and beautiful hope and ambition, and I have gone on growing and growing. I feel it—seeing more clearly, feeling more intensely, thinking more deeply—and loving more passionately, more unselfishly that beautiful Spirit of Art that has now become dearer than my life's blood to me—and all this I owe to you. I know I have not expressed myself at all well, but you will understand me I think, and you will not mind my telling you all this.

As you have for so long been so good an influence in my life, I want you to go on forever! I will send you everything I write and you must tell me what you think. I want you to be more severe and exacting than ever, the better I do—because, I do not want to outlast the years, but the centuries. That is very conceited of me, but is it not worthwhile to aim at the stars, tho[ugh] one never gets beyond a mountain top?

I don't think I am going to ask you to excuse me for taking up so much of your time because I cannot go on being grateful to you in silence without your knowing how much cause I have to be grateful to you for!

Ever believe me,
Yours in all gratitude,

Sarojini Chattopadhyay

My most humble respects to Charles Nathaniel[8]

To M. Govindarajulu Naidu

Girton College, Cambridge[9]
9 October 1896

Well, I am at Girton after all! And there is something strikingly comical in my coming to Girton! Fancy me! No I shan't love it—I

---

[8] The Gosses' pet tomcat.
[9] A college for women founded in 1869.
[10] By Charlotte Bronte, first published in 1853.

shall like it here in time, but there's a difference between liking a thing and loving it—it will cramp my development in some ways, it will strengthen [it] in others—I don't care what happens. Everybody, of course, here as elsewhere tho' I have been only a few hours here, makes a pet of me—you see I am far the youngest and a curiosity—so I shan't be left long to myself! However, Govindu, I love you and that is quite enough. Good night.

To M. Govindarajulu Naidu

[Girton College, Cambridge]
10 October 1896

Well Govindu, I know if I had my way I should not stop here more than one term. I shall get to like my work, get to like the girls, get used to the ways—and then the library will be my delight and the garden my paradise—but for all that I shall be lonelier here than ever I have been. I shall rebel against the groove all must get into—the narrowly broad, the crampedly independent existence. O Govindu, Govindu! it makes me writhe to think of it—however, as some one said, 'souls carry their own atmosphere wherever they go'—so I will too be very [. . .] be very near and help me from being lonely.
Good night and God bless you.

To M. Govindarajulu Naidu

Girton College, Cambridge
11 October 1896. Sunday

Dear one, have you been very near me today? All the morning I had to myself and spent it in a long walk around the grounds, exulting with passionate joy over the crimson and gold of autumn mysteries—then in the afternoon, I did different things—the isolation of numbers is very great and I am lonely but never mind—I love you dear, I love you and be near me. Good night. God bless you.

To M. Govindarajulu Naidu

Girton College, Cambridge
16 October 1896

Govindu, I am feeling better; tho' I still keep my room. They are all so kind and nice here, they bring me flowers and books and fruit. I have been reading *Villette*[10] and thinking of you Govindu, thinking how dear your love was to me, and longing to be clasped to your heart for just one moment—my love, my Govindu! Just one moment. Then I could bear this isolation better. Your gray eyes bless me, my dear, my dear, and your lips kiss me even now. God bless you—strange shrine is this shelter of unawakened hearts for your dear image, but if my heart is its holy of holies it is well. These girls are children, children, whose souls have not been wakened yet—and towards them I feel sometimes as a mother for have I not loved and loved and offered things they cannot dream of.

SUBHAS CHANDRA BOSE

The Sum Total of Good I Can Do

Subhas Chandra Bose set sail for England on 15 September 1919. He joined Cambridge as a student and found it to be remarkably different from 'a police-ridden city like Calcutta where every student was looked upon as a potential revolutionary and suspect.' Bose was only in his early twenties but was thoroughly politicized, and was also prepared to make huge sacrifices. In some of the letters that the future nationalist leader wrote to his childhood friends like Hemanta Kumar Sarkar and Charu Chandra Ganguly, Bose conveys the worries of a student who cannot be indifferent to his studies, or money, or the wretched cold outside his room. However, in some of the other letters, particularly those written to his brother, Sarat Chandra Bose, we witness the struggle of a young man, successful in gaining entry into the prestigious Indian Civil Service, agonizing over the question whether a highly regarded job in the British-led bureaucracy was the best way he could serve his country. Not all these letters were written in English, though some were, including the one Bose penned on 22 April 1921 in which, after seven months of torment, he announced his resignation to the British Secretary of State for India.

—Ed.

These letters are taken from *Subhas Chandra Bose, An Indian Pilgrim*, edited by Sisir K. Bose and Sugata Bose, published by Oxford University Press India, New Delhi, 1997. Reprinted by special permission from the Netaji Research Bureau, Kolkata.

The following four letters were written to Sarat Chandra Bose.

Cambridge
16-2-'21
Wednesday

My dear brother,

I was expecting copies of some of the photographs taken at Shillong. I suppose they are on their way now.

Has Saroj Babu started an independent firm of his own? It appears so, from the letter he has written to me.

Your letter of the 20th Jan. reached me on Saturday last. I am glad to learn how the children are getting on. I am told Asoka has improved considerably of late. From what I know of the Bolpur School I think it is a jolly good idea to send Bimal there. I hope *Bardidi* will approve of this plan.

You have received my 'explosive' letter by this time. Further thought confirms me in my support of the plans I have sketched for myself in that letter. The only difficulty is what I may call social opposition. No man of the world will approve of my rash enterprise. The ordinary man lacks the idealism which alone can conceive of a life different from the one we ordinarily live. I am sure you will support me. If C.R. Das at this age can give up everything and face the uncertainties of life—I am sure a young man like myself, who has no worldly cares to trouble him, is much more capable of doing so. If I give up the service, I shall not be in want of work to keep my hands full. Teaching, social service, co-operative credit work, journalism, village organisation work—there are so many things to keep thousands of energetic young men busy. Personally, I should like to take up teaching and journalism at present. The national college and the new paper 'Swaraj' will afford plenty of scope for my activity.

As for my livelihood, I hope to earn enough to make ends meet—either as a teacher in the National College or as a member of the Editorial Staff of any of the nationalist papers, or as both. My wants are few and I shall be satisfied with little.

When I persuaded myself, a few months ago, that I should accept the service at present, my idea was to save an amount roughly equivalent to the money spent over me and then to resign the service and join public life. That amount I wanted to set apart for the higher education of Gopali or Sati or for the upbringing of *Bardidi's* children. I felt (and I still feel) that I owed a duty to the members of our family—having myself enjoyed the benefit of an education abroad. But I have begun to doubt whether that is the best way I can fulfil the moral responsibility which hangs on my shoulders. I have further begun to think that the sum total of good I can do if I resign the service is more than what I can do if I stick to the service and simply save money. It is for you to decide whether I can better fulfil the moral responsibility which rests on me by resigning the service or remaining in it. Personally I have no doubt that I can do much more if I am not in the service. A life of sacrifice to start with, plain living and high thinking, wholehearted devotion to the country's cause—all these are highly enchanting to my imagination and inclination. Further, the very principle of serving under an alien bureaucracy is intensely repugnant to me. The path of Arabindo Ghosh is to me more noble, more inspiring, more lofty, more unselfish though more thorny than the path of Romesh Dutt.

I have written to father and to mother to permit me to take the vow of poverty and service. They may be frightened at the thought that that path might lead to suffering in the future. Personally I am not afraid of suffering—in fact, I would rather welcome it than shrink from it.

I am pretty well here. How are you all doing?

I shall keep all this a secret until a decision is arrived at.

Yours v. affly,
Subhas

P.S.—If I resign, I intend to return home as soon as possible. The Tripos comes off early in June and the results will be declared within a fortnight. So I shall be in a position to return in June along with *Bardada*. I shall of course have to refund to the India Office the total sum I get as allowance by that time. I shall get the second instalment of the allowance (£50/-) by the end of March and the third instalment by the end of June.

S.C. BOSE

Cambridge
23-2-'21

My dear brother,

I did not hear from you by the last mail. You were too busy at the time—I presume.

I have aleady written to you more than once about my desire to resign the Civil Service and take up public service instead. I have submitted this desire of mine to a severe analysis and to a mature deliberation. I can assure you that I have not arrived at such a decision in a moment of mental excitement. The decision may be a regrettable one from a certain point of view but it is based on my whole outlook on life. Ever since the result of the ICS was declared, I have been asking myself whether I shall be more useful to my country if I am in the service than if I am not. I am fully convinced now that I shall be able to serve my country better if I am one of the people than if I am a member of the bureaucracy. I do not deny that one can do some amount of good when he is in the service but it can't be compared with the amount of good that one can do when his hands are not tied by bureaucratic chains. Besides, as I have already mentioned in one of my letters, the question involved is mainly one of principle. The principle of serving an alien bureaucracy is one to which I cannot reconcile myself. Besides, the first step towards equipping oneself for public service is to sacrifice all worldly interests—to burn one's boats as it were—and devote oneself wholeheartedly to the national cause.

You will realize that the conditions under which an ICS man has got to live and work are incompatible with my temperament, training and general outlook on life. Under these circumstances it would be a most illogical thing for me to accept conditions in the midst of which I am sure to feel miserable. On the other hand I know that a life of sacrifice, of suffering and even of poverty is heartily welcome to me if only it is in the interests of our national cause.

I have already said more than once that the uncertainties of life are powerless to intimidate me. I am fully aware that I am deliberately courting pecuniary loss and physical discomfort. But I am prepared for the untoward effects of my action—both immediate and remote.

The illustrious example of Aurobindo Ghose looms large before my vision. I feel that I am ready to make the sacrifice which that example demands of me. My circumstances are also favourable. Our family is fairly well-to-do (except for *Bardidi* and her children) and I have no pressing worldly responsibilities. I believe I have an ascetic frame of mind which will enable me to bear with patience any misfortune which may visit me in future. Lastly, I am unmarried and hope to remain so. Who can ever expect such easy circumstances?

My plan is to return home in June after taking my degree—with *Bardada* if possible. I desire to take up teaching work in the National College on my arrival in Calcutta. In addition to this I intend to join the staff of one of the nationalist daily papers in Calcutta. I have other plans also in my mind viz. social service, mass education, cooperative credit society and the organisation of a research department for political and economic problems in connection with the National Congress. But these plans will be taken up later on when men and money are forthcoming. In any case I shall have plenty of work to do to keep my hands full when I arrive in India.

I am sure you will respond favourably to this proposal of mine. The only obstacle is that hardly any one else among our relatives will approve of my eccentric plans. There will be a terrible hue and cry everywhere but I do not think that that should scare us if we take our stand on truth.

You have done all that you could for me and all that I could expect from you—and without being solicited either. I feel that I have been placed under a kind of moral obligation—the meaning and depth of which I do not sufficiently comprehend. The result is that I feel that my proposal to resign is, to say the least, a cruel one. Such a proposal means that the sum of Rs 10,000/- spent for my sake will yield no return whatsoever. But when I appeal to you to consent to my resignation I do so, not as a personal favour but for the sake of our unfortunate country which is in dire need of wholehearted devotees. You will have to look upon the money spent for my sake as a gift laid at the feet of the mother without any expectation of return in any shape or form.

This is my last letter to you on the subject of my resignation. I am making a similar appeal to father and mother also. I am sure I shall get your consent. The next riding examination comes off on or about the 23rd April. I hope to get a reply to this before that date and in all probability I shall not have to appear at the next riding examination.

I realize that it will require more strength of mind on your part to consent to my proposal than has been required of me in formulating this proposal. But I am fully confident that you possess the requisite strength of mind. I am sure that if you are convinced of the soundness of my proposal you will not allow any other consideration to withhold your consent.

Aurobindo Ghose is to me my spiritual guru. To him and to his mission I have dedicated my life and soul. My decision is final and unchangeable, but my destiny is at present in your hands.

Can I not expect your blessings in return and will you not wish me Godspeed in my new and adventurous career?

Your v. affly,
Subhas

P.S.—Glad to receive your letter of the second inst: and to learn that all of you are doing well.

We are pretty well here. How are you all doing?

Subhas

Oxford
6-4-'21

My dear brother,

Your letter of the 12th March was to hand duly. I have been profoundly impressed by the sentiments expressed in that letter. I am gratified to find that you corroborate my point of view even though you do not accept my conclusions.

Since the 15th of August last, one thought has taken possession of me—viz. how to effect a reconciliation between my duty to father (and mother) and my duty to myself. I could see from the very outset that father would be against my proposal—in fact, my idea would seem to him preposterous. It was not without a shudder therefore—shudder at the thought of causing him pain—that I asked you to communicate my intention to father. In fact, I did not then have the heart to write to him direct. That was in September last and the result of that attempt you know very well.

Since then the struggle has been going on in my mind—a struggle intensely painful and bitter in view of the issues involved. I have failed to arrive at any reconciliation. We who have grown up under the influence of Swami Vivekananda on one side and Aurobindo Ghose on the other—have, fortunately or unfortunately, developed a mentality which does not accept a compromise between points of view so diametrically opposed. It is quite possible that I have been nurtured on a wrong philosophy. But it is the characteristic of youthful minds to have more faith in themselves than in others. It is perhaps an unfortunate fact but it is a fact all the same.

You know very well that in the past I had occasion to cause great pain not only to father and mother but to many others including yourself. I have never excused myself for that and I shall never do so. Nevertheless, conditioned as I was by temperament and circumstance, there was no escape for me out of an intellectual and moral revolt. My only desire then was to secure that amount of freedom which was necessary for developing a character after my own ideals and for shaping my destiny after my own inclination.

Since then, circumstances have considerably changed. Bereavement after bereavement has overtaken us. Father and mother are not in the same state of health in which they were some years ago. It will be cruel—exceedingly cruel—for me to cause them grievous pain in their present state of mind and health. I know I shall never be able to excuse myself in afterlife for being instrumental in bringing so much pain and worry. But what can I do? Should I abandon my own point of view?

I realise that all along I alone have been instrumental in introducing so much discord into our otherwise quiet family. The reason is that certain ideas have taken possession of me and these ideas have unfortunately been unacceptable to others.

Father thinks that the life of a self-respecting Indian Civil servant will not be intolerable under the new regime. And that home rule will come to us within ten years. But to me the question is not whether my life will be tolerable under the new regime. In fact I believe that even if I am in the service, I can do some useful work. The main question involved is one of principle. Should we under the present circumstances own allegiance to a foreign bureaucracy and sell ourselves for a mess of pottage? Those who are already in the service or who cannot help accepting service may do so. But should I, being favourably situated in many respects, own allegiance so readily? The day I sign the covenant I shall cease to be a free man.

I believe we shall get Home Rule within ten years and certainly earlier if we are ready to pay the price. The price consists of sacrifice and suffering. Only on the soil of sacrifice and suffering can we raise our national edifice. If we all stick to our jobs and look after our own interests, I don't think we shall get Home Rule even in fifty years. Each family—if not each individual—should now bring forward its offering to the feet of the mother. Father wants to save me from this sacrifice. I am not so callous as not to appreciate the love and affection which impels him to save me from this sacrifice, in my own interests. He is naturally apprehensive that I am perhaps hasty in my judgment or over-zealous in my youthful enthusiasm. But I am perfectly convinced that the sacrifice has got to be made—by somebody at least.

If anybody else had come forward, I might have had cause to withdraw or wait. Unfortunately nobody is coming yet and the precious moments are flying away. In spite of all the agitation going on there, it still remains true that not a single civil servant has had the courage to throw away his job and join the people's movement. This challenge has been thrown at India and has not been answered yet. I may go further and say that in the whole history of British India, not one Indian has voluntarily given up the civil service with a patriotic motive. It is time that members of the highest service in India should set an example to members of the other services. If the members of the services withdraw their allegiance or even show a desire to do so— then and then only will the bureaucratic machine collapse.

I therefore do not see how I can save myself from this sacrifice. I know what this sacrifice means. It means poverty, suffering, hard work and possibly other hardships to which I need not expressly refer but which you can very well understand. But the sacrifice has got to be made—consciously and deliberately.

Father says that most of the so-called leaders are not really unselfish. But is that any reason why he should prevent me from being unselfish? If anybody wants to be unselfish he will unavoidably cause suffering and worry in his own family. We cannot complain that other people are not self-sacrificing if we ourselves are not prepared to be so.

From the above considerations I conclude that on behalf of our family I must come forward with my little offering and since this sacrifice must be undergone we might as well do so with a light heart. Father is afraid that I am ruining my career and that I may bring untold suffering on myself in future. I do not see how I can persuade him that the day I resign will be one of the proudest and happiest moments of my life.

Your proposal that I should resign after returning is eminently reasonable but there are one or two points to be urged against it. In the first place it will be a galling thing for me to sign the covenant which is an emblem of servitude. In the second place if I accept service for the present I shall not be able to return home before December or January, as the usual custom stands. If I resign now, I may return by July. In six months' time water will have flowed through the Ganges. In the absence of adequate response at the right moment, the whole movement might tend to flag and if response comes too late it may not have any effect. I believe it will take years to initiate another such movement and hence I think that the tide in the present movement must be availed of. If I have to resign, it does not make any difference to me or to anyone of us whether I resign tomorrow or after a year but delay in resigning may on the other hand have some untoward effect on the movement. I know full well that I can do but little to help the movement—but it will be a great thing if I have the satisfaction of having done my bit.

As to my programme when I return home—that will depend on the conditions then existing in Bengal and on the needs of that province. Apart from the work I do, I shall have to devote a lot of time to a study of the different problems of our national life. Only a profound study of these problems can equip a man intellectually for the task of intelligent service.

A couple of years' service—specially under Lord Sinha's regime— will not help me in my future work. A couple of years' work as district officer will no doubt afford valuable experience. But it will take about eight years to be a district officer and two to three years in order to be a sub-divisional officer. The first year is devoted more or less to official, or rather clerical, work.

The movement—as you say—is now in a nebulous and chaotic condition. But it is for us to shape it in the proper manner. It will serve no useful purpose if we adopt the Asquithian policy of wait and see. The movement will either succeed or fail. If it succeeds, it will do so in spite of our indifference which one may call criminal. If it fails, the responsibility will be ours for having kept aloof from the movement.

I have no exaggerated opinion about the progress of events at home. If I were sure that the movement would progress favourably, I could easily have waited. The apprehension of failure or slackening impels me to throw myself into the movement before it is too late to mend matters.

I do not know who has spread the rumour in Calcutta that I have resigned already. Some people perhaps presume to know more about myself than I do.

The application for a military commission refers to myself though there has been some misunderstanding on this score. The Indian students at Cambridge have been agitating for admission into the Officers' Training Corps there. I was one of those who applied in Michaelmas Term 1920, for enlistment. But we only wanted training during our stay at Cambridge. I expressly mentioned in the application that I was a probationer in the ICS. It is clear that when I resign the ICS, I can have nothing to do with HM's Army.

I may do some teaching work immediately I return but as a permanent profession I shall choose journalism. That will help me to earn my living as well.

If for any reason I happen to change my decision regarding resignation, I shall send a cable to father as that will relieve his anxiety.

How are you all doing? We are all pretty well here.

Yours v. affly,
Subhas

Cambridge,
20-4-'21

My dear brother,

I have not heard from you for the last two weeks. I am particularly anxious on *Mejdidi's* account.

I do not know how the rumour spread in Calcutta about 2 months ago that I had resigned. I had written only to one man in Calcutta about my desire and he has not given it out. I believe the expectations of certain people took shape in the form of a rumour which soon gained currency.

I am going to send in my resignation day-after-tomorrow. I have written this week to two persons in Calcutta about it and have requested them not to make a fuss over it. The fact that I am definitely going to resign has leaked out here only within the last few days. Unfortunately it seems to have created a sensation among the Indian Community. I am afraid, therefore, that some of the people here will send word to India and some people there will try to make a sensation over it. I am anxious to avoid creating a sensation for several reasons. In the first place, I dislike both sensation and popular applause. Secondly, if there is no sensation there is not likely to be any difficulty about my getting home as soon as possible. Thirdly, I would like to hide the fact of my resignation from father's knowledge, in view of Mejdidi's present state of health. I have not written to father anything about my resignation since I heard of Mejdidi's illness. But I am afraid it is impossible to keep it a secret. Still, I shall try my best.

I had a very stormy time at Oxford—stormy—from the mental point of view. I shall write to you in my next letter all the reasons which finally persuaded me to choose the path of resignation.

You need not bother about sending me any money at present—especially in view of the unfavourable rate of exchange. Some of my friends have offered to lend me sufficient money which will keep me going till I reach home. I have not hesitated in accepting the offer because I have been assured that they are lending out of their surplus stock which they have at present. I shall borrow in pounds and if the rate of exchange improves during the next few months, it will be convenient for me to repay the amount from India. They will not lose anything by lending me the money (except the bank rate of interest) whereas it may be of great help to me. I expect the rate of exchange to improve during the next few months.

I shall apply for a passage early next week. I intend to leave for home by the end of June. I shall try for a berth in the Messageries Maritimes and failing that, in the BISN or City Line.

You have said too many kind words about me in your letters which I know how little I deserve. The magnanimous spirit revealed in your letters has touched me profoundly. I know that that spirit is worthy of you and all I shall say is—I am proud of you. In spite of the difference of opinion, I feel sure that no one could have expected a more cordial and sympathetic response from one's elder brother.

I know how many hearts I have grieved—how many superiors of mine I have disobeyed. But on the eve of this hazardous undertaking my only prayer is—may it be for the good of our dear country.

Yours v. affly,
Subhas

Letter of resignation from the Indian Civil Service.

16, Herbert Street
Cambridge
22-4-'21

The Right Hon. E. S. Montagu MP
Secretary of State for India.

Sir,

I desire to have my name removed from the list of probationers in the Indian Civil Service.

I may state in this connection that I was selected as a result of an open competitive examination held in August, 1920.

I have received an allowance of £100/- (one hundred pounds only) up till now. I shall remit the amount to the India Office as soon as my resignation is accepted.

I have the honour to be Sir,
Your most obedient servant,
Subhas Chandra Bose

The following letter was written to Sarat Chandra Bose.

The Union Society
Cambridge,
23-4-'21

My dear brother,

I have not heard from you for the last two weeks. I learn from father's letter that you had been to Cuttack during Easter Week. I am anxious to know how Mejdidi is doing, but all of you are maintaining what appears to me a suspicious silence about her.

I had a talk with the Censor of Fitzwilliam Hall, Mr Reddaway, about my resignation. Contrary to my expectations, he heartily approved of my idea. He said he was surprised, almost shocked, to hear that I had changed my mind, since no Indian within his knowledge had ever done that before. I told him that I would make journalism my profession later on and he said that he preferred a journalistic career to a monotonous one like the Civil Service.

I was at Oxford for three weeks before I came up here and there the final stage of my deliberation took place. The only point which had been taxing me for the last few months was whether I should be justified morally in following a course which would cause intense sorrow and displeasure in many minds and especially in the minds of father and mother.

I wrote to you in one of my previous letters that I felt that, having had the advantage of an education abroad, I should try my best to extend the same advantage to some other members of our family or at least to contribute to the material welfare of our family in some other way. Strictly personal questions did not in any way trouble me as I did not have any worldly ambition to start with and as I had further resolved to live a life of celibacy. But it occurred to me that before I turned my back on all family interests I should be convinced that I was really acting under the inspiration of some higher duty. The apt saying of Christ that he who hates his brother and says that he loves God is a hypocrite—reminded me that it is often possible to neglect mundane duties under a delusion of working for higher ends.

I have always felt that it is unfair from our point of view to place such a huge financial burden on your shoulders—though I could never effect any other practical solution of our financial problem. Consequently I felt that I should try to decentralize the burden and take some responsibility on my shoulders. This appeared to me all the more imperative since in order to help father to retire you would have to take over some further financial responsibility. I wrote to you what I felt on this matter and received your reply to it. The reply was magnanimous as it could be and you tried therein to absolve me of the moral obligation under which I felt I had been placed. Nevertheless I feel that I have not been absolved of the moral obligation and shall not be absolved—until and unless I prove to my own satisfaction that I have done sound and solid work in the career which I am now going to follow.

I need not make it a secret that I felt I was responsible more to father, mother and yourself for what I did, than to anyone else. You have tried to absolve me of the moral obligation though moral obligation which is deeper than legal obligation cannot be disowned at the will of either or both parties. The obligation I own to father and mother is not to displease them to the best of my ability. They are inspired by a desire to look after my own interests and they are naturally afraid that if I resign the Civil Service I shall be courting financial ruin and poverty for myself in the future. I have not been able to persuade them that the course I intend to follow will bring me the greatest amount of happiness—that real happiness cannot be measured in terms of pounds, shillings and pence and that if I stick to the service I shall always feel that I am a criminal who has not got the courage of his convictions. Their view follows naturally upon a materialistic interpretation of life but I quite realize that out of their affection for me they are anxious to see me getting on well in life instead of being plunged once more into a sea of tainties.

My position therefore is that in entering upon a new career I am acting against the express wishes of father and mother and against your advice though you have sent me your 'warmest felicitations in whatever course I choose'.

My greatest objection to joining the service was based on the fact that I would have to sign the Covenant and thereby own the allegiance of a foreign bureaucracy which I feel rightly or wrongly has no moral right to be there. Once I signed the Covenant, it would not matter from the point of view of principle whether I served for three days or three years or thirty years. I have come to believe our hands clean of any connection with the British Government. Every Government servant whether he be a petty chaprasi or a provincial Governor only helps to contribute to the stability of the British Government in India. The best way to end a government is to withdraw from it. I say this not because that was Tolstoy's doctrine nor because Gandhi preaches it—but because I have come to believe in it.

I have come to believe, further, that the national liberty which we want cannot be attained without paying for it dearly in the way of sacrifice and suffering. Those of us who have the heart to feel and the opportunity to suffer should come forward with their offering. I do not expect that those who have been long in the service and have financial responsibilities to shoulder can do this. Nevertheless each family in this wide land of ours must come forward with its own humble tribute and as long as we do not do our duty, we have no right to complain that the leaders are selfish.

I feel that we have not yet contributed our share and therefore I should make the sacrifice. Sacrifice and suffering are not in themselves very attractive things but I can't avoid them as I have been convinced that without them our national aspirations can never be fulfilled. It is purely an accident that I should be coming forward for the work and not somebody else. If we would approve of the sacrifice in the case of a third person there is no reason why we should not approve of it in our own case.

Besides, I find that fortunately I am fitted for this task by my temperament and previous training.

These considerations lead me to think that I am right in giving up the service—that father's desire that I should serve is unreasonable and is actuated only by natural affection for me and solicitude for my worldly prosperity.

My resignation will bring some amount of suffering—it may for instance hinder *Sejdada's* promotion later on. But I think we should accept some amount of suffering as inevitable.

I hope it will not appear from this long letter that I am sermonising. Any such thing is farthest from my mind. My desire in writing the above has been to tell you what considerations have led me to decide upon a course of action which is opposed to the wishes of almost all of you. I have taken up an attitude of disobedience only after being convinced that sacrifice and suffering are inevitable for gaining one's ends and that under the circumstances I am best fitted to undergo the sacrifice.

It is not for me to judge whether this constitutes a moral justification for acting on my own initiative in the face of all advice to the contrary. I know I have hurt father beyond measure and I shall never excuse myself for having done so. Time alone will prove whether I am right or not. If you think that I have been guilty of rashness and indiscretion I pray that you will suspend your judgment and restrain your condemnation till my folly is thoroughly exposed by time. If you think I am not wrong in my choice I am sure your blessings and good wishes will always attend on me in my future career.

I received a letter from mother saying that in spite of what father and others think she prefers the ideal for which Mahatma Gandhi stands. I cannot tell you how happy I have been to receive such a letter. It will be worth a treasure to me as it has removed something like a burden from my mind.

I sent in my resignation a few days ago. I have not yet been informed that it has been accepted.

C.R. Das has written, in reply to a letter of mine, about the work that is already being done. He complains that there is a dearth of sincere workers at present. There will consequently be plenty of congenial work for me when I return home.

I intend to sail for home by the end of June. I shall apply for a berth as soon as my resignation is accepted. You need not bother about sending me any money now. I have been offered a loan which will keep me going till I reach Calcutta.

I am relieved to learn that *Mejdidi* has come round. I am therefore writing to father to say that I have resigned.

I hope and pray that he will be able to stand this piece of bad news.

I have nothing more to say. The die is cast and I earnestly hope that nothing but good will come out of it.

I have not heard from you for three weeks at least. Your silence surprises me. Are you doing quite well?

We are all pretty well here. How are you all doing? Does Ami still remember me? He will be a big boy by the time I return.

Yours v. affly,
Subhas

JAWAHARLAL NEHRU

In the Modern World

Jawaharlal Nehru was not just a great political leader, he was also a wonderful stylist. While his intellectual inquiry into India's past comes across well in the books that he wrote, his brilliant fluency and intuitive grasp of the rhythms of language is conveyed more in his speeches and, often, also in his letters. In these letters written to his sister Vijayalakshmi Pandit ('Nan' was the name that her English governess gave her, shortened from the Hindi 'nanhi', in the same way that she called Nehru's second sister 'Betty' for 'beti' or daughter), Nehru is in his element, dynamic, a man on the move, caught in the swirl of history, touching quickly and easily on a wide variety of subjects. Here he is, on a luxury liner and telling his sister in his letter that he is thinking of the violence in Canton: 'That I suppose is the contrast of the modern world. There are several Spaniards here whose friends and relatives are fighting in Spain. Meanwhile they dance and flirt here.' There is a lot that Nehru asks about the family, and he also offers a great deal of information about himself. At the same time, the real weight of history also imposes itself on each inquiry: 'I have no news of India at all. Except for your letters, no letter from India—I do not know what is happening in Cawnpore, whether the strike is on or off.'

—Ed.

These letters are taken from *Before Freedom: Nehru's Letters to his Sister,* edited by Nayantara Sahgal, published by HarperCollins Publishers India, New Delhi, 2000.

Biancamano
Nearing Suez
9 June 1938

Darling Nan,

I had set apart part of today and tomorrow for letter writing so that I might post my letters at Port Said. I had decided not to make the trip to Cairo (from Suez and back to Port Said). This was an expensive business and not worthwhile for a few hours. It is curious that for so many years every time that I have passed through Suez I have thought of going to Cairo and ultimately desisted. Only when I went by air I passed through Cairo. So I decided again to stick to the steamer through the Suez Canal. A little while ago I had a cable from Cairo informing me that the Wafd Party welcomed me and that Nahas Pasha who was in Alexandria would like to meet me there. For this purpose they wanted to send a private plane for me to Suez—I could not very well refuse and so the time allotted to letter writing is now no more. Soon we shall be in Suez.

We have had a good voyage and there are a number of interesting people on board. There is an Italian mission, headed by an ambassador, returning from a goodwill visit to Japan. There are Chinese representatives going to Geneva. There are many persons from Shanghai—European businessmen and others. Italians predominate. Then there are Americans, Scandinavians, Indians of course and a few Englishmen. The English are not much in evidence. We have two royal highnesses, two excellencies and numerous counts and countesses. The RHs are the Duke of Aosta and his mother who came on board at Massana in the Red Sea.

11/6

This letter had to be interrupted and then we got down at Suez. I fear I shall not be able to write many or long letters as there are many interruptions. I have got to know many people on board and they come to me and want to have talks. Some of them are not interesting but I cannot ignore them. But there are quite a number of interesting folk and my autobiography, of which there are a number of copies on board, has made me a desirable acquaintance. I think I am a pretty useful ambassador for India. I succeed in impressing people with the strength and vitality of our national movement and they are convinced that big things are going to happen in India and we are going to come into our own.

The Duke of Aosta informed us that the Italian mission from Japan had been greatly impressed. The Duke, by the way, is a fascinating person. I did not know who he was for two or three days, that is I did not recognise him although I knew he was on board. He was standing near us one day and asked a member of the Italian mission to introduce us. He is 6ft 6 and very schoolboyish. As he was sitting by us, clad in shorts, an ADC arrived and whispered to him something to the effect that Her Royal Highness his mother considered it desirable that he should get into trousers! We were reaching Suez and there might be officials to meet him there. And so in some disgust he went and got into trousers and came back. Then he got hold of my autobiography from Bee[1] and has been reading it since. He speaks English perfectly.

Some of the Italian mission people are also charming and interesting—they are excellencies and counts. Then there is a beautiful Danish Countess coming from Shanghai and odd persons from various parts of the world.

You will remember that Mrs Rau[2] asked me to sit at her table. I had decided to do no such thing and so I told her later that I had already fixed my table. I took the table Raja had reserved for me and Bee joined me there. I think Mrs Rau has been slightly cool, and I have not had any long talk with her. But we meet daily of course and exchange a few words of greeting etc. In spite of her numerous accomplishments, I have scored in one matter at least. I can swim and dive and neither Mrs Rau nor Lila[3] can do so. In the last eight days the swimming pool has been a great attraction and I have spent a good deal of time there. On some evenings I have gone as late as 11 p.m. and remained there till midnight. Mrs Rau and Lila have tried to learn swimming without much success. It is not easy to learn on board a ship.

---

[1] Batlivala acting as his secretary.
[2] Pandita Kshama Rau, a Sanskrit scholar.
[3] Lila, her daughter; a tennis star.

It is chilly in the Mediterranean and I am afraid there will not be so much swimming as there used to be. So far we have had crowds of men and women displaying huge expanses of flesh, disporting themselves in the pool or outside.

Clothes have been at a discount throughout the Indian Ocean and Red Sea. Shorts and a vest, or something much less even, are all that is considered proper by men and women. Even the famous suits I had made in Bombay were out of place and I wished that I had more shorts and vests or sports shirts. The two suits have not turned out to be great successes. As for the shoes, my first attempt to wear them during my visit to Cairo was a ghastly failure and I was in pain most of the time. So I propose to stick to my Peshawari chappals. Most people wear chappals here. The Duke of Aosta swears by them and says they are spreading fast in Italy and Abyssinia. The army and navy are adopting them. They were first introduced by Aosta's brother who had brought them from Kashmir when he went to do mountain climbing. They are called Karakorum shoes in Italy.

Bee has been functioning as my secretary on board and has proved helpful. She accompanied me to Cairo and Alexandria during my visit to Nahas Pasha. She is very popular on board and the Duke manages to roll up frequently for a talk with her. She speaks fairly good French and that helps her to get on with the motley crowd on board. I must say I feel very small when I meet people—there are many on board—who can speak fluently in several languages. The Danish Countess I have mentioned above speaks quite a number with the most delightful ease.

I am enclosing a typed letter which I am sending to Kripalani for members of the working Committee. You may show it to Pantji,[4] Rafi etc but not to too many persons or any who are not reliable. Of course show it to Ranjit.

As I write a fancy dress ball is going on though there are very few fancy dresses. We had a gorgeous farewell dinner tonight. And this reminds me that Nahas Pasha gave us a stupendous and magnificent lunch—one of the best-cooked meals I have ever had.

---

[4] Govind Ballabh Pant, at this time premier of the United Provinces.

I do not yet know what will happen to me after I land in Genoa. Krishna Menon will meet me at Genoa and that means that we shall proceed to Spain. Strange when I think of what is happening there and the horror of Canton and compare it to the life on this luxury liner. That I suppose is the contrast of the modern world. There are several Spaniards here whose friends and relatives are fighting in Spain. Meanwhile they dance and flirt here. A young Chinaman was talking to me the other day. I spoke of the terrible bombing of Canton. 'I come from Canton,' he replied, 'that is my home town', and his face grew hard and stern, and that was the end of the topic. Nothing more could be said. How many of his relatives and friends and dear ones might be dead and dying.

Always this contrast comes up before me. Here on board I have been surrounded by an atmosphere of friendliness and even some respect. Partly this is due to my book which many had read, partly to the thought that I was someone who counted. Anyway this atmosphere has been far more in evidence than on any previous voyage.

Send this letter when you have done with it, and Ranjit has seen it, to Betty. I am writing to her briefly.

Love to the children and Ranjit and you,

Your loving brother,
Jawahar

Ormonde House
St. James' Street
S.W. 1 London
23 June 1938

Darling Nan,

I have not written a single letter to India since my arrival in Europe ten days ago. I have tried hard but failed to find the time. Soon after arrival in Genoa I went by plane to Marseilles—a lot of trouble there about formalities to enable us to go to Spain—then five days in Barcelona—journey to Paris and three days there. Today I arrived here. I could and want to write so much about Spain but I must not do so now. This letter is supposed to be a brief one to be followed by another when I have the chance.

On arrival here I met Indu today. She looked fairly well but not as well as I had expected and hoped. Your letter reached me today. It is because of this that I am finding some time late at night to write. You mention the possibility of an operation. One need not be anxious about this but it is obviously desirable to take all precautions and to have the best medical aid available. Purandare is no doubt good but, everything considered, it seems to be obviously better that you should have the operation in Vienna or elsewhere in Europe. I want you to consider this. The question of your ministerial work need not come in the way much as in any event you will have to suspend it if you have the operation. I do recommend strongly that you should come to Europe soon.

My programme is still uncertain. I expect to remain here till the night of 17th July and then go to Paris for five or six days. This is certain. After that Indu and I go to Switzerland, Munich, Czechoslovakia and Vienna. Perhaps further to Budapest and Turkey.

This is uncertain. I want to be back in Geneva early in September and return to India in October.

This flat is good but expensive. We are paying 9 guineas a week for two bedrooms and a sitting room etc. The quarter is expensive. If a letter can reach me by the 17th July it might be sent direct here. From 18th to 22nd or 23rd I shall be in Paris and letters reaching me there can be sent to Hotel Bourgoyne and Montana, 7 rue de Bourgoyne, Paris (Cables Bourgonotel Paris).

The press in various countries has said a lot about me. I enclose a silly article which appeared here today.

I enclose also for Tandon's[5] benefit a menu of a new vegetarian restaurant to which Indu took me. Observe the uncooked food.

In haste.

Love,

Your loving brother,
Jawahar

---

[5] Purshottam Das Tandon.

Goodfellows
Lechlade
Glos.
25 June 1938

Darling Nan,

After a day in London I have come here with Indu to Sir Stafford Cripps' country home for the weekend. It is a well-run charming house situated in delightful surroundings. We return tomorrow night.

My first night in London I went to see (with Indu) a workers' play in a new purely workers' theatre—the Unity Theatre. We were taken there by Susan Lawrence, an oldish lady who was minister once and whose name you might have heard. I went to this play especially to see Paul Robeson. Unfortunately he did not sing but he acted very well. Indeed the whole cast of worker amateurs did remarkably well. Robeson promised to sing at one of my meetings in London.

Do you know that there is a ferry train service now between Paris and London? I came by it. Got into the train in Paris, went to sleep in a second class wagon lit and woke up in England. I was tired perhaps but there was no sensation of crossing the sea at all. It might have been different if the sea had been at all rough. This ought just to suit you.

In Paris I broadcasted but I am not quite sure if the actual broadcasting took place then or later from a disc. I was told to do so in French—an embarrassing business. I wrote out something in English, had it translated and then read it out.

I have no news of India at all. Except for your letters, no letter from India—I do not know what is happening in Cawnpore, whether the strike is on or off.

Why should Pantji be exercised over an article in the *Leader*?

I hope you will agree to my suggestion and come over to Europe for your operation and treatment. The children will be in school and in any event you will be *hors de combat* during your treatment.

I am just going to meet the village, trade union committee and have a heart to heart talk with the English worker.

Love,
Jawahar

Ormonde House
St. James' Street, London
S.W. 1
2 July 1938

Darling Nan,

This visit to London is likely to tire me out. After a week or so of it I feel exhausted and sleepy all the time and I have two and a half weeks more of it. I can find no time for letters or even the pettiest purchases. The India League has provided me with a very efficient secretary—a Somerville girl—but I can hardly find time to give her any instructions.

There is so much I could write to you. I do not know where to begin but anyway there is no time. Today Indu and I went to pay a visit to Mr and Mrs Sidney Webb. It was almost a pilgrimage for the Webbs occupy a unique place not only in England but in the world of international socialism. Even before the work Lenin translated, some of their works were translated into Russian. They are both eighty now and still most vigorous of mind. Sidney has some difficulty in talking but Beatrice is quite extraordinarily keen-minded and full of interesting and instructive conversations. She came for a long walk with us in the country and walked fast and well. She was beautiful when she was young and she is beautiful still. It was a privilege to meet this aged couple who have taught so much to generations of socialists and intellectuals. They live about fifty miles from London.

Tomorrow we are going to Canterbury to spend a day with the delightful old dean there.

I am not diverting the foreign newspapers etc which were being sent to me to Allahabad. They will continue to go there. I thought that they would be of more use to you and others there. When you have finished with them you can send them on to the AICC office.

Love,
Jawahar

London
4 and 5 July 1938

Darling Nan,

Your letter. Obviously you had to go to the cholera-stricken areas. One cannot keep away whatever the risk—but I am worried about your general health and I do think you should get rid of your troubles. All the family, except me, seems to compete in ill-health—you, Ranjit, Indu, Betty, Raja—the children have their own troubles. Only I continue to be disgustingly healthy.

Meetings, discussions, interviews etc follow each other in quick succession leaving us no time for thought or any other work. I have just had a somewhat exhilarating experience. This was a meeting at Chatham House, a famous and noted die-hard centre. Lothian presided. Perfectly politely and quietly, I laid it on thick on old Anglo-Indians and others till they grew red in the face and excessively irritated. One Indian—a person of the name of Lalkaka—spoke astoundingly. Having dealt with other questions I finally turned to Lalkaka and said that it had been an interesting experience as for long years the type represented by him had been extinct in India. Mr Lalkaka, I added, was the final argument for Indian independence. Game and set, said Agatha, and so the meeting ended. (Don't get this into the press as the rules of Chatham House forbid this!)

I am here for another two weeks—every half hour taken up, and a long list of people wanting to see me and unable to find time.

My broadcast in Paris was in French. Was it picked up in India? You say it was. Are you sure?

Love,
Jawahar

You have not sent me your photographs. Indu's photos are very good but like yours huge size and enormously expensive. Each £ 3-3-0.

Will you ask Upadhyaya to get for me six copies each of my photographs taken in Ceylon and Bombay in 1931. Three of each should be sent to me. The rest kept.

Blickling Hall
Aylsham
9 July 1938

Darling Nan,

As I was leaving London this morning I received your letter with Betty's. Betty had already sent me a similar letter. Everything connected with Jal's death has been a painful business. It seems as if a malign fate was pursuing him and his people.

From what you write to me it is clear to me that you must take yourself in hand or else you will have to face far greater trouble. I appreciate all your reasons. But you cannot possibly carry on in this fashion. You will grow increasingly inefficient even in your work and may have to stop suddenly. My strong advice to you is to have a frank talk with Pantji and your other colleagues and take leave for treatment, and then come over to Europe, say for three months. The best course would be to go to Vienna direct and then elsewhere. I am writing to Pantji also.

Indu and I are at Lothian's place for the weekend. It is really beautiful—both the house and the park and gardens. As Indu said, it is like the pictures of great houses in *Good Housekeeping.* But apart from the house, the company is interesting. There are Lord and Lady Astor, Agatha Harrison, Grace Lancaster, General and Lady Ironside, Tom Jones, and Sir Arthur Salter. Tom Jones is supposed to be a remarkable man and the power behind many prime ministers. The gallant general is at present in a high command—I think the defence of London is one of his jobs—but apart from this he has had a life full of interesting incidents. He was in Archangel when the Soviets were fighting for their life; in Persia just when Riza Khan emerged (indeed according to him it was he who gave R.K. the push); in Turkey when the Greeks were fighting the Turks. He is evidently in intimate touch with all manner of present day problems and is a most interesting person to talk to.

This London programme of mine has been a little too much for me and I developed a cold. The doctor most unnecessarily has been dosing me and has even given me ultraviolet rays (for vitality I suppose). I have got this cold in control and it will gradually fade off. I have still a heavy week in London.

Then I go to Paris. As soon as I can I want a week or ten days of absolute quiet when I can rest and do some arrears of writing etc. Probably I shall go with Indu to the south of France for this. Then to Czechoslovakia and further East. I have drawn up no programme yet. Haven't had any time to think of it.

Grace Lancaster is in a state of suppressed excitement here. She told me that she had never previously stayed at a big country home. She has been boosting you up to Lady Astor.

Love,

Your loving brother,
Jawahar

Overleaf is a note for Ranjit

Blickling Hall
9 July 1938

My dear Ranjit,
Thank you for your letter. I was delighted to learn of all the improvements at Khali.

I am glad you have appointed Harijans as Hon. Magistrates.

You will read my letter to Nan and so I shall not write more now. If I had the time of course I could write so much more.

Love,

Yours affly,
Jawahar

Paris
22 July 1938

Darling Nan,
I am so terribly behindhand with my letters that I do not know what to write. There is a world to write if I had the leisure to sit down

for a significantly long time with pen and paper. But I cannot delay writing to you simply because I cannot write at length.

Last night I left London after four weeks' stay. This was, as you know, a very full and busy stay and I think it has made a difference in people's minds. I am told that I have impressed people. The real fact of the matter is that world events and especially the possibility of India not cooperating in a war, have shaken up people. This prospect is a most disturbing one and even die-hard Tories talk now (though rather vaguely) of independence for India.

I hope to be in Paris for six days and then to go to a French seaside place for a rest and writing work—probably for ten days. I think the best address for me will continue to be c/o India League 165 Strand London WC2.

24/7

I had to go away so suddenly that this letter remained unfinished.

I have just come back from the World Peace Conference. There was an exciting incident there this afternoon. The delegates wanted very much to hear Passionaria of Spain, the platform had decided not to allow her to speak. Gradually feeling arose and there was a demonstration in the body of the hall. As this did not subside for some time the chairman and platform retired leaving the dais empty. Ellen Wilkinson tried to go up on the platform but was pushed back rudely. This irritated me and I went up and had an argument. Later the president and others came back and made the president of the Spanish Cortes (Parliament) speak and tell us that the Spanish delegation and the Spanish Govt. had decided that only one person should speak on behalf of Spain and so Passionaria could not speak. After this statement the delegates had to subside but there was great resentment. The conference soon ended after the resolutions were formally passed.

The whole incident was very revealing and showed the difficulty of various groups pulling together. Lord Cecil the permanent president of the IPC[6] apparently threatened to resign if Passionaria spoke, so

---

[6] Probably, International Peace Conference, referred to earlier in the letter as World Peace Conference.

also some others, and for fear of creating a split and thus injuring the cause of Spain, the others restrained themselves. And yet Passionaria was out and out the extraordinary personality of the conference. She represents in an outstanding way the unconquerable spirit of Spain. A maternal, domestic looking person, whose Father was a miner, with infinite vitality and earnestness, she has become the symbol of Spain. She is said to be a very powerful orator who can sweep audiences completely off their feet. I met her in Barcelona and was tremendously impressed by her. She was magnificent. But with all these qualities she happens to be a communist and hence the objection of some superior folk who threaten to resign. As a matter of fact there were not very many communists among the delegates and yet nearly everybody was keen on hearing her. After this incident I hurriedly got a bouquet of flowers and presented it to her on behalf of the Indian delegation.

The conference was very representative and hundreds of organisations were represented. There were over 1000 delegates. My speech in it was not pleasing to Cecil and some others as I brought in imperialism and British policy.

Yesterday I received your letter and Pantji's telegram. I am worried over the cholera and plague situation in the UP. What a terrible burden this must be on you. I suppose you know best what to do about your health. But do look after it.

Your two photographs have reached me. They were badly packed and are somewhat bent. Who was responsible for this? The PA?

From your letter and from brief news in the papers, it appears that there is a great deal of internal trouble within the Congress.

25/7

This letter gets more and more delayed. The temptation to write more is strong but then other things take my time. So I hasten to end this letter and send it off to you.

Your loving,
Jawahar

The enclosed snap was taken by Lady Cripps.

Paris
26 July 1938

Darling Nan,

Your letter of the 21st reached me this morning. I am glad you are coming. I hope I shall know soon so that as far as possible I might be able to adjust my programme. For the present my programme is to stay in Normandy till the 4th August—Paris 5th and 6th, Munich 7th, 8th—and then Czechoslovakia for a week.

I think also that Vienna might be ruled out in your case. Conditions there are too bad. The only places you might go to are Paris and London. If Alexander is very keen on your going to England you had better go there. I do not know what kind of arrangements you require made. You might write to Agatha Harrison and she will gladly help. I expect to be in England again by mid-September. I should like to meet you sooner if I can manage it.

I am taking a week in Normandy for some rest, though I have a great deal of writing work to do there. In London some doctor friends insisted on giving me ultraviolet rays and injections to tone me up and add to my vitality.

Dr Sun Fo (son of Sun Yat Sen and president of the Legislative Yuan in China, now a kind of ambassador extraordinary in Europe) is returning to China by air within a few days, probably by the KLM. His plane will stop at Karachi, Allahabad and Calcutta. I should like him to be welcomed on our behalf at all these places. I am writing to Subash and Kripalani.

Let me know as soon as you can when you are due to sail and reach here. Better send a cable.

Your loving,

Jawahar

A cable will be sent to Kripalani informing him of Dr Sun Fo's departure.

Hanoi

22 August 1939

Darling Nan,

I have just arrived here at 11 a.m. and I find that I have to leave for China in another plane at 3 p.m. today. Two seats have been booked for me by the Chinese authorities. I wish someone had been there to take advantage of this. Even apart from the extra seat, I rather miss a companion. I suppose I am getting old.

I have sent a diary of my journey to the *Herald* from Saigon today. But the air mail is a weekly service and so it will take time to reach, as will this letter.

I had a great reception from Indians at Bangkok and Saigon. Everywhere they insist on my breaking journey and I talk about a future possible visit. Here at Hanoi also there are a good number of Indians—merchants from South India chiefly. A Sindhi, with a huge shop of the usual Sindhi kind, called the Palais des Srienées,[7] has brought me to his house. I have invited the Indians in the town to meet me before I go. They had practically no notice of my arrival.

After sticking to my sherwani right through Calcutta, in spite of the sweltering heat, I discarded it the next day. And then we flew so high that I felt cold! These quick changes of temperature are somewhat disconcerting.

I am taking this opportunity of writing to you as I am not sure of the postal service from China. I shall of course write but the letters might be delayed. Tonight I shall sleep in China and tomorrow by eleven in the forenoon I ought to be in Chungking.

I had an alarming experience in Calcutta yesterday morning. I had to get up at 3 a.m. and get ready quickly. In spite of every effort I was delayed by two or three minutes. I sent off all my luggage. When I put on my pyjamas the इजरबन्द[8] slipped on one side and I could not tie it. I had no time to pull it out properly and so I tucked it in as best I could and marched out. The wretched thing would not remain up and I had to hold on to it all the time. At that frightfully early hour, the

---

[7] Name not legible in original letter.
[8] Izarbandh (pyjama cord).

Chinese Consul turned up at my hotel, and the Sass Brunners, who were as usual most affectionate. At the aerodrome at 4 a.m. there was a crowd of Congressmen and others. Imagine my plight—holding on to my pyjamas, accepting bouquets, shaking hands, doing नमस्कार[9] etc. etc. It was a terrible ordeal for an hour!

Love,
Jawahar

---

[9] Namaskar (greetings).

MULK RAJ ANAND

Lions and Shadows in the Sherry Party in Harold Monro's Poetry Bookshop

'There is a sherry party in Harold Monro's poetry bookshop this evening at six,' Nikhil Sen told me one Friday afternoon, in the British Museum Reading Room. 'Meet me in Jacob Schwartz's bookshop and we will go there. I have been asked. You can gatecrash.'

I waited on the pavement till six by Jacob Schwartz's bookshop, because it was closed. I was nervous about being late to the party and yet timid in my callow Indian student's soul to barge in and meet the great people on my own. I hoped that Nikhil and Jacob had not already gone into Harold Monro's bookshop, but might be having a drink in the Museum Tavern to get boozed enough to shoot their mouths off on equal terms, without betraying the fact that one of them was a would-be poet and the other a collector of first editions to sell to American fans.

I soon saw them coming towards me from the Museum Tavern, with Gwenda Zeidmann between them, all smiles from the liquor.

'Hello! Hello! Hello!' Gwenda greeted me, fawning on me as Elizabeth Barrett Browning might have done on her pet dog Flush.

'Why so glum?' she asked me as she came and kissed me on both cheeks.

'Plucking up courage to go into the lion's den,' I said.

This extract is taken from *Conversations in Bloomsbury*, published by Oxford University Press India, New Delhi, 1981.

'That's the spirit!' said Jacob. 'Keep up your sense of humour . . . That's the way the English keep their ends up.'

I smiled but was all nerves. I had begun to look like the 'melancholy gentleman', I had christened the Englishman.

'He is writing a novel *à-la-Joyce* and feels tentative about it—and yet thinks it will be a masterpiece,' Nikhil said in a vein of half mockery.

'Let him be,' said Gwenda protectively carrying me along. 'It is his first novel . . . Anyhow, you will never sit down an hour a day to write one.' And she turned to me.

'Only don't you go the whole hog with Joyce . . . He releases one. But ends up in the language of night . . . There's Harold looking for us . . .'

Indeed, the host was looking anxiously towards the street corner from his doorway.

'Waiting for Eliot,' he said, plastering his brown hair nervously as an abject smile covered his sensitive lean face with dark eyes . . . 'Gwenda dear—do help my wife to serve drinks . . . And oh Jacob— I shouldn't ask them to that table you have laid out with the books— let them sign their first editions only if they feel like it . . .'

'Mr Anand,' Nikhil presented me.

'Oh you were here a month or so ago?'

'Yes,' I said, shaking hands with Harold Monro, smiling to shake off my morbid shyness.

Suddenly, I felt that there was an uncanny gap between me and people, as though I was inferior and others were superior. I realized that all of them being older than me, and part of a metropolitan world, had been privileged to take part in a living culture, whereas, apart from two Shakespeare plays and Thackeray's *Henry Esmond*, I had read only the books of poetry which Professor Harvey used to lend me in Khalsa College, Amritsar. I came from a world where everyone was hampered, where desires were frustrated, and happiness thwarted by the elders, who were all-important. And inside me was the longing to be free, to expand my consciousness, to live and to be on equal terms with the men of learning like those Professor Bonamy Dobrée was familiar with.

As we entered, Bonamy Dobrée, who was just putting his coat on a rack, turned to us, and shook hands with each one of us.

Then he saw Eliot and went to greet the poet who entered, a handsome figure, with the pale cast of thought on his face, relieved by a demure smile.

'There's Aldous Huxley—and D.H. Lawrence,' Nikhil said, 'both standing in a farther corner in conclave with a lady.'

'Who is she?' I asked Nikhil.

'Edith Sitwell of Gold Coast Custom's fame.'

Indeed, she had an African necklace of heavy beads and amulets on her neck. Her face, with the aquiline nose, was tanned.

Professor Dobrée beckoned Nikhil and me towards T.S. Eliot.

'Tom—this is Nikhil Sen, an admirer of yours, and Mulk Anand, a fresh arrival . . . Student of Philosophy.'

I bowed shyly and muttered: 'Good evening, Sir.' And, sweating, confused, small against his tall presence, I stood there, head bent, emptied of all thought, as though the deeply conditioned respect for the elders had emerged in me.

Mr Eliot gave his limp hand first to Nikhil then to me.

'He knew the poet Iqbal,' Nikhil said. 'The poet of new Islam . . . He has sent him here.'

My face was flushed.

'Iqbal was in Cambridge,' said Bonamy Dobrée. 'A student of McTaggart.'

I felt that, beyond Iqbal, I wanted to understand the thoughts which he had imbibed in Europe. I hoped T.S. Eliot would reveal his innermost mind. I wanted immediately to ask him about the myths from India he had referred to in his poem, *The Waste Land*.

But from the reserved, tight-lipped, urbane presence came only an implied condemnation of Iqbal in a brief sentence:

'Not the same depth in Islam as in Hindu and Buddhist thought . . .'

'Perhaps the Arabs did have a sense of brotherhood,' Professor Dobrée put in. 'A kind of democracy . . . And they conquered all North Africa. Even Spain. I have gone through the Koran. Mohammad had God like fire in his head.' And he looked away as though guilty for not mentioning Jesus.

'They took much from the Jews—and Mohamet owed a good deal to the Christian revelation,' Mr Eliot said in a solemn voice.

'Mr Eliot is a Boston Brahmin,' said Nikhil impertinently and then turned to fetch sherry from the tray Gwenda had brought near them.

'They had poets like Attar, Rumi, Nizami, Saadi, Hafiz,' I said, from an uprush of stirrings of the mystic Persian poets in me. I impetuously recited a verse from Rumi in Persian and then rendered it into English: 'Everyone separated from his origin, wants to return to it.'

'Vague mysticisms!' Eliot said, and took a glass of sherry from Gwenda.

'When is mysticism not vague?' asked Professor Dobrée in a falsetto. And he took a cigarette from the tray in Gwenda's hand and lit it.

'Iqbal is quite clear, Sir, in his reply to Goethe's *West Ostlicher Diwan*,' I asserted, in a voice which went out of my control from the need to defend my mentor. 'He indicates the approach towards the whole Self and not the parts. He has not built a system. He thinks the concern of poetry is to make the human person . . . He wants poetry to set us free . . .'

'Tut! Tut!' Professor Dobrée exclaimed, 'Cliches! I suppose–he talks in terms of "pearls of wisdom" . . .'

'Perhaps he means digging down,' Eliot helped me.

I was sweating with confusion. I beckoned the courage to look up.

'The sage of Lahore is rather like you, Sir,' I said, the Oriental courtier in me coming from the constant reference to religion. 'Metaphysics and Islam seem to converge in his poems.'

'Isn't Lahore where Kipling lived and worked?' the poet asked.

'And where he wrote *Kim*,' Professor Dobrée added. 'What wonderful elastic prose!'

'Including the distortion of the Bengali Babu!' asserted Nikhil and sipped his sherry.

'You are a wog!' mocked Professor Dobrée.

Gwenda came smilingly towards me, as I had no sherry. I took a glass, warming to her for the attention.

Then I felt I must communicate to these intellectuals that I had learnt to love the life of imagination from Iqbal, and that, against such a poet, Kipling's writings seemed fantastically low-minded.

'If I may say so, Professor Dobrée,' I burst out, in spite of my efforts to control myself, 'I have read *Kim* twice. It is a fairy tale glorifying a young boy. Going about with that exotic Hooi Sipi Lama,

who keeps revolving the wheel of life. A little hero of the Empire—
a fantasy boy . . .'

'And superior to all the Indians put together!' said Nikhil, cynically
waving his head. Then he lifted his sherry glass and said: 'Here's to
the bard of the British Empire!'

As the 'wog' drank the toast, the faces of both Eliot and Dobrée
became slightly pale at his drunken words.

They did not lift their glasses, shifted their postures slightly and
looked around boredly.

Without lifting my eyes, I was looking for a way out of my false
start, for another beginning, but could not get out of the vicious circle
of my nationalist obsessions.

'There's a lilt in the Barrack Room ballads,' T.S. Eliot suggested
airily and sipped his sherry. 'One must not ignore his skill as a poet
. . . I believe the Oriental poets still use the old metaphors of the
nightingale and the rose.'

There I agreed with him. Even Iqbal used traditional imagery.

'Those delightful Jungle books!' added Dobrée. 'It makes the animals
live as in some Arabian fables.'

'"Lesser breeds beyond the law!"' Nikhil muttered, and gulped his
sherry.

'Come, come, the British did give you roads—and justice!' said
Professor Dobrée to Nikhil, rapping his shoulder.

'And exploited us for more than a century,' Nikhil protested.

Mr Eliot was taciturn.

I felt waves of warmth rise in my body and become sweat.

'So says Gandhi, the sage of non-violence,' I put in from the rush
of my stored up bad temper.

'Not very non-violent . . . What with all his burstings out!' said
Professor Dobrée.

Eliot's face was uplifted to the ceiling. He blushed and said: 'Gandhi
seems to be an anarchist . . . Sometimes, I feel the Indians should pursue
their culture and leave government to the British empiricists . . .'

Luckily Mrs Harold Monro, in an elegant black dress, came up
bearing another tray of sherry glasses, followed by her husband.

'Perhaps Harold will arrange for a recital by Mr Anand of some of
Mohamet Iqbal's poems,' Eliot conceded.

'Of course,' agreed Mr Harold Monro, leading both Eliot and Dobrée away towards Edith Sitwell, who was coming towards them anyhow.

'How do you do,' she greeted both Nikhil and me, as she passed.

My pride had made me rigid. I wanted to correct Mr Eliot for mispronouncing Mohammad. The thwartings which had made me a rebel at home throbbed behind my head. I moved towards the sherry tray, surprised that two of the most self-conscious writers should be so removed from the actualities of India. Maybe they were for noble thoughts and could forgive Kipling everything for his lilts. I wondered if either of them had read E.M. Forster's *A Passage to India*, which I had devoured after Professor Foxwell of University College told me about it. I was sorry I had got flustered. The mention of that might have been my trump card. They would find the Burtons and Tutons odious, because they themselves were not Imperialists.

'Let us meet Mr Huxley there,' Nikhil said, after snatching two glasses of sherry from Mrs Monro's tray, gulping them, and taking up a third one. 'Eliot is arrogant! Mother Love or Mother Hate! Mostly incommunicado. Fighting a sex war with his wife . . . !' And, turning to D.H. Lawrence, he asked: 'Mr Lawrence, woman has become a urinal to most people.'

'This is Mr Nikhil Sen, would-be Hindu husband, speaking!' Gwenda said.

'They are practical people and arrange marriages, with dowry and the rest,' said Huxley.

'My pet—Mr Anand!' Gwenda said. 'He is a student of philosophy, but is writing a forward novel some of which Nikhil showed me.'

'I am not sure which philosophy you are studying,' said Lawrence and coughed a wheezy cough. 'But I hope you can trust your eyes, nose, mouth, skin and the human sense against the ethereal Tagory.'

'David, there are post-Tagoreans in India,' said Aldous Huxley. 'And men like Gandhi have common sense plus the *Gita*. At one time, I myself thought all Indians were like Edward Lear's: "Old Man of Thermopoly, who never could do anything properly . . ." '

'And now?' queried Nikhil.

'I am changing my mind. I think Krishna is right when he says: "Live in action" to Arjuna.'

'Actually, the statement is cryptic,' I put in.

'Those are phrases, Aldous,' Lawrence began. 'What I admire in the Hindus is their sense of mystery.' And he twisted his face as though he wished to escape from the room and us all.

I turned around to see if I was the only tense person in the party. No. They all seemed to be summits of mountain peaks, above and away from each other, faces getting more and more flushed and averted from each other, held back in tenuous control of their opposing wills. Literature had not softened them.

I felt I had come here looking for something I could not define, to end my remoteness, to become part of the intimate circle of creative men. Instead, I had entered a world of conflicting personalities, involved in various ways of transcending dailiness. I was distressed that there were lurking prejudices in all of them about the East.

'I understand Indians have written very few novels,' said Lawrence, confirming my prognostications. 'Only fables with moral lessons.'

'They were moralists and wanted a sense of harmony,' Huxley explained. 'They felt the world is unreal. Life is completely unauthentic. They feel that we can understand more than we can know—by Yoga.'

'If they cut out the Maya business!' said Lawrence. 'They seem really to be pantheists of sorts. I have seen some prints of their wall paintings. They seem alive. The crowds are on the move—vivid, intense. More than in Gauguin's Tahiti pictures.'

Lawrence's face lit up as he said this.

'Mr Laurence Binyon, there, knows about Ajanta,' said Nikhil. 'He thinks those paintings are superior to anything of that time in the world.'

Mr Binyon was talking in whispers to Harold Monro, his head shyly bent down.

'I hear the women do not cover their breasts in some parts of India,' Lawrence said, 'where they have matriarchy.'

'In Malabar,' said Nikhil.

'Same in Sigriya paintings and in Ceylon villages,' said a sandy-haired, swarthy gentleman of middle height, who had just shaken hands with Aldous Huxley.

'Leonard Woolf,' Nikhil breathed to me.

I knew that Mr Woolf had been in Ceylon, but had retired prematurely from the Civil Service, was married to Virginia Woolf and ran the Hogarth Press.

'The Sigriya wave came from Ajanta,' said Nikhil.

'Wherever the wave came from, it is a very alive art,' said Mr Woolf

He took off his glasses to clean them and to get a better view of us all. And then he continued: 'In the Kandyan hills we can still see lovely, big-breasted women—the opposites of the flat-chested Miss Quested of Morgan Forster's novel.'

The heat of the room mixed with echoes from my inebriated heart. I recalled the mango breasts of my aunt Devaki, as she bathed on the bathroom sill. My eyes nearly half-closed as the ripe hard breasts of my dead beloved Yasmin pressed on to me.

'Is Forster still alive?' Lawrence asked.

'And kicking?' said Leonard Woolf.

'Kicking against the pricks,' Nikhil repeated a cliché.

'Actually,' corrected Huxley, 'he is a timid person . . . He had very little to say, but has said it very well.'

'Aldous, we must go,' suggested Lawrence. 'I promised to go to supper with Catharine Carswell.'

'Mr Huxley,' I said, 'come back to India—this time with—love.'

Aldous Huxley looked away, paled, smiled and said: 'Perhaps I will. I worried too much about trivialities during my first visit. And I wrote from my petit-bourgeois cares and preoccupations.' I felt he was more open-minded than Eliot or even Dobrée, as he took Lawrence's arm and led him towards the poet.

'There is Mr Murry,' Huxley said. 'Perhaps come specially to meet you, David Herbert.'

Lawrence seemed reluctant to go that way. The coldness of Eliot, standing erect and towering over the mousy coloured Murry and the dapper Dobrée seemed to hold him back.

'Come to us,' I said to Lawrence.

'Well you know, I feel much more at home with the Ceylonese. They are not so spiritual.' His head was bent with some recollections of Lanka.

'You are not above a mystique of your own,' put in Huxley, lifting his thick glasses to confront Lawrence.

Lawrence's beard nearly touched his chest, as he sighed and dreamily uttered in despair:

'The Hindus put themselves in the prison of God a long time ago . . . I daresay we have our prisons—Jesus and the Resurrection myth . . . We must drift and find . . . The sealed treasures . . . In men and women . . . Not by return to the old vomit . . . But—by the return to ourselves.'

Nikhil dared to say: 'We have had quite a few liberations. "Neti! Neti!" we said long ago—"Not this! Not this!" But we don't hide our ignorance. Come and see. We are still sifting the grain from the chaff . . .?'

'In the science laboratories!' Aldous Huxley added with a smile.

Lawrence smiled at Nikhil, then looked up tiredly at Huxley, with wrinkled brows, took his arm gently and began to tread the grey carpet as though to escape from this prison.

'Mr Sen,' said Huxley to appease Nikhil who had been snubbed, 'Lawrence generally takes himself wherever he goes.'

'Don't we all,' said Edith Sitwell coming towards Lawrence. 'But we do warm to other people—at least some of us! I like the Italians.'

'Very human—but crooked!' muttered D.H. Lawrence blushing. 'Edith, you were up on the hill. I grew up below and know human nature in the raw.'

'Don't talk class, David,' intervened Aldous Huxley.

'We are proud of you,' said Edith Sitwell with genuine warmth. 'Oh, Osbert wants you to come up for a week-end. And Sacheveral wrote from France, saying he looked for you in your hotel. We will be meeting at Lady Ottoline Morel's for lunch . . .' Her cordiality broke down D.H. Lawrence's resistance. He smiled and bowed to her.

'You know, I like your imagist poems the best,' Edith Sitwell said.

'I am issuing some more soon,' said Lawrence.

Harold Monro came up and negotiated D.H. Lawrence towards Mr Murry, who was still deep in conversation with Eliot and Dobrée.

Nikhil and I followed Lawrence and Huxley from sheer curiosity to discover how the prejudices of the literary coteries could be got over through hypocritical handshakes. Suddenly, Nikhil turned, put his arm around me, and dragged me towards the sherry table.

'Tied up in knots—all of them!' he said, his face pale, his eyes shining, his lips dry. And he gulped another whole glassful of sherry.

I took a sherry glass and went towards the author of *Keats and Shakespeare*, wondering how a man who looked like a publisher's commercial traveller could have written such a classic.

Murry had stepped aside and narrowed the distance between Lawrence and Eliot.

The two lions feigned humility, bowed and shook hands. Aldous Huxley came forward and offered a cordial handshake to Eliot, Murry and Dobrée.

'As I was saying,' Murry continued to Eliot, ostensibly to cover the distances, 'Paul Valery has made Monsieur Teste silent with his own despair.'

'Maybe a kind of suicide!' said Lawrence.

'One cannot just die,' said Huxley. 'There is always the church, and there is Bergson's Metanoia. And Shaw's life-force.'

'Indeed one has to face life,' said Dobrée.

'There are still some anchors available,' said Eliot.

'No safe harbours,' said Lawrence.

There was silence at his solution to the being-in-the-world situation.

I felt that each of these Europeans was clinging to his 'I'. In India we said 'We' and spoke to others as 'Thou'. They exploded in impatient voices. Our contradictions were expressed somewhat more softly. They tended to be self-sufficient, away from each other. We were still joined together in the family, the community, and even in the broken brotherhoods. But if they were not humble, they did not conceal their uncertainties, as we did, behind the mantras. They had some intellectual integrity. Perhaps they were new people. We had searched and asked questions and pronounced philosophical judgements long ago. The real existence was in an ineffable state, defined in ambiguous ways: 'It is understood by those who understand it not!'

'How's your health?' Eliot asked Lawrence, in a last effort at bonhomie.

'As well as it can be in this sick world,' Lawrence answered shyly, dipping his red beard in his chest again. 'No sun here. I go south with Huxley as soon as I can . . .' And he shook hands, smiled without looking at the adversary and proceeded towards the door.

After Lawrence, Huxley (who bowed all round) and Murry (who smiled a sheepish smile) had left, Bonamy Dobrée went towards his raincoat on the hat stand.

Harold Monro followed and brought Eliot's coat and helped him.

I caught Professor Dobrée in an unguarded moment, when he was picking up his felt hat and, beckoning my foolhardy courage, I said:

'May I give you my short novel to read?'

'Certainly,' he said. 'But it will be a week before I can touch it . . . And oh, Mulk, go and see Mr Eliot one day with Iqbal's poems. Telephone his secretary and ask for an appointment . . . And you and Nikhil and I must get together in the Etoile on Wednesday for lunch.'

Eliot bowed to both Nikhil and I, without relaxing the reserve of the formal Englishman by adoption. And while I had felt relieved at Bonamy Dobrée's peacemaking, I recalled the phrase of the poet 'How unpleasant to meet Mr Eliot!' which I had seen somewhere. Perhaps I had taken his siding with Kipling as an insult.

I went and helped myself to sherry.

'Gwenda and I and you and Nikhil and Jacob will help my wife wash up glasses,' said Harold Monro after seeing the guests off to the door. 'Then we will go and have a Chinese dinner.'

This American's cordiality was heart-warming. And we all went towards the little kitchen to help Mrs Monro, except Nikhil.

Laurence Binyon, who had hardly spoken to anybody, but was looking at the new poetry books, now made towards the door. Nikhil went up to him and said: 'Sir, may we come and see you at the BM?'

'By all means,' said Mr Binyon with utmost politeness.

I was too overwhelmed by the presence of these legendary literary men. I felt that they did not know very much about my country, and what they knew was through Kipling, or through superficial impressions, except for Leonard Woolf, who had lived and worked in Ceylon and even resigned from the Civil Service, because he did not want to be a part of Imperialist rule. And Aldous Huxley felt differently from others, and even different from himself of the days of *Jesting Pilate*, because he had doubts about our benign white sahibs. All the others seemed to believe, more or less, in the 'Empire on which the sun never sets'. I, who had been to jail in the Gandhi movement, was fuming inside. I had left home because my pro-white-sahib father had beaten my mother for my going to jail. And I had learnt to be a rebel.

While I helped to clean the glasses, I realized that I had taken umbrage about wrong words said about India, and for being considered 'lesser breeds beyond the law'. The humiliation for being inferior seemed like a wound in my soul, which would never heal. The more I licked it the more it became tender. And I decided in my mind that I would fight for the freedom of my country forever, though I may admire these English writers for their literary skills. The thing that disturbed me was that I might get a scholarship from the Silver Wedding Fund of King George and Queen Mary, which my Professor in University College had recommended me for. And then I would be a hypocrite, hating British rule in India and living on its dole.

QURRATULAIN HYDER

Red Indians in England

Nirmala was on her way to Fitzwilliam Library when she caught sight of Gautam.

'Nirmala! I have been looking for you everywhere . . . how are you?' he exclaimed, rushing down the road towards her. 'I met a most formidable female professor in your college who was thoroughly unhelpful in tracking you down. How are you, Nirmal?'

She closed her eyes for an instant. This *was* Gautam who stood before her, talking to her excitedly.

'How do you happen to be here?' she asked.

'I've come from London to see you.'

'I believe you are in regular foreign service now.'

'That's right.'

'Enjoying life?'

'Hmm . . .'

The conversation came to an abrupt end. Gautam noted that Nirmala was no longer a chatterbox—she had become serious, sober, quiet. 'Come along, Kamal told me he would meet us at the Koh-i-Noor,' he said.

Students in flapping black gowns were passing by. She gestured towards them, saying 'That's Denis . . . That one is Cyril, the good-looking blond fellow, he's the son of a lord and Champa Baji's new boyfriend. She often comes here from London to meet him. They're

This extract is taken from *River of Fire*, published by Kali for Women, New Delhi, 1998.

referred to as Nabob Cyril and his Bibi after the famous painting of his ancestor and his Indian common-law wife.'

Gautam looked shocked. After a pause he asked, 'So has she found love and happiness at last?'

Nirmala gave a short laugh. 'I remember there was an English or American movie called *It's Love I'm After*—we went to see it at the Plaza in Hazrat Ganj. Boys at the University used to give new year titles to the girls, and that year Champa Baji was given the title: *"It's Love I'm After"*! Once she even became a sort of jogan. She let her hair fall over her shoulders and wore an ochre sari—that phase lasted a couple of months.'

Gautam remained silent.

'I have a feeling,' Nirmala was saying, 'that Champa Baji will eventually become like Mrs Shunila Mukerji. Do you know Mrs Mukerji?'

'Yes, I do.'

'Time cheats us outright and goes on cheating us,' said Nirmala. 'Shunila Debi must have been an unusually attractive woman twenty years ago. Men used to consider it a privilege if she spoke a few words to them; now she's a lonely old lady who rounds up young men and takes them home for fish curry. Time betrayed her.'

A drop of rain fell on her eyes. She wiped her face with her handkerchief and continued: 'For Champa Baji, this is the era of the Hon'ble Cyril Ashley, son of Lord Barnfield. Just as you were the son of Sir Deep Narain, and Amir of Sir Zaki Reza.'

'Nirmal, you're being very unfair to Champa,' Gautam said quietly.

'No, Gautam, this is a fact. Champa Baji has been disappointed and she has disappointed us, too. The other day Kamal was saying, how is it that Champa has slowly lost her magic? And Talat said rightly, Champa Baji is the same, we have grown up.'

Gautam looked at her ruefully. Nirmal continued, 'She was in Paris and left whatever she was doing to come here. Now she's trying to get into Girton. She can't seem to decide any thing about herself. I think she's one of those people who need some kind of emotional support.'

The sound of a trumpet rose from Jesus Lane. Gautam stopped walking.

'I don't know who it is,' said Nirmala, 'he often plays very sad tunes.' A shower of rain had made her hair wet. 'Amir is also in London, has come here as a Pakistani diplomat. Nowadays he's busy showing his water colours to Roshan Ara.'

They had reached Koh-i-noor. 'Gautam,' Nirmal asked thoughtfully, 'Why are people so second-rate?' He kept quiet. A group of undergrads passed by.

'Nirmal,' Gautam stopped again.

'Yes?'

'Will you marry me?'

'No.'

'Why? Nirmal—' The words choked in his throat.

'Because,' she said in a very clear and deep voice, 'You are second rate, too. Come, let's go inside.'

Nirmal had really grown up. They entered the restaurant.

Roshan Ara Kazmi met Commander Amir Reza on a bright and sunny Id day on the lawns of Woking Mosque. The place was swarming with the small Muslim community that lived in and around London, mostly from India and Pakistan. A few English girls who had married Muslim students were dressed self-consciously in bright saris or shalwar-kameez. There was that special happiness in the air which Muslims experience in abundance on no other festival as they do on Id-ul-Fitr. Roshan had come from Cambridge with her friends and was introduced to Amir Reza by a common acquaintance. Amir was elegantly dressed in a grey suit and black lambskin qaraquli called a Jinnah cap. Jawaharlal Nehru, who was a product of UP's Indo-Muslim feudal culture, had made the black sherwani and white churidar pajama (basically the formal upper-class Muslim dress) the Indian diplomats' attire. The Pakistanis had to be different—therefore they continued to wear western dress.

Roshan had acquired a string of Commonwealth scholarships and was tipped to become a formidable professor in the future. However, she was instantly captivated by Amir Reza, and then her intellect was of no help. While she was talking to him Talat came along, her Lukhnawi gharara rustling on the English grass.

'Adab, Bhaiya Saheb, Id mubarak,' she said zestfully. Kamal followed her. Both of them had met Roshan in Cambridge. There was an exchange of pleasantries and small talk.

'Oh, Sir Feroze Khan Noon and Lady Afternoon are here! Must go and say Id mubarak to them. Excuse me,' Amir Reza walked away hurriedly.

'And pray who is Lady Afternoon?' asked Aley Hasan of the BBC Hindi Section, who had joined them.

'Sir Feroze's second wife, Austrian lady,' Talat informed him. 'Sir Feroze Khan Noon said in a speech the other day in London, that we Muslims produced such great men as Chengiz Khan and Halaku Khan. The poor fellow doesn't know that they were not Muslim!'

Kamal and Aley Hasan laughed.

Roshan didn't like the leader of her country and his wife being ridiculed by Indians. She kept quiet. But she was puzzled by the abrupt departure of the fabulous Commander.

'Why did he leave in such a hurry?' she asked Talat.

Talat grinned. 'See, we are Bharatis, and he belongs to Pakistan's armed forces, therefore he avoids us if he can.'

'Why should he do that? You wouldn't try to steal defence secrets from him, would you?'

'Roshan—do you have a divided family? I mean, close relatives who are divided between India and Pakistan?'

'No, I am a native of Lahore.'

'So you won't understand this dilemma, and anyway we belong to Nehru's India. We give a sort of complex to people like Cousin Amir,' Talat added loftily.

'Oof, this is the kind of holier-than-thou attitude of you Indians that we resent,' Roshan Kazmi said, frowning. She ambled away, crossed the lawn and joined the little group which had surrounded Sir Feroze and Lady Noon. Amir led her gallantly towards the tea stalls.

Talat laughed. 'Kamman, do you see what I see?'

'Yeah.'

'I think she will do. He is getting on and he needs a doting wife. She was absolutely goggle-eyed.'

'Don't start match-making, for God's sake.'

'Nothing could be more auspicious than today for this,' Talat replied cheerily.

Champa was sharing a broken-down flat with Comrades June Carter and Neil Brigg, both of whom had been introduced to her by Cyril.

June was teaching some obscure Slavonic language at the University, Neil was an engineer. Both were members of the Communist Party of Great Britain. On weekends the comrades got together at Feroze's or Surekha's place and talked till the early hours of the morning. Champa didn't meet Gautam anywhere—she heard that he had become an important person and was always extremely busy. Kamal was at Cambridge, Hari Shankar was posted to New York.

On the first day of her job as reader in a small publishing house, she woke up at six in the morning and quickly got ready. The ever-helpful Mrs Shunila Mukerji had found her this job.

After gulping down a cup of tea she dashed out and boarded a bus for Maida Vale. She had met Bill Craig several times but had never seen Shanta. Mrs Nilambar, too, had surfaced in London—she had left her husband, come to Britain to get her novel published and was living with Bill because divorce was not yet allowed by Hindu law.

A massive sandalwood Ganapati sat on the mantelpiece in William Craig's drawing-room in his house on Warwick Avenue. Bill was sprawled on the sofa, absorbed in *The Times,* a stocky, balding man in early middle-age. 'Do you know how to proof-read? It's quite easy.' He placed a bundle of yellow papers in front of her, got up and sauntered towards the kitchen. Clad in a brown-and-yellow sari of rich south Indian silk, Shanta came downstairs. Tall, sturdy and handsome, a blue-eyed Chitpawan, she crossed over to a corner table and began typing briskly.

'Bonjour, Madame!' Champa tried to impress her.

'Hello. I have heard a lot about you from Gautam. How do you do,' she said casually, still typing away at great speed. She certainly had very superior airs. Successful Indo-Anglian novelist and business partner of a noted British publisher. She didn't bother to speak to Champa again.

Bill brought her a cup of coffee. He was good-natured, and also had a glad eye. Shanta didn't accompany them to the office. She was leaving for Paris in the afternoon.

'What is your programme in life?' Bill asked his new employee during lunch break. He used to proof-read people, too.

'Haven't a clue.'

'Are you very confused?'

'Yes.'

'Are you also caught in the Net?'

'Yes.'

Bill reverted to gloomy silence. They were all caught in the Net. Himself, and Cyril Ashley and all other Western European intellectuals. The representatives of New Asia living in the West were suspended in mid-air, between diverse hells. Their Christian and Jewish and Muslim and Hindu and Buddhist souls were suffering all kinds of agonies. Arnold Toynbee had written ten fat books about them and still hadn't come to a satisfactory conclusion. Bill was a trader in words. He believed in their might and muddle, and their hollowness.

Shanta was also entangled in the Net. Their private hells, individual catacombs and separate universes were all the more painful as there was no way out, except for those who had become Marxists and thought they had found the Final Answer.

'We have recently lost our Indian Empire and there's going to be a great demand for nostalgic novels about the Raj. You write, I'll build you up as the modern Flora Annie Steele.'

'Who was Flora Annie Steele?'

'Never mind. You begin a novel about Lucknow, right away.'

They began to eat. He said, 'Mulk Raj Anand is old hat, we need young people like you. You write a novel about Old Lucknow—you must know somebody from the ex-royal family of Oudh?'

'I myself belong to the ex-royal family of Oudh,' she answered recklessly.

'Jolly good!' he exclaimed. 'My father is an Old India Hand, he was an indigo planter in eastern UP. Germany developed the chemical blue dye and Britain's indigo trade came to an end. Father sold his estate in Ghazipur district to a Muslim zamindar and returned to England. I was schooling in Mussoorie. We came back to our damp and cold house in Cobham, Surrey. Father still lives there. He would love to help you in your writing with his reminiscences. For instance, he can tell you about Sir Harcourt Butler and his favourite singer, Zohra Bai of Lucknow. Sir Harcourt was Lieutenant-Governor of the United Provinces in the 1920s, and was called the last of the Nabobs.

'I can take you to Cobham to meet Dad off and on. Shanta will be away in France for nearly a month. Let's meet at the Writers' and

Artists' Club in Haymarket tomorrow evening, and we'll discuss this project in some detail.'

'Princess Champa of India!' Bill Craig gravely introduced her to his friends in the Club.

'No titles please, we're a democracy,' she said modestly. She had realised with acute anxiety that Bill knew the Lucknow Gang—her fantasising had gone too far. In Paris she had told the Frogs that she was a niece of the Nizam of Hyderabad—then she ran into some Hyderabadis and immediately stopped being a royal niece.

In the Club an English journalist looked at her in absolute fascination. 'You know something, Princess,' he gushed, 'the beautiful Maharani of a Punjab state,who died here recently, was called the Rose of India. I think you are lovelier than her. What should we call you?'

'I'll ask Dad the botanical name of this flower. Let's go to Cobham, Saturday week,' said Bill with a glint in his eye.

'Sorry, couldn't make it earlier, had to rush off to Russia. Here is a little souvenir for you from Moscow,' he said, placing a parcel on the table.

She opened it eagerly and took out a gypsy shawl. 'Oh, Gautam, how *sweet*!' she cried as though she was still in Water Chestnut House.

Tenderly he wrapped the stole round her shoulders. She blushed. 'Some day I'll take you to Outer Mongolia. You very much want to go there, don't you?' he said.

Nirmala nodded vigorously. 'And Alma Ata.'

'And Alma Ata. And Samarkand-o-Bukhara. The works. Do you remember Thomas Moore's *Lala Rukh*?' He ordered lunch. The owner of Koh-i-Noor was a fellow Kayastha, a Mathur from Old Delhi.

'Lala Rukh,' he resumed, 'was Aurangzeb's daughter. She set forth in a caravan for Kashmir where she was to wed the King of Bokhara, and her barge sailed on the Indus. Say, *hoon, hoon,* that's the tradition, when you listen to a story you keep saying *hoon*.'

'Yes. But Talat's mother once told us that if you heard a story in the day time, travellers lost their way,' she answered, luxuriating in the warmth of the colourful shawl.

A fair and lanky girl came in. She had a long nose and wore ballerina glasses. Smoking a black cigarette, she smiled myopically at Nirmala and sat down at a corner table.

Although the unusual-looking undergraduate was beyond earshot, Nirmala whispered to Gautam: 'Light from Pureland . . .'

'Light—let me think: Roshni?'

'Roshan,' Nirmala responded in a more confidential undertone: 'Subject: Philosophy. Current interest: A.R. of the Holy Navy.'

Gautam burst out laughing, feeling immensely relieved. No, old buddy Nim hadn't changed—there was still hope for him.

'Have you ever met him in London?' she asked.

'At diplomatic receptions, yes. He was correctly cordial with me. So was I.'

'Although I have noticed that Pakis are more friendly with H's.'

'You mean they don't drop their aitches-ha-ha-'

'Yeah. But they avoid fellow M's from India. And vice versa. Anyway. So A.R. has also become very F.O.N.D. of R.O.S.H.A.N. And she is positively ga-ga—'

'Honey,' he cut her short, laughing. 'You would be a complete flop if you joined MI5.'

'And Bhaiya Saheb has started painting once again. Even made her portrait. Although, let's face it, she's no oil painting.' She winked at Gautam and giggled, the way she used to all those years ago in Lucknow. It seemed that in an instant they had crossed the razor-thin bridge of time.

Nirmala continued. 'When B.S. showed Talat that portrait she said its caption ought to be, Think and Be Sad.'

She fell silent. Gautam was left standing alone on that invisible and fragile bridge. Frightened by his loneliness he said with great urgency, 'Nirmal, can you still change your mind about me?'

In a flash she recollected the smoke-filled kitchen of Water Chestnut House when Talat had predicted—some day he will land up in England and take you round the sacred fire. Good old Talat.

Last time she had said no in a huff. She wouldn't now, but she kept quiet all the same.

'You know they say khamoshi means neem-raza, half-consent. Shall I take it as that?'

Students were drifting in and out of the door.

'Hello!' Michael called out and came towards them. Gautam had met him at Surekha's place. They shook hands, and Gautam fished out a tiny gift bottle of vodka and presented it to him.

'Oh! Thanks. Now I'll get drunk like a lord. Which reminds me— the future Lord Ashley is giving a bottle-party to-night. Would you care to join us? It's a sort of celebration.'

'Thank you, but I must leave right after lunch. What's the celebration for?'

'Cyril has received a grant to work on Anglo-French relations in eighteenth century India, post-Plassey—1756 and all that!'

'1066 and all that!' Gautam responded cheerily.

'Yes, and he has engaged Miss Champa Ahmed as his research assistant for the project! Soon she'll be leaving Bill Craig's office to come here. She has a diploma in French from Paris, you know. Cyril has found just the person to go through French documents, etc.'

Michael returned to his table, and for some reason Gautam became very tense. There was silence. The food arrived and they began to eat. Then he said reflectively, 'I was sorry to hear what you told me about Champa last time. I'm sure she is more sinned against than sinning.'

Nirmala tried to fight back sudden tears. He was still thinking about Champa. This man had just proposed to her again and was still thinking about Champa.

'I personally think that we shouldn't discuss Champa Baji any more—the topic has become really boring,' she said and tried to look busy finding something in her handbag. 'For you Champa Baji is a paragon, but perhaps you forget, Gautam Mashter, that we have known her from childhood, almost.'

'This is very funny!' Gautam was peeved. 'Why do all of you keep harping upon your childhood? Those who don't happen to know you or Champa Ahmed from their infancy, are they donkeys?'

Now he had come in the range of a powerful arc lamp. Just as she found herself in that bright light confronting Gautam, so this relentless critic of human weaknesses, the guru, considers a fraud like Champa to be a paragon.

'See, you started narrating a dastaan in the day time and you lost your way,' she commented sadly.

'I did not,' he replied emphatically. 'Let me finish the story . . .' He took a deep breath. 'So, there was this poet Framroze in Lala Rukh's entourage, and she fell in love with him. Therefore she banished him from the royal caravan because she was on her way to marry the King of Bokhara, remember?'

'*Hoon.*'

'When she reached Kashmir she discovered that Framroze was her royal fiancé in disguise. Therefore, Nim, do not banish the poor poet in a hurry.'

'Was he, is he, also in love with her?'

'Yes.'

'Are you sure?'

'Yes, I am quite sure.'

'*Hoon.*'

'Nirmal! Don't misunderstand me, I have nothing to do with Champa. You were right in calling me second rate. Please try to understand me . . .' Now he sounded like the hero of a trashy Hindi film.

'Oh, Nirmala . . .' He slipped into the dark once again. He was a mere schoolboy. Who says men are wise and all-knowing? Sitting at that table in front of him, Nirmala felt she was growing like a flowering creeper, like a tree, like mercury inside a barometer. She was attaining Knowledge. Now she too would switch off the artificial lights and slip into Darkness. That state of being in the Darkness, is the highest of all states. She would sit there and peer out. From now on she would put on the Cap of Solomon[1] whose fable Qadeer had narrated to her, once, in the outhouse of Gulfishan.

Everybody cannot find the Cap of Solomon. I am grateful to you, Gautam, that you helped me grow up and showed me how to find this magical cap.'

'Finish your cup, Nirmala,' he said gently.

She was playing with her coffee spoon. 'I was merely being Eliotonian, Gautam Mashter,' she replied gravely.

'May I come to see you next week?' he asked.

---

[1] According to Muslim lore, if one wore that cap one became invisible but could still see others.

'Yes, if you like.' She carefully placed three coffee spoons in a row. 'That makes a fairly short measurement . . .' she remarked, smiling wanly, '. . . of one's life! Doesn't it?'

A Red Indian sat upon a log sending out smoke signals under a full spring moon.

'Hey, you make excellent rings,' Talat said as she strolled by. The smoking Red Indian jumped down and joined the group winding its way to the dining hall. They began to sing, '*We'll make Lady Astor wash dishes when the Red Revolution comes/We'll make Mr Churchill smoke woodbine when the Red . . .*'

They had rented a farmhouse in a village for the annual conference of the Federation of Indian Students Unions of Great Britain. The Cold War was at its height. Inside, some Red Indians were making fierce anti-American speeches. A Scottish comrade was playing his guitar and belting out a ballad in praise of Joseph Stalin. Talat and Feroze walked across to the lounge where Professor Hyman Levy sat on a leather sofa surrounded by ardent young men and women. Talat spotted Roshan Kazmi in the gathering and greeted her warmly. Outside, around the bonfire, a group was singing:

> *One great vision unites us*
> *Though remote be the lands of our birth,*
> *Foes may threaten and smite us*
> *We shall bring peace to the world . . .*

A mixed crowd of English, Welsh, Scottish and East Pakistani students had been invited to attend the conference. The host Indians were Reds of many hues, most of them, like Talat and Kamal, Nehruites. Faiz Ahmed Faiz, who was in jail in Pakistan, was their hero as well. Both West Bengal and East Pakistan were united in their devotion to the revolutionary poet, Qazi Nazrul Islam. Most young progressives in England believed that Pakistan would soon have a red revolution because conditions there were as bad as those in pre-1917 Russia. And India would shine like a beacon for the rest of humanity.

The students had also invited a few pro-India socialist M.P.s and Left intellectuals like Professor Hyman Levy, author of *Literature in the Age of Science.* He had come all the way from Scotland. With his shock of white hair, Semitic nose and intense yet benign look, he was the model left-wing Jewish intellectual. London School of Economics was full of them, all friends of India.

'I am ashamed of the way my country treated you for two hundred years,' he was saying to the young people sitting in a semi-circle before him. Roshan passed a little note to Talat. 'Point for reflection— Britain is his country, Israel is his country, too . . .' Talat glared at her.

He turned towards Roshan, 'I'm thrilled to see so many brilliant young Indian women gathered here tonight . . .'

Roshan pursed her lips.

Talat saved the awkward moment. 'We must have been a great disappointment to you, sir, the way we behaved in 1947. All the humanism of the humanists could not save us.'

Talat was quite unpredictable. That hot afternoon in April 1941, she had suddenly got up and started dancing in front of the row of glistening Buddhas in Sarnath. Now she stood up and declaimed as though she was on the stage of the Old Vic, taking part in *Murder in the Cathedral.*

Clear the air! Clean the sky! Wash the wind, take stone
From stone and wash them.
The land is foul, the water is foul, our beasts and
Ourselves are defiled with blood.
A rain of blood has blinded my eyes.
I wander in a land of barren boughs: if I break them they Bleed,
I wander in a land of dry stones: if I touch them they bleed.
How can I ever return to the soft quiet seasons?

She sat down again, as abruptly as she had stood up.

How do I return to the soft quiet seasons? he repeated to himself, smoking furtively. He wore a pork-pie hat, his face was half-hidden in the upturned collar of his overcoat and he looked like a shadowy figure in a Cold War spy novel.

'Didi, an American agent!' a youthful Bengali whispered to Talat. 'I noticed him lurking out there while you were reciting that reactionary Royalist's poem—I'll go and see. Come on, comrades!'

'Don't behave like a schoolboy,' Talat scolded him and peeped out. She recognised the profile of her cousin Amir, and grasped the situation in an instant. He had come here to haul up poor Roshan and didn't want to be seen by the Bharatis. A delicate and dangerous mission, indeed! She felt a surge of affection for him and slipped out of the lounge. Then she accosted him merrily.

He looked embarrassed.

'Bhaiya Saheb! Adaab! Do come in. There are so many of your countrymen here attending this conference. And look, you are a diplomat. I've seen your High Commissioner and his Begum hobnobbing with Krishna Menon at so many parties, so don't make life difficult for yourself. Come in! You must have gone to Cambridge to see Roshan and were told that she is here—right?'

He smiled and patted her head, 'My clever little sis!' he said with some emotion.

Talat was touched. He had never been demonstrative with his family—Bhaiya Saheb must be growing old, he has become wiser and sadder, she decided and led him to a secluded corner of the barn. He sat down on a bench. 'I'll ask Zarina to get you a cup of hot coffee. Relax.' She ran off, came back and perched like a monkey on a haystack. 'Remember, Bhaiya Saheb, you used to be in the Forward Bloc in Lucknow. Most of these people will probably also get over all this when their student days are over. It's a necessary phase in young adulthood.'

'Yes, Dadi Jan. You have always been the Wise One of the clan.'

Zarina brought him coffee and left, and gradually he relaxed. He felt he was back in the barnyard at Kalyanpur.

'How is my rakhi-sister, Nirmala?' he asked. 'I don't see her here.'

'She is not well—admitted to the University Hospital for a check-up.'

Talat reminded him painfully of Gulfishan and Tehmina and Champa. How could life be so pitiless that it had turned Champa into a tramp? Did this self-righteous slip of a girl know that she had over-simplified matters by adhering to mercurial political ideologies? How could intelligent people divide life into black and white?

He had been an Indian student himself fifteen years ago, organising similar conferences. Tonight he was a different person, inhabiting a separate world. A very different person indeed, in the spring of 1953. And he was dreadfully tired. How can I return to the soft quiet seasons once again?

'Now take this tamasha, for instance,' he continued, 'you are like a bunch of Salvation Army people.'

Talat promptly broke into, '*Onward Christian soldiers, marching on to war.*'

'It will only create intense nostalgia when you recall these evenings and faces in the future. Every moment, every season brings with it the memory of times past. Still, you hold conferences and sing community songs, and you are always organising.'

Talat blinked.

'You never see the inner drama,' he went on, 'you do not acknowledge what is really happening. You're simply not looking, all you do is to keep plotting, keep setting traps. But I'll still escape. You,' he added after a pause, 'cannot waylay me. I shall always be separate, and always be wandering. Now please go and call Roshan, I feel responsible for her and it is getting late.'

Talat left. He lit another cigarette and listened to the song they were singing in the hall—*Way down upon the Swanee River, far, far away/That's where my heart is turning ever, that's where the Old Folks stay.* He used to sing this haunting American slave song around the bonfire at La Martiniere. Unwittingly, he joined in the refrain—

All the world is sad and weary, everywhere I roam.
Take me back to my old . . .

Suddenly he noticed Talat standing in front, looking at him in wonderment. She literally couldn't believe her ears. He stopped, sheepishly. Roshan came forward, carrying her overnight bag, and they said goodnight to Talat and left.

Advancing towards his car he said gruffly, 'Do you realise that a report has been sent against you to the Educational Advisor? Remember, you are here on a prestigious government scholarship.'

'You,' she said defiantly, 'have the moral outrage of someone who has found me in a den of iniquity. Who do you think you are—Senator Macarthy? There are many East Pakistanis here also, attending the conference as observers.'

'Yeah, but they are Bengalis.'

'What do you mean? Aren't they Pakistanis like you and me?'

'Sure, but they are Bengalis,' he replied obstinately and opened the limousine door for her.

On the way to London from the Fedin Conference Talat discovered that she had broken a sandal. She got off the train, dived into a shoe shop and after acquiring a new pair, caught a bus to St. Johns Wood. The moment she entered her flat the telephone rang.

It was Chacha from BBC. Sajida Begum, an eminent educationist, had to be interviewed right away. 'She has come to England after attending some conferences in western Europe and is due to go back home.' With the exuberance and boundless energy of a twenty-four-year-old, Talat ran out again to do his bidding.

The BBC canteen on Oxford Street was full of cheerful din as usual. Members of the Middle Eastern and Eastern Services were floating in and out of the hall. Indians and Pakistanis usually sat together because most of them belonged to the pre-Partition All India Radio. The Urdu Section included Siddique Ahmad Siddiqui, affectionately called Chacha or Uncle, Taqi Saiyid and Yawar Abbas, Attiya Hosain and Hamraz Fyzabadi. Ejaz Hussain Batalvi, Zarina, Feroze and Talat were frequent broadcasters.

The canteen had no teaspoons. 'Since it probably had no teaspoons during the war, it shall never have any—the British are great believers in tradition,' Chacha had once said dryly.

A rotund, prosaic, bespectacled lady sat in a corner, stirring sugar in her cup with a fork. She was talking to Feroze who had come a day earlier from Cambridgeshire. Talat joined them.

'No spoons,' the lady complained.

'British tradition, ma'am,' Talat replied dutifully.

Sajida Begum resumed her conversation with Feroze. 'In Copenhagen I was interviewed over Denmark's BBC,' she said, continuing to ignore Talat. Feroze who had known her in Aligarh before she migrated to the new country, introduced her to Talat. Sajida Begum was also a novelist.

'Feroze tells me you work in the telegraph office,' she said patronisingly.

'Yes, ma'am. Right now I am on leave for a fortnight.'

'Then you will go back to delivering telegrams door-to-door?'

'No, ma'am, I'm a cub-reporter on Fleet Street.'

'She got a by-line for her very first story,' Feroze tried to rescue Talat.

'You write stories, too? Romantic or progressive?'

Feroze gave up—then grinned: 'She is going to write a novella about her cousin, Comdr. Amir Reza. *The Life and Times of a—of—a—*'

Talat got the hint. 'Its title is going to be *Romance de la Rose* because our house in Lucknow is called Gulfishan and he used to speak in French.'

Sajida Begum's eyes gleamed behind her spectacles. Her attitude towards Talat changed instantly.

'Do you often see him over here?'

'No. When he is not flirting with upper-class English girls, he goes to Cambridge singing, "Lydia, O Lydia, O Encyclopaedia".'

'Why?'

'Have you heard of Miss Roshan Kazmi? That' s why . . .'

Sajida Begum looked worried. 'Well, I have no ulterior motive nor any vested interest in him,' she said in the dreary monotone of bores. 'My brother knows him and has asked him to look after me while I am here. Being so young and inexperienced, you see, I do feel lost sometimes.'

On the way down to the basement studios Feroze whispered to Talat, 'You know how ancient she is? Thirty-five! Almost Attiya and Champa Baji's age.'

'St. Johns Wood is becoming curiouser and curiouser. Sajida Apa has also rented a flatlet over there because she was told that all writers and artists live in that mohalla. Now she's busy cultivating Bill Craig and Shanta because she wants them to publish her new novel,' Talat informed her friends in the BBC canteen a few days later.

On a Sunday morning Sajida Begum dropped by at Greville Place and said to Talat darkly, 'This Champa Ahmed seems to be the number two person in Bill's office—Shanta is not around. I suspect there's more to it than meets the eye. Talat, you must warn Shanta—let's meet her this evening. A stitch in time saves nine . . . .'

'Yes, and strike while the iron is hot. But it is none of my business, Sajida Apa. Besides, I'm going to interview Mr and Mrs Max Factor for the Women's Page this evening. They're here from Hollywood and are staying at the Dorchester.'

'You must be joking! Max Factor is a lipstick, not a human being. Tomorrow you'll say you are going to see Mr Lipton or Miss Brooke Bond! Don't take me to be such a simpleton, Talat Reza.'

Dusk fell on Park Lane. Footmen stood at the entrance to the Dorchester Hotel, announcing the arrival of guests. Famous film stars, leading fashion columnists, debutantes, people who inhabited the glossy pages of *The Tatler* and *Country Life*. Countless diamonds glittered on Mrs Max Factor's mink coat as she glided into the Blue Room.

'. . . Father, Jewish immigrant from Balkans, started shop small back-room Hollywood. Max Factor, Empire at present . . .' Talat jotted down rapidly. Mrs Max Factor spoke to her for a full twenty minutes in an exclusive interview—Talat's Conjeevaram sari did the trick.

Talat happened to be one of the two women from the subcontinent who had found temporary work as a journalist on Fleet Street—the other was a Keralite married to an Englishman. Talat had come to be known as 'the sari reporter', her sari a kind of press card which gave her easy access to celebrities.

The following week Talat received an excited call from Sajida Begum. 'I met Amir Reza again. He is more handsome than Girigiri Peck, isn't he? You and Kamal do not stop talking, but he is so quiet one wonders what he's thinking about.'

'Nothing much, Sajida Apa, nothing much.'

'Well, to me he appeared ever so thoughtful and a little sad when we dined at Istamboul last evening.'

'And a Hungarian violinist played *Night in a Spanish Garden* especially for you.'

'How did you know?'

'I guessed, Sajida Apa. So, my no-good cousin is taking you to fancy restaurants!'

'You see, it happened like this—I met him at a party and somebody said, let's go to Istamboul. Amir asked me if I would like to go along. I thought they were going to Turkey, so I said Yes! How was Mrs Max Factor? A real person? Listen, that reminds me, you told me about an

English goldsmith the other day who pierced the Queen's ears for the Women's Page . . .'

'For the Coronation,' Talat corrected her.

Sajida Begum paused awhile then said, 'And then you interviewed the Queen's beautician?'

'Yes, Mrs Henry Holland—she's Oscar Wilde's daughter-in-law.'

'She must be very expensive.'

'I should imagine so, although she gave me a free facial in her beauty parlour on Bond Street,' Talat added nonchalantly.

Sajida Begum disappeared from the scene for a while. 'I'm leaving for a six-week study tour of Britain,' she said before going underground. 'Study tour' was a rather dubious term, anyway.

A reasonably slim lady wearing fashionable goggles and the latest 'sheath' dress over her shalwar entered the BBC canteen one afternoon. Nobody could recognise her—she had been transformed by Oscar Wilde's daughter-in-law!

'The importance of being earnest in the pursuit of you-know-who,' said Talat in an aside.

'Hear, hear! how witty some people have become around here,' said Feroze meanly and blinked. She still could not believe her eyes.

However, Sajida Begum in her new incarnation failed to cheer them up, for a few days earlier Nirmala had been diagnosed with tuberculosis of the lungs in Cambridge. Kamal had made a frantic call to Amir Reza and both of them had accompanied a very scared Nirmala to the Chest Hospital in London. Hari Shankar was not available on the phone in New York.

Sajida Begum was waiting to be complimented on her new urchin cut, which did not suit her. Then, suddenly realising why they were so quiet, she sighed. 'Very sad. I rang up Capt. Reza to congratulate him on his promotion and he told me. I hope it is not galloping TB.'

'Don't be ghoulish, Sajida Apa,' said Talat angrily, 'Nirmala is okay. She'll soon be taken to Lidhurst Sanatorium, for full recovery.'

'An aunt of mine had T.B., she died in Bhawali Sanatorium,' Sajida Begum responded smugly.

'*Thoo—thoo*, Sajida Apa, that must have been in 1853. TB is completely curable today.'

Sajida Begum persisted, 'Heroines of old Urdu novels always died of tuberculosis of the lungs. French novels, even . . . remember Camille?'

'Shoo—shoo, Sajida Apa!' the girls chorused furiously. Placidly, she moved on to another table and was greeted by the members of the Urdu unit.

'Capt. Reza told Mummy that Nirmal would be out of the woods in no time,' said Zarina. 'He came to see us yesterday.'

They carried their cups of coffee from the counter and Zarina said to Surekha and Feroze, 'My father began legal practice as Sir Zaki Reza's junior in Allahabad and Lady Reza was a friend of Mummy's. After her death, Mummy says, Reza used to come to our place with his governess, Nina, but he hated her. He's still a little orphan, deep within. He comes to 'The Laurels' for solace and advice, which he gets in plenty from Mummy.'

Zarina's mother was an expansive and warm-hearted English-woman, everybody's refuge in trouble. Gautam also went to see her whenever he needed to, and his barrister father had also been a friend of Sir Zaki's in Allahabad.

'Now Capt. Reza is very worried about you, Talat, because these two Macarthy characters have been sent to witch-hunt in the BBC.'

'The BBC has refused to be witch-hunted, if that's the correct expression,' Talat replied.

'Yeah . . . And he is distressed about Roshan. She went off to Rumania even though he had told her not to. "Stupid woman", he growled, "sacrificing her chance of a Fulbright for the sake of dancing about in a one horse-town like Bucharest."

'Aye, aye, sir, I said.

' "And she is here on a government scholarship and her father is a senior army officer. And do you know what she told me? That she went to the youth festival because she wanted to psychoanalyse the Commies! And she travelled on fake travel papers which the Rumanians had issued. Was it an honourable thing to do?" he thundered.

'Aye, aye, sir, I agreed. It was not an honourable thing to do. Oh, he was livid. After he left, Mummy said Roshan should be mothering this Little Boy Blue instead of behaving like an Independent Brainy Woman. Men don't like it. Still, the frequency of their quarrels is increasing, which means they'll get married soon. Mummy said Nirmal will be out of the hospital and we'll all go to the Woking Mosque for the Kazmi-Reza wedding sooner than you expect. Insha Allah.'

'Do you remember that painting book, Talat,' asked Kamal, 'in which two English children roam the countryside in a tiny red car?'

'Yes, I do. They stop at a road-house marked "Teas", and John fills the car's tank with a toy petrol tin . . . And they pluck bright red apples from a very green tree—it was just like this place,' said Talat looking around, 'and there was a blue stream and a china white motor-boat and a windmill and horse-carts, and cottages of pre-war England. I even remember the names of the colours we used—cobalt blue, crimson lake, viridian. We used to get loads of such books on our birthdays, published by some mysterious "Father Tuck, London E.C.4." They're still there, in Khyaban.'

The waitress brought the bill. 'There has been a terrible world war but England's countryside is still the same, spread out like John and Mary's painting book,' Talat continued.

'We are the same, too, we carry all of our past with us wherever we go,' said Kamal.

Gautam was listening to their conversation in silence. He understood the importance of their childhood for these people, including Nirmala, and recalled with a pang how irritated he had been when she had mentioned hers that morning in the Koh-i-Noor. After that, he was meeting her again for the first time, a TB patient now, because he had been away on the Continent. If he had married her in Lucknow her life could have been very different, she may not have been lying in a sanatorium hovering between hope and despair. Half of Nirmala's lungs were soon to be removed. Had intellectual flirtation with Champa been so important for him? What is it that a man really wants?

Hari Shankar, who had flown in from New York, was absorbed in studying the willow pattern on the crockery. 'This is so typically English,' he remarked.

'Let's go,' said Kamal abruptly, rising from his chair. Quietly, they walked down towards Gautam's sleek American limousine.

The sanatorium sprawled over a low hill, surrounded by magnificent parkland. Inside, there were flowers everywhere and smiling staff faces, gleaming corridors and beautiful drawing-rooms. In this haven of rest and comfort people waited for their end, watching television; or recovered and went back into the world to live until some other kind of end overtook them.

Nirmala's room was surrounded by gardens on three sides.

'Isn't it like Kishwar Apa's room in Nishat Mahal Hostel?' she said cheerfully to Talat. Gautam smiled sadly as she turned to him. 'See, we had three hostels in Chand Bagh—Nishat Mahal, Naunihal Manzil and Maitri Bhawan—'

Gautam nodded. They were addicted to their past because it was safe and intact, more so for Kamal and Talat because there was no fear of Partition in it. 'We were day students, as you know, but had so many friends in the hostels, didn't we, Talat? And also in Lady Kailash Hostel—I say, have you started work for the Majlis Mela?' she asked Talat eagerly.

'You'll be with us for next year's Mela, Insha Allah,' replied Kamal.

'Insha Allah,' she repeated with a cheery smile. After a while she said, 'Bhaiya Saheb brought me to the hospital, he has been here several times.'

'Cho chweet,' Hari mimicked the girls. Everybody laughed.

Nirmala continued, 'He told Roshan—she had come with him last time—what rakhi was all about, Pakistan notwithstanding. It's also Lucknow *wazedari*. Everyone has been here to see me except Champa Baji and Cyril. Well, I don't expect Cyril to come, I hardly knew him, but Champa Baji . . .'

There was silence. Then Hari mimicked some more people and made everybody laugh again. It was time to leave.

Suddenly Nirmala broke down. 'You all will go away and I'll be left alone again—it's terrible when one's family and friends turn into Visitors.'

A nurse came in and gave them all a broad smile.

'Your Lucknow friends are over there, under the apple trees. Oh, they're leaving! Should we follow them to Lidhurst?' asked Cyril, looking out of the road-house window. 'I came here with the intention of taking the road to Lidhurst but you didn't seem too keen,' he added.

Cunningly, she tried to divert his attention. 'Look, Shakespearean actors!' A touring company had just arrived at the inn, wearing Elizabethan costumes. They were also on their way to Lidhurst to enact a few scenes for the patients at the sanatorium.

Nirmala had already been taken to the hospital when Champa started working for Cyril Ashley in Cambridge. She could not tell him why she had such a bad conscience about Nirmala. In fact, she hadn't told him anything about herself or the way she used to confide in Gautam—she hadn't even told him about Gautam or Amir. Western men weren't interested in a girl's past, they weren't nosey. Thank God.

They boarded a launch and sailed downstream. The *Luisa Jane* passed through overhanging trees and creepers which formed dark watery tunnels. Cyril looked bored, like a husband. Everything seemed slightly worn out, including Cyril Ashley himself. The launch stopped in front of a boat-house and they went ashore.

A large Scandinavian woman stood on the wooden balcony overhead, and a number of people walked through the primroses carrying fishing rods.

Champa and Cyril spent several days in a riverside inn and went for long walks in the forest. 'Champa,' said Cyril one afternoon as he sat down on an up-turned canoe in the boathouse. 'Tell me about your own milieu.' He had discovered that this woman from a distant land had become strangely dependent on him. She was insecure, but he thought she might be comforted by memory.

He had become nosey too! 'Are you also going to write a novel about me?' she asked unhappily.

'No. Who is?'

'Bill—William Craig.'

'No, I don't wish to write a novel about you. You're not a freak, there are thousands of girls like you everywhere in the world, clever, sensitive, pretty.'

So these three words describe me fully. She closed her eyes and tried to remember her own world. The drab locality in Banaras, cots scattered in the courtyard, Father reading depressing files of criminal cases. She cut out Banaras and went straight to Chand Bagh, Lucknow.

She began telling Cyril about the Lantern Service, the Forest of Arden, the swimming pool, the American community songs sung around the bonfire . . .

Cyril interrupted her. 'Look who's coming straight out of your Moon Garden!' he exclaimed.

She looked up. Kamal emerged from the crowd of holiday-makers. 'Hello, Champa Baji, Cyril,' he said. 'We saw you the other day at a road-house, but were in a hurry to reach Lidhurst.' He sat down on another up-turned canoe.

'I was just telling Cyril about Lucknow,' she said, looking a bit crestfallen.

'How interesting!' Kamal smiled politely.

Champa heard the sadness in his voice and continued rapidly, with a certain bravado, 'I was telling him about India—the smell of hay on a hot summer afternoon in the compound of our kothi in Banaras, the neighing of horses, the bullock-carts passing by . . . You know, when the wheels of a bullock-cart creaked in the distance at night our maid-servants used to say, "This creaking of the wheels indicates that the goddess Bhavani is angry".'

Kamal listened to her in grim silence.

'In the languid afternoons, the pankha coolie dozed outside—we have those long verandas with Georgian pillars in our country-home in Banaras district.' She added hastily, 'Now, of course, the house is fast crumbling. It may soon vanish. No, Cyril, you won't comprehend, your perceptions are different.'

'I shall tell you . . . ' said Kamal, leaning forward. He had suddenly entered a world which was far away and with which he was deeply in love. He wanted to escape from the tensions of the present, and set out on his own journey.

'Nirmala is not well at all—in Lucknow, her mother must have gone to the Hanuman temple in Aligunj and then proceeded to some Imambara and prayed to Imam Hussain for her speedy recovery. Gyanwati used to sing in the mode Yaman—

The House of the Prophet, the Children of Ali,
How I adore Hasan and Hussain, sons of Zahra . . .!

'Can I translate this classical melody and the emotions they convey to me, into English? And during winter, at the time of weddings in our joint family, quilted curtains were dropped in the veranda of our ancestral mud-brick house in Kalyanpur and the mirasins crooned, *May the shadow of Ali fall on my Shyam Sunder Banra*[2]. Can any western sociologist understand the beauty of this scene, this fusion of Muslim and Hindu imagery in a song sung at Muslim marriages? And the peasants of my village sang the Ballad of Alha-Udal: *Alha sat by the Jamuna, Syed rushed forward crying, Ali—Ali—and ordered Udal: listen, sonny, King Prithvi has come with massive troops—drive him away.*

'Do you remember, Champa Baji, you and Gautam once came with us to Kalyanpur in the winter vacations, we sat under the tattered canopy of our village theatre and our nautanki orchestra played our favourite theatrical tunes! They were such good musicians. They staged *Laila Majnun* for us—Qadeer's nephew Master Chapati played Majnun— and he sang *Praise be to the Lord, Laila, I have come in thy Presence.*

'And he sang:

Laila, thy face is my Qibla. The ringlets of thy hair my faith,
To circumvent the Kaaba, I have come to thy Court.

'The mystic import of such ghazals was readily understood by our common people—the West doesn't have an equivalent in its culture.'

Champa and Kamal were now transported to the mandap, sipping ginger tea out of clay cups. Master Chapati was singing:

Like Zuleikha when I fell in love with thee, Laila
I came to thy bazaar to be sold like Joseph—

They sat on cane stools watching Laila Majnun against the backdrop of a crudely painted fountain, a palace and the full moon. The nautanki percussionist played *kaharva* on his tabla. A motor launch went past noisily, they returned from Kalyanpur. 'Our nautanki staged a first class *Nala Damayanti* and *Indersabha,*' said Kamal proudly and lighted Cyril's cigarette.

---

[2] Banna or Banra—bridegroom, derived from Ban Raj or Forest Prince or Krishna, Shyam Sunder; dark and handsome Krishna.

Champa asked him: 'Do you remember Vasanti's song, *The jogan has gone forth in the search?*'

You won't get anything out of this search, my good woman, he wanted to tell her crossly. 'It is an exercise in futility,' he said aloud, 'I mean, remembering the old songs—Pankaj Mallik for instance.'

'Yes, *I was going to meet my man, fully made up and with braided plaits,*' she said. 'How can you know, Cyril, who is Pankaj Mallik and Arzoo Lucknawi and Kallan Qawwal and Ustad Fayyaz Khan, what importance they have in our lives . . . And Jigar Moradabadi who says: '*A million suns went past and we continued to wait for the morn.*' And Kalidas: '*Passing over the Vindhyas and the Sindhu in the company of cranes, the cloud went forth carrying the message. . .*'

Now Kamal wanted to come back to earth but Champa sat before him like the conscience of time. He felt she was flying about like a leaf in the maelstrom of eons. He frowned.

'Kamal, listen—' she was saying, 'it is night-time, dogs bark, the bazaar is filled with silence. Birds are asleep, chowkidars are guarding the watermelon fields, gardeners are rattling the gondni's rattlers. In a short while the grindstones shall start moving—'

'Sarshar?'[3] Kamal asked her. She nodded and was lost in thought again.

'We used to assemble in Hari's tower room and solve the world's problems. Life was still very undefined. Sometimes we were picked up by strong beams of light; often we were surrounded by mists. We spent our youthful days in this light and shade of intellectual hide-and-seek. We aquired a kind of Gandhian humility, but it was not born of a sense of superiority. We felt as though the blood of mankind was on our hands and we had to wash it off. And, then, look what happened.' He spread his hands in front of Cyril Ashley—'One morning we discovered that our own hands were drenched in blood, and we saw that all those fine people—intellectuals and authors and leaders— many of them had blood-stained hands too. Most of them were not willing to atone. They ran away, or took different avtars, but there were some genuine human beings, as well.'

---

[3] Pandit Ratan Nath Sarshar, nineteenth century Urdu novelist of Lucknow.

'Like Qadeer and Qamrun?' Champa asked humbly.

Silently he took her permission to speak about them. They appeared like holy, shining beings.

'Yes, Qadeer and Qamrun, Ram Autar and Ram Daiya, our peasants and betel-leaf sellers, our chikan embroiderers who lose their eyesight doing intricate needlework for a pittance. They are our real backbone, Cyril.'

Champa was still far away. She said, 'Kamal, ask Gautam if he also remembers the wood-apples falling with a soft thud on the grass in Badshah Bagh . . .'

He pondered. How shall I tell her that Gautam has probably forgotten her? But, can he forget her? He must remember her, just as he remembers the river and the mossy houses and wood-apple trees. Kamal looked anxiously at his watch. 'Er . . . Excuse me, Champa Baji, I've just come from Sir Ronald Grey's house—he's the surgeon, lives in a village close by—because I had to speak to him about Nirmal. May I take your leave? Bye, Cyril.' He got up and strode away.

It was strange, he hadn't shown any surprise at finding her with Cyril in a boat-house. Everybody knew everything about her. She stood on a pinnacle, fully exposed. Why did I let this happen to myself, why? She looked at Cyril in abject terror. She had come back to the present like a wood-apple falling with a thud on English grass. She was living at the mercy of circumstances. Perhaps it was already much too late.

PART II

R.K. NARAYAN

My America

At the American consulates, the visa issuing section is kept busy nowadays as more and more young men seek the Green Card or profess to go on a student visa and many try to extend their stay once they get in. The official handles a difficult task while filtering out the 'permanents' and letting in only the 'transients'. The average American himself is liberal-minded and doesn't bother that more Indian engineers and doctors are swamping the opportunities available in the country possibly to the disadvantage of the American candidate himself.

I discussed the subject with Prof. Ainslee Embree of Columbia University, who has had a long association with Indian affairs and culture. His reply was noteworthy. 'Why not Indians as well? In course of time they will be Americans. The American citizen of today was once an expatriate, a foreigner who had come out of a European or African country. Why not from India too? We certainly love to have Indians in our country.' There are, however, two views on this subject.

The elderly parents of Indians settled in America pay a visit to them, from time to time (on excursion round ticket), and feel pleased at the prosperity of their sons or daughters in America. After a Greyhound tour of the country and a visit to Niagara, they are ready to return home when the suburban existence begins to bore them, whether at New Jersey or Queens or the Silicon Valley neighborhood of California. But they always say on their return, 'After all, our boys

This essay is taken from *Frontline*, October 1985.

are happy there. Why should they come back to this country, where they get no encouragement?'

Our young man who goes out to the States for higher studies or training, declares when leaving home, 'I will come back as soon as I complete my course, may be two years or a little more, but I will definitely come back and work for our country, and also help our family . . .' Excellent intentions, but it will not work that way. Later, when he returns home full of dreams, projects and plans, he only finds hurdles at every turn when he tries for a job or to start an enterprise of his own.

Form-filling, bureaucracy, caste and other restrictions, and a generally feudal style of functioning, exasperate the young man and waste his time. He frets and fumes as days pass with nothing achieved, while he has been running around presenting or collecting papers at various places. He is not used to this sort of treatment in America, where, he claims, he could walk into the office of the top man anywhere, address him by his first name and explain his purpose; when he attempts to visit a man of similar rank in India to discuss his ideas, he realizes that he has no access to him, but can only talk to subordinate officials in a hierarchy.

Some years ago a biochemist returning home and bursting with proposals, was curtly told off by the big man when he innocently pushed the door and stepped in. 'You should not come to me directly, send your papers through proper channels.' Thereafter the young biochemist left India once for all, having kept his retreat open with the help of a sympathetic professor at the American end. In this respect American democratic habits have rather spoilt our young men. They have no patience with our official style or tempo, whereas an Indian at home would accept the hurdles as inevitable *Karma*.

The America-returned Indian expects special treatment, forgetting the fact that over here chancellors of universities will see only the other chancellors, and top executives will see only other top executives and none less under any circumstance. Our administrative machinery is slow, tedious, and feudal in its operation, probably still based on what they called the Tottenham Manual, creation of a British administrator five decades ago.

One other reason for a young man's final retreat from India could also be attributed to the lack of openings for his particular qualification.

A young engineer trained in robotics had to spend all his hours explaining what it means to prospective sponsors, until he realized that there could be no place for robots in an over-crowded country.

The Indian in America is a rather lonely being having lost his roots in one place and not grown them in the other. Few Indians in America make any attempt to integrate in American cultural or social life. So few visit an American home or a theater or an opera or try to understand the American psyche. An Indian's contact with the American is confined to his colleagues working along with him and to an official or seminar luncheon. He may also mutter a 'Hi!' across the fence to an American neighbor while lawn-mowing. At other times one never sees the other except by appointment, each family being boxed up in their homes securely behind locked doors.

After he has equipped his new home with the latest dish-washer, video, etc., with two cars in the garage and acquired all that the others have, he sits back with his family counting his blessings. Outwardly happy, but secretly gnawed by some vague discontent and aware of some inner turbulence or vacuum, he cannot define which. All the comfort is physically satisfying, he has immense 'job satisfaction' and that is about all.

On a weekend, he drives his family fifty miles or more towards another Indian family to eat an Indian dinner, discuss Indian politics, or tax problems (for doctors particularly this is a constant topic of conversation, being in the highest income bracket). There is monotony in this pattern of life, so mechanical and standardized. In this individual, India has lost an intellectual or an expert; but it must not be forgotten that the expert has lost India too, which is a more serious loss in the final reckoning.

The quality of life in India is different. In spite of all its deficiencies, irritations, and general confusion, Indian life builds up an inner strength. It is through subtle inexplicable influences (through religion, family ties and human relationships in general). Let us call them psychological 'inputs' to use a modern terminology, which cumulatively sustain and lend variety and richness to existence.

Building imposing Indian temples in America, installing our gods therein and importing Indian priests to perform the *puja* and festivals, are only imitative of Indian existence and could have only a limited value. Social and religious assemblies at the temples (in America) might mitigate boredom, but only temporarily.

I have lived as a guest for extended periods in many Indian homes in America and have noticed the ennui that descends on a family when they are stuck at home. Children growing up in America present a special problem. They have to develop themselves on a shallow foundation without a cultural basis, either Indian or American. Such children are ignorant of India and without the gentleness and courtesy and respect for parents, which forms the basic training for a child in an Indian home, unlike the American upbringing whereby a child is left alone to discover for himself the right code of conduct.

Aware of his child's ignorance of Indian life, the Indian parent tries to cram into the child's little head all possible information during an 'Excursion Fare' trip to the mother country.

In the final analysis America and India differ basically, though it would be wonderful if they could complement each other's values. Indian philosophy lays stress on austerity and unencumbered, uncomplicated day-to-day living. On the other hand, America's emphasis is on material acquisitions and a limitless pursuit of prosperity.

From childhood an Indian is brought up on the notion that austerity and a contented life is good, and also a certain other-worldliness is inculcated through the tales a grandmother narrates, the discourses at the temple hall, and through moral books. The American temperament, on the contrary, is pragmatic.

The American has a robust indifference to eternity. 'Visit the church on a Sunday and listen to the sermon if you like but don't bother about the future,' he seems to say. Also, 'dead yesterday and unborn tomorrow, why fret about them if today be sweet?'—he seems to echo Omar Khayyam's philosophy. He works hard and earnestly, and acquires wealth, and enjoys life. He has no time to worry about the after-life, he only takes the precaution to draw up a proper will and trusts the Funeral Home round the corner to take care of the rest.

The Indian who is not able to live on this basis wholeheartedly, finds himself in a half-way house; he is unable to overcome the inherited complexes while physically flourishing on American soil. One may hope that the next generation of Indians (American-grown) will do better by accepting the American climate spontaneously or in the alternative return to India to live a different life.

Dom Moraes

Changes of Scenery

I arrived in England in August 1954. The P & O liner *Strathmore* decanted me at Tilbury. I was sixteen years old. My possessions were a suitcase full of clothes and a steamer trunk full of books.

I also carried a small portable typewriter, only slightly younger than I was. My father had used it in Burma and China, where he had been a war correspondent. The London editor of his newspaper, the *Times of India,* an amiable man named Mulgaonkar, met me off the ship, and escorted me on the train trip to London. Showers had fallen as the *Strathmore* docked, but the clouds had moved away and from the train window the landscape, rinsed by rain, looked newly washed. Though I had never seen it before, I recognised it from books.

There were occasional glimpses of very green countryside. Mostly there were endless, uniform rows of redbrick houses that faced away from me; clothes hung up to dry in their backyards, given shapes by the wind. They faced other, identical houses. Pink-skinned people went in and out of the houses; typewriter ribbons of road unwound between them. The traffic was slow and intermittent; it was still early in the day. I identified shops that were not yet open, and an undertaker's establishment that was. Near London I began to see Black people, shabbily dressed, and groups of long-haired youths in Edwardian clothes. I recognised them as Jamaican immigrants and Teddy boys, from novels read under the humid sun of Bombay.

This essay is taken from *Voices of the Crossing*, edited by Ferdinand Dennis and Naseem Khan, published by Serpent's Tail, London, 2000.

London seemed familiar too, when we reached it. It was then still identifiable as an English city. Its great grey buildings aroused a sense of history in me. I knew the streets by name. Somewhere in the labyrinth they formed, a key to my future lay. Somewhere in it there were poets I had read. Soon I might meet them. I certainly knew I would meet Stephen Spender, who had read my poems in India and had published some of them in *Encounter.* So, though I had never been to England before, it did not seem to me a strange or an unknown country. It seemed to me the destination I had been trying to reach for years, a hidden place inside myself, to arrive in which was a relief and a sudden freedom.

Through Mulgaonkar I found a small flat in Knightsbridge. It was really a bedsitter, but had an attached bathroom, an electric kettle and a minuscule electric stove. I lived in it for several months. I had two years to wait before my Oxford college would admit me. Though I was too young for university, it was in this flat, in a small way, that I started my literary career. I did it all the wrong way round. A young English writer would have entered university and met other writers there. Then for a couple of years he might have been led by what used to be called a bohemian life. Finally he would have found his way into the literary establishment, and rubbed shoulders with the great men and women authors of his time.

Thanks to Stephen Spender and his wife Natasha, the last bit came first where I was concerned. The Spenders were very caring people; they felt I would be lonely in London. They invited me to lunch every Sunday at their house in St. John's Wood. These Sunday lunches were attended by other guests, usually famous writers. The first one was Cyril Connolly, who told me my suit didn't fit and reduced me to tremulous silence. I was nearly always silent, unable to think of anything to say. I listened to the conversation around me, however, and came to the conclusion that great writers were no less silly than other human beings, and quite often much sillier. It was a valuable discovery for a young man to make.

Stephen also introduced me to older writers like E.M. Forster and Walter de la Mare. So my poems were read and criticised by several people whose work had formed part of my mind. I sometimes could not believe my good luck, and was grateful for it. Stephen then tried to introduce me to writers nearer my own age. During the week he occasionally asked me to lunch near the *Encounter* offices in Haymarket. The others present were young poets whose work he liked. One, Oliver Bernard, took me into Soho, in whose cagelike pubs and drinking clubs a wide selection of artistic fauna was to be found. I met some good writers and painters there, and found friends in Francis Bacon and George Barker. I also encountered David Archer.

Why nobody has ever written a biography of David is beyond me. He was a great man. He was tall and, when I met him, fiftyish and rather bald, with the flushed face of a drinker, and very kind, bespectacled eyes of that pale blue colour which physiognomists have described as a mark of criminal tendencies. Archer walked with an awkward tensity of body, a Prussian stiffness, a bundle of newspapers always clamped under his left arm. He looked as though he were afraid he would explode. He had a rich father, whose fortune he had slowly demolished through his patronage of the arts. Whenever David had money, he gave it away, almost at random, but mostly to needy writers and to the sailors he liked to sleep with.

He had started a literary bookshop in the 1930s. This was in Parton Street, a cul-de-sac off Red Lion Square. From this shop, under the imprint of The Parton Press, he published three of the most important books of poetry of the decade. These were the first books of George Barker, Dylan Thomas, and David Gascoyne. During the war the shop and David moved to Glasgow. Here the Parton Press produced W.S. Graham's first book. The war ended; David came back to London and opened the third Parton Bookshop in Greek Street, Soho. It was a beautiful establishment on two floors; besides the section which sold new books, it contained a library, a coffee shop, and an art gallery where homeless poets sometimes slept.

This bookshop became bankrupt very soon, due to its proprietor's habit of never accepting any money from his customers. Indeed he often gave them whatever was in the till, feeling they looked in need of a square meal. Before this happened, he offered to publish my first book of poems. I protested that he had not read any. 'But, my dear boy, I only ever read detective stories,' he said. 'I never read any of the poets I published. But I can smell a poet, if you see what I mean.' He then seemed to realise the possible implications of his remark. 'I don't mean that none of you ever bathe,' he added hastily, 'except Dylan, you could certainly smell him, what?' For some reason he always talked like a Wodehouse character.

But in July 1957 he published my first book, *A Beginning*. We had to distribute it by carrying it round the bookshops, some of whom grudgingly accepted a few copies on sale or return.

But suddenly and unexpectedly it started to get good reviews everywhere, from rather well-known poets. The bookshops started to order copies. Then it won the Hawthornden Prize.

My father was educated at Oxford. Afterwards he entered Lincoln's Inn and emerged from it a qualified barrister. He returned to Bombay, where his legal career proved brief and unsatisfactory. He joined the *Times of India,* which was owned by a British company and where most of his colleagues on the editorial staff were English. In 1937 he married his college sweetheart. A year later I was born. With all his British connections, it was rather surprising that he was a strong supporter of the Indian Freedom Movement. Jawaharlal Nehru was a friend of his. When the government cracked down on the Congress party, my parents hid several leaders, wanted by the police, in our flat, where they shared my nursery.

If his British employers knew about this, they did not let it affect them. As a journalist my father was brilliant. They made him the first Indian war correspondent, and he was despatched to the Burma front, and later to China. During his absence, a lengthy one, my mother, who was gifted and pretty and a practising pathologist, went quietly mad. My father returned. In 1946 he accepted the editorship of the *Times of Ceylon,* and we spent the next two years in Colombo. Then he went back to Bombay and his old paper, which in 1949 sent him on an assignment to Australia and New Zealand. From Australia the Indian prime minister, Nehru, asked him to travel through southeast Asia and report on the state of the nations there.

My father, because he was very worried about my mother's mental health, had taken us both with him. When we had got back to India, she had a complete breakdown, became violent, and had to be committed to a mental hospital. She had still been in it when I left for England. It was possibly this that forced my father to send me there two years before I could be admitted to Oxford. There was nobody at home to look after me. Also, I continually told him how much I hated India and actually feared it. I had the same feelings about it as I did about my mother. I felt she had betrayed me and that I had no home. There were other reasons. I had never learnt, and I could not speak, any of the Indian languages, only English.

At this time, very shortly after Independence, there was a kind of chauvinism in Indian attitudes. It was felt that an adolescent of Indian birth in a newly independent India *had* to speak an Indian language, *had* to feel Indian. I rebelled against this assumption, but was constantly reminded of it by my schoolmates and the adults I met. Since my childhood I had spent much of my time reading, and the language I read was English. That was also the language I wrote in, and writing in it was the most important part of my life. Sometimes in Bombay I was told that I should not even speak it, or not exclusively; it was unpatriotic. My inclinations, even then, were to do the opposite of what others told me I should do.

My father knew all the powerful people in his country. Because he was now the editor of the largest and most influential English language newspaper, he was one of them. They talked to him as an equal, and often took his advice, and to them it did not seem to matter that he could only speak to them in English. He felt, however Westernised he was, that he was Indian. He felt that he belonged to India. He did not understand my reaction to the country of both our births, but he knew it existed. He also, I think, realised that he could not change it. That was why he surrendered and why he sent me to England two years before it was necessary. However reluctantly, however sadly, he realised that in India I felt an outsider.

In England I never felt an outsider. I lived in London for a year and made several friends, not all of them literary. Then for a year I travelled in Europe, and stayed for long periods in Paris and Rome. When I returned to London I felt I had come home. In October 1956 I had to make another adjustment; I went up to Jesus College, Oxford. At that time most young men did National Service before university, and at eighteen I was the youngest person in my college. But I was more grown up than most of the other undergraduates. I had travelled more widely than anyone else in college, I had published poetry in several reputable literary magazines, and, important in a society of young males, I had experience with women.

A Beginning was published and reviewed in my first year; it won the Hawthornden Prize in my second. I was not yet twenty. I was the youngest person ever to win the award, and the first non-English writer. The results were a cyclone of publicity, which was bad for me. What was good was that I received offers from national magazines and newspapers to review books and write feature articles. I began to know a lot of people, none of whom except for Mulgaonkar, were Indians, until Ved Mehta arrived in Oxford. He was blind, and had written an autobiographical book. He became my friend not because he was an Indian, but because he was a writer. Nearly all his other friends were Indians, though they were not writers.

They were his friends because they were Indians. They found comfort and reminders of home in one another's company. I needed no such reassurances. It didn't matter to me where my friends came from, nor even, any longer, where I came from. The language I wrote was the language spoken and understood by everyone around me. I fitted into English life, but the concept of 'home' was difficult for me to hold on to. One lived where one was; different places were only changes of scenery. Once I had left Oxford, publishers and television companies hired me to write books and documentary scripts. Magazines and newspapers paid me to travel. Sometimes I was sent to India, and I found I did not have any quarrel with it now.

During this time I had a number of adventures with women; then I married. Judy was English. She could hardly have been more English. She came of a county family, generations of which had lived in Buckinghamshire. Her father was dead, but her mother was still young. At weekends we visited her in the country. We bought a house in Islington. We had a son. Judy was a very good person, but I was hardly an ideal husband. I travelled too much, sometimes into dangerous situations like wars; I drank too much. After six years, we decided to separate. Soon after this I was offered the editorship of a magazine in Hong Kong. The position involved constant travel in southeast Asia and Australia. I took it.

Three years later the United Nations hired me as a literary adviser. I was based in New York, but travelled incessantly, and produced two books. My UN agency then lent me to the Government of India to write television films. I did not now dislike India, but the work bored me, and I resigned and wrote a biography of Mrs Indira Gandhi, whom I knew well, and also a book on Bombay. Judy and I remained friends. Whenever I visited London I saw her, and our son Heff. During one of these visits from India, it occurred to me that England was the country I knew best, and I was tired of travel. I had lunch with my literary agent, who was also a friend, and announced my intention of returning to England and setting up shop there.

I had expected him to be delighted. He was appalled. 'Don't you realise,' he said, 'that you've been away ten years? It's a hell of a long time. The editors and television producers have all changed; even the publishers are different now. You'd have to start from scratch. If I were you, I would go back to India, make it your base, and write about Asia.' This conversation had a shattering effect on me. It was not easy to accept the role of a man everybody had forgotten. I talked to other close friends and, usually with reluctance, they gave me the same advice as my agent. So I flew back to India. Changes of scenery had become part of my life. I might as well be a part of the Indian scenery as that of another place.

Last time I went back to London it was winter. That was three years ago. I had flown in from Israel. In Jerusalem I had met one of the closest friends I have ever had, the poet T. Carmi. I had said goodbye to him for the last time; he was dying of cancer. Judy had died two years earlier also of cancer; she had been tragically young. But Heff still lived in London, where he was a successful music mixer. He owned a house in Islington, not the same one Judy and I had had, and I stayed with him there. He developed a bad cold and had to stay in bed much of the time. One day, feeling very fatherly, I decided to make him some soup. I put it on to cook and looked out of the window at the English winter.

It was evening; I saw uniform redbrick houses, rooftops and television aerials under the dull, stationary clouds. It was by no means a romantic or beautiful view, but to me tremendously evocative. The familiar smell of London came in through the window, and mingled with the smell of chicken soup. I had first come here as a refugee, fleeing from his birthplace to another country of which he had had great expectations. England had fulfilled most of my expectations, but I no longer belonged here or anywhere. This, to me, seemed an important piece of knowledge, which it had taken over half a century to acquire. In London I had visited the pubs and restaurants I had once frequented, at least those that remained, and had talked to old friends.

I had done what I had come for. Next day I was to fly back to India. There I had poems to finish, and a woman whom I loved to meet. I took the soup in to Heff, who sat up and blew his nose. We talked about my departure while he consumed the soup. 'You seem very happy today,' he said. 'Is it because you're in London, or because tomorrow you're going back to India?' It was a very good question. I looked at him, thought of several matters I had never told him of, and offered the only possible reply. 'Honestly,' I said, 'I don't know.'

Farrukh Dhondy

Speaking in Tongues

When I was sixteen I left my home town of Poona and went to Bombay, the big city, to do a course in Chemical Engineering at the University. I was bewildered and lonely in Bombay and I hated Chemical Engineering and every wretched equation connected with its study.

I lived in the flat of a grand-uncle of mine, a great and generous man who was a staunch Gandhian and would only wear clothes of homespun cotton and eat a strict vegetarian diet. These were the early sixties, the Gandhian agenda was at an end and my grand-uncle's experiments with truth had been boiled down to prayer, to astounding and sometimes disgusting feats of yoga and to the personal distribution of hundreds of umbrellas to the poor during the monsoons.

All of it, including the lectures in thermodynamics and changing suburban trains in the Bombay rush hour, drove me mad. Yet I knew that I had contrived to deserve all of it, a punishment for the twin sins of literalness and vanity.

It was the practice amongst all those who passed their 'Intermediate' year of a science college, throughout the length and breadth of India, to apply either to medical institutes or one or other college of technology. My mark at the exam had been good, even exceptional— no great feat of the intellect in any objective terms, but singular enough to get me a coveted place on the most coveted course. I had

This essay is taken from *Voices of the Crossing*, edited by Ferdinand Dennis and Naseem Khan, published by Serpent's Tail, London, 2000.

to apply and I had to accept the place when it was offered, if only so that I could spend the next few months, out of short-sighted vanity, impressing my classmates and teachers with the fact.

The sin of literalness was inherent in the residue of Indian nationalism from which we all suffered, from resonating slogans about being useful to the country, building the nation and finding a career in a field which would in the near future demand irrigation with talent—well-paid talent. The literal bent of mind made me and my advisers, teachers, friends and most of all my family elders, look no further than the expansion of Indian industry, medicine, economics and law.

After a few months of being on the Chemical course, I gave up the struggle with the vengeful Bombay monsoon and with suburban trains. I discovered a tram that ran the length of Bombay from where I lived to the doorstep of the college. It took a couple of hours each way, but it afforded me seating space for the whole journey and every morning I would set out on it with paperbacks I had bought from the pavement bookshops.

I read Lawrence Durrell's Alexandria Quartet end to end, four books with a secret interconnection of a time-space continuum which only I of all the tram-travellers could understand! Here was a richness of language, contrived, self-conscious, sentimentally exaggerated, that precisely answered the needs of my loneliness, my Bombay blues.

Here was a story about people who lived in Egypt and weren't all white. People who were taken as seriously as the satirised British caricatures or the Bohemian British philosopher-hero. If Arabs could be written into the narrative web of what I prematurely thought was a masterpiece, then so could Indians. I wanted to be a writer. No more Chemical Engineering. Here was a brighter conceit.

I left Bombay and went to Delhi, telling my parents that I had renounced all career ambitions, braving their grave and desperate disapproval and, again from the pavement bookstalls, I began the reading that privately promised me membership of the club of aspiring writers. Reading Durrell's letters, essays and travelogues took me to Henry Miller and to D.H. Lawrence, to Cavafy and Kazantzakis in translation. A lot of it was a waste of time, none of it was evaluated in any deep sense and I didn't know anyone with whom I could discuss what I was voraciously reading. Durrell seemed to have formed, with Miller and the memory of Lawrence (someone whom neither Miller nor Durrell had ever met), a small, charmed, special, knowing, literary sect. God, I wanted to be part of that sect!

There was no way in. I was back in Poona and wanting to get out of India. The real test of vanity would be to apply to the big universities, and for several snobbish and historical reasons there seemed to be only two that fitted this bill, Oxford or Cambridge, and that's what I did.

Growing up in India in those years meant listening to and taking part in two debates about writing, one public, one internal. The public debate was not a widespread preoccupation of the general populace. Within this populace, in the two or three decades after Independence from colonial rule, there was a debate about which language would be used in official transactions and which languages would be the medium in schools and universities. The debate had a literary adjunct. Should Indian writers write in English at all?

To admit that one thought in English was somehow to admit that one's mind still wore the uniform of the departed conqueror.

There had been a handful of Indian writers in English, both in fiction and non-fiction, but to use English at all was seen by some to be a betrayal of the Indian consciousness and since one didn't possess any other, a betrayal of the material of one's experience.

I can't quite say how or why this debate fizzled out, but it's certainly true that those writers and poets whose first or best language happened to be English, because it was the language of their disciplined reading and of their critical awareness, began to assert the right of English to be recognised as Indian, shoulder to shoulder with Urdu, Hindi, Bengali or Gujerati. India emerged from its blinding nationalism as its intellectual and economic commerce with the world grew, using English as the language of communication. That was the start and finish of the open debate.

The internal debate was a very old one which, crudely stated, proposed the substitution of Odes to Nightingales with Odes to Bulbuls and addresses to roses which are sick, with addresses to lotuses or jasmine buds similarly afflicted. It was a canker of a debate and gave rise to silly self-questioning—where the relationship between people called Wooster and Jeeves could be funny, could there be an Indian equivalent? The answer is, of course, yes, there could be a hundred interesting, even hilarious formats exploring the relationship between particular classes of Indians in an ironic servant-master relationship. The trick was to find the pattern in the carpet, the story in day to day goings on.

Two literary events settled the internal debate in the years in which I was plotting my exit, working at my exams in order to win a scholarship and get a place at one of the 'chosen' Universities. I wasn't Jude the Obscure but I did understand how he felt.

The first intervention was that of a novelist called John Wain who was booked to speak at the Poona Philosophical Society, a sleepy gathering of academics who met once a fortnight to discuss Bertrand Russell's contentions on God or unravel the connections between Vedanta and Atomic Physics in a narrow tutorial room of the gothic, black-stoned Ferguson College.

The John Wain lecture was heavily oversubscribed and had to be moved to a lecture theatre in the same place because very many citizens had turned up in the mistaken belief that Mr Wain was a famous cowboy. The crowd grew shifty when they didn't recognise their hero, but Mr Wain, probably amazed at the response to his coming, braved the crowds with an address on the state of the English novel with allusions to Kingsley Amis and Iris Murdoch which passed through the audience like gamma rays from a distant galaxy. Nevertheless they clapped, as much I thought, for the relief of its end as for the lecture itself.

A few weeks later a magazine called *Encounter,* which was widely read in India, carried an article by John Wain on his trip to Poona. He didn't mention the lecture but he made a story out of his visit to the little bungalow in the middle of our college where our Principal, the logician and philosopher Mr Damle, lived. Mr Wain described the house, the furnishings, the tea, the conversation and the small army of cockroaches which invaded the floor and his consciousness to the exclusion of everything else. The end of the essay was a lament for Indian education. I read it with fascination. It was an invitation to test reality against prose, because here it was, the Eng Lit essay by a published person about my own college in Poona. The descriptions were precise, recognisable. The jerky and finally pathetic personality of our college Principal was well captured and the pathos of his house and position as a 'logician' poignantly and even sympathetically sketched.

Of course it wasn't the whole story. John Wain would have had to stay longer to know how Professor Damle rose to prominence in the society of Brahmins who ran the college and awarded him his turn at the helm. There was more to the diminutive Damle than tea, tarnished Aristotelian logic and cockroaches.

But Wain had done me a service. He had seen that pattern in the carpet which had grown dusty with my footsteps. It was not only possible to write about Principal Damle, it was irreverent, precise in its own way and interesting.

The second comet to cross this gaze towards a literary horizon was V.S. Naipaul's book *An Area Of Darkness.* It was a beginning. It was a brown man, albeit from abroad, trying to see India without nationalistic spectacles, without guilt, almost without ideology. It was refreshing. Everyone who read English argued about it. It was in India bigger than Rushdie was later to be in Iran.

The book was condemned for being in the tradition of Katharine Mayo and Beverly Nichols who had written disparagingly of India in the thirties and forties, at the height of the nationalist movement against the British Raj. I knew that it was no such thing. It was a nail in the cross of blind nationalism, and this crucifixion felt necessary.

The book was not so much a travelogue but more of an imaginative excursion that no-one had dared to take. It was not a great formal invention—a trip across India with the travelogue in mind and a sharpness of perception that only a foreigner could bring to the subject. It was a book waiting to be written and this expatriate descendant of indentured Indian labour rushed in, with genius, where others feared to tread.

Despite these examples, I came to Cambridge University to study Physics, not English Literature. We called it 'reading Natural Sciences', but that was part of the appeal, speaking in tongues. There were ideas, fashions and conceits in the styles, conversations and in the very air of the place.

For me the strongest of these, the most ensnaring idea and the one that has stayed with me the longest was the conviction that one poem is demonstrably better than another and that the demonstration consists of a critical dialogue with the text in hand, calling upon the richness of experience that went into its construction.

The idea came from the work of F.R. Leavis and his associates and it mattered not whether you were reading History or Slavonic Studies, it had spread through the intellectual fabric of the place as fluoride spreads through water. Even those who were articulately against fluoridation drank it. The big idea spreads naturally to novels, to music, to philosophies, to religious experience and ultimately to values and ways of life. For a would-be writer, this powerful idea is a curse. It's an inhibition. Even though the newly learnt critical art makes it self-evident that D.H. Lawrence is a finer writer than Lawrence Durrell or Henry Miller, the analysis of writing makes it harder to do it. It was a common cry: the critical cramps the creative.

Or that was a way of dodging the truth which was that I was not convinced, not totally convinced that anyone would want to read any story I had to tell. My material hadn't found me.

When I had finished my studies in England there was no home in India to go back to. After a spell of depressing unemployment my father had found a job as an immigrant engineer in Iran. The rented house in the narrow lanes of a casbah in Isphahan was now 'home'. Or it was England and the challenge of writing something that someone would want to read? I chose London and took a job as a school teacher because a friend advised me to 'go to the Inner London Education Authority, they take anybody!'

Before I got employment as a teacher I drifted, doing odd jobs, washing dishes, painting houses, selling the occasional article to journalist agencies. The anonymity of this life was on the one hand exhilarating, a freedom from all bonds of social responsibility and a temptation to live in a totally 'existential' mode, imitating Jean Genet or characters in Camus for kicks, and on the other a condition of total powerlessness. It was not that I was kicked in the head every day by racist mobs, though it did happen once or twice, nor that white people spat on you in public, but more the fact that you didn't exist as a social entity in the fabric of Britain. You were nobody.

Politics is the pursuit of dignity. I signed up. I had been a member of a very close-knit Indian Workers' Association in the Midlands and now I signed up to the secretive and serious cabal called the Black Panther Movement.

Despite being called a Movement, it hadn't thought very hard about where it was going. It spent a lot of time on 'discipline' which could mean anything from not being late for the six or seven weekly 'collective' meetings or initiating agitational activity in the Leninist mould—printing a paper, selling it at tube stations and street markets, waiting for the contradictions of racist bourgeois society to catch up with it. The group grew without direction even though there were clear tendencies emerging within it. Some of the members wanted to turn the young immigrant organisation, mostly Afro-Caribbean with a smattering of smart Asians, into a Baden-Powell troop, helping old ladies with their housing and shopping. Others wanted to turn to undeclared and sinister purposes bordering on imitation of the Irish Republican Army's robbing of banks, planting of bombs and arms practice. I belonged to the soft faction which started a literary group to read our poems to each other, canvassed for there to be a regular paper to be written and printed by ourselves and for 'organisational work' in the immigrant communities.

There were other groups of blacks with the same dilemmas at the time. It was a game with several serious consequences. People fought the police, they were tried for agitation, for conspiracy, for riot, for bodily harm, grievous and aggravated. Some went to jail, some went mad. The flat in which I lived was fire-bombed one dawn and I jumped from the second floor window, with any cover I could grab as I suffocated, onto the exploded glass on the pavement. Par for the course.

I began teaching in schools to earn some money and was immediately drawn to the challenge of it. The schools that would employ me had a vast number of black children and they didn't quite know what to do with them. I didn't know either but was determined to find out in my first few hours facing a class. To not do so would be to invite destruction. They were naughty children, bewildered in the main by the process of liberal schooling. They expected either a tight slap or they expected to get away with it and hone their skills of defiance against the will and prepared tasks of the teacher.

The 'Movement' published an amateur paper called *Freedom News*. In the interests of proletarianism, a few of us swallowed our literary education and pride and contributed whole-heartedly to what we knew in our heart of hearts was a poor cousin of Lenin's *Iskra* and a tatty version of the professional hippy newspapers of the sixties and early seventies. But there was nothing else. There was no other rag or bag which represented the voice of angry or posturing immigrants.

For *Freedom News* each week, or whenever it emerged, I wrote an anonymous 'story' about life in a tough multiracial London school. An editor working at a publishing house, a young white man with some sympathy for left-wing causes, used to buy the newspaper from the pavement sellers and read the pieces from the chalk zoo. He enterprisingly sought me out.

The 'comrades' who sold the newspapers were conspiratorially reluctant to relay to him the name of the author of the pieces. He may after all be a secret police agent or a member of the CIA.

Martin Pick, after an abortive foray into the wrong 'bad' school— he was guessing and chose the one with the naughtiest reputation– found me and offered me my first writing contract for a book of short stories.

Britain was ready for 'multicultural' writing before it existed.

The demand for it came with unbearably ponderous baggage. If young black and brown people could see themselves in stories it would build their confidence in their identity. It was deemed psychologically traumatic for the black and brown readers of Britain to not recognise themselves in books and turn page after page to imagine white men being heroic and white women being beautiful. These pseudo-political considerations are of course garbage, but into such a pool of expectation I cast my first stories. Macmillan published *East End At Your Feet* and the editors immediately began talking about a second book and a third.

There was no way that the money being offered for these stories, novels or memoirs would have kept me alive. I had to continue teaching, but there was no shortage of demand for such writing.

The Americans had fielded a genre of 'black' writing in the sixties, shifting the pendulum from James Baldwin's pensées to the radical, mother-fucking rhetoric of Eldridge Cleaver, Bobby Seale and George Jackson. These rebel writers, following Malcolm X, gave a white American readership the opportunity to expiate the discomfort and guilt of race in the USA by doing no more than buying a book and talking about it at dinner parties.

In Britain there was no race war. Some of the rhetoric and a few of the confidence tricks of such a war had crossed the Atlantic and a petty imitative game had started and petered out. A con man calling himself Michael X wrote his own autobiography full of fantasy and mendacious claims. As a 'writer' and revolutionary he had certainly found his material—bullying rhetoric which was the written equivalent for white readers of being whipped for a fee in Bayswater. He came to a sad end, running from himself and his discovered frauds to Trinidad where he murdered a few people, among them a British woman with aristocratic connections who had followed him there to live on his 'commune'. When the bodies of his victims were discovered he fled to Guyana and was captured deep in the savannah, defeated and played out. They hanged him and even as they did, his supporters in England appealed for mercy for this 'writer' and 'victim of racism'.

Finding a voice is inseparable from finding an audience. And yet once I had found a particular audience through four or five books whose stories came from the new ghettos, the frightened communities, I wanted to put a distance between the sympathy of this audience and myself. The sympathy had turned sour, become perverse. It was making its own demands and there were other writers expanding into the vacuum with autobiographical hard luck stories.

Winning sympathy for oneself through writing defeats the ironical object of writing. Gaining the reader's sympathy for one's characters, good ones and bad ones, as perhaps Dickens does, and George Eliot, Tolstoy, D.H. Lawrence and Joseph Conrad do, is a better way to write. It's braver, and riskier to sympathise with the nasty, to turn away from the easy target. 'Truth can never be told so as to be understood, and not be believ'd.'—William Blake

Ved Mehta

Naturalized Citizen No. 984–5165

One fresh autumn day, I present myself with two witnesses at the New York offices of the United States Immigration and Naturalization Service, at 20 West Broadway, to be examined under oath on a petition which I am about to file. A rather stylish-looking young man, who introduces himself as Seth Roberts, an attorney for the Service, ushers the three of us into his room and calls on us to raise our right hands and swear to tell the whole truth and nothing but the truth. We do. Mr Roberts asks the witnesses to wait in an outer office. 'We will now go through your petition—No. 832653—so that you can confirm your written statements under oath,' he says to me. 'Please be as direct as possible. Remember, you are under oath.'

I slip into the compliant role of one who is known only by his serial numbers, and give more or less the same old answers to more or less the same old questions that the men of the Service have been putting to me since I first came to America, in August of 1949. I keep my thoughts about who I am and why I want to become an American to myself.

'What is your name?' he asks, rather formally.

'Ved Parkash Mehta,' I respond.

'Where do you live?'

'1010 Fifth Avenue, in New York City.'

'Have you ever used any other names?'

This essay is taken from *A Ved Mehta Reader*, published by Yale University Press, New Haven, 1998.

'No.'

'When and where were you born?'

'I was born on March 21, 1934, in Lahore, in British India.'

'What is your marital status?'

'Single.'

'What is your present occupation?'

'Writer.'

'Your sex is . . .'

'Male.' The ritual has its absurd side.

'When were you lawfully admitted to the United States as a permanent resident?'

'December 3, 1964.'

'How long have you resided continuously in the United States?'

I embark on the complicated answer I have given in my petition—that I have lived in America almost twice as long as in the country of my birth, and the reasons—but Mr Roberts interrupts me, telling me helpfully that all I need to say is 'Ditto.'

'For the past five years you have been present in the United States for an aggregate period of . . . ' he intones.

'Fifty-two months.'

'Do you plan to reside permanently in the United States?'

'Yes, I do.'

Questions about my parents, my American employers, my other American residences, my foreign travels, my travelling companions, my willingness to fight in the American armed forces follow quickly. Then, abruptly, my examiner slows down and, with a grave air, reads out from my petition, 'The law provides that you may not be regarded as qualified for naturalization under certain conditions: if you knowingly committed certain offenses or crimes, even though you may not have been arrested therefore. Have you ever, in or outside the United States, knowingly committed any crime? Just answer "Yes" or "No".'

'No.'

'Or been arrested, charged, indicted, convicted, fined, or imprisoned for breaking or violating any law or ordinance, including traffic regulations?'

'No, never.'

'You need only answer "Yes" or "No".'

Now he comes to my present and past membership in or affiliation with organizations, associations, funds, foundations, parties, clubs, societies, and similar groups in the United States and in other countries. He examines me closely about each group that I have listed, and at one point solemnly asks, 'Is this Century Club, this Century Association, a subversive organization?'

Next come the clinchers.

'Are you now, or have you ever, in the United States or in any other place, been a member of, or in any other way connected or associated with, the Communist Party?'

'No.'

'Have you ever knowingly aided or supported the Communist Party, direct or indirectly, through another organization, group, or person?'

'No.'

'Do you now or have you ever advocated, taught, believed in, or knowingly supported or furthered the interests of Communism?'

'No.'

'Have you borne any hereditary title, or have you been of any order of nobility in any foreign state?'

The question, on various applications and petitions, has always interested me, making me wonder if loyalty to a title, class, or caste could be considered as subversive as loyalty to the Communist Party. In any case, I don't have any titles. I do belong to the Kshatriya, or warrior and ruling, caste of the Hindus. But all he wants is a 'Yes' or a 'No'.

'Have you ever been a patient in an institution or been treated anywhere else for a mental or nervous illness or disorder?'

It occurs to me to wonder if psychoanalysis would be considered such treatment, and I put the question to Mr Roberts.

'No,' he says, and he adds, a little flippantly, 'That's just arty.'

Now come a few relatively simple questions on the order of 'Have you ever claimed in writing, or in any other way, to be a United States citizen?' And then he says, 'The law further provides that you may not be regarded as qualified for naturalization if, at any time during the period for which you are required to prove good moral character, you believed in polygamy, or have been a polygamist. Have you?'

'No.'

'If you have committed adultery. Have you?'

Such questions seem to be an invasion of privacy, and yet they appear on all the applications and examinations for would-be legal aliens or immigrants or naturalized citizens. I've always wondered what people who have never been here and have no knowledge of the country make of the adultery question, for instance. Do they imagine that there are no adulterers here and Americans don't want to start anything new—or that there are already too many adulterers and they don't want any more? But then, of course, adultery is considered a crime.

'No,' I reply.

'If you have profited by the immoral earnings of ladies.'

'No.'

'If you have knowingly, for gain, encouraged or helped an alien to enter the United States illegally. Have you?'

'No.'

'If you have trafficked in or profited by the sale or use of narcotics or marijuana. Have you?'

'No.'

'I'm sure you haven't been a drunkard.'

I shake my head.

'Do you live alone?'

'Yes.'

'Congratulations! You have passed your moral examination.'

I stand up, relieved, but sit down again immediately, remembering that I still have to pass an examination in American history and the Constitution.

'What is the highest court in the land? . . . How many states are there in the United States? . . . What happens if the President dies? . . . Do you believe in the Constitution and form of government of the United States? . . . That's all . . . . Sign here . . . . And here.' It is strange that this examination is so perfunctory when the moral examination was so lengthy.

Mr Roberts ushers me out and closets himself with my witnesses—first one, then the other—to check up on me and my answers. Finally, all smiles, he conducts the three of us into the office of the supervisory attorney of the Citizenship Section, a kindly elderly man, who has a hefty file open in front of him. Mr Roberts hands him my signed and attested papers, and the supervisory attorney adds them to the file, shuffling papers of many colors and sizes. 'You have a big file,' he remarks.

In an adjacent room, a woman with a Spanish accent is being put through her catechism. She seems to be on the verge of hysteria.

'Will you fight for this country?'

'I never fighting. You ask my neighbors. Never fighting.'

'The question is,' the attorney patiently says, 'if someone attacked this country, would you take up arms to protect the country?'

'I no understand.'

'You know what a bad man is?'

'Yes.'

'Would you stop a bad man doing bad things to America?'

'Yes,' the woman says in delight.

'You've passed,' says the attorney in the adjacent room.

I have a sudden sense of déjà vu as many similar scenes from my own past rush through my mind.

The supervisory attorney is shaking my hand and saying, 'Good luck in court. The judge puts on quite a show when he swears in new citizens.'

I first started dreaming of leaving India and coming to the United States when I was five years old and my father sent me to an American missionary boarding school in Bombay, eight hundred and fifty miles away from our home, in Lahore. My father had studied in the West and was a doctor and a government servant. He was so fair-skinned and spoke English so fluently that our servants said he could easily pass for an Englishman. He sported a bowler hat, carried a walking stick, was an avid tennis and bridge player, and was one of the first Indians to be accepted into British clubs. I wanted to grow up to be like him. Soon after I arrived at the boarding school, my father entered into correspondence with one of the missionaries there, Mrs G. Ross Thomas. He had learned that she would soon be returning to America, and he commissioned her to take me with her and enroll me in a good New England school. It was Mrs Thomas who gave me my first few lessons in English, and I was soon able to write letters home in

English. They were all more or less the same: 'My dear Mummy and Daddy, how are you? I'm quite well and happy. Thank you. Your loving son, Vedi.' Actually, I was often sick and miserable, but I didn't know how to say that in English.

Mrs Thomas used to tell me stories about America. I got the impression that no one in America ever told a lie, or stole, or cheated, or needed to be washed. The passengers who rode American trams were so honest that they didn't even use tickets—they just dropped the fare in a piggy bank for the driver to collect when he was ready. There were no newspaper sellers there—just a big newspaper stand with a big hat in front, and people were trusted to pick up the newspaper they wanted and pay for it by dropping change in the hat. At street corners, there were electronic policemen who stopped the traffic and waved it on. They had no whistles or guns—just lights—but the drivers always obeyed. I remember I once asked Mrs Thomas who did the dirty jobs in America, and she said there was no dirt there. That night, I dreamed that I was turned away at the gates of America because I wasn't clean enough. The Americans had found out that I liked to play in the mud. After I woke up, I began dreading that they would also find out about the tin of sweets: when the school matron was out making her rounds, I would steal into her room, climb onto her dressing table, take a big tin down from a shelf, pry open the top with her comb, and help myself to a fistful of lemon drops and sticky orange sweets. One day, after I had been at the school for a couple of years, Mrs Thomas did not appear. The matron told me that Mrs Thomas had left because a war had broken out in America (it was just after Pearl Harbor), and that for the time being America was not open to foreigners like me.

It was not until some seven years later, when I was fourteen or fifteen, that I finally began making serious preparations to go to America as a student. I first had to see an Indian doctor in New Delhi, to get a medical examination for a 4-E, or student, visa. He gave me a complete going over, which took several visits. He inspected my scalp, my gums, my nails, and my feet, checked me for amoebic dysentery, gave me a Wasserman test, took a chest X-ray, and immunized me against smallpox, typhoid, and cholera. He then handed me the record of all this in a folder and sent me over to the American Embassy to get my visa. As I sat waiting to see the consul in charge, I had visions of America as the one clean, rich, healthful haven in a poverty-stricken, disease-ridden world. I couldn't get over the idea that all the people in the country—even servants—would speak English, wear shoes, live in their own houses, and ride around in their own motorcars. My English had not made much progress since Mrs Thomas left, and, according to a test I had taken some time earlier at the American Embassy, I had a vocabulary of only a few hundred words. But I found myself looking forward to the day when I would take out my first 'date,' talk to her in fluent English, take her to a drive-in movie theatre showing 'Forever Amber,' and spend the time kissing. My reverie was abruptly interrupted: I was being summoned into the consul's office. The consul started off by lecturing me. He said that I was very lucky to have been certified by a trustworthy Indian doctor as a fit applicant for America. He said that Indian doctors as a breed were known to be susceptible to string-pulling, blandishments, and bribery, and that there were plenty of opportunities for succumbing to such inducements. There were more 'go-getting' Indians all the time, and they would stop at nothing to get themselves across to what the consul called 'God's country'. In fact, he said, if America were to throw open its doors to all comers, hundreds of millions of Indians would migrate there and settle over the land like a plague of frogs. The consul issued me a 4-E, and informed me that it was valid only for a period of twelve months, that if I intended to stay longer I would have to apply for a year's extension, and that if I happened to leave the United States at any time before my 4-E expired I would be forced to reapply for it and to take all the medical tests over again. I was so excited I wanted to touch his feet, but instead I thanked him stiffly, as I imagined that my father and his English friends would have done.

I felt no qualms about saying goodbye to India and having to make do in America from one extension of my visa to the next, for I was already accustomed to migration: a couple of years earlier, I had lost my bicycle, my Meccano sets, my books, my carpentry tools, along with my childhood, in Lahore, when it became part of the new nation of Pakistan, and my family and I, leaving our house and abandoning all our belongings and savings, had to flee for our lives. We were now living in newly independent India as members of a floating population of eight million Hindu and Sikh refugees. I felt that I would be no more a stranger in America than I was in independent India.

I spent my first three years in America as a student in a small boarding school in Little Rock, Arkansas—the only school in America that would take me, with my meagre knowledge of English. (At the start, I was still apt to confuse 'chicken' with 'kitchen', and say, 'Please get me kitchen from the chicken.') The school, it turned out, had never had a student from another state, let alone another country. In fact, much to my surprise, it was an all-white school, and my fellow-students didn't know what to make of me; they seemed to think I was as exotic as a Kalahari Bushman. The girls I tried to persuade to be my dates politely turned me down. They viewed me with curiosity but no romantic interest. I myself felt anything but exotic—even though, every year, to get my 4-E extended, I had to reduce my American experiences to cold forms and send them off to Washington. I also had to go down to the local post office every January and reduce my life to a United States Department of Justice Alien Address Report Card, which, in compliance with a certain law—Section 265, 8 U.S.C. 1305—I would mail to the United States Immigration and Naturalization Service, Alien Address Report Processing Center, in Rockville, Maryland. My father had once told me that foreigners were liable to be stopped and required to show their passports, so I made sure that I had mine in my pocket whenever I left the school grounds. For a time, I even developed a nervous habit of tapping my pocket any time I heard footsteps behind me, expecting a policeman to call out 'Halt!'

I took refuge from omnipresent authorities and policemen—and also from the elusive dates and curious students, who were as alien to me as I was to them—in the enveloping walls of the school library, where I set about struggling with Chaucer, Shakespeare, Milton, Johnson, Pope, Byron, and Joyce. I was obliged to compress into my three Arkansas high-school years twelve years of American schooling, feeling all the while like a tadpole washed ashore who had to learn quickly to become a frog—or perhaps even a prince, without ever being kissed by the storybook princess.

With my Arkansas diploma in my suitcase, I headed west to college in southern California, the promised land within the promised land—only to discover, to my dismay, that although I now had at my command a sizable English vocabulary, few people there could understand my Arkansas drawl. To clear up my pronunciation, I launched a self-improvement campaign, American style, and soon became a gung-ho Californian.

During my four years as an undergraduate in California, I made many friends. I remember that one of them used to try to tempt me to sneak across the Mexican border to Tijuana to take in a game of jai alai, but I never went, because I still feared the footsteps of the law—although I had long since come to realize that they weren't always following me. I knew that I could travel anywhere within the country, however, and began planning to go to New England to find out what a Connecticut Yankee might be like. But, as it happened, from California I proceeded to England, to continue my studies. When I arrived at London's Heathrow Airport, I was exhilarated to discover that, as a subject of the British Commonwealth, I was allowed to whiz through Customs and Immigration while 'foreigners' impatiently waited in line.

In my ten years in the West—I had spent seven years in America, and I spent three more in England without being able to go home— I became more and more Indian even as I became more and more Western. I would lecture girls—I had no special difficulty getting dates now—on the fecklessness and folly of romantic love, and the wisdom and constancy of arranged marriages. India became a little island in my head, where I could go and speak Punjabi and act like a Punjabi. I would put old 78-r.p.m. records of Indian film music on the gramophone and daydream about an arranged marriage to a beautiful Punjabi girl in a rustling silk sari, the two of us sitting and eating pomegranate seeds in a hill station with fog closing in.

After England, I did return to India, in the summer of 1959, only to have my fantasies about my homeland rudely dispelled. Everywhere I went, I was assaulted by putrid odors rising from the streets, by flies relentlessly swarming around my face, by the octopuslike hands of a hundred scabrous, deformed beggars clutching at my hands and feet; I could not escape the choking dust, the still, oppressive air, and the incinerating heat of a summer in India. I found myself thinking of the cool, gracious comfort of a Southern mansion in Nashville— airconditioned from wine cellar to maids' quarters—where I had once been the guest of a college friend whose father made his money by importing Indian jute. I found myself longing for the ice-cold pitchers of freshly made mint julep waiting at poolside for the swimmers. My time in the Western world had spoiled me, and I could now hardly wait to get back. Fortunately, I had arranged to take up graduate studies in New England in the autumn, so I lost no time in getting to the American Embassy in New Delhi to pick up a visa. I submitted to another round of medical and bureaucratic scrutiny, and, at the end of it, again received a single-entry, twelve-month 4-E. It contained no record of my ever having been in America before.

Back in America, I completed my studies, and thereby outgrew my 4-E. I began earning my keep by writing, and was informed by the immigration authorities that I must apply for a change of status and obtain a new kind of visa if I wanted to stay on in the country. They suggested an H-1, which was granted to actors, opera singers, and other artists of 'distinguished merit and ability' who wanted to live and work in America for a time. I applied for and eventually got my H-1, and became part of a community of legal aliens and expatriates in New York who had come from many lands and spoke many languages. They were all experts on the advantages and disadvantages of the different kinds of visas. None of them held the H-1 in very high esteem, because every time an H-1 left the country he had to satisfy American officials abroad that he was still an artist of 'distinguished merit and ability' before he was allowed back in. Most of them aspired to the 'green card'—the popular name for the alien-registration-receipt card, which shows its holder to be a 'permanent resident', eligible to apply for naturalization after five years of residence.

After I had been an H-1 for several years, I got tired of proving to the far-flung, intercontinental network of American immigration officials that I was an artist of 'distinguished merit and ability,' and decided to plump for a green card. As a 'permanent resident', I would be able to leave and re-enter the country as I pleased and still continue to be an Indian national. I could live and work here as long as I chose without ever committing myself to becoming an American citizen. (Charlie Chaplin had done it for forty years.) But I could not work for the federal government, although I could be drafted into the armed forces and was obliged, if I was called upon, to fight for the United

States. Moreover, if I happened to stay away for more than a year I would risk losing my new status altogether. I decided to take the limitations along with the privileges, and put in for a green card. I was required to submit numerous documents, including yet another medical report, to swear that I had never been a Communist, never committed adultery, never trafficked in drugs or women, and so on—to answer, in fact, the same questions that the immigration authorities had been asking me on and off for years—and to produce not, this time, proof of 'distinguished merit and ability' but 'Evidence of Exceptional Ability in the Sciences or the Arts'. I was obliged to retain counsel to help me find my way through the labyrinthine procedures; to remain in the country for a year while my petition was being reviewed; and, ultimately, to appear, with my counsel, as a petitioner at a hearing in the New York offices of the Immigration and Naturalization Service. My petition was granted, and I received my green card shortly thereafter. It was a bit like a credit card—a laminated affair bearing my photograph, my alien-registration number (A7 828 521), and a list of the conditions governing the card's use. For the next ten years, I possessed dual status as an Indian national and a permanent resident of the United States. Then, one day in September of 1974, I decided to give up my nationality and become a naturalized American.

As a first step, I was required to file another petition with the Immigration and Naturalization Service. The application form was a forbidding document. It read, in part:

1. You must send with this application the following items (1), (2), (3), and (4):

(1) Photographs of your Face . . . .

(2) Fingerprint Chart—A record of your fingerprints, taken on the fingerprint chart furnished you with this application . . . .

(3) Biographic Information—Complete every item in the Biographic Information form furnished you with this application and sign your name on the line provided . . . .

(4) US Military Service—If your application is based on your military service, obtain and complete Form N-126 . . . .

2. Fee . . . .

3. Alien Registration Receipt Card . . . .

4. Date of Arrival . . . .

5. Examination on Government and Literacy—Every person applying for naturalization must show that he or she has a knowledge and understanding of the history, principles, and form of government of the United States. THERE IS NO EXEMPTION FROM THIS REQUIREMENT, and you will therefore be examined on these subjects when you appear before the examiner with your witnesses. The application details the various public school classes, correspondence courses, and prescribed text-books available for the purpose. You will also be examined on your ability to read, write, and speak simple English . . . .

My oral examination by Mr Roberts was one of the requirements for filing this petition. I came away from that examination feeling agitated and ambivalent. By then, I had no particular reservations about renouncing my Indian nationality. My last visit home, in the summer of 1974, had left me profoundly depressed. I felt out of sympathy with the government—the main industry in the country. Its policies bore no relation to the humane ideals of independent India's founding father, Mahatma Gandhi, and were directed more and more toward serving the interests of the middle-class politicians, who had little use for the poor and even less use for civil liberties. Yet I knew I could not become a nationalist reformer, so committed to the land of my birth that I would stay and fight the system from within. I was a writer, not a politician, and, because I had by now spent the better part of my life outside India, I could not think of myself as altogether Indian. I was a member of a worldwide community of expatriates, whose thoughts, feelings, and dreams were a jumble of languages and countries. Now that the moment for becoming an American was at hand, however, I found myself wondering, as I often had before, whether I should not perhaps become an Englishman instead. After all, I had grown up under the British raj and, in a sense, like an English child: playing in my father's clubs, going to a hill station every summer, studying in an English university. But then I had also grown up at the time of India's struggle for independence: going to political rallies, hearing about the heroic deeds of Gandhi and Nehru, spurning many British ways as I grew older—even while I embraced others—and all the time trying to overcome the apish habits of the colonial mind. Could I ever really feel comfortable calling myself an Englishman? Even if I somehow managed to swim against the historical tide, would I not, as a 'brown gentleman', always feel inferior to 'real' Englishmen? As before, I knew the answers to these questions. I also knew that it was the momentousness of the step that made me dwell on them once more.

On the other hand, it had not been a simple matter to decide to become an American. Few of those who are born and die citizens of the same country, I reflected, ever consciously commit themselves to their own citizenship, but we who change citizenship by choice must commit ourselves voluntarily to the history and the heritage, the pride and the guilt of our adopted homeland. So, just as America, through its Immigration Service, had once again examined my personal history, I once again began conducting a private investigation of America. For instance, there was the matter of the Vietnam War. I had been against it even at the beginning, and had wondered then whether I should become an American while it was still continuing, especially since I had been born an Asian. What if America thought one day that India was going Communist? Would Americans go to fight there also? Then there was the bomb. No Asian can forget that it was dropped only on an Asian country. And there was the issue of Richard Nixon and Watergate. Was America headed toward totalitarianism? I had reached my decision to file my citizenship papers only after President Nixon resigned. Fighting, though, was still going on in Vietnam. Later, I had taken note of the problem of the Vietnam refugees, whom some Americans were trying to send back to their homeland. I was an Asian about to become an American citizen at a time when many of my countrymen-to-be wanted to expel a group of Asians. But I found reassurance on this point in the remarks of another countryman-to-be—George Meany, the president of the AFL–CIO. 'Frankly, I think the attitude of people who say, "Dump these refugees in the sea; send them back"—to me it's really deplorable,' he said to the press. 'We are a nation of immigrants. And to turn our backs on people who are fleeing from oppression, fleeing for their lives, and say to them that we are going to dump them in the sea—this to me is about as contrary to American tradition as anything that I ever heard of . . . . We [would be] denying the history, the background, the traditions of this country as a haven for the oppressed.'

Since the American Revolution, the United States had indeed admitted, altogether, almost fifty million immigrants and refugees, yet the history of immigration was not as uniformly noble and honorable as Meany made out. The inscription on the Statue of Liberty reads, 'Send these, the homeless, tempest-tossed to me. I lift my lamp beside the golden door.' Until 1921, when a quota system was established, the golden door was open to just about all comers, with the exception of Asians, who were subjected to special restrictions. More than a million and a half poor refugees from the Irish potato famines of the eighteen-forties were among those who readily found a home here. Then, in 1924—the year the Statue of Liberty was designated a national monument—Congress passed a permanent-quota law. It was the first piece of major immigration legislation and, as amended in 1929, rigidly regulated the flow of immigrants to this country for thirty-six years. It fixed the total number of immigrants at a hundred and fifty thousand a year, and apportioned to each country a quota of two per cent of the number of that country's ex-nationals living in the United States at the time of the 1920 census. Immigrants from the countries of northwestern Europe were, in effect, granted an allotment of more than seventy per cent of this so-called national origins quota, while those from the countries of Southern and Eastern Europe, who had been streaming across the Atlantic since the beginning of the century in ever-increasing numbers and were by then thought to threaten the predominantly Anglo-Saxon complexion of the country, were allotted proportionately low quotas. Historians usually give at least two reasons for the passage of the 1924 act: fear of political radicals, and the influence of contemporary theories of eugenics. At the time, there was much left-wing agitation in the trade unions, and part of the blame for this was placed on Poles, Italians, and Jews; Poles, Italians, and Jews also became targets of eugenicists, who called them 'undesirables' and 'biological degenerates', and whose ideas loomed prominently in the congressional hearings and debates on the bill. The eugenicists tried to show through laborious research that the human race was divided into superior and inferior types, and that America had been built up by the superior types, who originated in Northern Europe, and was now being inundated by the inferior types, who originated in Southern and Eastern Europe. The eugenicists claimed that the inferior types were genetically incapable of performing 'decently' in a free, democratic society, and that they or their children would end up by destroying it. One eugenicist—Dr Harry H. Laughlin, of the Eugenics Record Office of the Carnegie Institution, of Washington—made several studies for the House of Representatives Committee on Immigration and Naturalization as its 'expert eugenics agent.' He testified before the committee on 'the relative degeneracies of the several types in each of the nativity groups in the population of the United States', and produced an array of charts and statistics to prove that the more recent immigrants to the United States tended to have a greater incidence of insanity, feeble-mindedness, crime, delinquency, leprosy, epilepsy, tuberculosis, blindness, deafness, deformity, and dependency than their predecessors. At one point, he said:

> America is a melting pot . . . . If we succeed for many centuries as a great nation, historians should be able to look back and always find us exercising great vigor and vigilance in sorting out the immigrant material which applied for admission to the United States. We should be found admitting only sound metals, and those in such proportions as would alloy well with the earlier American elements already in the crucible, and should take great care to reject and eliminate all dross. The American bell should vibrate without discord.

Some of the more fanatical eugenicists actually suggested that the 'undesirables' already in the country could be humanely got rid of with carbonic-acid gas. The amended 1924 act continued to govern United States immigration policy until 1965, when the national-origins quota system was finally abolished in favor of a two-part system—one part, for the Western Hemisphere, based on the principle of first-come-first-served, and the other, for the Eastern Hemisphere, on a principle of giving preference to the skilled and the talented. This system, however, continued to regulate the number of immigrants, allotting a hundred and twenty thousand a year to the Western Hemisphere and a hundred and seventy thousand (with a maximum of twenty thousand from a single country) to the Eastern Hemisphere. (Since 1965, the total number of immigrants has actually been about four hundred thousand a year, because parents, spouses, and children of American citizens are permitted to immigrate freely.) All the immigrants who had been admitted since 1924, however, constituted a very much smaller proportion of the population, which numbered well over two hundred million, than immigrants did in 1900, when the population was only seventy-six million. But these more recent immigrants, because they tended to congregate in the big cities, seemed much more numerous than they actually were.

It would have been easier, I concluded, to have been born an American in the first place, but since I hadn't, I reasoned, it was easier to make a commitment to America than to most other countries I could think of. Coming from India, I could never become casual about America's open society, with its political freedoms and its economic opportunities. I felt that America, as a 'young' country, was less weighed down by history, tradition, class, and caste, which block change in India and in so many other countries. Since America was also an affluent country, the distinctions of class and privilege that did exist here had less importance than they had elsewhere. And, since America was a big country, it could more easily assimilate immigrants. I happened to share some of these feelings and thoughts with an American friend who moves in psychoanalytic circles. 'Rationalizations,' he said. 'Of course, you may consciously think that you are becoming an American citizen because Nixon resigned or because of what Meany said or because of your expectations of America, but, unconsciously, you are trying to reject part of your childhood.'

Two weeks after my naturalization hearing with Mr Roberts, I receive a letter from the Department of Justice—of which the Immigration and Naturalization Service is a part—summoning me to court, but I am to appear only if in the interval between my naturalization examination and my designated day in court I have not been absent from America; have not been married, divorced, separated, or widowed; have not joined the Communist Party; have not claimed exemption from military service or changed my willingness to bear arms for America; and have not committed crimes of any sort or acted immorally in any of a number of possible ways. Although I had a moment of alarm a few days back, when I received another communication from the Department of Justice, requiring me to be fingerprinted immediately, because 'fingerprints previously submitted are unsatisfactory,' I decide that the latest letter is a good omen, since I know I have kept clean.

And so I duly appear at the imposing United States Courthouse in Foley Square. It is 8 a.m., and with me are two old friends who are part of my 'family' here now—a young woman whose ancestors probably came over on the Mayflower, and a young playwright with an ability to bring a sense of occasion to any event. I take my place in a line of would-be citizens from all over the world—on this particular day, West Indians predominate—who are waiting patiently in the corridor outside the courtroom. I wonder about their many countries and their pasts, and what prompted them to converge here today, but there is already something American-seeming about them; they could be a crowd on the platform of a New York subway station. We are called one by one to a desk in the courtroom, where we have to sign our certificates of naturalization and surrender our precious green cards. Many people resist giving up their green cards, especially when they are told that they will have to wait a couple of weeks for their certificates of naturalization to be processed and sent to them by registered mail. I, too, feel a pang of reluctance as I realize that I will be in limbo—no longer a permanent resident and not yet stamped and certified a naturalized citizen. There are about a hundred and fifty of us in line, and it is about two hours before all of us are through with the signing. Those of us who arrived first take seats in the courtroom with our friends and families; the rest have to stand. Everyone has been given a welcome kit, and we pass the time looking it over. There is an individual letter from the President, a thumbnail history of the Pledge of Allegiance and the music to which it is set, and a souvenir booklet containing the text not only of the Constitution and the Declaration of Independence but also of 'Rules for Saluting the Flag', 'The Star-Spangled Banner', 'American's Creed', 'The Meaning of American Citizenship', 'The Duties of a Citizen', 'Rights and Privileges of a Citizen', 'The Five Qualities of the Good Citizen', and the song 'America', along with some blank pages for 'Memories of the Occasion'.

Shortly, United States District Judge Inzer B. Wyatt, a heavyset elderly man in black robes, comes in and takes his place on the bench, and the hubbub in the room subsides. The court clerk, a big, Italian-looking man, perhaps a naturalized citizen himself, calls out the names of a few people who have not shown up to sign their certificates—he mispronounces even the simplest foreign names—and then says, 'In the matter of Audor Baeder.'

The young attorney of my naturalization examination steps up and says, 'Good morning, Your Honor. My name is Seth Roberts, and I represent the Immigration and Naturalization Service. In the matter of Petition No. 822451'—apparently, the number refers to the person called Audor Baeder—'petitioner was a member of a proscribed organization while he lived in Hungary. After thorough investigation, the Immigration and Naturalization Service found him eligible for naturalization. I therefore move that his petition be granted.'

'All right. This will be received, and on your statement the recommendation is accepted and the motion granted,' the Judge says, in a big, deep voice.

'In the matter of Mui Lin Ho,' the court clerk says.

Mr Roberts then explains to the judge that Petition No. 825497 failed her immigration examination, because she was unable to speak, read, or write English, and that she did not appear for re-examination when summoned on three separate occasions. He therefore moves that her petition be denied for lack of prosecution. He makes half a dozen similar motions to deny petitions, and the Judge accordingly denies all of them.

'Your Honor, I now wish to present one hundred and forty-eight petitioners for naturalization,' Mr Roberts goes on. 'These petitioners have all been examined, and it was determined that they all are eligible for naturalization. I therefore move that their petitions be granted and that they be admitted to citizenship upon taking the Oath of Allegiance. Of these petitioners, twenty-five have requested a change of name. The Service has no objection . . . and I therefore move that their requests for change of name be granted.' He further moves that two of the petitioners be exempted from taking the Oath of Allegiance, on the ground that they are under fourteen years of age, and that a third petitioner be administered a modified Oath, on the ground that he is a conscientious objector.

The judge, who sounds as though he were from the South, grants these motions, too. He seems to have a little flair: he manages to vary the routine replies, branching out from 'The motion is granted' into

'So granted,' 'I think I have no choice but to grant the motion,' and the like.

The court clerk tells all of us petitioners who are to take the Oath to stand and raise our right hands.

'I hereby declare . . .' the clerk says, leading us.

'I hereby declare . . .' we respond.

'On oath . . .'

'On oath . . .'

And so he takes us through the Oath of Allegiance: '. . . that I absolutely and entirely renounce and abjure all allegiance and fidelity to any foreign prince, potentate, state, or sovereignty, of whom or which I have heretofore been a subject or citizen; that I will support and defend the Constitution and laws of the United States of America against all enemies, foreign and domestic; that I will bear true faith and allegiance to the same; that I will bear arms on behalf of the United States when required by the law; that I will perform noncombatant service in the armed forces of the United States when required by the law; that I will perform work of national importance under civilian direction when required by the law; and that I take this obligation freely without any mental reservation or purpose of evasion: So help me God.' (The conscientious objector is later led through the Oath by himself, and does not have to agree to bear arms.)

I repeat the powerful, magisterial words of the Oath and am moved by them. At the same time, I feel that I can never altogether renounce the country in which I was born: never renounce my mother tongue, my Indian childhood, my Indian memories, my brown skin and distinctive Indian features—never entirely stop being an Indian.

'Fellow-citizens,' the Judge is saying, in his sonorous voice. It feels strange to be so addressed. 'It is a privilege to be the first to address as fellow-citizens those who have been admitted this morning to citizenship by the Oath just taken. It is also a pleasure and a privilege to welcome on this solemn and significant occasion the relatives and friends of our new fellow-citizens. I am sorry that our accommodations in this, the largest courtroom in the building, are not sufficient to provide a place to sit down for all of you. I observe with regret that some of you are obliged to stand. But my remarks will be sufficiently, short so that you may be consoled by the thought that you will not

be obliged to stand very long. First, you have all been found to be of
good moral character. That means a lot. It means that you have, to this
point in your lives, conducted yourselves uprightly and honorably.
And, second, you have been found to be attached to the principles of
the Constitution of the United States and well disposed toward the
good order and happiness of the United States, and that is important
also. We like to think on occasions such as this, when we are reminded
of it, that this is a government of law, a government by consent of the
governed, a government of, by, and for the people. When you go to
Washington—and I hope that all of you will someday go to our capital
city—I ask you to look at the beautiful white marble building of the
Supreme Court of the United States, and, above the towering but
graceful columns at the front of the building, read what is written
there in only four words: "EQUAL JUSTICE UNDER LAW". . . . You
have doubtless noticed the discussion and debate in the last few days
over the refugees who have come to our country from Vietnam. It
would be inappropriate for us to consider the merits of that debate
and discussion. But you must have been struck, as most of us have
been struck, by how often in this debate and discussion it is said we
are a nation of immigrants. And it is true. We are a nation of immigrants
such as you ladies and gentlemen who are before me as new citizens
this morning. The United States has absorbed the strengths of all its
immigrants, and this fusion of many different strains and virtues has
greatly contributed to our present strength, and it has also greatly—
indeed, essentially—helped to make democracy work . . . We will ask
the clerk to lead us all in a Pledge of Allegiance to the flag.'

I am touched by the Judge's words. Yet I wonder what he can know
of the inner life of each of the immigrants sitting or standing before
him, of what each must have gone through to arrive in his courtroom,
and of what each must be feeling about this occasion at this moment.
As we rise to say the Pledge of Allegiance, my young woman friend
kisses me, and my writer friend shakes my hand and says,
'Congratulations. This is great. My grandfather, too, was an immigrant.
He was from Poland.'

As I pledge allegiance, I recall coming across some words of Learned
Hand, who, swearing in another generation of citizens some thirty
years ago in New York's Central Park, said:

We have some right to consider ourselves a picked group, a group of those who had the courage to break from the past and brave the dangers and the loneliness of a strange land. What was the object that nerved us, or those who went before us, to this choice? We sought liberty, freedom from oppression, freedom from want, freedom to be ourselves . . . Liberty lies in the hearts of men and women; when it dies there, no constitution, no law, no court can save it . . . The spirit of liberty is the spirit of Him who, near two thousand years ago, taught mankind that lesson it has never learned, but has never quite forgotten; that there may be a kingdom where the least shall be heard and considered side by side with the greatest. And now, in that spirit, that spirit of an America which has never been, and which may never be; nay, which never will be except as the conscience and courage of Americans create it; yet in the spirit of that America which lies hidden in some form in the aspirations of us all . . . in that spirit of liberty and of America I ask you to rise and with me pledge our faith in the glorious destiny of our beloved country.

After the ceremony, I go with my friends to have lunch at Fraunces Tavern, the inn dating from American Revolutionary times. We feast on New England chowder, spicy shrimp curry à l'Indienne with Major Grey chutney, and a bottle of Pouilly-Fuissé. 'I am no longer a guest in your country,' I say. 'Now I, too, can sign petitions and march and protest in public when I feel like it, without worrying about abusing hospitality.' One of my friends suggests that I wait until I have my certificate of naturalization in hand.

A couple of weeks later, my certificate of naturalization—No. 9845165—arrives in the mail. It looks very much like an AT&T bond, except that it has my photograph on it, and it reads, in part:

Petition No. 832653
Alien Registration No. A7 828 521.

Be it known that at a term of the District Court of The United States held pursuant to law at New York City . . . the Court having found that VED PARKASH MEHTA . . . intends to reside permanently in the United States (when so required by the Naturalization Laws of the United States), had in all other respects complied with the applicable provisions of such naturalization laws, and was entitled to be admitted to citizenship, thereupon ordered that such person be and (s)he was admitted as a citizen of the United States of America.

After using the certificate to obtain an American passport, I put it in my safe-deposit box, which I felt was an appropriate place for the deed to Learned Hand's hidden kingdom.

A.K. RAMANUJAN

Some Indian Uses of History on a Rainy Day

I

Madras,
      1965, and rain.
Head clerks from city banks
curse, batter, elbow
in vain the patchwork gangs
of coolies in their scramble
for the single seat
in the seventh bus:

they tell each other how
Old King Harsha's men
beat soft gongs
to stand a crowd of ten
thousand monks
in a queue, to give them
and the single visiting Chinaman
a hundred pieces of gold,
a pearl, and a length of cloth;

This poem is taken from *Selected Poems*, published by Oxford University Press India, New Delhi, 1976.

so, miss another bus, the eighth,
and begin to walk, for King Harsha's
monks had nothing but their own two feet.

2

Fulbright Indians, tiepins of ivory,
colour cameras for eyes, stand every July
in Egypt among camels,

faces pressed against the past
as against museum glass,
tongue tasting dust,
amazed at pyramidfuls
of mummies swathed in millennia,
of Calicut muslin.

3

1935. Professor of Sanskrit
on cultural exchange;
                        passing through; lost
in Berlin rain; reduced
to a literal, turbanned child,
spelling German signs on door, bus, and shop,
trying to guess *go* from *stop*;
                        desperate
for a way of telling apart
a familiar street from a strange,
or east
from west at night,
the brown dog that barks
from the brown dog that doesn't,

memorizing a foreign paradigm
of lanterns, landmarks,
a gothic lotus on the iron gate;

suddenly comes home
in English, gesture, and Sanskrit,
assimilating
                the swastika
on the neighbour's arm
in that roaring bus from a grey
nowhere to a green.

V.S. NAIPAUL

The Ceremony of Farewell

In my late thirties the dream of disappointment and exhaustion had been the dream of the exploding head: the dream of a noise in my head so loud and long that I felt with the brain that survived that the brain could not survive; that this was death. Now, in my early fifties, after my illness, after I had left the manor cottage and put an end to that section of my life, I began to be awakened by thoughts of death, the end of things; and sometimes not even by thoughts so specific, not even by fear rational or fantastic, but by a great melancholy. This melancholy penetrated my mind while I slept; and then, when I awakened in response to its prompting, I was so poisoned by it, made so much not a doer (as men must be, every day of their lives), that it took the best part of the day to shake it off. And that wasted or dark day added to the gloom preparing for the night.

I had thought for years about a book like *The Enigma of Arrival*. The Mediterranean fantasy that had come to me a day or so after I had arrived in the valley—the story of the traveler, the strange city, the spent life—had been modified over the years. The fantasy and the ancient-world setting had been dropped. The story had become more personal: my journey, the writer's journey, the writer defined by his writing discoveries, his ways of seeing, rather than by his personal adventures, writer and man separating at the beginning of the journey and coming together again in a second life just before the end.

This extract is taken from *The Enigma of Arrival*, published by Vintage Books, New York, 1987.

My theme, the narrative to carry it, my characters—for some years I felt they were sitting on my shoulder, waiting to declare themselves and to possess me. But it was only out of this new awareness of death that I began at last to write. Death was the motif; it had perhaps been the motif all along. Death and the way of handling it—that was the motif of the story of Jack.

It was a journalistic assignment that got me started. In August 1984 I had gone to the Republican Convention in Dallas for the *New York Review of Books*. I had found nothing to write about. The occasion was overstaged, scripted in advance, and in itself empty; and I was oppressed by the idea of thousands of busy journalists simply finding new words for stories that had in effect been already written for them. It was only back in Wiltshire, away from the oppressiveness and handouts of the convention center, that I began to be able to acknowledge what I had responded to: not the formal, staged occasion, but the things around the occasion. And suddenly, where there had been nothing to write about, there was a great deal: the experience of a week, all new, which, without the writing, would have vanished and been lost to me. With the discovery of that experience came the language and the tone appropriate to the experience.

It was out of that excitement, finding experience where I thought there had been nothing, and out of that reawakened delight in language, that I began immediately afterwards to write my book. I let my hand move. I wrote the first pages of many different books; stopped, started again. Then from apparently far away the memory of Jack, peripheral to my life, came to me; and with it the conviction that to write of Jack was the best way to get started, to summon up the material of *The Enigma of Arrival*, to set the scene and themes, to indicate the time-spread of the book I was intending to write. For some weeks I made many starts, allowing my hand to run; starting at different points.

There were interruptions. A bad molar. It was extracted—quite suddenly, it seemed. An extraction wasn't at all what I had been expecting when I went to the dentist, who usually saved things; and there came to me a sense of decay, uneffaceable, as I felt, through the anesthetic, the dentist's strong fingers pushing at the painless tooth; a sense of death. Two days later, with a salty rawness in my mouth, there was a prize-giving lunch for an old writer friend in London—

this occasion mixed up with looking for a new flat in London, and the special gloom of looking at old flats, other lives, other views. Then Mrs Gandhi was shot dead by her bodyguard in Delhi. Immediately after that there was a visit to Germany for my publisher in that country: the shock of East Berlin, still in parts destroyed after forty years, seedlings grown into trees high on the wrecked masonry of some buildings, a vision of a world undoing itself: new to me: I should have gone long before to look. On the morning of my last day in Germany, in West Berlin, I went to the Egyptian Museum. I returned to Wiltshire to the news that my younger sister, Sati, had had a brain hemorrhage in Trinidad that day: just at the time I was leaving the museum. She was in a coma; she was not to recover. For more than thirty years, since the death of my father in 1953, I had lived without grief. I took the news coldly, therefore; then I had hiccups; then I became concerned.

When I had left Trinidad in 1950, when the little Pan American Airways System plane had taken me away, Sati was seven weeks short of her sixteenth birthday. When I next saw her and heard her voice she was nearly twenty-two, and married. Trinidad had since become almost an imaginary place for me; but she had lived all her life there, apart from short holidays abroad. She had lived through my father's illness in 1952 and death in 1953; the political changes, the racial politics from 1956, the dangers of the street, the near-revolution and anarchy of 1970. She had also lived through the oil boom; she had known ease for many years; she could think of her life as a success.

Three days after her death, at the time she was being cremated in Trinidad, I spread her photographs in front of me on the low coffee table in the sitting room of my new house in Wiltshire. I had been intending for years to sort out these family photographs, put them in albums. There had always seemed to be time. In these photographs, while she had lived, I had not noticed her age. Now I saw that many of the photographs—her little honeymoon snapshots especially—were of a young girl with slender arms. That girl was now someone whose life had been lived; death had, painfully, touched these snapshots with youth. I looked at the pictures I had laid out and thought about Sati harder than I had ever thought about her. After thirty-five or forty minutes—the cremation going on in Trinidad, as I thought—I felt purged. I had had no rules to follow; but I felt I had done the right thing. I had concentrated on that person, that life, that unique character; I had honored the person who had lived.

Two days later I went to Trinidad. The family had wanted me to be with them. My brother had gone on the day of our sister's cremation. He had arrived six hours after the cremation; he had asked then to be taken to the cremation site. My elder sister drove him. It was night; the pyre after six hours was still glowing. My brother walked up alone to the glow, and my sister, from the car, watched him looking at the glowing pyre.

Two weeks before, my brother had been in Delhi for Mrs Gandhi's cremation. In London, then, he had written a major article; now, that writing barely finished, he had come to Trinidad. Modern airplanes had made these big journeys possible; had exposed him to these deaths. In 1950, when I left Trinidad, airplane travel was still unusual. To go abroad could be to fracture one's life: it was six years before I saw or heard members of my family again; I lost six years of their lives. There was no question, in 1953, when my father died, of my returning home. My brother it was, then aged eight, who performed and witnessed the terrible final rites of cremation. The event marked him. That death and cremation were his private wound. And now there was this cremation of his sister: still a pyre and aglow after his airplane flight from London. Soon an airplane took him back to London. And airplanes took other members of the family to other places.

I stayed on in Trinidad for the religious ceremony that took place some days later and was complementary to the cremation. Sati had not been religious; like my father, she had had no feeling for ritual.

But at her death her family wished to have all the Hindu rites performed for her, to leave nothing undone.

The pundit, a big man, was late for this ceremony. He had been late for the cremation as well, I had heard. He said something now about being busy and harassed, about misreading his watch; and settled down to his duties. The materials he needed were ready for him. A shallow earth altar had been laid out on a board on the terrazzo of Sati's veranda. To me the ritual in this setting—the suburban house and garden, the suburban street—was new and strange. My memories were old; I associated this kind of ritual with more country scenes.

The pundit in his silk tunic sat cross-legged on one side of the altar. Sati's younger son sat facing him on the other side. Sati's son was in jeans and jumper—and this informality of dress was also new to me. The earth rites the pundit began to perform on the veranda appeared to mimic Sati's cremation; but these rites suggested fertility and growth rather than the returning of the body by way of fire to the earth, the elements. Sacrifice and feeding—that was the theme. Always, in Aryan scriptures, this emphasis on sacrifice!

There was a complicated physical side to the ceremony, as with so many Hindu ceremonies: knowing where on the altar to put the sacrificial flowers, knowing how to sing the verses and when, knowing how and when and where to pour various substances: the whole mechanical side of priesthood. The pundit led Sati's son through the complications, telling him what offerings to make to the sacred fire, to say *swa-ha* when the offerings were placed with a downward gesture of the fingers, to say *shruddha* when the fingers were flicked back from the open palm to scatter the offering onto the fire.

Then the pundit began to do a little more. He became aware of the people on the veranda who were his audience and he began, while instructing Sati's son, partly to address us in a general religious way. He told Sati's son it was necessary for him to cool his lusts; he began to use texts and words that might have served on many other solemn occasions. Something else was new to me: the pundit was being 'ecumenical' in a way he wouldn't have been when I was a child, equating Hinduism—speculative, many-sided, with animist roots—with the revealed faiths of Christianity and Mohammedanism. Indeed the pundit said at one stage—talking indirectly to us as though we were a Trinidad public assembly and many of us were of other faiths—that the Gita was like the Koran and the Bible. It was the pundit's way of saying that we too had a Book; it was his way, in a changed Trinidad, of defending our faith and ways.

In spite of his jeans, Sati's son was serious. He was humble in the presence of the pundit, not a formally educated man, for whom—on another day, in another setting—he might have had little time. He seemed to be looking to the pundit for consolation, a support greater than the support of ritual. He was listening to everything the pundit said. The pundit, continuing to add moral and religious teaching to the complicated ritual he was performing with earth and flowers and flour and clarified butter and milk, said that our past lives dictated the present. Sati's son asked in what way Sati's past had dictated the cruelty of her death. The pundit didn't answer. But Sati's son, if he had been more of a Hindu, if he had more of a Hindu cast of mind, would have understood the idea of karma, and wouldn't have asked the question. He would have yielded to the mystery of the ritual and accepted the pundit's words as part of the ritual.

The pundit went on with the physical side of his business. That was what people looked to a pundit for; that was what they wished to see carried out as correctly as possible—this pressing together of balls of rice and then of balls of earth, this arranging of flowers and pouring of milk on heaps of this and that, this constant feeding of the sacred fire.

Afterwards the pundit had lunch. In the old days he would have eaten sitting cross-legged on blankets or flour sacks or sugar sacks spread on the top with cotton. He would have been carefully fed and constantly waited on. Now—sumptuously served, but all at once—he ate sitting at a table in the veranda. He ate by himself. He ate great quantities of food, using his hands as he had used them earlier with the earth and the rice and the sacrificial offerings of the earth altar.

Sati's husband and her son sat with the pundit while he ate. They asked him, while he ate, and as though being a pundit he knew, what were the chances of an afterlife for Sati. It was not strictly a Hindu question; and it sounded strange, after the rite we had witnessed.

Sati's husband said, 'I would like to see her again.' His voice sounded whole; but there were tears in his eyes.

The pundit didn't give a straight reply. The Hindu idea of reincarnation, the idea of men being released from the cycle of rebirth after a series of good lives—if that was in the pundit's mind, it would have been too hard to pass on to people who were so grief-stricken.

Sati's son asked, 'Will she come back?'

Sati's husband asked, 'Will we be together again?'

The pundit said, 'But you wouldn't know it is her.'

It was the pundit's interpretation of the idea of reincarnation. And it was no comfort at all. It reduced Sati's husband to despair.

I asked to see the Gita the pundit had been using during the ceremony. It was from a South Indian press. After each verse there was an English translation. The pundit, in between his ritual doings and his chanting of a few well-known Sanskrit verses, had made use of the English translations from this Gita.

The pundit said he gave away Gitas. Then, using an ecumenical word (as I thought), he said he 'shared' Gitas. People gave him Gitas; he gave people Gitas. One devout man bought Gitas a dozen at a time and passed them on to him; he passed them on to others.

And then, his pundit's duties done, his lunch over, the pundit became social, expansive, as, from my childhood, I had known pundits to be when they had done their duties.

He began to tell a story. I couldn't understand the story. An important man in the community had asked him one day: 'What do you think is the best Hindu scripture?' He, the pundit, had replied, 'The Gita.' The man had then said to somebody else present, 'He says the Gita is the best Hindu scripture.' There should have been more to the story. But there was no more. Either that was the end of the story so far as the pundit was concerned—a mentioning of famous local people, a bearing of witness in the presence of famous people. Or he had found that the story was leading him into areas he didn't want to go to; or he had forgotten the point of the story. Or in fact the point was as he had made it: that he thought the Gita was the most important Hindu scripture. (Though, at the very end, just before he left, he said that his pundit's duties left him little time to read the Gita.)

And to add to the intellectual randomness of the occasion, the pundit began without prompting to speak, and with passion, about the internal Hindu controversy between the conservatives, on whose side the pundit was, and the reformists, who the pundit thought were hypocrites. I had thought that this issue had died in Trinidad fifty years before and was part almost of our pastoral past, when the life of our community was more self-contained. I could not imagine it surviving racial politics and the stresses of independence. But the pundit spoke of it as something that still mattered.

The pundit was a relation, a first cousin. And the great irony—or appropriateness—of the situation was like this. I had discovered through the adventure of writing—curiosity and knowledge feeding off one another, committing one not only to travel but also to different explorations of the past—I had discovered that my father had been intended by his grandmother and mother to be a pundit. My father hadn't become a pundit. He had instead become a journalist; and his literary ambitions had seeded the literary ambitions of his two sons. But it was because of his family's wish to make him a pundit that my father, in circumstances of desperate poverty before the first war, had been given an education; while my father's brother had been sent to the fields as a child to work for eight cents a day. The two branches of the family had ever after divided. My father's brother had made himself into a small cane farmer; at the end of his life he was far better off than my journalist father had been at the end of his. My father had died in 1953, impoverished after a long illness; my father's brother had contributed to the cremation expenses. But there had been little contact between our families. Physically, even, we were different. We (except for my brother) were small people; my father's brother's sons were six-footers. And now, after the ups and downs of fortune, a pundit had arisen in the family; and this pundit, the heavy six-footer who had performed the rites on my sister's veranda, came from my father's brother's family. This pundit had served my father's family, attended at the first death among my father's children. Some of the pundit's demeanor would have been explained by the family relationship, his wish to assert himself among us.

The other, internal irony was that my father, though devoted to Hindu speculative thought, had disliked ritual and had always, even in the 1920s, belonged to the reformist group the pundit didn't care for and dismissed now as hypocrites. My sister Sati had no liking for ritual either. But at her death there was in her family a wish to give sanctity to the occasion, a wish for old rites, for things that were felt specifically to represent us and our past. So the pundit had been called in; and on the terrazzo floor of my sister's veranda symbolical ceremonies had been played out on an earth altar, laid with a miniature pyre of fragrant pitch pine and flowers and sugar which, when soaked with clarified butter and set alight, made a sweet caramel smell.

We were immemorially people of the countryside, far from the courts of princes, living according to rituals we didn't always understand and yet were unwilling to dishonor because that would cut us off from the past, the sacred earth, the gods. Those earth rites went back far. They would always have been partly mysterious. But we couldn't surrender to them now. We had become self-aware. Forty years before, we would not have been so self-aware. We would have accepted; we would have felt ourselves to be more whole, more in tune with the land and the spirit of the earth.

It would have been easier to accept, too, because forty years before, it would have been all so much poorer, so much closer to the Indian past: houses, roads, vehicles, clothes. Now money had touched us all—like a branch of a tree or a twig dipped in gold, according to some designer's extravagant whim, and made to keep the shape of the twig or the leaf. Generations of a new kind of education had separated us from our past; and travel; and history. And the money that had come to our island, from oil and natural gas.

That money, that unexpected bounty, had ravaged and remade the landscape where we had had our beginnings in the New World. When I was a child the hills of the Northern Range which I looked at when I traveled up to Port of Spain on the ten-mile-an-hour train were bare—primary forest still in parts. Now halfway up those hills there were the huts and shacks of illegal immigrants from the other islands. Small islands surrounded by sea: plantation barracoons, slavery and Africa quarantined and festering together for two centuries: immigrants from those islands had altered our landscape, our population, our mood.

Where there had been swamp at the foot of the Northern Range, with mud huts with earthen walls that showed the damp halfway up, there was now a landscape of Holland: acres upon acres of vegetable plots, the ridges and furrows and irrigation canals straight. Sugarcane as a crop had ceased to be important. None of the Indian villages were like villages I had known. No narrow roads; no dark, overhanging trees; no huts; no earth yards with hibiscus hedges; no ceremonial lighting of lamps, no play of shadows on the wall; no cooking of food in half-walled verandas, no leaping firelight; no flowers along gutters or ditches where frogs croaked the night away. But highways and clover-shaped exits and direction boards: a wooded land laid bare, its secrets opened up.

We had made ourselves anew. The world we found ourselves in— the suburban houses, with gardens, where my sister's farewell ceremony had taken place—was one we had partly made ourselves, and had longed for, when we had longed for money and the end of distress; we couldn't go back. There was no ship of antique shape now to take us back. We had come out of the nightmare; and there was nowhere else to go.

The pundit gave his last instructions. One brass plate with consecrated food was to be placed somewhere; another plate of food was to be cast into the river that had borne away her ashes: a final offering. Then, a big man dressed in cream-colored silk, the silk showing the heaviness above his waist, the pundit got in his car and drove away. (Such memories I had of Sunday visits, holiday excursions, with my father to his family house—my father's brother's house—forty years and more before: flat sugarcane fields all around, grass tracks between the fields, scattered huts and houses on stilts and tall pillars, dimly lit at night, animals in some yards, bonfires of grass to keep away mosquitoes, grocery shops with pitched corrugated-iron roofs, and silence.)

A visitor, an old man, a distant relation of my sister's husband, began—perhaps because of the ceremonies that had taken place—to talk of our past, and of the difference between us, originally from the Gangetic plain, immigrants to the New World since 1845, and the other Indians in other parts of the island, especially in the villages to the northwest of Port of Spain.

This man said, 'Those other people haven't been here since 1845, you know. They've been here long, long before. You've heard about Columbus? Well, Queen Isabella opened this place up to everybody, provided they was Catholics. And that was when the French came in. They was Catholics, you see. Now, you hear about a place in India called Pondicherry? That was the French place in India, and that was where they bring over those Indians near Port of Spain from. So those Indian people up in Boissière and places like that, they not like us—they've been here four, five hundred years.'

History! He had run together the events of 1498, when Columbus had discovered the island for Queen Isabella on his third voyage; 1784, when the Spanish authorities, after three hundred years of neglect, and out of a wish to protect their empire, opened up the island to Catholic immigration, giving preference and free land to people who could bring in slaves; and 1845, when the British, ten years after slavery had been abolished in the British Empire, began to bring in Indians from India to work the land. He had created a composite history. But it was enough for him. Men need history; it helps them to have an idea of who they are. But history, like sanctity, can reside in the heart; it is enough that there is something there.

Our sacred world—the sanctities that had been handed down to us as children by our families, the sacred places of our childhood, sacred because we had seen them as children and had filled them with wonder, places doubly and trebly sacred to me because far away in England I had lived in them imaginatively over many books and had in my fantasy set in those places the very beginning of things, had constructed out of them a fantasy of home, though I was to learn that the ground was bloody, that there had been aboriginal people there once, who had been killed or made to die away—our sacred world had vanished. Every generation now was to take us further away from those sanctities. But we remade the world for ourselves; every generation does that, as we found when we came together for the death of this sister and felt the need to honor and remember. It forced us to look on death. It forced me to face the death I had been contemplating at night, in my sleep; it fitted a real grief where melancholy had created a vacancy, as if to prepare me for the moment. It showed me life and man as the mystery, the true religion of men, the grief and the glory. And that was when, faced with a real death, and with this new wonder about men, I laid aside my drafts and hesitations and began to write very fast about Jack and his garden.

October 1984–April 1986

SALMAN RUSHDIE

Eating the Eggs of Love

I first read Omar Cabezas' book, *Fire from the Mountain*, on the plane from London to Managua. (The English title is much less evocative, though shorter, than the Spanish, which translates literally as 'The mountain is something more than a great expanse of green'.) Now, on the road to Matagalpa, travelling towards the mountains about which he'd written, I dipped into it again. Even in English, without any of the 'Nica' slang that had helped make it the most successful book in the new Nicaragua (its sales were close to 70,000 copies), it was an enjoyable and evocative memoir of 'Skinny' Cabezas' recruitment by the FSLN, his early work for the Frente in León, and his journey up into the mountains to become one of the early guerrillas. Cabezas managed to communicate the terrible difficulty of life in the mountains, which were a hell of mud, jungle and disease (although one of his fans, a young Nicaraguan soldier, thought he had failed to make it sound bad enough because he had made it too funny). But for Cabezas the mountains were something more than a great expanse of unpleasantness. He turned them into a mythic, archetypal force, The Mountain, because during the Somoza period hope lay there. The Mountain was where the Frente guerrillas were; it was the source from which, one day, the revolution would come. And it did.

Nowadays, when the Contra emerged from The Mountain to terrorize the *campesinos*, it must have felt like a violation; like, perhaps, the desecration of a shrine.

This extract is taken from *The Jaguar Smile*, published by Henry Holt, New York, 1997.

Forested mesas flanked the road; ahead, the multiform mountains, conical, twisted, sinuous, closed the horizon. Cattle and dogs shared the road with cars, refusing to acknowledge the supremacy of the automobile. When the trucks came, however, everybody got out of the way fast.

Tall cacti by the roadside. Women in fatigues carried rifles over their shoulders, holding them by the barrels. Moss hung in clumps from the trees and even from the telephone wires. Children pushed wooden wheelbarrows full of wood. And then, as we neared Matagalpa, we came upon a sombre procession carrying a distressingly small box: a child's funeral. I saw three in the next two days.

It had begun to rain.

I was pleased to be getting out of Managua again. Matagalpa felt like a real town, with its church-dominated squares, its town centre. It was like returning to normal, but normality here was of a violent, exceptional type. The buildings were full of bullet-holes left over from the insurrection years, and dominating the town was a high, ugly tower which was all that remained of the National Guard's hated command post. After the revolution, the people had demolished the Guardia's fearsome redoubt.

The ice cream shop had no ice cream because of the shortages. In the toy shop the evidence of poverty was everywhere; the best toys on display were primitive 'cars' made out of a couple of bits of wood nailed together and painted, with Coca-Cola bottle tops for hubcaps. There were, interestingly, a number of mixed-business stores known as 'Egyptian shops', boasting such names as 'Armando Mustafa' or 'Manolo Saleh', selling haberdashery, a few clothes, some toiletries, a variety of basic household items—shampoo, buckets, safety-pins, mirrors, balls. I remembered the Street of Turks in *One Hundred Years of Solitude*. In Matagalpa, Macondo did not seem so very far away.

The faces in the Egyptian shops didn't look particularly Egyptian but then neither did the orientally named Moisès Hassan, mayor of Managua. In the cafés, I met some more familiar faces. Posters of the Pope and of Cardinal Obando y Bravo were everywhere, the Cardinal's scarlet robes rendered pale pink by the passage of time. Sandinistas, unconcerned about the company they were keeping, drank hideously sweetened fruit squashes, including the bright purple *pitahaya*, and munched on the glutinous kiwi-like *mamón,* beneath the watching Cardinal. I talked to Carlos Paladino, who worked in the office of the *delegado* or governor of Matagalpa province, about the regional resettlement policy.

Large areas of the mountainous and densely jungled war zone in the north-eastern part of Jinotega province had been evacuated, and the population relocated in southern Jinotega, and Matagalpa province, too. It had been a 'military decision', that is, compulsory. The army had been having trouble fighting the Contra because the scattered civilian population kept getting in the way. The people were also in danger from the Contra, who regularly kidnapped *campesinos,* or forced them to grow food for the counter-revolutionary soldiers, or killed them. But wasn't it also true, I asked, that many people in those areas sympathized with the Contra? Yes, Paladino replied, some men had gone to join them, leaving many women with children behind. The large number of one-parent families of this type had become quite a problem. But in many cases the men would return, disillusioned after a time. The government offered a complete amnesty for any *campesino* who returned in this way. 'We don't hold them responsible,' Paladino said. 'We know how much pressure the Contra can exert.'

Resettlement brought problems. Apart from the single-parent issue– how were these women to be involved in production when they had to look after their children?—the resettled northerners were people who were utterly unfamiliar with living in communities. They had led isolated lives in jungle clearings. Now they were being put into clusters of houses built close together. Their animals strayed into their neighbours' yards. Their children fought. They hated it. Many of them were racially different from the local *mestizos:* they were Amerindians, Miskito or Sumo, with their own languages, their own culture, and they felt colonized. 'We made many mistakes,' Carlos Paladino admitted.

The plan was to have child-care centres at each co-operative settlement, but so far they had only been able to put in eleven such centres in over fifty communities. They had also managed to build some schools, some health-care facilities; but there was still a lot of resentment in the air.

The lack of resources (and, no doubt, the haste with which the operation had been carried out) had meant that in some places the authorities had been unable to provide the resettled families with completed houses. The 'roof only policy', as it was called, offered the uprooted families exactly what its name suggested: a roof. They had to build the walls out of whatever materials they could find. It was not a policy calculated to win hearts and minds. But, Paladino insisted, the state was doing its best, and international volunteer brigades and relief agencies were helping, too. There were even some unexpected individual initiatives. 'A few days after the mine blew up and killed the thirty-two bus passengers,' he told me, 'a tall, fair-haired man appeared in the area, a foreigner, with fifteen hundred dollars to give away. He was just carrying it in his pockets, and looking for the families of the thirty-two, to hand over the money. It was his savings.'

Progress remained slow. 'It isn't easy,' Carlos said. 'Eight new communities have been destroyed by the Contra in the last six months. Hundreds of *campesinos* die in the attacks every year.'

Our best defence is the people in arms. 'The people are more and more able to undertake their own defence. In November 1985 at Santa Rosa hundreds of Contra were killed. Since then, in the attacks on the new co-operatives, hundreds more.'

But the Contra were doing damage, all right. For a country in Nicaragua's position, the loss of an estimated forty per cent of the harvest was a crippling blow.

When Carlos Paladino came to work in Matagalpa, he was highly critical of the way the revolution had handled the resettlements, and won the approval of the regional *delegado*, Carlos Zamora, for his new approach. He went into the jungle, with his staff, and lived with the peasants for months, to learn about their way of life and their needs, before attempting any resettlement. This altered the layout of the new settlements, and greatly increased the officials' sensitivity to the people's wishes. Paladino became an expert on Miskito Indian culture, and had started writing about it. In his spare time (!) he was doing a history degree. Not for the first time, I felt awed by the amount people were willing to take on in Nicaragua.

After I'd been talking to him for more than an hour, I discovered that Paladino had been in hospital twenty-four hours earlier, having a .22 bullet removed from his lung. It had been there since before the 'triumph', the result of an accident: he had been shot in training by a careless cadet. He opened his shirt, after I had bullied him to do so, and showed me the scar. It was an inch away from his heart.

I stayed in a wooden chalet in the mountains high above Matagalpa, and that night the *delegado,* Carlos Zamora, and his deputy, Manuel Salvatierra, dropped by to inspect the *escritor hindú.* Zamora was small, slight, moustachioed; Salvatierra of much bigger build. They were old college friends. We sat down to a dinner of beef in hot pepper sauce, squash with melted cheese, and banana chips.

On the 19th, Zamora volunteered, the Contra had moved a thousand men into Jinotega province. Their plan had been to attack one of the two hydro-electric stations and cut the power cable. They had also intended to ambush *campesinos* on their way to Estelí. 'They failed completely,' he said with satisfaction. 'Our intelligence was good enough. But 700 of them are still in the region, still in Nicaragua. The rest have returned to Honduras.'

Salvatierra stressed the Contra's morale problem. 'They're scared of us,' he said. 'Dollars won't help that.'

I changed the subject. Was it true that it cost six head of cattle to get a car serviced? They laughed. 'Or ten hectares of maize,' said Carlos Zamora. So, then, I said, if prices are that high, tell me about corruption. They looked embarrassed, not unexpectedly, but they didn't refuse to answer. Yes, Zamora said, there was, er, some. 'About the car service,' he said. 'You see, a mechanic will tell you that a certain part is unavailable, or can be ordered for crazy money, but he just happens to have one at home, for a price.'

The black market accounted for maybe forty per cent of the country's liquid assets. 'Anything that can be bought can be sold down the road for more,' Salvatierra said. 'There is an old woman who hitchhikes from Matagalpa to León every day, with a suitcase full of beans, mangoes and rice. She earns 5000 córdobas a day. I earn about 3000.'

Zamora and Salvatierra had been 'bad students' in Managua when the FSLN recruited them. Zamora's father was a garage mechanic. (I had accidentally hit on the right subject when I talked about servicing motor cars.) 'He wasn't against the revolution but he wasn't for it, either.' I said that it seemed at times that the revolution had been a struggle between the generations—the Frente's '*muchachos*', kids, against

the older generation of Somocistas and cautious, conservative *campesinos.*
No, no, they both hastened to correct me. But the impression stuck.

'How old are you?' I asked them. They giggled prettily.

'Thirty,' Carlos Zamora said. He had fought a revolution and was
the governor of a province, and he was nine years younger than me.

Later, when a little Flor de Caña Extra Seco had loosened things
up, the old stories came out again: of the battle of Pancasàn in 1974,
at which the Sandinistas suffered a bloody defeat, but after which, for
the first time, the *campesinos* came to the Frente and asked for arms, so
that the defeat was a victory, after all, the moment at which the
muchachos and the peasants united; of Julio Buitrago; of the local boy,
Carlos Fonseca, who was born in Matagalpa. Sandino and Fonseca
were both illegitimate, they told me. 'So what's the connection between
bastards and revolutions?' I asked, but they only laughed nervously. It
wasn't done to joke about the saints.

I tried to get them to open up about the period in the '70s during
which the Frente had split into three 'tendencies', after a bitter dispute
about the correct path for the revolution. (The 'proletarian faction',
led by Jaime Wheelock, believed that a long period of work with the
campesinos, to politicize and mobilize them, was the way forward, even
if it took years. The faction that favoured a prolonged guerrilla war,
and based itself in the mountains, included Carlos Fonseca himself;
and the third faction, the *terceristas*, which believed in winning the
support of the middle classes and proceeding by a strategy of large-
scale urban insurrection, was led by Daniel Ortega and his brother.
The factions united, in December 1978, for the final push to victory,
and it was the *tercerista* plan that carried the day.)

Zamora and Salvatierra denied that there had been any internal power
struggles; the division had been tactical and not a real split. 'I've never
heard of a revolution without a power struggle in the leadership,' I said.
'Wasn't it true that Jaime Wheelock was accused of being responsible
for the split? Wasn't it true that Daniel Ortega became President because
the *tercerista* faction won the internal fight?' No, they said, anxiously. Not
at all. 'The directorate has always been very united.'

That simply wasn't true. Where had they spent the insurrection
years, I asked; 'In the cities,' Zamora replied; Salvatierra nodded.
Now I understood: they belonged to the urban-insurrectionist, *tercerista*

faction, the winning team. They didn't want to seem to be gloating over the victory.

To stir things up, I said that the case of Edén Pastora suggested that the divisions were deeper than they cared to admit. After all, Pastora had been a *tercerista* himself, he had been the famous 'Commander Zero', glamorous and dashing, who had led the sensational attack on the Palacio Nacional, taken the entire Somocista Chamber of Deputies hostage, and obtained the release of fifty jailed Sandinistas plus a half-million dollar ransom; and there he was today, in exile in Costa Rica, having tried to lead a counter-revolutionary army of his own . . . He had been defeated by the Sandinistas, but surely his break with the revolution he helped to bring about was significant? There were grins and embarrassed laughs from the *delegado* and his deputy. 'Edén Pastora wanted personal glory,' Salvatierra said. 'He joined the wrong army in the first place.'

The next day I drove up into the north. I knew that the road I was on, the one that went up past Jinotega and headed for Bocay, was the one on which the Contra mine had exploded, killing 'the thirty-two', and even though that had happened a good deal further north than I was going, I felt extremely fearless as we went over the bumps. 'How do you protect the roads?' I asked the army officer who was accompanying me. 'It's impossible to guarantee total safety,' he replied.

'I see,' I said. 'Yes. By the way, how do you know when there's a mine in the road?'

'There's a big bang,' came the straight-faced reply.

My breakfast of rice and beans—'gallo pinto', it was called, 'painted rooster'—began to crow noisily in my stomach.

There were vultures sitting by the roadsides. Low clouds sat amongst the mountains. The road-signs were punctured by bullet-holes. In the jeep, the driver, Danilo, had a radio, or rather a 'REALISTIC sixteen-band scanner', on which he picked up Contra transmissions. We passed co-operatives with resolutely optimistic names: *La Esperanza. La Paz.* The mountains thickened and closed: wars of tree and cloud. There was a flash of electric-blue wings; then, suddenly, a peasant shack surrounded by trees and hedges clipped into cones, domes, rectangles, spheres, all manner of geometric shapes. To be a topiarist in a jungle, I reflected, was to be a truly stubborn human being.

Then there was a tree lying across the road, blocking our way. Was this it? Was this where Contra fiends with machetes between their teeth would burst from the foliage, and goodbye *escritor hindú*?

It was just a tree across the road.

The Enrique Acuña co-operative was named after a local martyr, who had been murdered by a wealthy local landowner after Somoza's fall. (The killer got away, fleeing the country before he could be arrested.) It was a 'CAS', a Cooperativa Agrícola Sandinista, that is, a proper co-op, with all the land held and farmed collectively. Elsewhere, in areas where there had been resistance to the co-operative idea, the government had evolved the 'CCS', the Co-operative of Credits and Services. In a CCS the land was owned and farmed by individuals, and the government's role was limited to supplying them with power, water, health care and distribution facilities. There was no doubt that the *campesinos* were encouraged to adopt the CAS structure, but the existence of the alternative was an indication of the authorities' flexibility; this was not, surely, the way a doctrinaire commune-ist regime would go about its business.

The houses were built on the 'miniskirt' principle: metal roofs stood over walls that were made of concrete up to a height of three feet, and of wood above that height. This had become the *campesinos'* favourite building method. The Contra couldn't set fire to the roofs, or shoot the occupants through the walls while they lay sleeping. The houses were arranged around wide avenues, with plenty of space between them. Pigs were snoozing in the shade. There was a tap with running water, and even a shower. In a ramshackle shed, a playschool was in progress: clapping games and songs. In the next room, there was a baby care centre with instructions for the care and diagnosis of diarrhoea pinned up on the wall, written out and illustrated by the children themselves. The disease was the main child-killer in the rural areas.

All around the co-operative's residential area was a system of trenches. The *campesinos* did guard duty on a rota basis, and many of the men were familiar with the workings of the AK-47 automatic rifle. They were also geniuses with the machete. The *campesino* who had hacked to pieces the tree that had held us up could have shaved you without breaking your skin. Alternatively, he could have sliced you like a loaf.

Last November, the Contra had attacked the Acuña co-operative, by daylight and in force: around 400 of them against thirty-two armed defenders. Arturo, the burly young man who was in charge of the defence committee, told me proudly that they had held out for three hours until help arrived from a neighbouring co-operative. In the end the Contra were beaten off, with thirteen dead and around forty wounded. 'We lost nobody,' Arturo boasted. Since then, the Contra had been seen in the neighbourhood twice, but had not attacked.

A thought occurred to me: if the opposition were correct, and the Sandinistas were so unpopular, how was it that the government could hand out all these guns to the people, and be confident that the weapons would not be turned against them? There wasn't another regime in Central America that would dare to do the same: not Salvador, nor Guatemala, not Honduras, not Costa Rica. While in tyrannical, 'Stalinist' Nicaragua, the government armed the peasantry, and they, in turn, pointed the guns, every one of them, against the counter-revolutionary forces.

Could this mean something?

I got talking to a group of five *campesinos* during their lunch break. They parked their machetes by hacking them into a tree-stump, but brought their AKs along. Did they know anyone who had joined the Contra? They knew of kidnaps, they said. But how about someone who had joined voluntarily? No, they didn't. The people were afraid of the Contra.

One of the *campesinos*, Humberto, a small man with a big-toothed smile, was an *indigène,* but he wasn't sure what sort. He wasn't Miskito or Sumo, he knew that. 'I'm trying to find out what I am.' He had lived in the north, in the area now evacuated. The Contra, he said, had kidnapped him, threatened to kill him, but he had escaped. A while later he heard that they were still after him, and intended to recapture him. 'This time they'd have killed me for sure.' So he was delighted to be resettled. 'It was hard at first, but, for me, it was a blessing.' He sat close to a matchstick-thin man with wiry black hair sticking out sideways from beneath his peaked cap. 'The same happened to me,' this man, Rigoberto, said. 'Just the same story. Me, too.'

Another of the quintet came from a coastal fishing community, where there had been no possibility of getting any land. The other two were locals. 'So do you think of this as your home now?' I asked. 'Or does it seem like just some temporary place?'

Arturo, the defence organiser, answered. 'What do you mean? We've put our sweat into this earth, we've risked our lives for it. We're making our lives here. What do you mean? Of course it's home.'

'It's our first home,' the fisherman, the oldest of the five, at around fifty, said. He was called Horacio, and as I listened to him the penny dropped. What he had said, and what the *indigène* Humberto had told me—'I'm trying to find out what I am'—were both connected to Father Molina's sermon in Riguero, to the idea that one's own country can be a place of exile, can be Egypt, or Babylon. That, in fact, Somocista Nicaragua had literally *not been* these people's home, and that the revolution had really been an act of migration, for the locals as well as the resettled men. They were inventing their country, and, more than that, themselves. It was by belonging here that Humberto might actually discover what he was.

I said, 'You're lucky.' The idea of home had never stopped being a problem for me. They didn't understand that, though, and why should they? Nobody was shooting at me.

The co-operative's day began at five a.m., when the workers assembled to hear the day's work rota from the representatives of the various (annually elected) committees. Then they went home, breakfasted on tortillas and beans, and were in the fields (coffee, rice) at six, working for around eight hours. After work there were adult education classes. Three of the five men I spoke to had learned to write since arriving here—Humberto, he confessed, 'not very well.' The classes went up to the fourth grade.

What did they do for fun? Cockfighting, cards, guitar music, the occasional social call at the neighbouring co-op, the odd trip into Jinotega or Matagalpa, and of course the various fiestas. But they seemed awkward talking about fun. 'In spite of the men lost to the war effort,' Arturo insisted on getting the conversation back to the serious stuff, 'we have kept up our levels of production.'

With the generosity of the poor, they treated me to a delicacy at lunch. I was given an egg and bean soup, the point being that these eggs were the best-tasting, because they had been fertilized. Such eggs were known as 'the eggs of love'. When people had so little, a fertilized hen's egg became a treat.

As I ate my love-eggs, which really did taste good, there were children playing in the shack next door to the kitchen hut. Their playing-cards were made out of rectangles of paper cut out of an old Uncle Scrooge comic book. *Waak! My money! You dratted* . . . Pieces of Huey, Dewey and Louie fled from the rage of the billionaire American duck. While on a radio, I promise, Bruce Springsteen sang '*Born in the USA*'.

The Germàn Pomares field hospital, on the road back to Jinotega, was named after the FSLN leader who had been killed in May 1979, just two months before the 'triumph'. Pomares had been a great influence on Daniel Ortega, and was one of the most popular Sandinista leaders. 'He was so loved,' my interpreter told me, 'that his death wasn't even announced on the news for six months.' I added this to my collection of depressing sentences, alongside the one about the 'cosmetic' nature of press freedom.

At the sentry box at the hospital gate everybody was supposed to hand in their weapons, but our driver, Danilo, hid his pistol under a sweatshirt I'd taken off as the day grew hotter. Stripping in the heat was one thing, but he would have felt underdressed, he agreed when I discovered his deception, without some sort of gun.

The hospital was just two years old. 'We have had to develop it quickly,' said the director, Caldera, an Indian-looking man with a picture of Che, made of tiny shells, hanging on his office wall. 'Never in the history of our nation have we had so many wounded.' The specialist staff were all Cubans. Nicaraguan doctors were gradually being trained to take over, but, at present, simply didn't have the skills required for this kind of surgery.

The average age of the patients was twenty-one. Ten per cent of them were regular soldiers, thirty per cent came from the peasant militias, and no less than sixty per cent were youngsters doing their military service.

'That's astonishing,' I said. 'Why so many military service casualties?' The reason, Caldera said, was that these kids were the main components of the BLI forces, the small commando units that would pursue the Contra deep into the jungle, into The Mountain. Military service in Nicaragua was no joyride.

In recent months, many of the hospital's patients had been mineblast victims, and almost all of these had died. Otherwise the main injuries were from bullet wounds. 'Eighty-three per cent heal completely,' said director Caldera, who knew his statistics. 'Six to seven per cent survive with disabilities.' That left ten per cent. I didn't ask what happened to them.

By chance, I visited the Pomares hospital when there were quite a few empty beds, and very few amputees. Usually, Caldera said, things were different. 'If it was always this way I could write poetry.' Another poet. There was no escape from the fellows.

I asked if they had to import blood. No, he said, the national blood donation programme provided enough. That struck me as fairly remarkable. It was a small country, and it had been losing a lot of blood.

The young men in the wards were all gung-ho, all volubly starry-eyed about the revolution—'Since my injury,' one teenager told me, 'I love this revolutionary process even more'—and all super-keen to return to the fray. I met a nineteen-year-old youth who had been fighting for six years. I met a shamefaced seventeen-year-old who had shot himself accidentally in the foot. I met an eighteen-year-old with wounds all over his body. 'First I was hit in the leg,' he said, 'but I could keep firing. Then the shrapnel, here,' he indicated his bandaged forehead, 'and my vision blurred. I passed out, but only for a moment.' I asked about the alarming gash above his right knee. 'I don't know,' he said. It looked too large to have arrived without being noticed, but he shook his head. 'It's funny, but I just don't know how I got it.'

They were all very young, yet already so familiar with death that they had lost respect for it. That worried me. Then, as I was leaving, I met a young woman in a wheelchair. She had been shot in the groin, and her face was glassy, expressionless. Unlike the boy soldiers, this was someone who knew she'd been shot, and was upset about it.

'And what do you think about the revolution?' I asked her. 'I've got no time for that junk,' she replied.

'Are you against it?'

'Who cares?' she shrugged. 'Maybe. Yes.'

So there were people for whom the violence was too much, and not worth it. But it also mattered that she had been entirely unafraid.

She had been in the presence of several officers of the state, and it hadn't bothered her a bit.

When I was back in my chalet, the mountains looked so peaceful in the evening light that it was hard to believe in the danger they contained. Beauty, in Nicaragua, often contained the beast.

BHARATI MUKHERJEE

Two Ways to Belong in America

This is a tale of two sisters from Calcutta, Mira and Bharati, who have lived in the United States for some thirty-five years, but who find themselves on different sides in the current debate over the status of immigrants. I am an American citizen and she is not. I am moved that thousands of long-term residents are finally taking the oath of citizenship. She is not. Mira arrived in Detroit in 1960 to study child psychology and pre-school education. I followed her a year later to study creative writing at the University of Iowa. When we left India, we were almost identical in appearance and attitude. We dressed alike, in saris; we expressed identical views on politics, social issues, love and marriage in the same Calcutta convent-school accent. We would endure our two years in America, secure our degrees, then return to India to marry the grooms of our father's choosing.

Instead, Mira married an Indian student in 1962 who was getting his business administration degree at Wayne State University. They soon acquired the labour certifications necessary for the green card of hassle-free residence and employment.

Mira still lives in Detroit, works in the Southfield, Michigan, school system, and has become nationally recognized for her contributions in the fields of pre-school education and parent-teacher relationships. After thirty-six years as a legal immigrant in this country, she clings passionately to her Indian citizenship and hopes to go home to India when she retires.

This essay is taken from the *New York Times*, 22 September 1996.

In Iowa City in 1963, I married a fellow student, an American of Canadian parentage. Because of the accident of his North Dakota birth, I bypassed labour-certification requirements and the race-related 'quota' system that favoured the applicant's country of origin over his or her merit. I was prepared for (and even welcomed) the emotional strain that came with marrying outside my ethnic community. In thirty-three years of marriage, we have lived in every part of North America. By choosing a husband who was not my father's selection, I was opting for fluidity, self-invention, blue jeans and T-shirts, and renouncing 3,000 years (at least) of caste-observant, 'pure culture' marriage in the Mukherjee family. My books have often been read as unapologetic (and in some quarters overenthusiastic) texts for cultural and psychological 'mongrelization'. It's a word I celebrate.

Mira and I have stayed sisterly close by phone. In our regular Sunday morning conversations, we are unguardedly affectionate. I am her only blood relative on this continent. We expect to see each other through the looming crises of aging and ill health without being asked. Long before Vice President Gore's 'Citizenship USA' drive, we'd had our polite arguments over the ethics of retaining an overseas citizenship while expecting the permanent protection and economic benefits that come with living and working in America.

Like well-raised sisters, we never said what was really on our minds, but we probably pitied one another. She, for the lack of structure in my life, the erasure of Indianness, the absence of an unvarying daily core. I, for the narrowness of her perspective, her uninvolvement with the mythic depths or the superficial pop culture of this society. But, now, with the apegoating of 'aliens' (documented or illegal) on the increase, and the targeting of long-term legal immigrants like Mira for new scrutiny and new self-consciousness, she and I find ourselves unable to maintain the same polite discretion. We were always unacknowledged adversaries, and we are now, more than ever, sisters.

'I feel used,' Mira raged on the phone the other night. 'I feel manipulated and discarded. This is such an unfair way to treat a person who was invited to stay and work here because of her talent. My employer went to the INS and petitioned for the labour certification. For over thirty years, I've invested my creativity and professional skills into the improvement of this country's pre-school system. I've obeyed all the rules, I've paid my taxes, I love my work, I love my students, I love the friends I've made. How dare America now change its rules in midstream? If America wants to make new rules curtailing benefits of legal immigrants, they should apply only to immigrants who arrive after those rules are already in place.'

To my ears, it sounded like the description of a long-enduring, comfortable yet loveless marriage, without risk or recklessness. Have we the right to demand, and to expect, that we be loved? (That, to me, is the subtext of the arguments by immigration advocates.) My sister is an expatriate, professionally generous and creative, socially courteous and gracious, and that's as far as her Americanization can go. She is here to maintain an identity, not to transform it.

I asked her if she would follow the example of others who have decided to become citizens because of the anti-immigration bills in Congress. And here, she surprised me. 'If America wants to play the manipulative game, I'll play it too,' she snapped. 'I'll become a US citizen for now, then change back to Indian when I'm ready to go home. I feel some kind of irrational attachment to India that I don't to America. Until all this hysteria against legal immigrants, I was totally happy. Having my green card meant I could visit any place in the world I wanted to and then come back to a job that's satisfying and that I do very well.'

In one family, from two sisters alike as peas in a pod, there could not be a wider divergence of immigrant experience. America spoke to me—I married it—I embraced the demotion from expatriate aristocrat to immigrant nobody, surrendering those thousands of years of 'pure culture', the saris, the delightfully accented English. She retained them all. Which of us is the freak?

Mira's voice, I realize, is the voice not just of the immigrant South Asian community but of an immigrant community of the millions who have stayed rooted in one job, one city, one house, one ancestral culture, one cuisine, for the entirety of their productive years. She speaks for greater numbers than I possibly can. Only the fluency of her English and the anger, rather than fear, born of confidence from her education, differentiate her from the seamstresses, the domestics, the technicians, the shop owners, the millions of hard-working but effectively silenced documented immigrants as well as their less fortunate 'illegal' brothers and sisters.

Nearly twenty years ago, when I was living in my husband's ancestral homeland of Canada, I was always well-employed but never allowed to feel part of the local Quebec or larger Canadian society. Then, through a Green Paper that invited a national referendum on the unwanted side effects of 'non-traditional' immigration, the Government officially turned against its immigrant communities, particularly those from South Asia.

I felt then the same sense of betrayal that Mira feels now. I will never forget the pain of that sudden turning, and the casual racist outbursts the Green Paper elicited. That sense of betrayal had its desired effect and drove me, and thousands like me, from the country.

Mira and I differ, however, in the ways in which we hope to interact with the country that we have chosen to live in. She is happier to live in America as expatriate Indian than as an immigrant American. I need to feel like a part of the community I have adopted (as I tried to feel in Canada as well). I need to put roots down, to vote and make the difference that I can. The price that the immigrant willingly pays, and that the exile avoids, is the trauma of self-transformation.

HANIF KUREISHI

Wild Women, Wild Men

When I saw them waiting beside their car, I said, 'You must be freezing.' It was cold and foggy, the first night of winter, and the two women had matching short skirts and skimpy tops; their legs were bare.

'We wear what we like,' Zarina said.

Zarina was the elder of the pair, at twenty-four. For her this wasn't a job; it was an uprising, mutiny. She was the one with the talent for anarchy and unpredictability that made their show so wild. Qumar was nineteen and seemed more tired and wary. The work could disgust her. And unlike Zarina she did not enjoy the opportunity for mischief and disruption. Qumar had run away from home—her father was a barrister—and worked as a stripper on the Soho circuit, pretending to be Spanish. Zarina had worked as a kissogram. Neither had made much money until they identified themselves as Pakistani Muslims who stripped and did a lesbian double-act. They'd discovered a talent and an audience for it.

The atmosphere was febrile and overwrought. The two women's behaviour was a cross between a pop star's and a fugitive's; they were excited by the notoriety, the money and the danger of what they did. They'd been written up in the *Sport* and the *News of the World*. They wanted me and others to write about them. But everything could get out of hand. The danger was real. It gave their lives an edge, but of the two of them only Qumar knew they were doomed. They had

This essay is taken from *Granta 39* (Spring 1992).

excluded themselves from their community and been condemned. And they hadn't found a safe place among other men and women. Zarina's temperament wouldn't allow her to accept this, though she appeared to be the more nervous. Qumar just knew it would end badly but didn't know how to stop it, perhaps because Zarina didn't want it to stop. And Qumar was, I think, in love with Zarina.

We arrived—in Ealing. A frantic Asian man had been waiting in the drive of a house for two and a half hours. 'Follow my car,' he said. We did: Zarina started to panic.

'We're driving into Southall!' she said. Southall is the heart of Southern England's Asian community, and the women had more enemies here than anywhere else. The Muslim butchers of Southall had threatened their lives and, according to Zarina, had recently murdered a Muslim prostitute by hacking her up and letting her bleed to death, halal style. There could be a butcher concealed in the crowd, Zarina said; and we didn't have any security. It was true: in one car there was the driver and me, and in another there was a female Indian journalist, with two slight Pakistani lads who could have been students.

We came to a row of suburban semi-detached houses with gardens: the street was silent, frozen. If only the neighbours knew. We were greeted by a buoyant middle-aged Muslim man with a round, smiling face. He was clearly anxious but relieved to see us, as he had helped to arrange the evening. It was he, presumably, who had extracted the thirty pounds a head, from which he would pay the girls and take his own cut.

He shook our hands and then, when the front door closed behind us, he snatched at Qumar's arse, pulled her towards him and rubbed his crotch against her. She didn't resist or flinch but she did look away, as if wishing she were somewhere else, as if this wasn't her.

The house was not vulgar, only dingy and virtually bare, with white walls, grimy white plastic armchairs, a brown fraying carpet and a wall-mounted gas fire. The ground floor had been knocked into one long, narrow over-lit room. This unelaborated space was where the women would perform. The upstairs rooms were rented to students.

The men, a third of them Sikh and the rest Muslim, had been waiting for hours and had been drinking. But the atmosphere was benign. No one seemed excited as they stood, many of them in suits and ties, eating chicken curry, black peas and rice from plastic plates. There was none of the aggression of the English lad.

Zarina was the first to dance. Her costume was green and gold, with bells strapped to her ankles; she had placed the big tape-player on the floor beside her. If it weren't for the speed of the music and her jerky, almost inelegant movements, we might have been witnessing a cultural event at the Commonwealth Institute. But Zarina was tense, haughty, unsmiling. She feared Southall. The men stood inches from her, leaning against the wall. They could touch her when they wanted to. And from the moment she began they reached out to pinch or stroke her. But they didn't know what Zarina might do in return.

At the end of the room stood a fifty-year-old six-foot Sikh, an ecstatic look on his face, swaying to the music, wiggling his hips at Zarina. Zarina, who was tiny but strong and fast, suddenly ran at the Sikh, threateningly, as if she were going to tackle him. She knocked into him, but he didn't fall, and she then appeared to be climbing up him. She wrestled off his tweed jacket and threw it down. He complied. He was enjoying this. He pulled off his shirt and she dropped to her knees, jerking down his trousers and pants. His stomach fell out of his clothes—suddenly, like a suitcase falling off the top of a wardrobe. The tiny button of his penis shrank. Zarina wrapped her legs around his waist and beat her hands on his shoulders. The Sikh danced, and the others clapped and cheered. Then he plucked off his turban and threw it into the air, a balding man with his few strands of hair drawn into a frizzy bun.

Zarina was then grabbed from behind. It was the mild, buoyant man who had greeted us at the door. He pulled his trousers off and stood in his blue and white spotted boxer shorts. He began to gyrate against Zarina.

And then she was gone, slipping away as if greased from the bottom of the scrum, out of the door and upstairs to Qumar. The music ended, and the big Sikh, still naked, was putting his turban back on. Another Sikh looked at him disapprovingly; a younger one laughed. The men fetched more drinks. (They were pleased and exhilarated, as if they'd survived a fight.) The door-greeter walked around in his shorts and shoes.

After a break, Zarina and Qumar returned for another set, this time in black bra and pants. The music was even faster. I noticed that the door-greeter was in a strange state. He had been relaxed, even a little glazed, but now, as the women danced, he was rigid with excitement, chattering to the man next to him, and then to himself, until finally his words became a kind of chant. 'We are hypocrite Muslims,' he was saying. 'We are hypocrite Muslims,'—again and again, causing the man near him to move away.

Zarina's assault on the Sikh and on some of the other, more reluctant men had broken that line that separated spectator from performer. The men had come to see the women. They hadn't anticipated having their pants pulled around their ankles and their cocks revealed to other men. (But it was Zarina's intention to round on the men, not turn them on—to humiliate and frighten them. This was part of the act.)

The confirmed spectators were now grouped in the kitchen behind a table; the others joined in on the floor. Qumar and Zarina removed their tops. The young and friendly man who owned the house was sitting next to me, exultant. He thought I was the women's manager and he said in my ear: 'They are fantastic, this is out of this world! I have never seen anything like this before—what a beef! Get me two more girls for Wednesday and four for Saturday.' But things were getting out of hand. The centre of the room was starting to resemble a playground fight, a bundle, a children's party. The landlord, panicking, was attempting to separate the men and the two women. He told me to help.

An older man, another Sikh, the oldest man in the room, had been sitting in an armchair from which he reached out occasionally to nip Zarina's breasts. But now he was on the floor—I don't know how— and Zarina was on his head. Qumar was squatting on his stomach with her hand inside his trousers. It didn't seem like a game any more, and people were arguing. The landlord was saying to me, 'This man, he's a respectable man, he's the richest man, one of the best known in Southall, he's an old man . . .' Zarina and Qumar were stripping him. Other men, having lost their tempers, were attempting to drag the women away.

The old man was helped to his feet. He was breathing heavily, as if about to have a seizure. He was trying to stop himself from crying.

His turban had been dislodged and chicken curry and rice had been smeared over him, which he was trying to brush off.

There was still the final part of the show. For this, the men sat cross-legged on the floor to watch the women pretend to have sex with each other. One man got down on his knees as if he were checking his car exhaust-pipe—and peered up Zarina's cunt. Beside me, the landlord was passing comment once more. Our Muslim girls don't usually shave themselves, he said. He disapproved of the neatly trimmed black strip of hair over Zarina's cunt.

The show lasted over two hours. 'It wasn't difficult,' Qumar said. They were exhausted. They would ache and be covered in bruises. They did two shows a week.

ABRAHAM VERGHESE

The Cowpath to America

One night in 1979, toward the end of my interneship at the Government
General Hospital in Madras, India, I was summoned from my bed to
the contagious-diseases ward, where an elderly Brahman priest with
rabies needed to be sedated. He was in one of two 'dog bite' rooms:
well-ventilated, high-ceilinged structures with no hard furniture, a
padlocked door, and wire mesh on one wall. When I admitted him,
two days previously, he had been lucid but had complained of fever
and a tingling around the site of a healed bite wound. Now, as I stood,
with the matron, peering into the cage, he was agitated and mumbling
incoherently. I fished out a needle from the tabletop sterilizer and
fitted it onto a syringe. I entered his room, squatted by his mat, gently
rolled him to one side, and injected pethidine (Demerol) into his
gluteus muscle. A plate of puri and potatoes lay untouched next to
him; water had been taken away, because the sight of it gave him
pharyngeal spasms.

I thought of my father's older brother, who was ten when he chased
away a dog that had strayed into the compound of the family home in
Kerala, South India. When the boy turned back to the house, the dog
came up behind him and bit him on the hand. The wound was treated
with a poultice by an Ayurvedic physician, but within a few weeks the
child developed fever and confusion. The family knew what this
meant. They made preparations to take him downriver by boat and
from there by car to Trivandrum and the nearest big hospital. But the

This essay is taken from the *New Yorker*, 23 and 30 June 1997.

little boy screamed in terror at the sight of the river, it threw him into a fit of choking. Nothing could induce him to get on the boat. He died in the house where he was born.

The night matron ushered me out. 'Cent per cent fatal, Doctor,' she said as she locked the door after me. Then she added, 'By morning? All over.'

She would have laughed at my stupidity if I had told her that, according to 'Harrison's Principles of Internal Medicine,' my American textbook, a rabid patient could survive. One patient, the book said, had been maintained for months on a respirator, in a state-of-the-art intensive-care unit, until the virus burned itself out. But then in America only a few human rabies cases occurred every year. Around twenty-five thousand people died of rabies annually in India. Our intensive-care beds were needed for people who had better chances of survival.

I walked back to my quarters, through a maze of walkways that led past the open wards. When I first entered the hospital, as a third-year medical student, the redolence of the wards had been exciting—vindication for the years of sitting through dry lectures on anatomy, biochemistry, and physiology. My hero was Professor K.V. Thiruvengadam. During my first day on the wards, as fifteen of us students trooped behind him on rounds, we came to a patient giving off a strange smell, and it seemed to animate Professor K.V.T. He rattled off a litany of odors—the acetone breath of diabetic coma, the freshly-baked-bread odor of typhoid fever, the stale-beer stench of scrofula, the sewer breath of a lung abscess, the just-plucked-chicken-feathers emanation of rubella—before arriving at the ammoniacal, mousy odor that rose from the patient before us. 'Hepatic coma,' he said, and he proceeded to demonstrate all its other signs.

K.V.T. could percuss a lung and predict precisely what the chest X-ray would look like. He would quote Thackeray, *Nature*, and the most recent edition of 'Harrison's.' As chief of medicine, he was a busy man, but he made us feel that there was nothing more important to him than guiding our fingers to feel what he felt, and guiding our eyes and ears to see and hear what he saw and heard.

But three years after I met him—half-way through my compulsory interneship—my excitement had worn off. It had given way to a sense of impotence. Oh, yes, our hospital performed open-heart surgery; we had a giant neurosurgical institute; and we provided yeoman service in many other areas. But the demands always outstripped the resources. In the lines that wove and doubled back on themselves at the door of the outpatient clinic each morning, almost every patient would have been deserving of hospital admission by American standards. But only some were picked for admission, and then often because the patient was a good 'teaching case.' At exam time, professional patients would come to the hospital and receive a week's lodging and food in return for being fodder for the examinees. Takedown Govindraj, for instance, would, if you got him as your assigned case, signal to you to get your pen out. (A few rupees would have had to pass between examinee and patient before this step.) 'Take down, Doctor,' he'd say, adopting the tone of the many clinicians who had used his body to instruct medical students. 'Take down: jaundice, spider angiomas, palmar erythema, Dupuytren's contracture, flapping tremor, breast enlargement, splenomegaly, shrunken liver, testicular atrophy.' He would point to each of the stigmata of cirrhosis and pronounce the words pretty well, considering that he spoke no English. But it was best for the examinee to know this stuff on his own. Takedown occasionally sent out for mutton *biriyani*, which was more protein than his liver could handle. The mild hepatic encephalopathy that resulted would cause him to say 'breast enlargement' while pointing to his balls.

The corridor outside the operating rooms was now dark and silent. The daytime cacophony of auto rickshaws, scooters, mopeds, cars, and buses outside the hospital walls and the crush of people within had lessened. The whitewashed pillars that held up the buildings were faintly visible. It was possible, in the dim glow of the metal-caged light bulbs, to ignore the betel-juice stains and to imagine the colonial era, when British medical officers had ruled like emperors here and had trained 'native' medical students, teaching them about Pott's disease and Hansen's disease and Sydenham's chorea and other white-male-eponym conditions, and instilling in them the desire to wear pith helmets and white cotton suits and own Raleigh bicycles and, one day, sail to England and bring home a cherished FRCP (Fellow of the Royal College of Physicians) or FRCS (Fellow of the Royal College of Surgeons).

Once again, I calculated how many days of my interneship I had left before I could leave India. I was twenty-five and restless and I had decided to pursue specialty training in America. I had been educated in India for the most part, but was born in Ethiopia, where my expatriate-Indian parents were teachers. By the time I reached medical school, my parents had emigrated to America. My older brother had finished engineering school in Madras and was now at M.I.T., in Cambridge. My parents had filed all the necessary papers, and I had a green card. The door was open for me to leave.

Most of my friends in India had, like me, grown up speaking English in the house, thinking in English, reading first Enid Blyton's Famous Five books and then the Hardy Boys. Increasingly, by the late seventies, it seemed as if we merely had our physical existence in India; mentally, we lived in a fantasy world that was somehow removed from the dust and the traffic and the chaos outside. It often appeared to me that my friends' parents and grandparents were doing the same thing we were. Their escape was the world of 'the old days', by which, strangely, they meant the British days and the era of the maharajas and princely states and the rituals of afternoon tea. Our escape was the America of 'Woodstock,' the documentary (which, like most things, came to India years after the actual event, but seemed to trigger its own revolution among the already Westernized kids I knew). For us, America was defined by the music of Crosby, Stills, Nash and Young and by the novels of John Irving and Joseph Heller. Our preference for America was also a form of rebellion against the British fixation of our elders. England seemed to be a dead-end place, particularly for a young medical student. You could get your FRCS (Farting Round the Countryside, we called it), but you would almost never be appointed a consultant. You either stayed as a perpetual interne or took your precious FRCS back to Madras and hung up your shingle and competed with all the other ' "phoren" returned' doctors on Sterling Road.

Those of us who planned to get to America abandoned British and Indian texts, which tended to be dogmatic, imperious tomes. 'Harrison's' had numerous authors, and it quoted the pivotal, and even controversial, studies—the Tuskegee study of untreated syphilis, for example—that formed the basis of modern practice. I would pick out names from the seven-page list of contributors to the seventh edition and read them aloud, enjoying the way the elegant titles rolled off my tongue and fantasizing about one day being the Hersey Professor of the Theory and Practice of Physic (Medicine), Harvard Medical School.

It was possible to get an internship as a foreign medical graduate (FMG) in America. Residency programs in many inner-city American hospitals needed foreign medical graduates, and recruited them vigorously. These were institutions that rarely attracted American medical-school graduates. The hospitals' residency programs were supported by Medicare educational money, and they served an indigent patient population. The annual influx of foreign medical graduates was vital to the hospitals' functioning.

Yet while it was possible to get an American interneship, it wasn't easy. First, you had to pass a daylong examination that tested your medical knowledge, and another that tested your proficiency in English. By the end of the sixties, the exam was no longer offered in India. The closest places where the exam could be taken ended up being in Thailand, the Philippines, and Singapore. It seemed to us that, through the seventies and eighties, the bar kept being raised; the exam became more specialized, with the two parts given at different times of the year. Undaunted, medical students, their heads buried in study guides, packed the twice-a-year charter planes that took off from Madras or Bombay. Fewer than fifty per cent of the students passed the exams; a larger percentage probably lost their virginity in Bangkok or Manila.

The biggest hurdle, though, came *after* the exams, with the attempt to get a visa from the American Consulate. In the late seventies, it was exceedingly difficult for an Indian doctor to obtain a visa to go to America. But this didn't stop people who had passed the exams from trying. The main visa officer was a black gentleman who, rumor had it, hated his posting. The lines outside the Consulate would form the night before. Most people were dressed in their consulate best, but some scruffy-looking touts wearing sarongs squatted in line all night and made a good living selling their spots to late arrivals. For a fee, a pundit whose credentials were dubious—after all, if he knew how to get a visa, what was he doing in Madras?—would coach you on how to be 'cent per cent successful'.

From the sweltering humidity outdoors I entered the spotless, air-conditioned antechamber of the Consulate, with its United States flag, its orange carpets, and its photograph of Jimmy Carter. My visit was routine, since I had a green card. But my classmates who were applying for tourist visas or work visas needed an 'interview' to prove that they planned to return to India. They carried with them surety bonds, land certificates, bank statements, and anything else that signified wealth in India, as proof that they were not going to America to *better* themselves—they were doing just fabulously in India, thank you very much. Relatives often transferred all their assets to an applicant for twenty-four hours, so that the applicant could be rich for one day. Or else 'instant wealth' agencies provided papers, good only for the few hours spent in the Consulate. And, of course, despite all the pledges to return, I didn't know anyone who had any intention of coming back.

If an applicant came out of the Consulate smiling, the line outside collapsed as people mobbed the apparently successful candidate: 'What did he ask? What did you say? What did he say?' Most people emerged with long faces and were shunned, as if they were contagious.

One morning, the visa officer turned down six consecutive doctors and told the seventh, who happened to be a friend of mine, and whom I'll call Vadivel, 'Spare me the crap about coming back with specialized knowledge to serve your country. Why do you really want to go?' Vadivel, who had held on to his American dream for so long that he could speak with the passion of a visionary, said, 'Sir, craving your indulgence, I want to train in a decent, ten-story hospital where the lifts are actually working. I want to pass board-certification exams by my own merit and not through pull or bribes. I want to become a wonderful doctor, practice real medicine, pay taxes, make a good living, drive a big car on decent roads, and eventually live in the Ansel Adams section of New Mexico and never come back to this wretched town, where doctors are as numerous as fleas and practice is cutthroat, and where the air outside is not even fit to breathe.' The consul gave him a visa. The eighth applicant, forewarned, tried the same tactic but was turned down.

At the entrance to the internes' quarters, which occupied the top floor of a three-storey building, the peon whose full-time job was to sit by the solitary phone and log the calls from the matrons and wake up the appropriate interne was snoring. A faint odor of ganja was in the air.

A door burst open and a fellow-interne, known as Mo, stumbled out of his room, almost knocking into me. He had his left hand raised above his head, and the fingers of his right were applying pressure to the antecubital vein. I guessed that Mo had mainlined with pethidine and had come out of his room so the sea breeze could fan the flames of his rush.

'Sorry, bugger,' he said.

Mo was part of a different kind of madness from what we would-be foreign medical graduates went in for. He belonged to the peth-and-poker crowd. There was a room in the men's hostel where a poker game was reputed to have gone on day and night for three years—with politicians, lawyers, and other *dadas* coming and going, and a percentage of the kitty going to the occupant of the room. Mo, like many in his group, had been in medical school for many years, consistently failing the anatomy viva voce. He had passed and become an interne when state elections brought one of his relatives into power, giving him the necessary pull to get through.

Tonight, the pethidine had taken away the barrier that usually kept him wary of me. 'Abe, you lucky bugger,' he said. He lowered his arm and clamped it over my shoulder. 'I wish I could go to America.'

I was about to mention what many of my classmates planned to do: get a position in England or Tanzania or Nigeria or the Caribbean and from there get a visa to America, because the odds were better than in Madras. Of course, he had to study and clear the exams first.

'No, bugger,' he said, anticipating my advice. 'If at all I go, I'll marry a green-card holder, then live there and do Stanley Kaplan till I pass. Or maybe do business in Las Vegas or something. But, no, I think I'll stay here. *Desh*—motherland—that's important to me.'

His voice took on a conspiratorial tone. 'I heard that one of our buggers, when he landed at Kennedy, he met a beautiful woman—a deadly blonde—and her brother outside baggage claim. She was *very, very* friendly. They offered him a lift in a white convertible. They took him to their apartment, and then you know what the brother did? Pulled a bloody gun out and said, "Screw my sister or I'll kill you." Can you imagine? What a country!'

Mo's deadly-blonde fantasy was just one version of the American dream that most of us had. And Vadivel had been right when he told the consular officer that doctors abounded in India; what was lacking was money to provide meaningful treatment to people in need. America was the land where there was no dichotomy between what the textbook said you should do and what you *could* do—or so we thought. In America, your talent and hard work could take you to the very top. It was the land of defibrillators on every ward and disposable *everything*, by God—no more mucking around in the murky waters of a lukewarm sterilizer for a needle that could actually penetrate skin. As for the deadly blonde . . .

I arrived in America a few months before my interneship was due to start. My graduation gift from my parents had been a fifteen-day airline ticket that allowed multiple stops around America. My mood was euphoric. On my first stop, I met a friend of a friend who was just finishing his interneship at an East Coast hospital. We slipped into the easy familiarity of expatriates. Over dinner at a Vietnamese restaurant, I told him the places I hoped to apply to.

He laughed. 'Don't be so bloody naïve, bugger,' he said. 'Learn from the experience of others. Look.' He pushed a chili-sauce bottle to the center of the table. 'This, my dear friend, is an Ellis Island hospital. Mark my words, every city has one. Such a place is *completely* dependent on foreign medical graduates, and that's where you will go. No ifs and buts. Think of it as a quarantine period, before you can move on and do your land-of-opportunity fantasy. Your elders and betters have passed through these places. Why should you think you are different?'

Now he put a saltshaker as far away from the chili-sauce bottle as he could. 'That,' he said, 'is a Plymouth Rock hospital—university-and medical-school-affiliated, of course. It has *never* taken a foreign medical graduate. Except for the occasional South African white or Brit or Australian, who—don't ask why—is a different species of foreign medical graduate from you and me. Don't even bother with that kind of place. The cowpath from India never goes through there. Unless you want to take a job as a bathroom sweeper.'

He could see that I resisted this argument, and my resistance irritated him. 'Look here. We foreign medical graduates are an *embarrassment* to this society, a *prob-lem*,' he said, waggling the index and middle fingers of both hands, as if placing quotation marks—a gesture I'd never seen in India. 'We are like the Mexican-migrant-worker *prob-lem*, or the Colombian-cocaine-export *prob-lem*. Alas, we *prob-lems* wouldn't exist if the United States economy didn't depend on us, if there wasn't a great need for the commodity we provide and which they are willing to pay for. *They* create the *prob-lem*. But that doesn't mean they have to *like* us, or treat us fairly.'

He signalled for the check. 'We are, my dear friend, like a transplanted organ—lifesaving, and desperately needed, but rejected because we are foreign tissue. But, as they say in America, tough shit.'

Contrariness made me visit a Plymouth Rock hospital in Boston. The secretary in the internal-medicine office was barely cordial. She soon ascertained what my appearance had already suggested: that I was a foreign medical graduate. I explained that, since I had never received a reply to my letter of inquiry, I thought that perhaps their letter to me had been lost in the mail. 'Not likely,' she said. There was a long silence.

A wiser traveller, I continued my journey across America. I discovered that the patient population at a Plymouth Rock hospital was not necessarily different from that at an Ellis Island hospital. What ultimately stigmatized an Ellis Island hospital was not its patients but its doctors. The very fact that it had become dependent on foreign medical graduates made American medical students avoid the place. At Ellis Island hospitals, I was welcomed by the secretaries in the residency offices and had interviews with program directors who were eager to sign me up. I thought that I could read their thoughts: Hmm . . . speaks well . . . not much of an accent . . . more of a British accent, if anything . . . great exam scores . . . not the never-raise-the-toilet-seat, spit-out-of-the-window type.

I applied to a new medical school—East Tennessee State University, in Johnson City, Tennessee, in the foothills of the Smoky Mountains. The residency program was so new that it had not clearly defined itself as foreign-medical-graduate-dependent or not. I was given a contract. My fellow-internes included a couple of Americans as well as foreign medical graduates from India, the Philippines, and Haiti.

On the first day of orientation, I was nervous. But nothing about the wards, the lab, the medical library, or the intensive-care unit was unexpected. I had simply arrived in the very situation I had visualized for years. I loved the way the charts were kept, with tabs separating order sheets, progress notes, laboratory results, nurses' notes, radiological reports, and consultants' notes. A call to the medical-record department would bring two or three volumes of the patient's old chart. By studying these, one could re-construct the waxing and waning of a disease over time. And after I discharged the patient I could follow him regularly in the outpatient clinic and add to the chronicle of his encounter with illness. I had been right about one thing in America: what you should do for a patient, you *could* do.

I was intensely aware of myself at all times. I realized that I was trying not to stand out, and would speak in a manner that was understood, even if it meant pronouncing 'gastroenterology' in one slurred ejaculation, rather than 'gastro-enter-ology.' I asked my senior resident, John Duncan, to show me how to tie my necktie in a thinner knot than the broad seventies knot I used. I studied sociological minutiae carefully, even keeping notes in my diary on the etiquette of the cafeteria line—how queue-jumping was permissible if you were heading for the salad bar, how having money ready when you got to the cashier was appreciated, how the sawdust-tasting entity appropriately called grits was to be avoided, how biscuits and gravy were tasty but sat in your belly like bricks, and, most important, where the Tabasco sauce was kept. Tabasco provided the only way I could keep my taste buds from atrophying completely. I wanted my foreignness to be forgotten. The highest compliment I received after three months of this was paid me by a nurse: she said, 'Doc, I don't know where you're from, but you're a good ole Tennessee boy in my book. Are you married?'

Each year in Tennessee, I encountered more second-generation Indians in the medical-school classes. I was fascinated by the contrast between their looks and their manner. It was like a trick of some sort—how, when they opened their mouths, the most fluent East Tennessee patois emerged. I thought (and perhaps I was wrong) that they were so American, so assimilated, that they had a confidence, a swagger, that we first-generation immigrants would never have. The FMGs jokingly, and jealously, referred to them as ABCDs: American-Born Confused Deshis.

In the third year of my medical residency, I spent my free weekends working in small emergency rooms in tiny towns tucked away in the Appalachian Mountains. The staff physicians in these little mining communities were mostly Indians, with a smattering of other foreign medical graduates. The few American doctors there were usually home-town boys who had returned after their training. I studied the Indian doctors: they represented a later stage in the life cycle of a foreign medical graduate.

One of these doctors invited me to his house. His wife and children were on vacation in India. We had a couple of beers. He seemed lonely, sinking deeper into his recliner as the evening wore on, his every sentence tinged with nostalgia. It struck me that in the privacy of his home he was more Indian than he might have been in India. If I was trying to integrate, and learn the rituals of Monday-night football and Moon Pies, cookouts and coon-hunting, squirrel stew and possum pie, this doctor had abandoned that strategy. Or else he had worked his way through that phase and arrived at this.

On the walls of his den were pictures of his family. 'That's my oldest daughter,' he said, pointing. 'Guess what—she's been accepted by Harvard as an undergraduate. Pre-med, of course.'

His face revealed more than just parental pride. He wanted her to succeed in a way that he, for all his financial success, never could. His daughter would soon penetrate the upper tier of medicine, which had been closed to him. She would step right into it, as if it were her birthright—sans accent and with an American medical degree. There was pride and vindication in his expression.

I wasn't ready to settle in the hinterland. I wanted to make it to Plymouth Rock. My mentor in Tennessee, an infectious-disease specialist named Steven Berk, had sparked my interest in that field and encouraged me to apply for a fellowship. Once again, in 1982, I sent out applications to the best programs in the country. But this time I actually received replies.

I asked myself what had changed. I had published a few papers by then, but Berk's strong letter of recommendation had helped; it said, 'Look beyond the foreign-medical-graduate label.' When Boston University made me a pre-emptive offer of a fellowship, before the official 'match' day, I accepted. I had finally penetrated the country club.

Boston was Mecca. It had three medical schools, each with years of tradition, and each owning or linked to several famous hospitals. I sat in lecture halls listening to speakers whose papers and textbook chapters I had read and who had been mythical figures to me. My fellow-trainees—all American graduates—found my propensity for hero worship amusing. Real fame in Boston that year belonged to Ray Flynn, Yo-Yo Ma, and Larry Bird.

Half of my fellowship training was spent in laboratory research, learning basic techniques. I embarked on a study of pneumonia using an animal model. The laboratory skills and the imagination required to be a first-class researcher were quite distinct from the skills demanded of a clinician. Either you had them or you didn't.

I soon noticed that in Boston, as in Tennessee, there wasn't much interest in the bedside exam. Most case discussions took place in conference rooms or labs. As a student in India, I had imagined that the ready availability of CAT scans and angiograms, the routine ability to float Swan-Ganz catheters into the heart and measure pressures, and so on, would have resulted in American doctors' becoming superb bedside sleuths. They had so many opportunities to confirm bedside findings with appropriate investigations. But instead their senses were rusty from lack of use, and there was little faith in the bedside exam.

I realized that the movers and shakers in medicine—the chairmen and the department heads with the magnificent tides—didn't get to their positions by seeing patients. Their fame and power had come from doing basic biological research, at which they were brilliant. American education, unlike didactic Indian education, encouraged innovative and original thinking, and this was where it paid off: if medicine was both art and science, no country in the world was better at the science than America. Typically, early in these doctors' careers they had explored and described an important phenomenon and written the seminal paper on it. They had then spent years refining that observation and assigning Younger Turks to pursue the spinoffs, all the while broadening their sphere of influence, writing textbook chapters on the subject, sitting on the National Institutes of Health and Veterans Administration committees that awarded funding. The necessary skills for such a rise were business acumen, Machiavellian cunning, and skill in the thrust-and-parry action of committees. And all the while the research ship had to be kept afloat. If you were looking for an outstanding clinician, someone whom other doctors would seek if they were ill, it was unlikely that you would find one in a position of power.

One of the professors I admired the most was a superb clinician and a gifted researcher. He let me run the clinical service without much interference. I presented the new consultations to him every afternoon, in his lab. Almost never did I present a patient with a condition that he hadn't seen before. On one occasion, I surprised him by something I'd said.

'That's just not possible, Abe,' he said. 'It can't be.' He wanted to see the patient. Our entourage marched over to the hospital. The professor, wrapped up in his thoughts, extended his hand. The patient, thinking that this meant a handshake, extended hers. But the professor's fingers had already slipped past the outstretched hand to grab the bedsheet and expose the part of the body in question, to see for himself what it was that seemed to defy his knowledge of how this particular disease worked. He showed us what we had missed—a finding that we thought was trivial but that was, in fact, crucial. He marched out, satisfied, having proved what it was that he had come to prove: that the rules of how infections behaved had not been broken. He left us to explain to the astonished patient that she had just received the opinion of the top infectious-disease expert in America.

I began to understand that if I still aspired to one of the heady titles that I had fantasized about as a student my life would have to take a path I hadn't anticipated. After two years, my research had barely begun to yield results. It would take several more years of committed laboratory apprenticeship before I could start exploring the research questions that really interested me. I had gone into medicine partly because middle-class Indian parents guided their children into either engineering or medicine, as if there were no other careers. But I had also chosen medicine because of Somerset Maugham's 'Of Human Bondage,' a book that when I was thirteen made medicine seem the most romantic of professions: 'humanity there in the rough, the materials the artist worked on,' in Maugham's words. In medical school Professor K.V.T. had embodied this approach to medicine for me. I was reluctant now to change paths. I had started to resent the time I was spending away from my patients. A new disease, AIDS, had emerged. While researchers chased after its cause, there was plenty of opportunity for a clinician to observe its manifestations at the bedside. I wanted to combine patient care and teaching with more modest research.

I had made the passage from India to Plymouth Rock. But there I discovered that one of the most important things America had to offer was the *choice* of how one could live and work.

After finishing my fellowship, in 1985, I went back to India. It was a nostalgic visit to see friends and relatives; my return ticket was safely in my pocket. Nevertheless, I wanted to find out whether India would feel different. I had a fleeting fantasy that I might discover a way of using my specialty in infectious diseases within India.

I carried with me an old but functioning gastroscope donated by a physician in Tennessee; I was to deliver it to a Methodist mission hospital in the state of Karnataka which was supported by an American congregation. But the customs officers in Bombay wouldn't release the gastroscope; they were convinced that I wanted to sell it. At the time, India had huge taxes on most imported items. I argued to no avail. The gastroscope never left customs and is probably still sitting there. I visited the isolated rural mission hospital anyway. The senior doctor, an ophthalmologist, had given his best years to the hospital. He was dedicated but poorly paid. His strong religious belief—something I lacked—was what kept him there. In the same hospital, I met a young anesthetist and his obstetrician wife, both fresh out of training. I thought that they were wonderful, compassionate physicians. But as their child neared school age they worried about the lack of good schools in the village. Their pay was insufficient to buy even the simplest luxuries that India's huge middle class took for granted. I couldn't see them staying there for more than another year or so. I couldn't see myself working there, either.

On a subsequent visit, four years later, I noted a new phenomenon sweeping Madras and other cities in India: NRI hospitals. These were nonresident-Indian hospitals, set up by Indian doctors living abroad who invested their foreign exchange in hospitals modelled on their counterparts in the West, right down to the modular furniture in the foyers. These hospitals offered everything from renal transplants to coronary-bypass surgery. But they were expensive and catered to the rich. The very rich, however, still went to Manhattan's Sloan-Kettering or the Texas Heart Institute.

I made rounds at one of these hospitals for two weeks. I gave a formal lecture. And I tried to imagine myself living and working in this setting, but I couldn't. I made excuses for myself on the plane returning to America. 'No one knows what to do with your specialty in India,' I told myself. 'Most physicians manage the infections they encounter without outside assistance, and they're not about to change to help you make a living. And, as for AIDS, Abe, they seem to think that it is and will remain an American problem. Money is the missing ingredient in India, not you. You're just not needed, Abe. If a new enlightened government ever comes along . . .' I never completely convinced myself.

My academic career, spent largely in smaller medical schools where patient care was valued more than research, brought me, eventually, to America's southernmost border—to a professorship at the Texas Tech University Health Sciences Center, in El Paso, and to a consultancy at R. E. Thomason Hospital, a county hospital. For the first time in America, I felt as if I had disappeared. I no longer stood out. The patients and their families walking the corridors of the county hospital looked like my kin from South India. They shared my skin color and took *me* to be Hispanic. When I was stopped in the corridors and asked questions in Spanish, I learned to respond with answers such as *'La cafetería es en el basement'*—border Spanglish, allowing one the liberty of throwing in English when nothing else could do the job. A sizable percentage of our patients were Mexican nationals. The hospital required only an El Paso billing address to provide service. As the sole not-for-profit hospital serving a population of almost seven hundred thousand, well over a third of whom were uninsured, we were overburdened and understaffed. But you'd have known this only if you read it somewhere. The wards were airy, and sunlight from big picture windows flooded the corridors, reflecting off the waxed floors and pale-blue walls of the internal-medicine ward. The security guards directed you to the choice *caldo de res* and *barbacoa* joints on Alameda Avenue; the nurses smiled, and if they felt embattled they didn't show it. As a doctor interested in infectious diseases, I had found a perfect niche in El Paso: treating Third World diseases—typhoid, amoebic liver abscesses, brucellosis—in a First World setting.

In 1993, I found myself in the South of India again, this time at the Oberoi Hotel in Bangalore, and I was having a strange conversation with the bellman. The annual struggle to fill our internship slots at Texas Tech had become desperate. Despite the fact that our medical students loved the experience at the county hospital, they had no intention of staying with us as internes. We had always been dependent on foreign medical graduates, and it appeared that we always would be. But visas for foreign medical graduates, which seemed to have been easier to obtain at the peak of the AIDS epidemic, were once again difficult to get. A new twist had been added: to have a chance for a visa, you had to have a contract with a residency program in America.

I had come to India to interview potential internes, pick the best, and hand out five contracts. These five graduates, contract in hand, would have a decent chance of getting their visas. Before I left El Paso, I had run a small ad in an Indian newspaper, specifying a very high score on the equivalency exam. I thought that I would get ten or twenty applicants. Four hundred people answered the advertisement, all of them meeting or exceeding the qualifications and overwhelming the fax machine in El Paso. I had picked seventy people to interview in Bangalore.

The bellman at the Oberoi was a bright young man, and it didn't surprise me when he told me he had a college degree. He hoped to rise in the catering field, he said. It had good prospects overseas.

'There have been many people inquiring about you, sir. Starting three days ago,' the bellman said.

'What do they want to know?'

'How you look. Whether you seem strict or not.' He grinned.

'What else?'

'Just silly people . . .'

'Tell me.'

'One fellow asked . . . I'm ashamed to tell you.'

'Go ahead.'

'He asked whether you are susceptible to . . .'

'To what?'

'"Monetary adjustments"—his exact words, sir, I swear.'

'Well, I'm not. Spread the word.'

'If you don't mind my suggesting, sir, leave a list with our telephone operator of people whose calls you want put through. She will not connect other calls.' I must have looked puzzled, because he went on to say, 'Otherwise, ministers and what-not will be bothering you all night.'

The lobby of the hotel the next morning looked like a variant of the Consulate scene. Even though I had given each person a specific time to appear over the next two days, it looked as if they were *all* there.

The hotel made its business suite available to me, and I began to work my way through the applicants. The secretary assisting me told me that people I had finished interviewing were being mobbed outside. 'What did he ask? What did you say.' My questions were designed simply to get to know the candidates and to pick out the brightest, smartest ones. But now, as an experiment, I began deliberately throwing in specific questions, such as 'How do you feel about Clinton?' and 'What are your views on homosexuality?' By the afternoon, I was getting polished but totally noncommittal answers to these questions, since nobody had any idea what my views were.

I asked one young man why he wanted to leave.

'I want to specialize in hematology oncology and then return to serve—'

'Save that for the Consulate. Really, why do you want to leave?'

He was startled. After a moment's silence, his face broke out into a naughty smile.

'*You* know, sir,' he said. I did, but I wanted to hear anyway. Reluctantly, almost ashamed, he went on, 'It's just hopeless—that's all I can tell you, sir. No jobs. And to get into specialty training here requires influence. And there are so many medical schools now that having a specialty degree here means less and less. And if you join government service, without some political pull you will be posted to some godforsaken place forever. And to set up a private practice— it's cutthroat, sir. Unless you have a rich father-in-law who builds a hospital for you.'

According to him, yet another wrinkle had been added to the protocol of leaving: you had to have an NOC—a no-objection certificate—which showed that India didn't mind your decamping. This seemed to me to be a brilliant obstacle set up by the Indian government to plug the brain drain. 'But,' he reassured me quickly, 'NOCs are no problem. They are easily obtained by lubricating the right person in Delhi.'

I asked him why it was that all those I had interviewed so far claimed to want to pursue hematology oncology after their residency in internal medicine.

'It's because that's the only category of subspecialty training not readily available in India, sir. Therefore, technically, an NOC can be issued. That's why we say that to you, sir.' He had dropped all pretense now. He was giving me the inside story. 'Everyone tells the consular officer that he wants to return and start a bone-marrow-transplant center in India. The consular officer said to someone the other day that if everyone who *said* that actually came back India would have more bone-marrow-transplant centers than *chai* shops.'

By the evening of the second day, I had my five candidates. I was exhausted. The gruelling process of talking to so many young doctors, and hearing why they wanted to leave, had given me a sense of being immensely fortunate—fortunate that my parents had emigrated, fortunate that I had got the residency in Tennessee, fortunate in my choice of specialty.

My journey to America had brought me full circle, back to India, and to a situation where I could pick others to make the voyage. The best I could do for the five doctors I had picked was to bring them to a county hospital like mine: Ellis Island. The rest was up to them.

Part III

Amit Chaudhuri

Oxford

Each year, in Oxford, new students come and old ones disappear; after a while, one knows the streets and by-lanes, all of which lead to each other, by heart; in the north, no one goes beyond Summertown, and the road leading to London goes out via Headington. On the first day of Michaelmas, men and gowns walk to matriculation ceremonies, and at the end of the year they wear these gowns again, unhappily, to take exams; then, after the exams, the town is nearly empty, and the days, because of that peculiar English enchantment called Summer Time, last one hour longer; and Oxford, in the evening, resembles what an English town must have looked like in wartime, the small shops open but unfrequented, an endangered, dolorous, but perfectly vivid peace in the lanes, as the eye is both surprised by, and takes pleasure in, a couple linked arm in arm, or a young man conversing with a woman on a polished doorstep, and then the early goodbyes. It is like what I imagine a wartime township to have been, because all the young people, with their whistling, their pavement to pavement chatter, their beer-breathed, elbow-nudging polemics, are suddenly gone, leaving the persistent habits of an old way of life, the opening and shutting of shops, intact, a quiet, empty bastion of civilisation and citizenry. It is because of its smallness, repetition, and the evanescence of its populace, that Oxford is dream-like.

This extract is taken from *Freedom Song: Three Novels*, published by Alfred A. Knopf, New York, 1999.

From the window of my room I could see a library and a faculty building, and a path, curving slightly, that led to college. Students, dressed in the oddest of clothes, in secretive overcoats, in long and black primitive skirts, men with earrings, women wearing gypsy ornaments, would gather each morning for lectures, or pass in and out of doors recklessly with books clutched to their bosoms, or sit on the steps in abandonment, as if they had forgotten their appointments. The path, which was flanked by hedges that turn bright red in the autumn, I could see far into; at one point, it ran over a canal, so that I sensed water there. This intuition of water came to me again when I was visiting Worcester College; it was an unhappy day, because I was still vacillating between Mandira and Shehnaz, falling asleep by one woman at night and spending the day with the other, but I had, for a forced, lucid period of time, come here to attend a seminar on Lawrence. On entering the first quad, I saw that the light—it was evening—behind the wall at the end of the garden was different; as if the sun had set there, so that I imagined a seashore and a horizon. Later, I learnt that there was a lake there.

Dr Mason's room was simple, with two sofas, adjacent to each other, and a study-table, next to which there was a chair on which he sat. It was a well-lit and warm room, but its colours were cool— furniture browns and wallpaper purples and magnolias and greys, the colours that create, in afternoon light or evening shadow, the abidingness of an English interior. Three undergraduates, myself, and two other graduate students sat on the sofa, while another undergraduate, bearded and with spectacles, placed himself on the window-sill and never said a word, but listened to the others' words, seeming to weigh them, and it was his silence that I deciphered for agreement or disapproval. Dr Mason was a polite, even kind, man, a very big man, not very old, facing us in his armchair. Some students had open copies of *The White Peacock* in their hands, and as we talked of Lawrence, extolled him, applauded him, and, most invigorating of all, corrected him, it seemed both strange and natural to hear our own voices. The mind focused itself upon the sphere of the room and the table lamp, and then dilated vaguely and darkly into a consciousness of Lawrence-country, and then focused upon the room again, and this dilation and constriction went on for a long time, like breathing. An hour later, we got up to leave. There was laughter, and a relaxed certainty with which we let each other go, almost released each other, into the night. How unique student life is, with its different rooms, its temporary enclosures and crystallisations, its awareness and memory of furniture and windows and spaces.

Early in the morning, light would frame the curtains of my window, although at times there was only a dull whiteness. When I parted the curtains, I would look out into the curving road to the next college, the closed doors of the library, and the pavements. The wind would make a piece of paper move, and, touching the window, I would sense the cold outside. As I am used to the sound of crows in the morning, this absence of noise would fill me with a melancholy which was difficult to get rid of because it seemed to have no immediate cause. It was only when I saw students, with their odd, comical gait, and their touchingly disguised sleepiness, walking down that road, growing, little by little, in number as the morning wore on, that I would feel an at-homeness and pleasure in their rhythm. It was around this time that Shehnaz too would set out from her college and come down the same road, indistinguishable from the other students, but with her own thoughtful gait, a backward-lookingness, happy in a simple way in having this opportunity to walk to her library in Broad Street, and devote a fresh day to copying out notes, stopping at my room for half an hour on her way there.

She was, essentially, a lonely person searching for the right company, a wise little girl in a woman's body, dressed in black trousers, a blue top and a coat, and black sneakers. Her hair was long and striking and untidy; solemnly, she carried a file full of papers under her arm, and a clumsy, oversized bag whose significance was that there was a tiny packet of Marlboro Lights in it. She had been married once, very briefly, and then divorced; later, she had an involvement in Oxford which came to nothing. It was towards the end of this involvement that I first met her, through a friend, and then we would exchange nods when we passed each other by on the bicycle-lined pavement of a street which led to a pub and a junction. Students, drolly crossing the street, or lavishly arguing, filled out the spaces in the street and the time between one meeting and the other upon this repeated route, so that the street, with its daily, inconsequential academic excitement and drama, has become indissoluble from the inner life of our early meetings, and Oxford, its climate and architecture, seems not so much a setting as a part of the heart of our friendship.

By the time she would get up to leave, the rest of the building would have woken up and be moving about. Noises were transmitted through walls and doors: a radio; a knowing, crowded murmur in the kitchen; footsteps in the corridor; the main door shutting; the firm but almost nonphysical sound of footsteps on the gravel; there were many lives in the building made transiently one by sound. I had a feeling of being surrounded, as on a ship or a train, by personal routines and habits that would not be known again, that had their natural place in some larger, more fixed habitat, and the morning noise had about it, therefore, the concentratedness, the temporariness, and the pathos of the noise of shared travel. It was at this time, after the sun had risen, and lives, without apparent reason, once more began excitedly, when there was shouting upstairs, windows opening, last-minute preparations, and a joy akin to that felt by passengers approaching a port, that Shehnaz would get up to leave, listening, with one ear, to the voices of other students, smiling at what they were saying. Everything they said she found worth listening to, especially if she had had a happy morning with me; she had an uncanny sensitivity to the presence of people in small spaces, in corridors, in doorways, as others have to landscapes, or to places. Being there in that corridor at that moment, as students sheepishly came out of rooms and vanished into the kitchen or the toilet, was a real experience for her.

Sharma lived in another room in the same building. Sometimes, in the morning, he would come down in his shorts to have coffee with me. Banging on the door in a forthright manner, he would enter, and if I happened to be midway through practising a raag, he would sit quietly on a chair and nod and shake his head in vigorous appreciation as I sang. The irrepressible bodily meaning of the words 'to be moved,' which we have come to associate with mental and aesthetic response, was apparent when one looked at him listening to music. Sometimes he would keep rhythm to the song, arbitrary temporal divisions that he slapped and pounded on the table, and when I had finished he would still be doing this, as if he could no longer stop. Later, he would walk around the room possessively, tapping the keys of my typewriter and reading aloud all the titles of the books on my shelf in order to make himself more conversant with the English language.

Once or twice, it happened that I had gone outside, leaving my door open, and then returned and closed it, thinking I was alone. But Sharma, in the meanwhile, had come and hidden himself in the clothes closet, from which, at a given moment, he emerged explosively. Towards the beginning of our friendship, he had told me very seriously that I was to help him improve his English. He was writing a thesis on Indian philosophy, but he longed to be a stylist. I would, thus, recommend to him a book whose language had given me pleasure, and he would read aloud passages from Mandelstam or Updike or Lawrence to me, either in the morning or at midnight, times at which I was sleepy, he reading sonorous lines in a loud and unstoppable voice, interrupting himself only to demand comments from me that were both fair and encouraging. His English had a strong, pure North Indian accent, so that he pronounced 'joy' a little bit like the French 'joie', and 'toilet' like 'twilit'. Yet this accent, I soon learnt, was never to be silenced completely; it was himself, and however he trained himself to imitate the sounds of English speech, 'toilet', when he pronounced it, would always have the faint but unmistakable and intimate and fortunate hint of 'twilit'. His sentence constructions were curious, with missing articles and mixed-up pronouns, but he compensated for these with an excess of 'thank yous' and 'sorrys', two expressions gratuitous in Indian languages and, therefore, no doubt, of great and triumphant cultural importance to him. His reading practice in the mornings, executed with the single-mindedness of a child practising scales by thumping the keys, remains for me one of the most relaxing memories of Oxford; me lying on the bed and patiently listening, a time of rootedness and plenitude, even of equable solitude, for with Sharma one is always alone, listening to him. Mandelstam, read by Sharma, took on a different, unsuspected life, odd, cubist, harmlessly egotistical, and atmospheric.

🙠

Mandira lived in a room in college. She had come to Oxford two years after me, and I first saw her in hall. She spoke English, I noticed, with a slight American accent, talked actively at the table, walked in what is called 'a brisk manner', and was surrounded by English friends. She was small and roundish, and a favourite with the porters and stewards, who would wink at her, or put an arm around her, and call her 'love' or 'dear', as the English do, and not take her very seriously. I did not like her, but, when I was bored, I would go to her room and drink a cup of tea. I gradually got over my tentativeness, and came to realise that a knock on her door would not be unwelcome, for she was always very hospitable in her disorganised way. The first five minutes would be spent in me settling down, after a preamble during which I decided where I should sit, on the armchair in a way that was both tortured and patient, and then open a bantering conversation with her in medias res; all this I took to be courtesy, but it made her uncomfortable, for I remember her as a compound of movement and aimless speed, putting the kettle on the boil, and then running down a flight of stairs to the kitchen for her carton of milk. Shyness made her quick, while I, by contrast, was slow. When she was gone for that minute, I would be alone in her room, with the photographs on the wall, the secret things and cups and clothes in her cupboard, the badly made bed, the wash-basin and mirror, the textbooks on the table and the floor, absorbing the materiality of the room and also its cheerful, fleeting makeshiftness, and not knowing what to think. She was not a very tidy person, but her attempt at order and creating the semblance of a household, even the clumsy tear at the spout of the milk carton, touched me. These undergraduate rooms were larger and more comfortable to look at than the box-like, modern rooms in my building. A light hung from the ceiling, enclosed by a comical, globe-like shade, and at evening it gave a light that was both encompassing and personal. The window opened onto a path to the garden and the hall, and all day, laughter and footsteps could be heard, coming and going, and these sounds too became a part of the room's presence.

In the morning, I looked forward to the small journey I made across the road, glancing right and left with avid interest for oncoming cars, to see if I had any mail. The pigeon-holes, after the poverty of Sunday, its forced spiritual calm, seemed to overflow humanely with letters on Monday, and even if I had not got any, that small walk did not lose its freshness and buoyancy, and a tiny and acute feeling of hope did not desert me in all my mornings. From about half-past nine to ten, there was a hubbub as students stooped or stood on tip-toe to peep into pigeon-holes, and sorted and sifted letters, and the mail-room had an air of optimism, of being in touch with the universe, found nowhere else in Oxford. When there *were* letters for me—the cheap, blue Indian aerogrammes from my mother—they lay there innocently like gifts from a Santa Claus, they did not seem material at all, but magical, like signs. Then I would miss the special feeling of mornings at home, I would think benignly of my mother's good health, and how she suffers from nothing but constipation, how for three days she will go without having been to the toilet, with an abstracted look on her face, as if she were hatching an egg. Secretively, she will concoct a mixture of Isab-gol and water, and stir it ferociously before drinking it. Then, one day, like a revelation, it will come, and she will have vanished from human company. My father, a great generaliser, collector of proverbs, shows no concern over her health, displays no bitterness.

The furniture in Mandira's room—the bed, the study-table, its chair, the cupboard, the bookshelves—was old, enduring. The armchair was solid and stoic, and seemed to cradle the space that existed between its thick arms; one felt protected when one sat in it. As I got to know Mandira better, as we became intimate and then grew increasingly unhappy, the room became her refuge, her dwelling, and when she said, 'I want to go back to my room,' the words 'my room' suggested the small but familiar vacuums that kept close around her, that attended to her and guided her in this faraway country. Because, for a foreigner and a student, the room one wakes and sleeps in, becomes one's first friend, the only thing with which one establishes a relationship that is natural and unthinking, its air and light what one shares with one's thoughts, its deep, unambiguous space, whether in daytime, or in darkness when the light has been switched off, what gives one back to oneself. The bed and chairs in it had an inscape, a life, which made them particular, and not a general array of objects.

That is why, when she spoke of her room, I think what she meant was the sense of not being deserted, of something, if not someone, waiting, of a silent but reliable expectancy.

The room had other rooms next to it and other rooms facing it. Sometimes, I would come up the staircase and enter the corridor to find Mandira leaning out of a half-closed door, talking to the American girl who lived opposite, who would be standing by her own door. Even when I was inside the room, they would continue their conversation, and I would sit on the chair and watch Mandira's back; from there I could listen to the voice of the invisible girl, and to her rising peals of laughter. For ten minutes they would say goodbye to each other, until there came a rounded silence, and Mandira closed the door. What was missing was the background sound of old people and children, of babies and mothers, of families; instead one heard people running up and down the staircase, or visitors approaching and knocking. There was a toilet near the room whose cistern gurgled candidly each time someone flushed it, and a bath to which men in dressing-gowns went solemnly in the evening, and women with towels around their heads, less solemn and with an air of freedom. From the bath everyone returned radiant and clean, and slightly ashamed. As I passed to or from Mandira's room, I would encounter them but not look at them, for I had learnt that the English do not consider it polite to look at each other, but nevertheless I remember the embarrassment of the men, and the opulent towels like Moorish turbans around the women's hair.

The first few weeks I knew Shehnaz, when we were still getting to be friends, were an uncomplicated time. We made appointments and did not keep them; we made appointments to discuss when we might meet; we liked each other but were occupied, like children, with other things to do. Sometimes I am nostalgic for that make-believe busyness, full of innocence, of having 'other things to do,' the prelapsarian background of lectures, bookshops, friends, our lives spent generously and routinely like rain-showers, stopping and starting again.

We decided to meet at the St. Giles' Café near the Oxfam Bookshop. 'Do you know where it is?' she asked me with a smile; these sociable questions she would invest with a mischievousness, so that they became funny and meaningful, and I would always pretend to be embarrassed answering them. I did know the St. Giles' Café; it was the only place in Oxford that served a strong and dark coffee, with a scorched South Indian flavour; a white froth, almost a scum, formed on the top even before they had put the milk in it. Unlike the coffee in the Senior Common Rooms, it was hot, and one could, with a certain satisfaction, admire the steam rising from the cup before one drank from it. The café was a small, ugly, and crowded place, full of students, and tramps minding their own business, hatted and bearded, with an unworldly look about them, like musicians. On either side of each table, there was a bench, and one had to squeeze past people to sit down, or have people squeeze past you as they got out. Thus, as one made small adjustments in position, one was always feeling grateful or obliged, strangely powerful or powerless; one shrank, and hunched, and then graciously expanded again, in regular, accordion-like time. Each table also had an introvert who sat in the corner throughout and looked at no one. When people were called to take their food from the counter, they were not addressed by their names, but by their orders—'Ham and eggs!' 'Plate of chips!' 'Bacon sandwich!'—and, calmly and without confusion, those who had been labelled so uniquely, rose and walked towards the counter. Whenever the door opened, a draught entered from outside, but the baked air inside, smelling of frying bacon, cushioned us from the cold and from other influences. The paradoxical confluence of timelessness and movement in the café made it an ideal place for a first meeting between two foreign students.

Yet that meeting, comically, was not to be. It was the beginning of summer, and some girls walked barefoot that day on Cornmarket Street. There was a hustle and bustle, a festive hurry, and even Ryman's, the stationery shop, had inspired-looking customers queueing up to pay for envelopes and sheets of paper and sellotape. Sharma and I were roaming around at our ease in loose shirts, two Indians who might never have met in India, feeling at home, giving studious attention, as if it truly mattered, to shop windows and an ancient organ-grinder edging our way towards Westgate, both of us feeling boyish, and I especially younger because I was wearing sandals. It began to thunder then, and rained very hard, as it does at home; girls screamed in

English, and people who were waiting for the bus panicked, but soon the crowds deployed themselves into neat dripping little squadrons, cheerful and brave, and the entrance of the Clarendon Centre and the great department stores were converted into shelters with an unfussy swiftness. I had never seen it rain like this in England before; water collected in the lanes and flowed past us as it does in Calcutta; and the English were excited at first and then reasonable and collected, telling each other jokes and enjoying themselves; it was all a little like but yet very unlike the wise dailiness with which an Indian outwaits a shower. Sharma looked at the sky and felt poetic and told me how he was reminded of his village. Thus I did not meet Shehnaz that afternoon but waited outside a shop that sold shoes and saw wet and laughing people running and appearing, and committed to memory the rare, leisurely couple who walked by, contented and soaked. Later, Shehnaz told me how she had cycled to the St. Giles' Café after it had stopped raining, but had found it empty except for its owners, the stentorian callers of 'Ham and cheese' and 'Bacon sandwich', who were silent now, and busy mopping up the wet floors.

Before I met Shehnaz, I led a domestic life with Sharma, a warm kitchen life of teas and conversations. In this country where afternoon comes suddenly, he was a desired and happy interference, sewing my buttons, cooking daal for dinner, advising me on which clothes to wear, forcing me to buy new ones. What brought us together, among other things, was a common love for the English language. Each night, till mid-night, he would recount with delight new idioms and words he had picked up during the day, and from these words he would become inseparable for about a week, using them in every context, just as a child who has been given a gift of new shoes spends a euphoric period wearing them everywhere. After lunch, we would sometimes watch black-and-white British films from the fifties on channel four, and Sharma would tell me how charming he found the rhythms and accents of Old English. He was a glum reader and connoisseur of dictionaries, an admirer of the *Collins'* and a baleful critic of the *OED,* and he had a special but clear-eyed insight into their limitations.

In Oxford, I would walk almost everywhere, because I had an inexplicable pride that prevented me from using buses. There were two kinds of local buses, the red double-decker and the small toy-like white-and-blue bus. When the double-deckers passed by, they looked grand and somehow inaccessible, while the white buses seemed warm and busy, with the people sitting in them clearly visible through the large windows. But sitting inside a bus was a different experience, unrelated to what one might have surmised from the outside. Once, I took a double-decker to Cowley Road. It was like entering another life, right from ascending the wide berth of the footboard at the entrance, clutching with great immediacy the pole-vaulter's pole that rose there from the floor, ignoring the stealthy staircase that crept primitively upward, to make one's way shyly inside, braving the curious but not unwelcoming glances of other people. As the scene changed from the civic architecture of High Street to the grey brick houses and Indian restaurants on Cowley Road, bodies circulated gently and continually inside, as people got in and got out; it was strangely but peacefully crowded, and one had to cling economically to a loop of leather or a horizontal rod travelling over one's head, and sway containedly from the top of one's head to the base of one's feet, and privately regain one's balance, as the bus went on its stately but mildly drunken, intemperate course. Another time, I took a less dramatic journey on a white bus to Summertown. Everything about it was small and detailed, from the coin handed for my fare to the driver, the neat black seats, the roof lowering over my head. Behind me sat a group of chattering boys and girls, and their impudent London accent filled the bus. Only a little way away from me sat the Indian bus driver in his blue uniform, but for some reason I thought of him as 'Asian', and he became for me mysterious and unclassifiable. At each stop, he greeted kindly old ladies in a hearty English manner, 'Hullo, dear! It's lovely day, innit?' and later bid them inimitable farewells, 'Have a nice day, dear!' but the way he was more English than the English was very Indian, and there was something surprising about his utterances.

Cowley Road was on the other side, East Oxford. Long ago I had accompanied Sharma in hope of seeing an erotic Japanese film, *The*

Realm of the Senses, to the Penultimate Picture Palace. After the roundabout, three roads ran parallel to each other—St. Clement's, Cowley Road, and Iffley Road. Full of spirit, we took the Cowley Road to the Picture Palace, but found, alas, that there were no tickets. The road was lined with Bangladeshi shops, and energetic little Muslim boys wearing skull-caps played on the pavement; they did not look foreign, but very provincial and East London. After darkness fell, the shops remained lit and open, and old Pakistani gentlemen in overcoats, holding crumpled carrier-bags in their hands, had a chance to meet each other inside and converse in idiomatic Punjabi. Politics was discussed; the Bhuttos; Kashmir; cowardly India; bullying India; and the Indian cricket team was dismissed, quite rightly, with a contemptuous but decorous burst of air from the lungs. 'Asian' couples with shopping-trolleys went down aisles stacked with boxes of chilli powder, packets of dried fruit, jars of pickles, and imported vegetables—roots and tubers—with the flecked soil of Bangladesh still upon them; the shopkeeper continued his conversation in full-throated asides while his hands worked at the till; and to pay him, finally, in pounds rather than in rupees was like a joke whose meaning we both shared. There was a row of Indian restaurants along the road; at six o'clock, Muslim waiters stood significantly by the windows, and at night, the interiors glowed a lurid red light. The furniture, selected with some tender and innocent idea of opulence in mind, was cheap and striking; honest Englishmen sat being served among fluted armrests and large, mendacious pictures of palm trees and winding rivers, helplessly surrendering to an inexhaustible trickle of Eastern courtesy; everything, including the waiters, smelled strongly of mint and fenugreek. The restaurants were seedy, but generous with life; and from the silvery letters of the sign outside, to the decor within, was a version of that style called the 'oriental'.

Meera Syal

Indoor Language

But today was our Christmas. My parents were celebrating it as they celebrated nearly everything else, with another *mehfil*. This was perfect for them but a major disappointment for me and all my other 'cousins' who wanted presents thrown in as part of the package, at least a nod towards what Christmas meant for the English. But I wanted to give myself a present, as no one else would, I wanted to see the fair. I knew mama did not want me to go, especially with Anita Rutter, but she assented with a slight nod of her head, and added as I rushed out of the door, 'Be back by five o'clock. I want you to help me cut the salad . . .'

Anita was peeking over my shoulder as she stood in the doorway, checking out the simmering pans and mountains of chopped vegetables crowding the kitchen. As we walked out of my gate, she said, 'Is it someone's birthday today?'

'No,' I replied. 'It's like our Christmas today. Dead boring.'

'Yow have two Christmases, do ya? Lucky cow.'

I had not thought of it this way before and suddenly felt elevated.

'I'm getting a pony for Christmas,' Anita said airily. She was wearing one of her old summer dresses and a cardigan I guessed must have been her mum's as it hung off her in woolly folds. I felt babyish and cosseted, wrapped up in my hooded anorak and thick socks and realised Anita must have been a lot older than I had previously thought.

This extract is taken from *Anita and Me*, published by New Press, New York, 1996.

'I'm gonna keep it at Sherrie's farm. In summat called a paddock. And then me and Sherrie am gooing to share a flat together. In London.'

I felt blindingly jealous. Sherrie was still her best friend then, and they had mapped out their life together already. I imagined them living in a penthouse flat in a place called the Angel (my favourite stop on the Monopoly board as it sounded so beautiful). They both wore mini-skirts and loads of black eyeliner and were eating toast whilst they looked out of their window. Before them stretched Buckingham Palace, the Tower of London, the Houses of Parliament and several theatres, all lit up, throwing coloured flashes onto their laughing faces, and tethered to a post attached to the breakfast bar was a sleek chestnut bay that looked just like Misty.

We passed the Big House which, as usual, showed no signs of life, save a thin twisting line of smoke curling up from its huge red chimney. Anita crossed herself quickly as we passed, muttering to herself.

'What yow dooing?' I asked.

'Quick! Do this! Do the cross over your heart!'

I hurriedly copied her, and broke into a trot behind her. We did not stop until we'd passed the grounds.

'Yow got to do that every time yow pass. Didn't yow know a witch lives there?'

I shook my head dumbly. I should have guessed, it explained everything. The sense of menace surrounding the place, the fact no one ever saw visitors or inhabitants arriving or leaving, or any lights blazing at night.

'It's a woman. She killed her kids and husband, but they could never prove it, see. She wants kids, needs the blood to keep alive. Remember Jodie from up the hill?'

Jodie Bagshot was a four-year-old girl from the top end of the village who had gone missing for three frantic days a few summers ago, and whose body was found caught in the bulrushes round Hollow Ponds, the deep water-filled old mine shafts at the back of the Big House. While she was missing, the village seemed to hold its breath. Mothers stopped their children playing anywhere except the yard and the adjoining park, where everyone could see them from their kitchen windows. Police cars and officers scoured every field and hedgerow with long sticks and alsatians, even going on into the night where we could see their torches flashing through the cornfields, like cyclopic aliens calling to each other under the high-domed summer sky. The radio was on constantly in every home, waiting for the latest newsflash, aware as they listened that the news itself was being made on their own doorsteps, with a dumb sense of shame that Tollington had finally been put on the map in this tainted way.

When Jodie's drowned body was discovered and the swift conclusion reached that she had tragically wandered off, a horrendous accident, no one else involved, Tollington breathed again. Pity for the girl's family was mingled with relief that it had not been some sick stranger roaming the village, an outsider bent on destroying the easy trust and unhampered wanderings of the village children. Those things happened to other people, people in cities, people who did not know their neighbours, not the good, reliable, nosey inhabitants of Tollington.

But soon afterwards, a rumour began, started by Sam Lowbridge who had made sure he was in the front row with the press when the body was hauled out of the water. 'Her was blue,' he said. 'Like every bit of blood wore gone from her little body . . .'

I remembered his testimony now, and shivered, seeing the triumph growing in Anita's face.

'Ar, the witch is after more kids now. Shame she can see right into yowr bedroom window, in't it?'

I swung my gaze across the fields and saw that our house was indeed directly, diagonally across from the Big House's gates.

'I don't care!' I blurted out. 'My mom knows loads of prayers anyway. She says them every night in my bedroom, before I sleep.'

Anita laughed. 'Them's no good! The witch is English, in't she? Yow need proper English prayers. Like Uncle Alan knows.'

The only one I could remember offhand from my Sunday sessions was the chant we uttered in unison which heralded the appearance of two plates of custard creams and paper cups of weak orange squash— 'For what we are about to receive, may the Lord make us truly thankful. Amen.' Me and Anita said it together, all the way to the Old Pit Head.

The fairground trailers were parked in what must have been the former car park attached to the old mine. A small brick office building near the base of the pit head had long crumbled away, and frost-withered hollyhocks and dandelions had broken through the concrete floor. This usually desolate rectangle was now a hive of activity as various stubble-brushed, burly men yelled to each other in smokey voices as they heaved around large lumps of machinery which would eventually become the Waltzer, the Octopus, the Helter Skelter and several sideshow stalls offering such delights as a free goldfish with every fallen coconut.

A row of caravans was parked alongside the back fence where a fire burned in a metal brazier and children's clothes hung stiffly on a makeshift washing line strung between two door handles. A group of pin-thin children were playing with some scrawny kittens near the brazier, whilst a tired, washed-out woman in a hairnet, stood leaning against her caravan door inhaling deeply on a cigarette. I was fascinated by these travelling people, envied them their ability to contain their whole home in a moving vehicle and imagined how romantic it must be to just climb in and move off once boredom or routine set in. How many countries had they visited, I wondered, how many deserts and jungles had they driven through, setting up their rides and booths on shifting sands or crushed palm leaf floors. Maybe they had even been to India.

I suddenly had a vivid picture of all my grandparents, dressed as they were in their photographs, being sedately whirled round in their waltzer cars. Dadima holding a goldfish in a plastic bag, Dadaji sucking on a candy floss, whilst Nanima sang along to the thumping soundtrack of 'All You Need is Love' and Nanaji kept time with a tapping sandalled foot, holding onto his turban with long brown fingers . . .

'Don't goo up there,' Anita warned me, indicating the caravans. 'Them's gippos, them is. Tinkers. Yow'll catch summat. Mum told me.' Then she waved and whooped at Fat Sally and Sherrie who were standing watching three young blokes putting the dodgem car floor down. They waved back and indicated we should come over.

As I got closer, I realised why I had not recognised them straight away. Sherrie was shivering in a short denim skirt and high heels, and had applied mauve eyeshadow all the way up to her eyebrows. Fat Sally was squeezed into a psychedelic mini-dress with a shiny scarf tied round the waist, and her lips looked wet and shimmery, like a goldfish.

'That's nice!' said Anita, pointing her finger at Fat Sally's mouth. 'Giz sum. Mom locked her door today, couldn't get nothing off her dressing table. Mean cow.'

Sherrie and Fat Sally giggled, Fat Sally rummaged in a pocket and brought out a small tub of Miners Lip Gloss which Anita grabbed and began smearing over her lips with a practised finger. They did not seem to have noticed me.

All three girls then scrutinised each other's faces, toning down a streak of blusher here, wiping a wet finger over a lipline there, whilst the three by now sweaty blokes stopped work and straightened up, looking over at us curiously. Anita, Fat Sally and Sherrie immediately pouted to attention, flicking their hair and digging each other in the ribs. Not to be outdone, I took my anorak hood down and wiped my nose. I could see the three musketeers clearly now, in a uniform of dirty denims and skinny rib sweaters, streaked with engine oil. The tallest of the three, a lanky, mousey youth with a poetic mouth, scratched his crotch absentmindedly, and muttered something to his companions, a short Italian-looking guy and a stockier blonde bloke with a smear of acne lying across his chin like scarlet porridge. They must have been about Sam Lowbridge's age, eighteen or so, just growing into their clumsy long limbs and carefully groomed bum-fluff upper lips.

Anita hissed, 'I'm having the tall one, roight?' and sauntered over towards them, her thin hips swaying to some far off radio which was playing 'This is the captain of your ship, your soul speaking . . .' I wondered if a soul was the same thing as a conscience and if Anita Rutter was following or ignoring hers at this moment in time. She sat down on the half-erected stage, right in the midst of them, and began talking to the Poet, each question punctuated with her short barking laugh. Pretty soon, all three guys were smiling along with her; I stood open-mouthed in admiration, wondering what spell she had cast, to turn these boy-men, whom I would have crossed streets to avoid had I seen them hanging around any corner near my school, into grinning, pliant pets.

Sherrie and Fat Sally were similarly impressed. 'Her always gets the best one,' muttered Sherrie, pulling her skirt down so that it momentarily covered her goosepimpled thighs.

'Look! He's only putting his arm round her! Cow!' breathed Fat Sally, who pulled her scarf tighter around her belly, as if constant optimistic pressure would finally reveal a waist as tiny and perfect as Anita's.

Anita suddenly seemed to remember we were waiting, and after a brief exchange with her new admirers, beckoned us over. I hesitated at first, wondering if it was five o'clock yet and if I should be getting back. But I sniffed something unfamiliar in the crisp late afternoon air, something forbidden and new, and I did not want to miss out.

'These am me mates, Sherrie and Sally. . .' Anita said, her hand resting proprietorially on the Poet's knee. 'This is Dave, that's Tonio, he's Italian like me dad, and Gary . . .'

Sherrie immediately plonked herself next to Tonio, once she realised she towered over him by about six inches. They seemed as relieved as each other to have not drawn the short straw and ended up with either spotty Gary or Fat Sally, who now faced each other sullenly over an empty dodgem car. There was an uncomfortable silence in which anger and pity overtook both their faces as they realised fate and their appearance had consigned them, inevitably, shamefully, to each other. If spotty Gary and Fat Sally had any illusions that they deserved better, they only had to look across and see their own miserable reflection in the other's eyes.

For one brief, mad moment, Gary's gaze flickered round wildly, seeking an alternative, hoping there might be someone else on whom he could hang his rapidly diminishing status. He came to rest on me, took in the winter coat, the scabbed knees, my stubborn nine-year-old face, and dismissed me with amusement and yes, relief. He had not got the short straw after all and I knew, I knew that it was not because I was too young or badly dressed, it was something else, something about me so offputting, so unimaginable, that I made Fat Sally look like the glittering star prize.

The Poet whispered something into Anita's ear which made her scream as if she'd been pinched.

'What? What!' hissed Fat Sally and Sherrie in unison.

Anita pulled them unceremoniously to one side and they huddled in a group, inches from my shoulder. I might as well have been invisible. The three lads did not seem surprised at this sudden withdrawal. This was obviously part of whatever ritual they were all going through and from which I was excluded, this gathering in of the troops to discuss tactics. The lads fell into their expected stance; they raised knowing eyebrows at each other, puffed out their chests and sat with their legs as wide as possible so that their jeans strained at the seams. I had seen the dogs in the yard do something similar when one of the bitches padded past. They would cock their legs in her face as if to say, 'Well, gerra load of this then, baby!' I was beginning to realise that what was happening in front of me was somehow related to this.

'What he say, goo on, tell us!' panted Fat Sally, almost salivating with anticipation.

'He said,' drawled Anita, 'he wanted to shag the arse off me!'

Fat Sally grabbed Sherrie in a bear hug and squealed madly. Sherrie began a squeak of delight and then stopped suddenly, pushing her off, realising that Anita was playing cool in the face of this compliment. I assumed it was a compliment by her smug expression. Now Anita was looking at me, inside my head it seemed. She knew exactly what I was thinking and even wrapped up in my duffle coat, I felt suddenly naked.

'Hey Meena,' Anita said almost tenderly. 'Know what that means, that he wants to shag the arse off me?'

I shrugged in what I hoped was a non-committal, I-Might-Know-But-I'm-Not-Telling-You sort of way.

'It means,' she continued, coming right up to my face, 'that he really really loves me.'

I nodded wisely. Of course, I had known this all along. Fat Sally and Sherrie turned their faces away, their shoulders shaking slightly. I didn't care. They were only jealous that Anita had taken time to let me in on their secret and I felt blessed.

'Ey! Nita!' called the Poet. He was holding up a packet of cigarettes, and suddenly all three girls had left me, falling upon the boys like puppies, giggling uncontrollably. It was only when I started walking away that I realised Anita had not even introduced me, they did not even know my name. I glanced back; the Poet was holding out the now open cigarette packet. Anita slipped one expertly into her mouth. It seemed that her lip gloss reflected the dying sun. I ran all the way home, crossing the road when I got to the Big House, muttering my prayer and desperate to be inside and anonymous.

I reached my front door at exactly the same time as papa. His suit looked crumpled at the knees and elbows and his tie hung loosely around his neck. He put his briefcase on the front step and lifted me up, nuzzling my neck. 'How's my beti?'

'Fine,' I lied. I opened the door to see mama on her knees, trying to push the windy yellow settee back against a wall.

'What the hell are you doing, Daljit?' barked papa, striding inside and pulling her up. 'Are you mad?'

'I was not going to lift it,' mama said weakly, surrendering herself to his embrace.

'Couldn't you wait?' papa shouted angrily. 'You will damage yourself like this.'

He sat mama down on an armchair and ordered me to fetch her a glass of water, which she sipped slowly, watching papa shove the settee into a corner and lay out a clean white sheet on the floor, ready for the evening's *mehfil*.

He glanced into the kitchen. The pans were heavy and silent on the stove, a large bowl of chapatti dough stood untouched at the counter.

'You haven't even made the roti yet,' he said. 'We should cancel tonight. Too much work.'

'Don't be silly, darling,' mama sighed. 'Everyone is coming. How will it look?'

This was one of her favourite get-out clauses, the mantra for her self-imposed martyrdom—what will people think?

'You could have waited till I got home,' papa continued, plumping up cushions. 'You don't have to do everything yourself.'

'Who else is there?' mama muttered, and then I remembered I was supposed to cut the salad. I went into the kitchen and opened the fridge where a huge tupperware full of freshly-cut tomatoes and cucumber stared back accusingly at me.

The first guests began arriving around seven o'clock. I was admiring myself in mama's dressing table mirror, deciding whether I liked this unfamiliar reflection staring back in a purple *salwar kameez* suit, stiff with yellow elephant embroidery around the cuffs and neckline. I liked the suit, but it did not quite go with the pudding basin haircut and chewed-down fingernails. I spotted mama's modest cache of make-up, a couple of Revlon lipsticks with round blunt heads, a goldplated compact case which when opened, played 'Strangers in the Night' in a tinkly offhand manner, and a tiny stub of black eyebrow pencil. I picked up one of the lipsticks, Pink Lady, and applied it carefully around my mouth, startled to see a glaring cerise grin appear on my face, seemingly hovering above it like the Cheshire Cat smile I had seen in one of the ink drawings in my Alice in Wonderland book. To finish off the stunning effect, I rifled through mama's jewellery case, a blue leather box with delicate filigree clasps, and chose a gold chain upon which hung a single teardrop-shaped diamond. Even though I was sure mama would not mind, I hid it under my vest.

'Meena?' mama called from downstairs. 'Door please!' I hurriedly opened the compact case and stuck my finger into its belly. The powder was surprisingly soft and crumbly, and I wiped a few smears around my nose and forehead, like I had seen mama do. I blew myself a kiss as I left, did I look gorgeous.

Auntie Shaila gave a shriek of alarm when I opened the door. *'Hai Ram!* What is this? Looking like a rumpty tumpty dancing girl already . . .' She tottered inside, dragging Uncle Amman behind her, his smooth, polished billiard ball head glistening with raindrops. 'Daljit! Eh! Look at your daughter!' Auntie Shaila continued, peeling off her overcoat, two woollen shawls and finally a thick pair of old bedsocks, revealing a glorious emerald green sari. 'Damn English weather. . . having to hide all the time under these smelly blankets . . . Daljit!'

Mama came bustling in from the kitchen, adjusting her sari *pulla,* and stopped short when she saw me pouting back. 'Meena! What have you done to your face?' she asked.

Auntie Shaila kissed mama and handed her a box of Ambala sweetmeats, sticky yellow *laddoos* pressing against the clear cellophane of the lid. 'Happy Diwali, sister. You see what happens to our girls here? Wanting to grow up so quickly and get boyfriends-shoyfriends . . . Isn't childhood short enough, eh?'

'She was just experimenting,' papa smiled, giving a jolly *namaste* to our visitors. 'Meena, go upstairs and wipe it off, good girl . . .'

'No!' I said, shocked by the sound of my voice. 'Where's Pinky? Where's Baby?'

Auntie Shaila's two daughters were the only other girls roughly around my age in our circle, and therefore I treated them as best friends in front of the adults, although I secretly thought they were boring and rather thick. I had planned a whole evening of ghost stories and plays in which we would take turns at playing a screaming blonde heroine being pursued by nameless wailing monsters. Auntie Shaila spoke carefully, as if addressing an idiot. 'Pinky and Baby are home with their dadima. Tonight is for grown-ups. And please no naughtiness tonight. Your mama is in a delicate way, you should be pressing her feet and asking for forgiveness. Now upstairs, and come back down wearing your own pretty face.'

After scrubbing my cheeks and lips clean with tissues, I opened my bedroom window and saw, as I had expected to, the lights of the fairground twinkling through the trees surrounding the Big House. I caught glimpses of the Octopus whirling round and round, its tentacles hung with chairs containing screaming, laughing passengers, their voices mingling with the thumping soundtrack of a pop song, 'One Two Three, Oh It's So Easy, Ba-by!' as my papa began tuning up his harmonium in the room below. I could see couples drawn by the music and lights, picking their way through the rows of cars which clogged the road up to the pithead.

I could make out another crowd of people pushing their way through the fairground punters, struggling against the flow and press of bodies. This crocodile of renegades moved slowly. I saw the flash of a jewelled sandal picking its way through the mud, a glittering nose ring caught by the flare of a neon bulb, a streak of vermilion silk exposed by a winter coat whipped up by the night air, and knew the rest of our guests had arrived.

By the time I had realised no one had noticed I was sulking and went downstairs, the front room was full of my uncles and aunties, all sitting cross-legged on the white floor sheet. Mama was handing round starters of kebabs and chutney whilst papa leafed through his tattered notebook containing ghazal lyrics, deep in conversation with Uncle Tendon, who cradled his *tabla* like a child. 'Ah Meena beti!' they called out as one, and I did the round of *namastes* and kisses, smiling through the lipstick assaults and the over-hard cheek pinching as my suit was praised and tweaked, my stomach tickled and jabbed, my educational achievements listed and admired, until I felt I was drowning in a sea of rustling saris, clinking gold jewellery and warm, brown, overpowering flesh.

The men, as usual, had divided up into two distinct groups. There were the ones like Uncle Tendon and my papa, the dapper, snapping, witty men in crisp suits who smoked and joked and retired to women-free corners where their whispered conversation, no doubt risqué, was punctuated by huge bear-hugs and back-slapping routines. Then there was the quieter type, like Auntie Shaila's husband, Uncle Amman, self-effacing, gentle shadows who followed their wives around playing the role of benevolent protector, but well aware that they were merely satellites caught in the matronly orbit of their noisy, loving wives.

Most of my Aunties were in the Shaila mode, plump, bosomy women with overactive gap-toothed mouths, fond of bright tight outfits accentuating every cherished roll and curve of flesh, bursting with optimism and unsolicited advice for everyone's children, upon whose futures they pinned all their unfulfilled desires. Mama was in the minority group of Auntie types, the slender, delicate soft-voiced women with the sloe-eyed grace captured by the Mughal miniature paintings hanging on our front room wall. Their serenity masked backbones of iron and a flair for passive resistance of which Gandhiji himself would have been proud.

As I watched my mother trying to force another kebab onto Auntie Shaila (mama looked like one of those tiny birds who hop in and out of hippos' mouths, negotiating molars nervously) I realised what part of my problem was—I had been born to the wrong type of Indian woman. If I had been given a mother like Auntie Shaila, the fat loud type who didn't mind the patches of sweat forming under their sari blouses after a good dance, I would not have to feel so angry at my body, the way it betrayed me by making me stand with my legs akimbo, hands on hips, the way it tripped me up into the dirt, skinning my knees—it was never meant to behave like the body of a lady. But next to mama, I would always feel lumbering and clumsy. Even in late pregnancy, she moved like a galleon in full sail, stately and calm, her belly leading the way. There was another baby inside there, as much as I had tried to ignore it, and I suddenly understood that mama would not be exclusively mine for very much longer.

A ripple of recognition passed through the room as papa began singing, his rich vibrato climbed slowly up my spine. I knew this song, a romantic song, naturally, of a lover singing to his beloved, telling her he was so sick with desire that he would follow her wherever she wandered like a shadow . . . *'Mera Saaya Sath Hoga, Tu Jahan Jahan Chalega . . .'* Uncle Tendon joined in with a soft heartbeat accompaniment and a collective sigh of longing swelled the air. Papa's voice swooped and soared like a swallow above our heads, notes catching in his throat, flowers caught momentarily in brambles before being tossed into the air, every face turned inwards, remembering the first time they heard this song.

I suddenly saw Auntie Shaila sauntering along Connaught Place, pencil-thin in her chic chiffon suit, stepping between the sprawled limbs of the young men lounging at the sidewalk cafes over their cold coffees and cheese *pakore*, humming the song to herself, pretending not to notice, but knowing for certain, that every eye was upon her. I saw mama singing the song to the wind as she cycled back from her all girls college, her long oiled plaits bumping against her back, swerving around the cows and trucks on the Karol Bagh Road, duty and desire already at war for her future. I saw papa, just like in the old photographs, hair slicked back, movie star fashion, Cary Grant baggy suit and lit cigarette hanging from his fingers, standing on the street corner opposite mama's flat, whistling that tune, blowing it through the peeling paint shutters where mama sat bent over textbooks she could not read because of the thumping of her heart, because that song told her that he was waiting for her outside, and would wait until she came. These were my versions of their stories and I set them free during papa's songs.

Papa's singing always unleashed these emotions which were unfamiliar and instinctive at the same time, in a language I could not recognise but felt I could speak in my sleep, in my dreams, evocative of a country I had never visited but which sounded like the only home I had ever known. The songs made me realise that there was a corner of me that would be forever not England.

I glanced around at my elders who looked so shiny and joyous in their best Diwali clothes. I had seen all of them at some point in their workday clothes of English separates and over-coordinated suits. But on occasions like Diwali, they expanded to fit their Indian clothes and at this moment, seemed too big and beautiful for our small suburban sitting room.

Papa finished singing, the last notes faded away to be replaced by rapturous applause and shouts of 'Wah! Kumar saab!'He radiated joy, achievement. I'd never seen him come home from work looking like this. He turned to me and my stomach sank; I knew what he was going to ask me. 'Meena beti, why don't you sing a song for your Aunties and Uncles?' They all began clapping and shouting, 'Hah! Let's hear your lovely voice! Come and show us how it is done.' 'No,' I mumbled uselessly. 'Don't want to . . . no . . .'

I knew I was already defeated, that false modesty was an expected response to any social request, that 'No' always meant 'Yes, I want to really but you will have to ask me at least five times before I can give in graciously and not look like a big fat show-off'. It applied to food, drink, money and especially public performance of any kind; I had seen mama literally force-feeding Auntie Shaila, who insisted she was not at all hungry and then proceeded to polish off a truckful of kebabs without chewing, ostensibly to please mama, but grateful she had been given permission to stuff her face without guilt. Of course, we all understood these complex rules of hospitality; our neighbours however did not.

Mama had been caught out quite badly when she once offered a lift down to the shops to the Mad Mitchells who lived next door, on the other side of the entry. Mr and Mrs Mitchell were a middle-aged brother and sister who lived with Cara, a moon-faced dopey woman who, it was rumoured, was their incestuous daughter. Whilst the couple were loud, argumentative, and swore as naturally as they breathed, Cara never said a word. We would often spot her wandering down the middle of the road humming to herself, dragging a squeaky shopping trolley as alarmed motorists swerved to avoid her.

Mama had been helping me into the car when all three Mitchells appeared at her side, wearing buttoned-up overcoats and their usual warm idiot grins.

'New car, Mrs K?'

'Oh yes,' mama smiled. 'So useful for getting to work.'

'Ay, bloody bosting car that, ain't it ma?' Mr Mitchell sighed.

'Bloody bosting,' agreed Mrs Mitchell, who was holding Cara's hand tightly.

'So am yow gooin down the shops then?' they said in unison.

'Why, yes,' mama said, still smiling. 'Can I give you a lift?' Now if she'd asked that question to an Indian, they would have replied, 'Oh no, we will walk, it is such a lovely day, please don't bother yourself, we enjoy strolling in the sleet, so good for the circulation . . .' etc, giving mama time to consider the request and the other room to withdraw gracefully, because if mama had not physically shoved them into the car, that obviously meant she was in a hurry and would rather not give them a lift at all.

Instead, the Mitchells said, 'Oh ta!' and piled into the back seat, leaving mama open-mouthed on the pavement. After we had dropped them off, we discovered a small patch of urine where Cara had been sitting. Mama had to scrub down the upholstery later that night, not wanting to do it in daylight where the Mitchells might see, and feel embarrassed.

'Hurry up Meena! No more pretending now, we have asked you enough times!' called Auntie Shaila, making everyone laugh.

I shuffled over to papa who shifted over, indicating a space beside him. I seethed with embarrassment and fury; what was wrong with these people? Why couldn't a No mean a bloody sodding No? Why was talking to them like trying to do semaphore in a gale?

'Which song, beti?' asked papa, running his hands over the keys, flexing his fingers in preparation.

'Any,' I said ungraciously.

Papa began an introduction to an old Hindi film song he had taught me. He paused where the verse began and nodded encouragingly. I took a breath and began, '*Yeh Raat Yeh Chandani Phir Kahan, Sunja Dil Ki Daastan . . .*'

I knew the song was about a sultry moonlit night in which a lover is thinking about his absent object of desire. I knew it was a romantic song, but as I sang, all I could think of was the Poet sniffing at Anita's hemline like a yard mutt. I became aware that some of the Aunties were giggling, whispering to each other behind their hands and then fixing me with long, fond stares. I could hear Auntie Shaila clearly, whispering not being one of her strong points. 'Va! She sings Punjabi with a Birmingham accent! Damn cute, really!'

I stopped dead, the harmonium carried on for a few bars after me and then breathed out and fell silent.

'I don't want to do this song,' I said to papa.

'But it sounds so lovely, really. You should sing your own songs, Meena.'

'Okay,' I said, took a deep breath and launched into a rendition of 'We Wear Short Shorts', complete with the gyrating dance routine I had seen Pan's People do to it on *Top Of the Pops*. I flicked my hair and kicked my legs as papa and Uncle Tendon gamely tried to match a key and rhythm to my show stopper, although their complex minor key riffs and passionate drum solos did not altogether complement the song. I finished by shouting 'Yeah man!', and doing the splits, accompanied by a loud ripping noise and after a moment's pause, a round of enthusiastic applause. Mama pulled me up and examined the large tear along the crotch of my trousers. 'Did you have to do that?' she hissed.

Papa laughed, 'Leave her! It was very groovy, Meena! That was what you call a good jam-in, hey Tendon saab?'

They slapped each other's backs and hooted uproariously.

The Aunties and Uncles just loved me; they crowded round patting me like a pet, over-enthusing about my talent and charisma whilst papa shot knowing winks to mama, who was slowly melting in the face of this public approval. 'Hai, such a performer!' shouted Auntie Shaila above the din. 'So sweetly done, so er modern! Where did you learn this song, Meena beti?'

'Off the radio,' I preened. 'It's my all time favourite song at the moment,' and then added, 'It's so brilliant I could shag the arse off it.'

There was a sudden terrible intake of breath and then complete silence, broken only by the harmonium emitting a death rattle as papa's fingers fell off the keys. In a split second, my beaming admirers had become parodies of Hindi film villains, with flared nostrils, bulging eyes and quivering, outraged eyebrows. They only needed twirling moustaches and pot bellies straining at a bullet laden belt to complete the sense of overwhelming menace that now surrounded me. In my dizzy state, I fancied I saw Anita Rutter perched on a dodgem car with a fag hanging out of her mouth, and laughing in reverberated echo as the heavens slowly crumbled and fell in blue jagged lumps around her.

'What did you say, Meena?'

It was papa, in a tone of voice I had not heard before, which shot right off the Outraged Parent clapometer.

'N . . . nothing papaji,' I stuttered, noticing that the Aunties and Uncles were now drifting away. This was a very bad sign. They were not even attempting group discipline on this particular crime. I was on my own. Papa stood up slowly and strode towards me. Papa has never hit me, never hit me, I told myself over and over again and yet I flinched when mama suddenly appeared at my side, putting a protective arm around me and shoving me towards the stairs. 'You better go upstairs, Meena,' she said quietly. I did not need to be asked twice and I fled.

MEERA SYAL

Gold Emporium

Not even snowfall could make Leyton look lovely. Sootfall was what it was; a fine drizzle of ash that sprinkled the pavements and terrace rooftops, dusting the rusty railings and faded awnings of the few remaining shops along the high road. They formed a puzzling collection of plucky bric-à-brac emporiums (All the Plastic Matting You'll Ever Need!) and defeated mini-marts (Cigs 'N' Bread! Fags 'N' Mags!), braving the elements like the no-hopers no-one wanted on their team, shivering in their sooty kit. Grey flecks nested in the grooves of the shutters of the boarded up homes, abandoned when new roads were put down and old ladies died; they settled silently on the graves in the choked churchyard, giving grace and shadow to long-unread inscriptions—Edna, Beloved Wife; Edward, Sleeps with the Angels— and dressed the withered cedars in almost-mourning robes of almost- black. Pigeons shook their heads, sneezing, blinking away the icy specks, claws skittering on the unfamiliar roof which had once been the reassuring flat red tiles of the methodist church and was now a gleaming minaret, topped by a metal sickle moon. The moon at midday, dark snow and nowhere to perch. No wonder they said Coo.

   An old man picked up a frozen milk bottle from his front step and held it up to the light, squinting at the petrified pearly sea beyond the glass. He'd seen an ocean like that once, in the navy or on the TV, he couldn't remember which now.

This extract is taken from *Life Isn't All Ha Ha Hee Hee*, published by New Press, New York, 1999.

'You waiting till the whole bloody house freezes then?' his wife called from inside. A voice that could splinter bone.

And then he heard them. Nothing more than an echo at first, muted by wind and traffic, but he felt the sound, like you always do when it brings the past with it. Clop-clop, there it was, no mistaking it. And then he was seven or ten again, in scratchy shorts with sherbet fizzing on his tongue, racing his brother to open up the coal shute at the front of the house before the cart drew up and the man with the black face and the bright smile groaned, his sack on his back, freeing swirls of dust with every heavy step.

'Come here!' the old man shouted behind him. 'Quickly! You hurry up and you'll see a . . . bleedin' hell!'

The horse turned the corner into his road, white enough to shame what fell from the sky, carrying what looked like a Christmas tree on its back. There was a man in the middle of the tinsel, pearls hanging down over his brown skin, suspended from a cartoon-size turban. He held a nervous small boy, similarly attired, on his lap. Behind him, a group of men of assorted heights and stomach sizes, grins as stiff as their new suits, attempted a half-dance half-jog behind the swishing tail, their polished shoes slipping in the slush. A fat man in a pink jacket held a drum around his neck and banged it with huge palms, like a punishment, daring anyone not to join in. 'Brrrr-aaaa! Bu-le, bu-le bu-le!' he yelled.

The old man understood half of that noise, it was brass monkey weather all right, but what did he mean by that last bit? They couldn't like the cold, surely.

'Another of them do's down the community centre then,' said his wife, sniffing at his shoulder.

Other neighbours had gathered at windows and doorways, the children giggling behind bunched fingers, their elders, flint-faced, guarding their stone-clad kingdoms warily, in case bhangra-ing in bollock-freezing weather was infectious.

Swamped, thought the old man; someone said that once, we'll be swamped by them. But it isn't like that, wet and soggy like Hackney Marshes. It's silent and gentle, so gradual that you hardly notice it at all until you look up and see that everything's different.

'Like snow,' he said, out loud.

Trigger, the horse, was enjoying himself. Anything was better than the dumpy pubescents he was forced to heave around paddocks in Chigwell for the rest of the week. This was an easy gig, a gentle amble past kind hands and interesting odours. Early this morning, he'd been woken by an old lady in a white sheet breaking coconuts beneath his hooves. She had sung for him. She smelt of pepper. There was none of the kisses and baby talk the stable girls lavished on him to impress the parents, but her patient worship had made him snort with joy. He stepped lightly now, considering he was carrying a heavy-hearted man on his back.

Deepak had noticed the hostile onlookers, albeit in fragments through the shimmering curtain that hid him from the world, but the cold stone in his chest, hidden beneath the silk brocade of his bridal suit, made them unimportant. He had explained his dank foreboding away many times, over many months now, using the dimpled smile and the mercurial tongue that had made him a business success and rendered matrons in the neighbourhood giddy with gratitude when he graced their kitty parties. Fear of commitment, he'd said to the stone in the spring. Any eligible bachelor taking the plunge is bound to feel some pangs of regret. She is as sweet as the blossom outside my window, and just as virginal. Fear of failure, he'd told the stone as he'd eyed up the passing girls from his pavement café, pluckable, all of them, bruised by summer evening blue. She doesn't need to prance around in thongs and halter necks, her beauty is beautiful because it's hidden and it will be mine. Fear of becoming my father, he'd smiled at the stone as he tramped through new-fallen leaves, recalling his parents' amazed faces as he'd confirmed his choice of bride. A Punjabi girl! They had almost wept with relief, having endured a parade of blonde trollops through their portals for most of their son's youth. Marrying her does not mean I will become my father, take up religion, grow nostril hair and wear pastel-coloured leisure wear, he told the stone playfully. We have choices. Wasn't that the reason his parents had come here in the first place? And now it was winter and the stone refused any further discussion on the matter. It was done.

And there they were, waiting. Ahead of him, the bride's welcoming committee stood in the doorway of the crumbling hall, garlands of flaming marigolds in their hands. His own Baraat, the menfolk from his side who were his companions on this journey from callow youth to fully paid up member of the respectable married classes, roared their arrival. Bow and be grateful, the man who will take your daughter off your hands for ever is here! His future mother-in-law teetered forward, her face shining; brown moon, white horse, grey snow. Deepak drew his tinsel curtain back over his eyes and felt the warm horse rumble and heave beneath him.

Chila looked at his toenails and felt a strange sense of dread. His feet were fine; brown, not too hairy, clean enough. But she could not tear her eyes from his toenails as they walked round the fire (about to be wed, head bowed submissively just in case anyone might suspect she was looking forward to a night of rampant nuptials). Ten yellowing, waxy nodules crowned each toe, curled and stiff as ancient parchment, a part of him she had never noticed before, feet that demanded attention because of their glaring imperfection, the feet of a man who might read *Garden Sheds Weekly* every evening instead of loving her. Chila told herself off. This was unfair, sacrilegious even, on your wedding day.

Or maybe it was just being prepared, like her mother was. Her mother who had handed over a parcel of brand new and frilly pink lingerie which she had bought as part of Chila's trousseau, ready to wear when her daughter finally moved in with Deepak tonight, man and wife, all official. Her mother who had coughed with embarrassment as Chila discovered the sprinkling of rose petals hidden amongst the Cellophane, shyly folding in on themselves like her own fingers were doing now. 'Sweet, Mum.' Chila smiled, ignoring the subtext in her mother's eyes, My poor baby will have the dirty thing done to her tonight. Chila had not had the heart to tell her the dirty thing had already taken place many months ago in a lock-up garage just off the A406.

'Move, didi!' her brother Raju hissed, pushing her round the holy fire. She could not look up even if she wanted, weighed down by an embroidered dupatta encrusted with fake pearls and gold-plated balls. The heavy lengha prevented her from taking more than baby steps behind her almost-husband to whom she was tied, literally, her scarf to his turban. She would have liked to wear a floaty thing, all gossamer and light, and skip around the flames like a sprite, blowing raspberries at the mafia of her mother's friends whose mantra during all her formative years had been, 'No man will ever want that one, the plump darkie with the shy stammer.' But she had shocked them all, the sour-faced harpies, by bagging not only a groom with his own teeth, hair, degree and house, but the most eligible bachelor within a twenty-mile radius.

She stole a sneaky glance at Deepak, who was checking his profile in the fractured reflection of the silver mirror ball above their heads, each winking pane with its own tiny flaming heart, a thousand holy fires refracted in its shiny orb. Bloody hell, he was fit and he was hers. She wanted to celebrate. But instead she was mummified in red and gold silk, swaddled in half the contents of Gupta's Gold Emporium, pierced, powdered and plumped up so that her body would only walk the walk of everyone's mothers on all their weddings, meekly, shyly, reluctantly towards matrimony. Chila tilted her head with difficulty and took in a deep gulp of air before she began the next perambulation, glad of the momentary rest while Deeps adjusted his headdress. She locked eyes with Tania, sitting straightbacked on the front row. She's looking a bit rough today, thought Chila, with an unexpected tinge of pleasure.

Tania shot Chila a reassuring wink and just managed to turn a grimace of discomfort into an encouraging smile. She ached all over and the new slingbacks she'd bought in five minutes flat yesterday had already raised blisters. She was squeezed between two large sari-draped ladies, fleshy bookends who exchanged stage whispers across her lap, giving a wheezy running commentary to the great drama unfolding before them.

'You see, how nicely she walks behind him? She will follow his lead in life. That is good.'

'Oh, now the father is crying. About time. Daughters are only visitors in our lives, hena?'

'Hai, they are lent to us for a short while and then we have to hand them over to strangers like—'

'Bus tickets?'

'Hah! But then where does the journey end, hah?'

'Hah! Yes. Only God knows, as he is the driver.'

'Now the sister is howling. I'd howl if I had a moustache like hers . . .'

ANURAG MATHUR

The First Letter Home

Beloved Younger Brother,

Greetings to Respectful Parents. I am hoping all is well with health and wealth. I am fine at my end. Hoping your end is fine too. With God's grace and Parents' Blessings I am arriving safely in America and finding good apartment near University. Kindly assure Mother that I am strictly consuming vegetarian food only in restaurants though I am not knowing if cooks are Brahmins. I am also constantly remembering Dr Verma's advice and strictly avoiding American women and other unhealthy habits. I hope Parents' Prayers are residing with me.

Younger Brother, I am having so many things to tell you I am not knowing where to start. Most surprising thing about America is it is full of Americans. Everywhere Americans, Americans, big and white, it is little frightening. The flight from New Delhi to New York is arriving safely thanks to God's Grace and Parents' Prayers and mine too. I am not able to go to bathroom whole time because I am sitting in corner seat as per Revered Grandmother's wish. Father is rightly scolding that airplane is flying too high to have good view. Still please tell her I have done needful.

But, brother, in next two seats are sitting two old gentle ladies and if I am getting up then they are put in lot of botheration so I am not getting up for bathroom except when plane is stopping for one hour at London. Many foods are being served in carts but I am only eating

This extract is taken from *The Inscrutable Americans*, published by Rupa & Co., 1991.

cashewnuts and bread because I am not knowing what is food and what is meat. I am having good time drinking thirty-seven glasses of Coca-Cola.

They are rolling down a screen and showing film but I am not listening because air hostess ladies are selling head phones for two dollars which is Rs 26 and in our beloved Jajau town we can sit in balcony seat in Regal Talkies for only Rs 3. I am asking lady if they are giving student discount but she is too busy. I am also asking her for more Coca-Cola but she is looking like she is weeping and walking away. I think perhaps she is not understanding proper English.

Then I am sleeping long time after London and when I am waking it is like we are flying over sea of lights. Everywhere, brother; as far as I am seeing there are lights lights. It is like God has made carpet of lights. Then we are landing in New York and plane is going right up to door so that we are not having to walk in cold. I must say Americans are very advanced. And as I am leaving airplane, air hostess is giving me one more can of Coca-Cola. Her two friends are also with her but why they are laughing so much I do not know. I think these Americans are strange but friendly people in their hearts. I hope she was not laughing for racial. Perhaps she was feeling shy earlier.

Then I am going to long bathroom. As I am leaving I am making first friend in America. This is negro gentleman named Joe who is standing at door and as I am opening it he is holding out hand so I am shaking it and telling him my name and he is telling me his. I am telling him if he is ever coming to Jajau he can ask for National Hair Oil Factory. If I have not returned from Higher Studies please tell Father that if negro gentleman named Joe is visiting Jajau he may kindly do needful.

In this way I feel each and every one of us is serving as Ambassador of our beloved Motherland. Joe is doubtful I feel because he says 'Far out, man, far out', but I am reassuring him that India is only sixteen hours away by plane and that is not very far. I think he is accepting this because he is not saying anything any more.

Next I go to place marked 'Baggage' as Father has advised and suddenly place I am sitting starts to move throwing me. It is like python we once saw in forest, only rattling and with luggage bouncing on its back and sometimes leaping to attack passengers. I am also throwing myself on bag before it is escaping. I think if I am not wrestling it down it would revert to plane and back home to India. I am only joking of course.

Before this I am meeting very friendly gentleman at Immigration desk. I do not know why all relatives had warned against this man, because he is so friendly. He is talking English strangely but is having kind heart because he is asking me about nuts and I am saying I am liking very much and eating many on plane.

'Totally, totally nuts,' he is saying, which is I feel American expression for someone fond of cashewnuts.

Before this he is showing friendliness by asking 'How is it going?' I am telling him fully and frankly about all problems and hopes, even though you may feel that as American he may be too selfish to bother about decline in price of hair oil in Jajau town. But, brother, he is listening very quietly with eyes on me for ten minutes and then we are having friendly talk about nuts and he is wanting me to go.

At Customs, brother, I am getting big shock. One fat man is grunting at me and looking cleverly from small eyes. 'First visit?' he is asking, 'Yes,' I am agreeing. 'Move on,' he is saying making chalk marks on bags. As I am picking up bags he is looking directly at me and saying 'Watch your ass.'

Now, brother, this is wonderful. How he is knowing we are purchasing donkey? I think they are knowing everything about everybody who is coming to America. They are not allowing anybody without knowing his family and financial status and other things. And we are only buying donkey two days before my departure. I think they are keeping all information in computers. Really these Americans are too advanced.

But, brother, now I am worrying. Supposing this is CIA, keeping watch or else how they can know about our donkey? Anyway please do not tell Mother and Father or they are worrying, but lock all doors and windows. If CIA wants to recruit me to be spy in Jajau, I will gladly take poison before betraying our Motherland.

Then I am going out and cousins are waiting and receiving me warmly. I will write soon after settling down.

Your brother,

Gopal.

Anita Desai

Vegetarian Summer

And so they began their careers as shoppers, Mrs Patton driving Arun in her white Honda Civic to the supermarkets along Route Two and opening out to him a vista of experience he had never expected to have. He was perplexed to find these stores and their attendant parking lots, bank outlets, gas stations, Burger Kings, Belly Delis and Dunkin' Donuts stranded on huge stretches of tarmac spread upon fields of meadow grass and summer flowers while in the distance the blue hazy line of woods smouldered and smoked against the blazing summer sky. Why would townspeople need to go into the country to shop? he wondered, but when he ventured to ask Mrs Patton, she could only give a little shake of her head and a small smile, not having understood his question: why should anyone question what was *there*?

She had already parked her car, swung out of it with her handbag, and was hurrying past the ranks of parked cars to the nest of stacked shopping carts in her eagerness to begin, while Arun trailed slowly after her, his eyes lingering over the cars that were not what he had previously known as cars—vehicles, designed to carry passengers from one point to another—but whole establishments, solid and rooted in their bulk, all laboriously acquired: weightage, history, even an inheritance. Their backseats piled with baby seats, dog blankets, boxes of Kleenex, toys and mascots adhering to their windows like barnacles. Each a module designed to contain and propel lives and dreams. Numberplates that read:

This extract is taken from *Fasting, Feasting*, published by Houghton Mifflin, New York, 1999.

'I love my Car'
'Another Day, Another Dollar'

and stickers that proclaimed:

'Guns, Guts and God
Make America Great.'

Histories inscribed on strips of plastic:

'My Daughter and I Both Go To College,
My Money and Her Brains.'

Certificates of pride:

'Dartmouth.' 'University of Pennsylvania.' 'Williams.'

And warnings:

'Baby on Board'
'I Brake for Animals'
'One Nuclear Accident
Could Spoil Your Whole Day'

Arun was dizzied by these biographies, these statements of faith. He could have lingered here, constructing characters, lives to go with these containers, all safely invisible, but Mrs Patton was waiting for him at the automatic doors. He could see her in her flat rubber-soled sandals, her yellow slacks and T-shirt that bore the legend *Born to Shop,* her hands on the cart she had chosen. As with his question regarding the location of the supermarket, she could not understand what was preoccupying him. 'Everything okay?' she asked as he caught up at last.

Once inside the chilled air and controlled atmosphere of the market, she showed him how to shop by her own assured and accomplished example, all the tentativeness and timidity she showed at home gone from her. He learnt to follow her up and down the aisles obediently, at her own measured pace, and to read the labels on the cans and cartons with the high seriousness she brought to the exercise, studying the different brands not only for their different prices—as he was inclined to do—but for their relative food value and calorific content. Together they wheeled the cart around and avoided walking past the open freezers where the meat lay steaming in pink packages of rawness, the tank where helpless lobsters, their claws rubber-banded together, rose on ascending bubbles and then sank again, tragically, the trays where the pale flesh of fish curled in opaque twists upon the polystyrene, and made their way instead to the shelves piled with pasta, beans and lentils, all harmlessly dry and odour-free, the racks of nuts and spices where whatever surprises might be were bottled and boxed with kindergarten attractiveness. Mrs Patton's eyes gleamed as they approached the vegetables, all shining and wet and sprinkled perpetually with a soft mist spread upon them, bringing out colours and presenting shapes impossible in the outside world. To Arun they seemed as unreal in their bright perfection as plastic representations, but she insisted on loading their cart with enough broccoli and bean sprouts, radishes and celery to feed the family for a month.

'But will they eat?' he asked worriedly as he helped her pull polythene bags off their rollers and open them, then fill and close them with a twist.

'What does it matter, Ahroon? *We* will,' she laughed gaily, at the same time weighing a cantaloupe in her hands and testing it for ripeness.

'Excuse me,' said a voice, and a woman leant over to pick her own cantaloupe: she wore a T-shirt that declared *Shop Till You Drop*.

This unnerved Arun but Mrs Patton did not seem to see.

Her joy lay in carrying home this hoard she had won from the maze of the supermarket, storing it away in her kitchen cupboards, her refrigerator and freezer. Arun, handing her the packages one by one—butter, yoghurt, milk to go in here, jam and cookies and cereal there—worried that they would never make their way through so much food but this did not seem to be the object of her purchases. Once it was all stored away in the gleaming white caves where ice secretly whispered to itself, she was content. She did not appear to think there was another stage beyond this final, satisfying one.

It was left to him to extract what he wanted from this hoard, to slice tomatoes and lay lettuce on bread, or spill cereal into a bowl; she watched, with pride and complicity. Arun ate with an expression of woe and a sense of mistreatment. How was he to tell Mrs Patton that these were not the foods that figured in his culture? That his digestive system did not know how to turn them into nourishment? For the first time in his existence, he found he craved what he had taken for granted before and even at times thought an unbearable nuisance— those meals cooked and placed before him whether he wanted them or not (and how often he had not), that duty to consume what others thought he must consume.

If she noticed his expression, she seemed incapable of doing anything about it. She had provided: she had foraged, she had gathered, she had put forth. Now she stood beaming, her arms crossed over that T-shirt that bore those ominous words, her eyes flashing the message of the bond between man and woman, between woman and child, brought to ideal consummation.

No, he had not escaped. He had travelled and he had stumbled into what was like a plastic representation of what he had known at home; not the real thing—which was plain, unbeautiful, misshapen, fraught and compromised—but the unreal thing—clean, bright, gleaming, without taste, savour or nourishment.

If Mr Patton ever noticed or watched this arrangement between his wife and the Indian boy they were giving shelter to that summer, he never referred to it or acknowledged it. He stopped on his way back from work to shop for steak, hamburger, ribs and chops. 'Thought you might not have enough,' he told Mrs Patton as he marched out onto the patio to broil and grill, fry and roast, and Mrs Patton looked suitably apologetic and deceitful. When she finally brought herself to tell him that Arun was a vegetarian and she herself had decided to give it a try, something she had meant to do for a long time now, he reacted by not reacting, as if he had simply not heard, or understood. That, too was something Arun knew and had experience of, even if a mirror reflection of it—his father's very expression, walking off, denying any opposition, any challenge to his authority, his stony wait for it to grow disheartened, despair—and disappear. Once again, its grey, vaporous chill crept into his life, like asthma.

AGHA SHAHID ALI

When on Route 80 in Ohio

When on Route 80 in Ohio
I came across an exit
to Calcutta

the temptation to write a poem
led me past the exit
so I could say

India always exists
off the turnpikes
of America

so I could say
I did take the exit
and crossed Howrah

and even mention the Ganges
as it continued its sobbing
under the bridge

so when I paid my toll
I saw trains rush by
one after one

This poem is taken from *A Nostalgist's Map of America*, published by W.W. Norton & Co., Inc., 1991.

on their roofs old passengers
each ready to surrender
his bones for tickets

so that I heard
the sun's percussion
on tamarind leaves

heard the empty cans of children
filling only with the shadows
of leaves

that behind the unloading trucks
were the voices of vendors
bargaining over women

so when the trees
let down their tresses
the monsoon oiled and braided them

and when the wind again parted them
this was the temptation
to end the poem this way:

The warm rains have left
many dead on the pavements

The signs to Route 80
all have disappeared

And now the road is a river
polished silver by cars

The cars are urns
carrying ashes to the sea

Rohinton Mistry

Swimming Lessons

The old man's wheelchair is audible today as he creaks by in the hallway: on some days it's just a smooth whirr. Maybe the way he slumps in it, or the way his weight rests has something to do with it. Down to the lobby he goes, and sits there most of the time, talking to people on their way out or in. That's where he first spoke to me a few days ago. I was waiting for the elevator, back from Eaton's with my new pair of swimming-trunks.

'Hullo,' he said. I nodded, smiled.

'Beautiful summer day we've got.'

'Yes,' I said, 'it's lovely outside.'

He shifted the wheelchair to face me squarely. 'How old do you think I am?'

I looked at him blankly, and he said, 'Go on, take a guess.'

I understood the game; he seemed about seventy-five although the hair was still black, so I said, 'Sixty-five?' He made a sound between a chuckle and a wheeze: 'I'll be seventy-seven next month.' Close enough.

I've heard him ask that question several times since, and everyone plays by the rules. Their faked guesses range from sixty to seventy. They pick a lower number when he's more depressed than usual. He reminds me of Grandpa as he sits on the sofa in the lobby, staring out vacantly at the parking lot. Only difference is, he sits with the stillness

This extract is taken from *Swimming Lessons and Other Stories from Firozsha Baag*, published by Vintage Books, New York, 1992.

of stroke victims, while Grandpa's Parkinson's disease would bounce his thighs and legs and arms all over the place. When he could no longer hold the *Bombay Samachar* steady enough to read, Grandpa took to sitting on the veranda and staring emptily at the traffic passing outside Firozsha Baag. Or waving to anyone who went by in the compound: Rustomji, Nariman Hansotia in his 1932 Mercedes-Benz, the fat ayah Jaakaylee with her shopping-bag, the *kuchrawalli* with her basket and long bamboo broom.

The Portuguese woman across the hall has told me a little about the old man. She is the communicator for the apartment building. To gather and disseminate information, she takes the liberty of unabashedly throwing open her door when newsworthy events transpire. Not for Portuguese Woman the furtive peerings from thin cracks or spyholes. She reminds me of a character in a movie, *Barefoot In The Park* I think it was, who left empty beer cans by the landing for anyone passing to stumble and give her the signal. But PW does not need beer cans. The gutang-khutang of the elevator opening and closing is enough.

The old man's daughter looks after him. He was living alone till his stroke, which coincided with his youngest daughter's divorce in Vancouver. She returned to him and they moved into this low-rise in Don Mills. PW says the daughter talks to no one in the building but takes good care of her father.

Mummy used to take good care of Grandpa, too, till things became complicated and he was moved to the Parsi General Hospital. Parkinsonism and osteoporosis laid him low. The doctor explained that Grandpa's hip did not break because he fell, but he fell because the hip, gradually growing brittle, snapped on that fatal day. That's what osteoporosis does, hollows out the bones and turns effect into cause. It has an unusually high incidence in the Parsi community, he said, but did not say why. Just one of those mysterious things. We are the chosen people where osteoporosis is concerned. And divorce. The Parsi community has the highest divorce rate in India. It also claims to be the most westernized community in India. Which is the result of the other? Confusion again, of cause and effect.

The hip was put in traction. Single-handed, Mummy struggled valiantly with bedpans and dressings for bedsores which soon appeared like grim spectres on his back. *Mamaiji*, bent double with her weak back, could give no assistance. My help would be enlisted to roll him over on his side while Mummy changed the dressing. But after three months, the doctor pronounced a patch upon Grandpa's lungs, and the male ward of Parsi General swallowed him up. There was no money for a private nursing home. I went to see him once, at Mummy's insistence. She used to say that the blessings of an old person were the most valuable and potent of all, they would last my whole life long. The ward had rows and rows of beds; the din was enormous, the smells nauseating, and it was just as well that Grandpa passed most of his time in a less than conscious state.

But I should have gone to see him more often. Whenever Grandpa went out, while he still could in the days before parkinsonism, he would bring back pink and white sugar-coated almonds for Percy and me. Every time I remember Grandpa, I remember that; and then I think: I should have gone to see him more often. That's what I also thought when our telephone-owning neighbour, esteemed by all for that reason, sent his son to tell us the hospital had phoned that Grandpa died an hour ago.

The postman rang the doorbell the way he always did, long and continuous; Mother went to open it, wanting to give him a piece of her mind but thought better of it, she did not want to risk the vengeance of postmen, it was so easy for them to destroy letters; workers nowadays thought no end of themselves, strutting around like peacocks, ever since all this Shiv Sena agitation about Maharashtra for Maharashtrians, threatening strikes and Bombay bundh all the time, with no respect for the public; bus drivers and conductors were the worst, behaving as if they owned the buses and were doing favours to commuters, pulling the bell before you were in the bus, the driver purposely braking and moving with big jerks to make the standees lose their balance, the conductor so rude if you did not have the right change.

But when she saw the airmail envelope with a Canadian stamp her face lit up, she said wait to the postman, and went in for a fifty paisa piece, a little baksheesh for you, she told him, then shut the door and kissed the envelope, went in running, saying my son has written, my son has sent a letter, and Father looked up from the newspaper and said, don't get too excited, first read it, you know what kind of letters he writes, a few lines of empty words, I'm fine, hope you are all right, your loving son—that kind of writing I don't call letter-writing.

Then Mother opened the envelope and took out one small page and began to read silently, and the joy brought to her face by the letter's arrival began to ebb; Father saw it happening and knew he was right, he said read aloud, let me also hear what our son is writing this time, so Mother read: My dear Mummy and Daddy, Last winter was terrible, we had record-breaking low temperatures all through February and March, and the first official day of spring was colder than the first official day of winter had been, but it's getting warmer now. Looks like it will be a nice warm summer. You asked about my new apartment. It's small, but not bad at all. This is just a quick note to let you know I'm fine, so you won't worry about me. Hope everything is okay at home.

After Mother put it back in the envelope, Father said everything about his life is locked in silence and secrecy, I still don't understand why he bothered to visit US last year if he had nothing to say; every letter of his has been a quick note so we won't worry—what does he think we worry about, his health, in that country everyone eats well whether they work or not, he should be worrying about us with all the black market and rationing, has he forgotten already how he used to go to the ration-shop and wait in line every week; and what kind of apartment description is that, not bad at all; and if it is a Canadian weather report I need from him, I can go with Nariman Hansotia from A Block to the Cawasji Framji Memorial Library and read all about it, there they get newspapers from all over the world.

The sun is hot today. Two women are sunbathing on the stretch of patchy lawn at the periphery of the parking lot. I can see them clearly from my kitchen. They're wearing bikinis and I'd love to take a closer look. But I have no binoculars. Nor do I have a car to saunter out to and pretend to look under the hood. They're both luscious and gleaming. From time to time they smear lotion over their skin, on the bellies, on the inside of the thighs, on the shoulders. Then one of them gets the other to undo the string of her top and spread some there. She lies on her stomach with the straps undone. I wait. I pray that the heat and haze make her forget, when it's time to turn over, that the straps are undone.

But the sun is not hot enough to work this magic for me. When it's time to come in, she flips over, deftly holding up the cups, and reties the top. They arise, pick up towels, lotions and magazines, and return to the building.

This is my chance to see them closer. I race down the stairs to the lobby. The old man says hullo. 'Down again?'

'My mailbox,' I mumble.

'It's Saturday,' he chortles. For some reason he finds it extremely funny. My eye is on the door leading in from the parking lot.

Through the glass panel I see them approaching. I hurry to the elevator and wait. In the dimly lit lobby I can see their eyes are having trouble adjusting after the bright sun. They don't seem as attractive as they did from the kitchen window. The elevator arrives and I hold it open, inviting them in with what I think is a gallant flourish. Under the fluorescent glare in the elevator I see their wrinkled skin, aging hands, sagging bottoms, varicose veins. The lustrous trick of sun and lotion and distance has ended.

I step out and they continue to the third floor. I have Monday night to look forward to, my first swimming lesson. The high school behind the apartment building is offering, among its usual assortment of macramé and ceramics and pottery classes, a class for non-swimming adults.

The woman at the registration desk is quite friendly. She even gives me the opening to satisfy the compulsion I have about explaining my non-swimming status.

'Are you from India?' she asks. I nod. 'I hope you don't mind my asking, but I was curious because an Indian couple, husband and wife, also registered a few minutes ago. Is swimming not encouraged in India?'

'On the contrary,' I say. 'Most Indians swim like fish. I'm an exception to the rule. My house was five minutes walking distance from Chaupatty beach in Bombay. It's one of the most beautiful beaches in Bombay, or was, before the filth took over. Anyway, even though we lived so close to it, I never learned to swim. It's just one of those things.'

'Well,' says the woman, 'that happens sometimes. Take me, for instance. I never learned to ride a bicycle. It was the mounting that used to scare me, I was afraid of falling.' People have lined up behind me. 'It's been very nice talking to you,' she says, 'hope you enjoy the course.'

The art of swimming had been trapped between the devil and the deep blue sea. The devil was money, always scarce, and kept the private swimming clubs out of reach; the deep blue sea of Chaupatty beach was grey and murky with garbage, too filthy to swim in. Every so often we would muster our courage and Mummy would take me there to try and teach me. But a few minutes of paddling was all we could endure. Sooner or later something would float up against our legs or thighs or waists, depending on how deep we'd gone in, and we'd be revulsed and stride out to the sand.

Water imagery in my life is recurring. Chaupatty beach, now the high-school swimming pool. The universal symbol of life and regeneration did nothing but frustrate me. Perhaps the swimming pool will overturn that failure.

When images and symbols abound in this manner, sprawling or rolling across the page without guile or artifice, one is prone to say, how obvious, how skilless; symbols, after all, should be still and gentle as dewdrops, tiny, yet shining with a world of meaning. But what happens when, on the page of life itself, one encounters the ever-moving, all-engirdling sprawl of the filthy sea? Dewdrops and oceans both have their rightful places; Nariman Hansotia certainly knew that when he told his stories to the boys of Firozsha Baag.

The sea of Chaupatty was fated to endure the finales of life's everyday functions. It seemed that the dirtier it became, the more crowds it attracted: street urchins and beggars and beachcombers, looking through the junk that washed up. (Or was it the crowds that made it dirtier?—another instance of cause and effect blurring and evading identification.)

Too many religious festivals also used the sea as repository for their finales. Its use should have been rationed, like rice and kerosene. On Ganesh Chaturthi, clay idols of the god Ganesh, adorned with garlands and all manner of finery, were carried in processions to the accompaniment of drums and a variety of wind instruments. The music got more frenzied the closer the procession got to Chaupatty and to the moment of immersion.

Then there was Coconut Day, which was never as popular as Ganesh Chaturthi. From a bystander's viewpoint, coconuts chucked into the sea do not provide as much of a spectacle. We used the sea, too, to deposit the leftovers from Parsi religious ceremonies, things such as flowers, or the ashes of the sacred sandalwood fire, which just could not be dumped with the regular garbage but had to be entrusted

to the care of Avan Yazad, the guardian of the sea. And things which
were of no use but which no one had the heart to destroy were also
given to Avan Yazad. Such as old photographs.

After Grandpa died, some of his things were flung out to sea. It was
high tide; we always checked the newspaper when going to perform
these disposals; an ebb would mean a long walk in squelchy sand
before finding water. Most of the things were probably washed up on
shore. But we tried to throw them as far out as possible, then waited
a few minutes; if they did not float back right away we would pretend
they were in the permanent safekeeping of Avan Yazad, which was a
comforting thought. I can't remember everything we sent out to sea,
but his brush and comb were in the parcel, his *kusti*, and some Kemadrin
pills, which he used to take to keep the parkinsonism under control.

Our paddling sessions stopped for lack of enthusiasm on my part.
Mummy wasn't too keen either, because of the filth. But my main
concern was the little guttersnipes, like naked fish with little buoyant
penises, taunting me with their skills, swimming underwater and
emerging unexpectedly all around me, or pretending to masturbate—
I think they were too young to achieve ejaculation. It was embarrassing.
When I look back, I'm surprised that Mummy and I kept going as long
as we did.

I examine the swimming-trunks I bought last week. Surf King, says
the label, Made in Canada-Fabriqué Au Canada. I've been learning bits
and pieces of French from bilingual labels at the supermarket too.
These trunks are extremely sleek and streamlined hipsters, the distance
from waistband to pouch tip the barest minimum. I wonder how
everything will stay in place, not that I'm boastful about my
endowments. I try them on, and feel that the tip of my member lingers
perilously close to the exit. Too close, in fact, to conceal the exigencies
of my swimming lesson fantasy: a gorgeous woman in the class for
non-swimmers, at whose sight I will be instantly aroused, and she,
spying the shape of my desire, will look me straight in the eye with
her intentions; she will come home with me to taste the pleasures of
my delectable Asian brown body whose strangeness has intrigued her
and unleashed uncontrollable surges of passion inside her throughout
the duration of the swimming lesson.

I drop the Eaton's bag and wrapper in the garbage can. The swimming-trunks cost fifteen dollars, same as the fee for the ten weekly lessons. The garbage bag is almost full. I tie it up and take it outside. There is a medicinal smell in the hallway; the old man must have just returned to his apartment.

PW opens her door and says, 'Two ladies from the third floor were lying in the sun this morning. In bikinis.'

'That's nice,' I say, and walk to the incinerator chute. She reminds me of Najamai in Firozsha Baag, except that Najamai employed a bit more subtlety while going about her life's chosen work.

PW withdraws and shuts her door.

Mother had to reply because Father said he did not want to write to his son till his son had something sensible to write to him, his questions had been ignored long enough, and if he wanted to keep his life a secret, fine, he would get no letters from his father.

But after Mother started the letter he went and looked over her shoulder, telling her what to ask him, because if they kept on writing the same questions, maybe he would understand how interested they were in knowing about things over there; Father said go on, ask him what his work is at the insurance company, tell him to take some courses at night school, that's how everyone moves ahead over there, tell him not to be discouraged if his job is just clerical right now, hard work will get him ahead, remind him he is a Zoroastrian: manashni, gavashni, kunashni, better write the translation also: good thoughts, good words, good deeds—he must have forgotten what it means, and tell him to say prayers and do kusti *at least twice a day.*

Writing it all down sadly, Mother did not believe he wore his sudra *and kusti anymore, she would be very surprised if he remembered any of the prayers; when she had asked him if he needed new* sudras *he said not to take any trouble because the Zoroastrian Society of Ontario imported them from Bombay for their members, and this sounded like a story he was making up, but she was leaving it in the hands of God, ten thousand miles away there was nothing she could do but write a letter and hope for the best.*

Then she sealed it, and Father wrote the address on it as usual because his writing was much neater than hers, handwriting was important in the address and she did not want the postman in Canada to make any mistake; she took it to the post office herself, it was impossible to trust anyone to mail it ever since the postage rates went up because people just tore off the stamps for their own use and threw away the letter, the only safe way was to hand it over the counter and make the clerk cancel the stamps before your own eyes.

Berthe, the building superintendent, is yelling at her son in the parking lot. He tinkers away with his van. This happens every fine-weathered Sunday. It must be the van that Berthe dislikes because I've seen mother and son together in other quite amicable situations.

Berthe is a big Yugoslavian with high cheekbones. Her nationality was disclosed to me by PW. Berthe speaks a very rough-hewn English, I've overheard her in the lobby scolding tenants for late rents and leaving dirty lint screens in the dryers. It's exciting to listen to her, her words fall like rocks and boulders, and one can never tell where or how the next few will drop. But her Slavic yells at her son are a different matter, the words fly swift and true, well-aimed missiles that never miss. Finally, the son slams down the hood in disgust, wipes his hands on a rag, accompanies mother Berthe inside.

Berthe's husband has a job in a factory. But he loses several days of work every month when he succumbs to the booze, a word Berthe uses often in her Slavic tirades on those days, the only one I can understand, as it clunks down heavily out of the tight-flying formation of Yugoslavian sentences. He lolls around in the lobby, submitting passively to his wife's tongue-lashings. The bags under his bloodshot eyes, his stringy moustache, stubbled chin, dirty hair are so vulnerable to the poison-laden barbs (poison works the same way in any language) emanating from deep within the powerful watermelon bosom. No one's presence can embarrass or dignify her into silence.

No one except the old man who arrives now. 'Good morning,' he says, and Berthe turns, stops yelling, and smiles. Her husband rises, positions the wheelchair at the favourite angle. The lobby will be peaceful as long as the old man is there.

It was hopeless. My first swimming lesson. The water terrified me. When did that happen, I wonder, I used to love splashing at Chaupatty, carried about by the waves. And this was only a swimming pool. Where did all that terror come from? I'm trying to remember.

Armed with my Surf King I enter the high school and go to the pool area. A sheet with instructions for the new class is pinned to the bulletin board. All students must shower and then assemble at eight by the shallow end. As I enter the showers three young boys, probably from a previous class, emerge. One of them holds his nose. The second begins to hum, under his breath: Paki Paki, smell like curry. The third says to the first two: pretty soon all the water's going to taste of curry. They leave.

It's a mixed class, but the gorgeous woman of my fantasy is missing. I have to settle for another, in a pink one-piece suit, with brown hair and a bit of a stomach. She must be about thirty-five. Plain-looking.

The instructor is called Ron. He gives us a pep talk, sensing some nervousness in the group. We're finally all in the water, in the shallow end. He demonstrates floating on the back, then asks for a volunteer. The pink one-piece suit wades forward. He supports her, tells her to lean back and let her head drop in the water.

She does very well. And as we all regard her floating body, I see what was not visible outside the pool: her bush, curly bits of it, straying out at the pink Spandex V. Tongues of water lapping against her delta, as if caressing it teasingly, make the brown hair come alive in a most tantalizing manner. The crests and troughs of little waves, set off by the movement of our bodies in a circle around her, dutifully irrigate her; the curls alternately wave free inside the crest, then adhere to her wet thighs, beached by the inevitable trough. I could watch this forever, and I wish the floating demonstration would never end.

Next we are shown how to grasp the rail and paddle, face down in the water. Between practising floating and paddling, the hour is almost gone. I have been trying to observe the pink one-piece suit, getting glimpses of her straying pubic hair from various angles. Finally, Ron wants a volunteer for the last demonstration, and I go forward. To my horror he leads the class to the deep end. Fifteen feet of water. It is so blue, and I can see the bottom. He picks up a metal hoop attached to a long wooden stick. He wants me to grasp the hoop, jump in the water, and paddle, while he guides me by the stick. Perfectly safe, he tells me. A demonstration of how paddling propels the body.

It's too late to back out; besides, I'm so terrified I couldn't find the words to do so even if I wanted to. Everything he says I do as if in a trance. I don't remember the moment of jumping. The next thing I know is, I'm swallowing water and floundering, hanging on to the hoop for dear life. Ron draws me to the rails and helps me out. The class applauds.

We disperse and one thought is on my mind: what if I'd lost my grip? Fifteen feet of water under me. I shudder and take deep breaths. This is it. I'm not coming next week. This instructor is an irresponsible person. Or he does not value the lives of non-white immigrants. I remember the three teenagers. Maybe the swimming pool is the hangout of some racist group, bent on eliminating all non-white swimmers, to keep their waters pure and their white sisters unogled.

The elevator takes me upstairs. Then gutang-khutang. PW opens her door as I turn the corridor of medicinal smells. 'Berthe was screaming loudly at her husband tonight,' she tells me.

'Good for her,' I say, and she frowns indignantly at me.

The old man is in the lobby. He's wearing thick wool gloves. He wants to know how the swimming was, must have seen me leaving with my towel yesterday. Not bad, I say.

'I used to swim a lot. Very good for the circulation.' He wheezes. 'My feet are cold all the time. Cold as ice. Hands too.'

Summer is winding down, so I say stupidly, 'Yes, it's not so warm any more.'

The thought of the next swimming lesson sickens me. But as I comb through the memories of that terrifying Monday, I come upon the straying curls of brown pubic hair. Inexorably drawn by them, I decide to go.

It's a mistake of course. This time I'm scared even to venture in the shallow end. When everyone has entered the water and I'm the only one outside, I feel a little foolish and slide in.

Instructor Ron says we should start by reviewing the floating technique. I'm in no hurry. I watch the pink one-piece pull the swimsuit down around her cheeks and flip back to achieve perfect flotation. And then reap disappointment. The pink Spandex triangle is perfectly streamlined today, nothing strays, not a trace of fuzz, not one filament, not even a sign of post-depilation irritation. Like the airbrushed parts of glamour magazine models. The barrenness of her impeccably packaged apex is a betrayal. Now she is shorn like the other women in the class. Why did she have to do it?

The weight of this disappointment makes the water less manageable, more lung-penetrating. With trepidation, I float and paddle my way through the remainder of the hour, jerking my head out every two seconds and breathing deeply, to continually shore up a supply of precious, precious air without, at the same time, seeming too anxious and losing my dignity.

I don't attend the remaining classes. After I've missed three, Ron the instructor telephones. I tell him I've had the flu and am still feeling poorly, but I'll try to be there the following week.

He does not call again. My Surf King is relegated to an unused drawer. Total losses: one fantasy plus thirty dollars. And no watery rebirth. The swimming pool, like Chaupatty beach, has produced a stillbirth. But there is a difference. Water means regeneration only if it is pure and cleansing. Chaupatty was filthy, the pool was not. Failure to swim through filth must mean something other than failure of rebirth—failure of symbolic death? Does that equal success of symbolic life? death of a symbolic failure? death of a symbol? What is the equation?

The postman did not bring a letter but a parcel, he was smiling because he knew that every time something came from Canada his baksheesh *was guaranteed, and this time because it was a parcel Mother gave him a whole rupee, she was quite excited, there were so many stickers on it besides the stamps, one for Small Parcel, another Printed Papers, a red sticker saying Insured; she showed it to Father, and opened it, then put both hands on her cheeks, not able to speak because the surprise and happiness was so great, tears came to her eyes and she could not stop smiling, till Father became impatient to know and finally got up and came to the table.*

When he saw it he was surprised and happy too, he began to grin, then hugged Mother saying our son is a writer, and we didn't even know it, he never told us a thing, here we are thinking he is still clerking away at the insurance company, and he has written a book of stories, all these years in school and college he kept his talent hidden, making us think he was just like one of the boys in the Baag, shouting and playing the fool in the compound, and now what a surprise; then Father opened the book and began reading it, heading back to the easy chair, and Mother so excited, still holding his arm, walked with him, saying it was not fair him reading it first, she wanted to read it too, and they agreed that he would read the first story, then give it to her so she could also read it, and they would take turns in that manner.

Mother removed the staples from the padded envelope in which he had mailed the book, and threw them away, then straightened the folded edges of the envelope and put it away safely with the other envelopes and letters she had collected since he left.

The leaves are beginning to fall. The only ones I can identify are maple. The days are dwindling like the leaves. I've started a habit of taking long walks every evening. The old man is in the lobby when I leave, he waves as I go by. By the time I'm back, the lobby is usually empty.

Today I was woken up by a grating sound outside that made my flesh crawl. I went to the window and saw Berthe raking the leaves in the parking lot. Not in the expanse of patchy lawn on the periphery, but in the parking lot proper. She was raking the black tarred surface. I went back to bed and dragged a pillow over my head, not releasing it till noon.

When I return from my walk in the evening, PW, summoned by the elevator's gutang-khutang, says, 'Berthe filled six big black garbage bags with leaves today.'

'Six bags!' I say. 'Wow!'

Since the weather turned cold, Berthe's son does not tinker with his van on Sundays under my window. I'm able to sleep late.

Around eleven, there's a commotion outside. I reach out and switch on the clock radio. It's a sunny day, the window curtains are bright. I get up, curious, and see a black Olds Ninety-Eight in the parking lot, by the entrance to the building. The old man is in his wheelchair, bundled up, with a scarf wound several times round his neck as though to immobilize it, like a surgical collar. His daughter and another man, the car-owner, are helping him from the wheelchair into the front seat, encouraging him with words like: that's it, easy does it, attaboy. From the open door of the lobby, Berthe is shouting encouragement too, but hers is confined to one word: yah, repeated at different levels of pitch and volume, with variations on vowel-length. The stranger could be the old man's son, he has the same jet black hair and piercing eyes.

Maybe the old man is not well, it's an emergency. But I quickly scrap that thought—this isn't Bombay, an ambulance would have arrived. They're probably taking him out for a ride. If he is his son, where has he been all this time, I wonder.

The old man finally settles in the front seat, the wheelchair goes in the trunk, and they're off. The one I think is the son looks up and catches me at the window before I can move away, so I wave, and he waves back.

In the afternoon I take down a load of clothes to the laundry room. Both machines have completed their cycles, the clothes inside are waiting to be transferred to dryers. Should I remove them and place them on top of a dryer, or wait? I decide to wait. After a few minutes, two women arrive, they are in bathrobes, and smoking. It takes me a while to realize that these are the two disappointments who were sunbathing in bikinis last summer.

'You didn't have to wait, you could have removed the clothes and carried on, dear,' says one. She has a Scottish accent. It's one of the few I've learned to identify. Like maple leaves.

'Well,' I say, 'some people might not like strangers touching their clothes.'

'You're not a stranger, dear,' she says, 'you live in this building, we've seen you before.'

'Besides, your hands are clean,' the other one pipes in. 'You can touch my things any time you like.'

Horny old cow. I wonder what they've got on under their bathrobes. Not much, I find, as they bend over to place their clothes in the dryers.

'See you soon,' they say, and exit, leaving me behind in an erotic wake of smoke and perfume and deep images of cleavages. I start the washers and depart, and when I come back later, the dryers are empty.

PW tells me, 'The old man's son took him out for a drive today. He has a big beautiful black car.'

I see my chance, and shoot back: 'Olds Ninety-Eight.'

'What?'

'The car,' I explain, 'it's an Oldsmobile Ninety-Eight.'

She does not like this at all, my giving her information. She is visibly nettled, and retreats with a sour face.

Mother and Father read the first five stories, and she was very sad after reading some of them, she said he must be so unhappy there, all his stories are about Bombay, he remembers every little thing about his childhood, he is thinking about it all the time even though he is ten thousand miles away, my poor son, I think he misses his home and us and everything he left behind, because if he likes it over there why would he not write stories about that, there must be so many new ideas that his new life could give him.

But Father did not agree with this, he said it did not mean that he was unhappy, all writers worked in the same way, they used their memories and experiences and made stories out of them, changing some things, adding some, imagining some, all writers were very good at remembring details of their lives.

Mother said, how can you be sure that he is remembering because he is a writer, or whether he started to write because he is unhappy and thinks of his past, and wants to save it all by making stories of it; and Father said that is not a sensible question, anyway, it is now my turn to read the next story.

The first snow has fallen, and the air is crisp. It's not very deep, about two inches, just right to go for a walk in. I've been told that immigrants from hot countries always enjoy the snow the first year, maybe for a couple of years more, then inevitably the dread sets in, and the approach of winter gets them fretting and moping. On the other hand, if it hadn't been for my conversation with the woman at the swimming registration desk, they might now be saying that India is a nation of non-swimmers.

Berthe is outside, shovelling the snow off the walkway in the parking lot. She has a heavy, wide pusher which she wields expertly.

The old radiators in the apartment alarm me incessantly. They continue to broadcast a series of variations on death throes, and go from hot to cold and cold to hot at will, there's no controlling their temperature. I speak to Berthe about it in the lobby. The old man is there too, his chin seems to have sunk deeper into his chest, and his face is a yellowish grey.

'Nothing, not to worry about anything,' says Berthe, dropping rough-hewn chunks of language around me. 'Radiator no work, you tell me. You feel cold, you come to me, I keep you warm,' and she opens her arms wide, laughing. I step back, and she advances, her breasts preceding her like the gallant prows of two ice-breakers. She looks at the old man to see if he is appreciating the act: 'You no feel scared, I keep you safe and warm.'

But the old man is staring outside, at the flakes of falling snow. What thoughts is he thinking as he watches them? Of childhood days, perhaps, and snowmen with hats and pipes, and snowball fights, and white Christmases, and Christmas trees? What will I think of, old in this country, when I sit and watch the snow come down? For me, it is already too late for snowmen and snowball fights, and all I will have is thoughts about childhood thoughts and dreams, built around snowscapes and winter-wonderlands on the Christmas cards so popular in Bombay; my snowmen and snowball fights and Christmas trees are in the pages of Enid Blyton's books, dispersed amidst the adventures of the Famous Five, and the Five Find-Outers, and the Secret Seven. My snowflakes are even less forgettable than the old man's, for they never melt.

It finally happened. The heat went. Not the usual intermittent coming and going, but out completely. Stone cold. The radiators are like ice. And so is everything else. There's no hot water. Naturally. It's the hot water that goes through the rads and heats them. Or is it the other way around? Is there no hot water because the rads have stopped circulating it? I don't care, I'm too cold to sort out the cause and effect relationship. Maybe there is no connection at all.

I dress quickly, put on my winter jacket, and go down to the lobby. The elevator is not working because the power is out, so I take the stairs. Several people are gathered, and Berthe has announced that she has telephoned the office, they are sending a man. I go back up the stairs. It's only one floor, the elevator is just a bad habit. Back in Firozsha Baag they were broken most of the time. The stairway enters the corridor outside the old man's apartment and I think of his cold feet and hands. Poor man, it must be horrible for him without heat.

As I walk down the long hallway, I feel there's something different but can't pin it down. I look at the carpet, the ceiling, the wallpaper: it all seems the same. Maybe it's the.freezing cold that imparts a feeling of difference.

PW opens her door: 'The old man had another stroke yesterday. They took him to the hospital.'

The medicinal smell. That's it. It's not in the hallway any more.

In the stories that he'd read so far Father said that all the Parsi families were poor or middle-class, but that was okay; nor did he mind that the seeds for the stories were picked from the sufferings of their own lives; but there should also have been something positive about Parsis, there was so much to be proud of: the great Tatas and their contribution to the steel industry, or Sir Dinshaw Petit in the textile industry who made Bombay the Manchester of the East, or Dadabhai Naoroji in the freedom movement, where he was the first to use the word swaraj, *and the first to be elected to the British Parliament where he carried on his campaign; he should have found some way to bring some of these wonderful facts into his stories, what would people reading these stories think, those who did not know about Parsis— that the whole community was full of cranky, bigoted people; and in reality it was the richest, most advanced and philanthropic community in India, and he did not need to tell his own son that Parsis had a reputation for being generous and family-oriented. And he could have written something also about the historic background, how Parsis came to India from Persia because of Islamic persecution in the seventh century, and were the descendants of Cyrus the Great and the magnificent Persian Empire. He could have made a story of all this, couldn't he?*

Mother said what she liked best was his remembering so well, how beautifully he wrote about it all, even the sad things, and though he changed some of it, and used his imagination, there was truth in it.

My hope is, Father said, that there will be some story based on his Canadian experience, that way we will know something about our son's life there, if not through his letters then in his stories; so far they are all about Parsis and Bombay, and the one with a little bit about Toronto, where a man perches on top of the toilet, is shameful and disgusting, although it is funny at times and did make me laugh, I have to admit, but where does he get such an imagination from, what is the point of such a fantasy; and Mother said that she would also enjoy some stories about Toronto and the people there; it puzzles me, she said, why he writes nothing about it, especially since you say that writers use their own experience to make stories out of.

Then Father said this is true, but he is probably not using his Toronto experience because it is too early; what do you mean, too early, asked Mother and Father explained it takes a writer about ten years time after an experience before he is able to use it in his writing, it takes that long to be absorbed internally and understood, thought out and thought about, over and over again, he haunts it and it haunts him if it is valuable enough, till the writer is comfortable with it to be able to use it as he wants; but this is only one theory I read somewhere, it may or may not be true.

That means, said Mother, that his childhood in Bombay and our home here is the most valuable thing in his life just now, because he is able to remember it all to write about it, and you were so bitterly saying he is forgetting where he came from; and that may be true, said Father, but that is not what the theory means, according to the theory he is writing of these things because they are far enough in the past for him to deal with objectively, he is able to achieve what critics call artistic distance, without emotions interfering; and what do you mean emotions, said Mother, you are saying he does not feel anything for his characters, how can he write so beautifully about so many sad things without any feelings in his heart?

But before Father could explain more, about beauty and emotion and inspiration and imagination, Mother took the book and said it was her turn now and too much theory she did not want to listen to, it was confusing and did not make as much sense as reading the stories, she would read them her way and Father could read them his.

My books on the windowsill have been damaged. Ice has been forming on the inside ledge, which I did not notice, and melting when the sun shines in. I spread them in a corner of the living-room to dry out.

The winter drags on. Berthe wields her snow pusher as expertly as ever, but there are signs of weariness in her performance. Neither husband nor son is ever seen outside with a shovel. Or anywhere else, for that matter. It occurs to me that the son's van is missing, too.

The medicinal smell is in the hall again, I sniff happily and look forward to seeing the old man in the lobby. I go downstairs and peer into the mailbox, see the blue and magenta of an Indian aerogramme with Don Mills, Ontario, Canada in Father's flawless hand through the slot.

I pocket the letter and enter the main lobby. The old man is there, but not in his usual place. He is not looking out through the glass door. His wheelchair is facing a bare wall where the wallpaper is torn in places. As though he is not interested in the outside world any more, having finished with all that, and now it's time to see inside. What does see inside, I wonder? I go up to him and say hullo. He says hullo without raising his sunken chin. After a few seconds his grey countenance faces me. 'How old do you think I am?' His eyes are dull and glazed; he is looking even further inside than I first presumed.

'Well, let's see, you're probably close to sixty-four.'

'I'll be seventy-eight next August.' But he does not chuckle or wheeze. Instead, he continues softly, 'I wish my feet did not feel so cold all the time. And my hands.' He lets his chin fall again.

In the elevator I start opening the aerogramme, a tricky business because a crooked tear means lost words. Absorbed in this, while emerging, I don't notice PW occupying the centre of the hallway, arms folded across her chest: 'They had a big fight. Both of them have left.'

I don't immediately understand her agitation. 'What . . . who?'

'Berthe. Husband and son both left her. Now she is all alone.'

Her tone and stance suggest that we should not be standing here talking but do something to bring Berthe's family back. 'That's very sad,' I say, and go in. I picture father and son in the van, driving away, driving across the snow-covered country, in the dead of winter, away from wife and mother; away to where? how far will they go? Not son's van nor father's booze can take them far enough. And the further they go, the more they'll remember, they can take it from me.

All the stories were read by Father and Mother, and they were sorry when the book was finished, they felt they had come to know their son better now, yet there was much more to know, they wished there were many more stories; and this is what they mean, said Father, when they say that the whole story can never be told, the whole truth can never be known; what do you mean, they say, asked Mother, who they, and Father said writers, poets, philosophers. I don't care what they say, said Mother, my son will write as much or as little as he wants to, and if I can read it I will be happy.

The last story they liked the best of all because it had the most in it about Canada, and now they felt they knew at least a little bit, even if it was a very little bit, about his day-to-day life in his apartment; and Father said if he continues to write about such things he will become popular because I am sure they are interested there in reading about life through the eyes of an immigrant, it provides a different viewpoint; the only danger is if he changes and becomes so much like them that he will write like one of them and lose the important difference.

The bathroom needs cleaning. I open a new can of Ajax and scour the tub. Sloshing with mug from bucket was standard bathing procedure in the bathrooms of Firozsha Baag, so my preference now is always for a shower. I've never used the tub as yet; besides, it would be too much like Chaupatty or the swimming pool, wallowing in my own dirt. Still, it must be cleaned.

When I've finished, I prepare for a shower. But the clean gleaming tub and the nearness of the vernal equinox give me the urge to do something different today. I find the drain plug in the bathroom cabinet, and run the bath.

I've spoken so often to the old man, but I don't know his name. I should have asked him the last time I saw him, when his wheelchair was facing the bare wall because he had seen all there was to see outside and it was time to see what was inside. Well, tomorrow. Or better yet, I can look it up in the directory in the lobby. Why didn't I think of that before? It will only have an initial and a last name, but then I can surprise him with: hullo Mr Wilson, or whatever it is.

The bath is full. Water imagery is recurring in my life: Chaupatty beach, swimming pool, bathtub. I step in and immerse myself up to the neck. It feels good. The hot water loses its opacity when the chlorine, or whatever it is, has cleared. My hair is still dry. I close my eyes, hold my breath, and dunk my head. Fighting the panic, I stay under and count to thirty. I come out, clear my lungs and breathe deeply.

I do it again. This time I open my eyes under water, and stare blindly without seeing, it takes all my will to keep the lids from closing. Then I am slowly able to discern the underwater objects. The drain plug looks different, slightly distorted; there is hair trapped between the hole and the plug, it waves and dances with the movement of the water. I come up, refresh my lungs, examine quickly the overwater world of the washroom, and go in again. I do it several times, over and over. The world outside the water I have seen a lot of, it is now time to see what is inside.

The spring session for adult non-swimmers will begin in a few days at the high school. I must not forget the registration date.

The dwindled days of winter are now all but forgotten; they have grown and attained a respectable span. I resume my evening walks, it's spring, and a vigorous thaw is on. The snowbanks are melting, the sound of water on its gushing, gurgling journey to the drains is beautiful. I plan to buy a book of trees, so I can identify more than the maple as they begin to bloom.

When I return to the building, I wipe my feet energetically on the mat because some people are entering behind me, and I want to set a good example. Then I go to the board with its little plastic letters and numbers. The old man's apartment is the one on the corner by the stairway, that makes it number 201. I run down the list, come to 201, but there are no little white plastic letters beside it. Just the empty black rectangle with holes where the letters would be squeezed in. That's strange. Well, I can introduce myself to him, then ask his name.

However, the lobby is empty. I take the elevator, exit at the second floor, wait for the gutang–khutang. It does not come: the door closes noiselessly, smoothly. Berthe has been at work, or has made sure someone else has. PW's cue has been lubricated out of existence.

But she must have the ears of a cockroach. She is waiting for me. I whistle my way down the corridor. She fixes me with an accusing look. She waits till I stop whistling, then says: 'You know the old man died last night.'

I cease groping for my key. She turns to go and I take a step towards her, my hand still in my trouser pocket. 'Did you know his name?' I ask, but she leaves without answering.

Then Mother said, the part I like best in the last story is about Grandpa, where he wonders if Grandpa's spirit is really watching him and blessing him because you know I really told him that, I told him helping an old suffering person who is near death is the most blessed thing to do, because that person will ever after watch over you from heaven, I told him this when he was disgusted with Grandpa's urine-bottle and would not touch it, would not hand it to him even when I was not at home.

Are you sure, said Father, that you really told him this, or you believe you told him because you like the sound of it, you said yourself the other day that he changes and adds and alters things in the stories but he writes it all so beautifully that it seems true, so how can you be sure; this sounds like another theory, said Mother, but I don't care, he says I told him and I believe now I told him, so even if I did not tell him then it does not matter now.

Don't you see, said Father, that you are confusing fiction with facts, fiction does not create facts, fiction can come from facts, it can grow out of facts by compounding, transposing, augmenting, diminishing, or altering them in any way; but you must not confuse cause and effect, you must not confuse what really happened with what the story says happened, you must not loose your grasp on reality, that way madness lies.

Then Mother stopped listening because, as she told Father so often, she was not very fond of theories, and she took out her writing pad and started a letter to her son; Father looked over her shoulder, telling her to say how proud they were of him and were waiting for his next book, he also said, leave a little space for me at the end, I want to write a few lines when I put the address on the envelope.

AMITAV GHOSH

The Imam and I

Even though Khamees never mentioned the subject himself, everyone around him seemed to know that he was haunted by his childlessness.

Once, on a cold winter's day, I dropped in to see him and found him sitting with his father in the guest-room of their house—one of the shabbiest and most derelict in the village. His father was sitting in a corner, huddled in a blanket, hugging his knees and shivering whenever a draught whistled in through the crumbling walls. He smiled when I stepped in, and motioned to me to sit beside him— a thin, frail old man with absent, wandering eyes. He had worked as a labourer in Alexandria during the Second World War, and he had met many Indians among the soldiers who had passed through the city at the start of the North African campaign. They had made a deep impression on his memory and at our first meeting he had greeted me as though he was resuming an interrupted friendship.

Now, after I had seated myself beside him, he leant towards me and ran his hands over my wool sweater, examining it closely, rubbing the material carefully between finger and thumb.

'That's the right thing to wear in winter,' he said. 'It must be really warm.'

'Not as warm as your blanket,' interjected Khamees.

His father pretended not to hear. 'I've heard you can get sweaters like that in Damanhour,' he said to me.

This extract is taken from *In an Antique Land*, published by Vintage Books, New York, 1992.

'You can get anything if you have the money,' said Khamees. 'It's getting the money that's the problem.'

Paying him no attention, his father patted my arm. 'I remember the Indian soldiers,' he said. 'They were so tall and dark that many of us Egyptians were afraid of them. But if you talked to them they were the most generous of all the soldiers; if you asked for a cigarette they gave you a whole packet.'

'That was then,' Khamees said, grinning at me. 'Now things have changed.'

'Do you see what my children are like?' his father said to me. 'They won't even get me a sweater from Damanhour so I can think of the winter without fear.'

At that Khamees rose abruptly to his feet and walked out of the room. His father watched him go with an unblinking stare.

'What am I to do with my children?' he muttered, under his breath. 'Look at them; look at Busaina, trying to rear her two sons on her own; look at Khamees, you can't talk to him any more, can't say a thing, neither me, nor his brothers, nor his wife. And every year he gets worse.'

He pulled his blanket over his ears, shivering spasmodically. 'Perhaps I'm the one who's to blame,' he said. 'I married him off early and I told him we wanted to see his children before we died. But that didn't work, so he married again. Now the one thought in his head is children—that's all he thinks about, nothing else.'

A few months later, in the spring, after nearly a year had passed and the time for my departure from Egypt was not far distant, I was walking back from the fields with Khamees and 'Eid one evening, when we spotted Imam Ibrahim sitting on the steps of the mosque.

Khamees stopped short, and with an uncharacteristic urgency in his voice he said: 'Listen, you know Imam Ibrahim, don't you? I've seen you greeting him.'

I made a noncommittal answer, although the truth was that ever after that ill-fated meal at Yasir's house the Imam had scarcely deigned to acknowledge my greetings when we passed each other in the village's narrow lanes.

'My wife's ill,' said Khamees. 'I want the Imam to come to my house and give her an injection.'

His answer surprised me, and I quickly repeated what Nabeel and his friends had said about the Imam's blunt needles, and told him that if his wife needed an injection there were many other people in the village who could do the job much better. But Khamees was insistent: it was not just the injection, he said—he had heard that Imam Ibrahim knew a lot about remedies and medicines and things like that, and people had told him that maybe he would be able to do something for him and his wife.

I understood then what sort of medicine he was hoping the Imam would give him.

'Khamees, he can't help in matters like that,' I said, 'and anyway he's stopped doing remedies now. He only does those injections.'

But Khamees had grown impatient by this time. 'Go and ask him,' he said, 'he won't come if I ask; he doesn't like us.'

'He doesn't like me either,' I said.

'That doesn't matter,' said Khamees. 'He'll come if you ask him—he knows you're a foreigner. He'll listen to you.'

It was clear that he had made up his mind, so I left him waiting at the edge of the square, and went across, towards the mosque. I could tell that the Imam had seen me—and Khamees—from a long way off, but he betrayed no sign of recognition and carefully kept his eyes from straying in my direction. Instead, he pretended to be deep in conversation with a man who was sitting beside him, an elderly shopkeeper with whom I had a slight acquaintance.

I was still a few steps away from them when I said 'good evening' to the Imam, pointedly, so he could no longer ignore me. He paused to acknowledge the greeting, but his response was short and curt, and he turned back at once to resume his conversation.

The old shopkeeper was taken aback at the Imam's manner; he was a pleasant man, and had often exchanged cordial salutes with me in the lanes of the village.

'Please sit down,' he said to me, in embarrassment. 'Do sit. Shall we get you a chair?'

Without waiting for an answer, he glanced at the Imam, frowning in puzzlement. 'You know the Indian doktór, don't you?' he said. 'He's come all the way from India to be a student at the University of Alexandria.'

'I know him,' said the Imam. 'He came around to ask me questions. But as for this student business, I don't know. What's he going to study? He doesn't even write in Arabic.'

'That's true,' said the shopkeeper judiciously, 'but after all, he writes his own languages and he knows English.'

'Oh those,' said the Imam scornfully. 'What's the use of those languages? They're the easiest languages in the world. Anyone can write those.'

He turned to face me now, and I saw that his mouth was twitching with anger and his eyes were shining with a startling brightness.

'Tell me,' he said, 'why do you worship cows?'

Taken by surprise I began to stammer, and he cut me short by turning his shoulder on me.

'That's what they do in his country,' he said to the old shopkeeper. 'Did you know? They worship cows.'

He shot me a glance from the corner of his eyes. 'And shall I tell you what else they do?' he said. He let the question hang in the air for a moment, and then announced, in a dramatic hiss: 'They burn their dead.'

The shopkeeper recoiled as though he had been slapped, and his hands flew to his mouth. 'Ya Allah!' he muttered.

'That's what they do,' said the Imam. 'They burn their dead.'

Then suddenly he spun around to face me and cried: 'Why do you allow it? Can't you see that it's a primitive and backward custom? Are you savages that you permit something like that? Look at you: you've had some education; you should know better. How will your country ever progress if you carry on doing these things? You've even been to Europe; you've seen how advanced they are. Now tell me: have you ever seen them burning their dead?'

A small crowd had gathered around us now, drawn by the Imam's voice, and under the pressure of their collective gaze, I found myself becoming increasingly tongue-tied.

'Yes, they do burn their dead in Europe,' I managed to say, voice rising despite my efforts to control it. 'Yes, they have special electric furnaces meant just for that.'

The Imam turned away and laughed scornfully. 'He's lying,' he said to the crowd. 'They don't burn their dead in the West. They're not an ignorant people. They're advanced, they're educated, they have science, they have guns and tanks and bombs.'

Suddenly something seemed to boil over in my head, dilemmas and arguments I could no longer contain within myself.

'We have them too!' I shouted back at him. 'In my country we have all those things too; we have guns and tanks and bombs. And they're better than anything you've got in Egypt—we're a long way ahead of you.'

'I tell you, he's lying,' cried the Imam, his voice rising in fury. 'Our guns and bombs are much better than theirs. Ours are second only to the West's.'

'It's you who's lying,' I said. 'You know nothing about this. Ours are much better. Why, in my country we've even had a nuclear explosion. You won't be able to match that even in a hundred years.'

It was about then, I think, that Khamees appeared at my side and led me away, or else we would probably have stood there a good while longer, the Imam and I: delegates from two superseded civilizations, vying with each other to establish a prior claim to the technology of modern violence.

At that moment, despite the vast gap that lay between us, we understood each other perfectly. We were both travelling, he and I: we were travelling in the West. The only difference was that I had actually been there, in person: I could have told him a great deal about it, seen at first hand, its libraries, its museums, its theatres, but it wouldn't have mattered. We would have known, both of us, that all that was mere fluff: in the end, for millions and millions of people on the landmasses around us, the West meant only this—science and tanks and guns and bombs.

I was crushed, as I walked away; it seemed to me that the Imam and I had participated in our own final defeat, in the dissolution of the centuries of dialogue that had linked us: we had demonstrated the irreversible triumph of the language that has usurped all the others in which people once discussed their differences. We had acknowledged that it was no longer possible to speak, as Ben Yiju or his Slave, or any one of the thousands of travellers who had crossed the Indian Ocean in the Middle Ages might have done: of things that were right, or good, or willed by God; it would have been merely absurd for either of us to use those words, for they belonged to a dismantled rung on the ascending ladder of Development. Instead, to make ourselves understood, we had both resorted, I, a student of the 'humane' sciences, and he, an old-fashioned village Imam, to the very terms that world leaders and statesmen use at great, global conferences, the universal, irresistible metaphysic of modern meaning; he had said to me, in effect: 'You ought not to do what you do, because otherwise you will not have guns and tanks and bombs.' It was the only language we had been able to discover in common.

For a while, after Khamees and 'Eid had led me back to their house, I could not bring myself to speak; I felt myself a conspirator in the betrayal of the history that had led me to Nashawy; a witness to the extermination of a world of accommodations that I had believed to be still alive, and, in some tiny measure, still retrievable.

But Khamees and his family did not let me long remain in silence. They took me back to their house, and after 'Eid had repeated the story of my encounter with Imam Ibrahim, Khamees turned to me, laughing, and said: 'Do not be upset, ya doktór. Forget about all those guns and things. I'll tell you what: I'll come to visit you in your country, even though I've never been anywhere. When you leave, I'll come with you; I'll come all the way to India.'

He began to scratch his head, thinking hard, and then he added: 'But if I die there you must remember to bury me.'

AMITAVA KUMAR

Flight

The Indian writer Rabindranath Tagore flew in a plane in 1932. He had awoken at three-thirty in the dark morning and was in the air at four. Tagore was travelling in what was then called Persia; at half-past eight the plane reached Bushire. 'Now comes an age in which man has lifted the burdens of earth into the air,' the writer noted in his travel diary. The achievement of flight did not always promise freedom for Tagore. On the contrary, he felt that the airplane was not in harmony with the wind. It roared like an animal in rage. A plane in flight suggested very strongly that human conflict had been raised from the level of the mundane world into the heavenly skies above.

Tagore had been awarded the Nobel Prize in literature in 1913 for his book of poems, *Gitanjali*. The thought that the earth lost its hold on man when he flew into the sky was not the result of poetic fancy. A few paragraphs later in his travelogue, Tagore had supplied the context for his thoughts. 'A British air force is stationed at Baghdad,' he wrote. 'Its Christian chaplain informs me that they are engaged in bombing operations on some Sheikh villages.'

The fields, ponds, and rivers of his childhood bound Tagore to the earth and its beauty. To fly was to lose this contact with the earth. Only the sense of sight remained for the one who was in the air, and it gave man the disease of aloofness. For Tagore, the man in the plane raining bombs below could not even in good faith ask himself who is kin and

This extract is taken from *Bombay-London-New York*, published by Routledge and Penguin Books India, 2002.

who is a stranger: he has put himself in a place from where he is unable to be aware of the difference and to judge accordingly. 'The men, women and children done to death there,' wrote Tagore, 'meet their fate by a decree from the stratosphere of British imperialism—which finds it easy to shower death because of its distance from its individual victims.' At the same time, the invention of the airplane impressed Tagore. He saw in the race of the inventors qualities of character like perseverance and courage. The sight of his four Dutch pilots ('immensely built, the personification of energy . . . their rude, overflowing health, bequeathed by generations brought up on nourishing food') evoked admiration and the thought that his own compatriots had been deprived of food and exhausted by toil.

This picture has now changed. The descendants of those who were, in Tagore's time, the subject peoples have now for long been flying planes. They also travel in planes. This situation also incites ambivalence. The travellers are often workers migrating long distances in search of work. In fact, such travel remains a part of the fantasy in the minds of the poor. There are many in the poorer countries of the world for whom the plane in flight represents the journey that, when undertaken in the future, will take them to the promised land. In airports all over the world, one can see the migrant workers from countries like Tagore's India, waiting to be taken to another place to work.

On the morning of 11 September last year, nineteen men, in their appearance not different at all from the others who stand in the visa lines outside the embassies and consulates of rich nations in cities like Calcutta and Cairo, Karachi and Khartoum, hijacked four American jets filled with fuel and people. The suicidal acts of the hijackers also gave a perverse twist to the old story of the difficult travel to the land of plenty and promise. According to reports that were published in the days following the attacks, it was revealed that the hijackers believed that their deaths promised them entry into the garden of heaven and the ministrations of seventy virgins. We can persist with Tagore's vision of the fiery bird raining death, but his universe is already lost, the simple oppositions between the earth and the sky rendered obsolete. Those who had been chained to the earth have also learned to claw their way into the air and wreak havoc from on high. There are new stories of travel, and now terror touches all.

Salman Rushdie's novel *The Satanic Verses* opens with an explosion in the air. A jet is blown apart while in flight, and two actors tumble out, 'like titbits of tobacco from a broken old cigar.' The two men, Gibreel Farishta and Saladin Chamcha, were passengers in the jumbo jet *Bostan*, Flight AI-420. In the night air around them 'floated the debris of the soul, broken memories, sloughed-off selves, severed mother-tongues, violated privacies, untranslatable jokes, extinguished futures, lost loves, the forgotten meaning of hollow, booming words, *land*, *belonging*, *home*.' Rushdie's fictional midair explosion was based on an actual event. On 28 June 1985, Flight AI-182 burst into flames off the coast of Ireland. The plane had taken off from Toronto and Montreal; it was headed for New Delhi and Bombay via London. All 331 people on board were killed. The plane's destruction was widely believed to be the work of Sikh extremists who wanted to avenge the Indian army's assault on the Holy Temple in Amritsar. Two Indo-Canadian Sikhs were arrested by the police and charged with first-degree murder. Flight AI-182 had indeed been packed with migrants. Rushdie's catalogue of the debris from the destroyed airliner furnishes a valuable, and touching, inventory of the baggage—the load of everyday experience—that immigrants carry with them. And the play of magic realism allows the writer to introduce, amidst the destruction, the miracle of rebirth. Gibreel Farishta and Saladin Chamcha survive death, and are transformed. This is an allegory of migration. Loss renews life. As Gibreel Farishta croons, even as he falls from 29,002 feet, 'To be born again, first you have to die.'

The sweet dream of reinvention is a radical one, but reality turns out to be more intractable. Rushdie's story of the passenger floating down to a part of London is not nearly as surprising as the actual, unheralded fall from the sky of a secret passenger at the edge of the same city. According to a July 2001 report in the *Guardian*, a body was discovered in a parking lot of a department store in west London. A workman in nearby Heathrow airport had seen a figure in jeans and a black T-shirt suddenly 'plummeting from the sky like a stone'. Where was the home of this dead man who was lying in a pool formed from his own split brains? The report said that the man who had fallen to earth was Mohammed Ayaz, a twenty-one-year old stowaway who had made a desperate attempt to escape the harsh life of a peasant in his village in

Pakistan on the Afghan border. The previous night, when a British Airways jet turned around to begin taxiing at Bahrain airport in preparation for takeoff, Ayaz had apparently sprinted through the dark and climbed into the huge chambers above the wheels of the Boeing. It could not have been an easy task to find one's way into the wheel bay. The report said: 'It involves climbing 14 ft up one of the aircraft's 12 enormous wheels, then finding somewhere to crouch or cling as the plane makes its way to the end of the runway and starts its deafening engines.' At that point, the plane would have accelerated to 180 mph.

Ayaz would not have known this, though one cannot be sure, but the undercarriage compartment 'has no oxygen, no heating and no pressure'. Within minutes, the temperature around Ayaz would have dropped below freezing. The report that I have been quoting had furnished, at this point, its own sense of journalistic pathos: 'At 18,000 ft, minutes later, while passengers only a few feet away were being served gin and tonic and settling down to watch in-flight movies, Ayaz would have begun to hallucinate from lack of oxygen.' The report had then added plainly: 'At 30,000 ft, the temperature is minus 56 degrees.' When, many hours later, the plane was still a few miles away from Heathrow, the captain would have lowered the wheels of the aircraft. It was at that time, when the plane was likely to have been between 2000 and 3000 feet, that Mohammed Ayaz's lifeless body must have been delivered into the morning air.

For seven months prior to his death, Ayaz had been working as a labourer in Dubai. His family is poor, finding a meagre livelihood from farming wheat, barley, corn, and onions. The agent who had secured a way for Ayaz to go to the Gulf had demanded money in addition to the cost of travel and visa. The family had had to borrow heavily. The money that Ayaz was going to earn would allow him to repay the debts in two years. But things didn't turn out the way Ayaz had expected. In Dubai, Ayaz's employer took away his passport. The salary he received was less than one-fourth of what the agent had promised. Ayaz was able to make barely enough to buy food. Ayaz did not tell his family of his plan to cross into Bahrain or his attempt to make his way to England. Ayaz's brother, Gul Bihar, told the reporter: 'He always spoke about going to work in America or England. But they don't give visas to poor people like us.'

The report in the *Guardian* had been sent to me in the mail by a friend. I was standing outside my house when the mailman brought the letter one morning, and I read the newspaper clipping while standing on my steps. As I began reading the first few paragraphs, I thought of the opening lines from Rushdie's *Satanic Verses* quoted above. Those lines were what first came to mind. But in seconds, the mood had slipped. The pain and despair that surrounded me as I read the report took me away from the pages of celebrated fiction. In much that I have written in the past few years, I have tried to understand how Indian writing has populated the literary landscape familiar to Western readers with people who look and speak differently and who have their histories in another part of the world. The presentation of this record by Indian writers has been a great, imaginative achievement. But a dead stowaway? So much that appears in Indian fiction today, particularly in its magical realist versions, appears banal if not also meretricious, when compared to the fragmentary account that emerges from a news story of a poor youth's struggle to cross the borders that divide the rich from the poor. The textbook of 'multicultural literature' carries no words of testimony of a young man narrating what flashed through his head as he went running in the dark behind a giant airplane that was about to pick up speed on the runway. It suddenly strikes me that Mohammed Ayaz could not have foreseen his death—and that seems to me to be more and more a triumph of his imagination.

The article in the *Guardian* also said that Ayaz was not the first to fall down from the sky. In October 1996, the body of a nineteen-year-old from Delhi, Vijay Saini, had dropped out of a plane at almost the same spot. Saini's corpse lay undiscovered for three days. (Vijay Saini's brother, Pradeep, according to the report, is the only person believed to have survived such a journey. The article said that the man was found at Heathrow 'in a disorientated state shortly after a flight from Delhi landed.') Then, two years later, a couple drinking in a pub in nearby Marlborough had seen another man tumble out of the sky. That body was never discovered. The police believe that it might have fallen in a reservoir. 'The undercarriage is always lowered at the same point, that is why they are falling at the same place,' an official told the *Guardian*. 'But it's an almost uncanny coincidence—these people fly right across the world in this way from different places, and they all end up in a car park in Richmond. If there are any more bodies to fall, that's where they will fall.' The West rushes up to meet the migrant, not as the promised land but, instead, a parking lot that becomes for him a desolate, temporary graveyard.

On 11 September bodies fell from the top floors of the north tower of the World Trade Centre. One writer, watching from the street below, wrote 'it looked like a desperate ballet: some seemed to be flying, their arms sweeping gracefully as they picked up speed. Others tumbled and some just dropped, rigid, all the way down.' As I reflect on that ghastly scene, months after it occurred, I find myself mentally moving Mohammed Ayaz from a parking lot in west London to the Twin Towers. He could have been one among the many migrant workers, dishwashers, messengers, cleaners, and restaurant help who perished on that day. But it doesn't work. I see him again and again in the wheelbay of the airplane. That thought won't go away. I also realize that I am perturbed by the thought that the hijackings and the mayhem that followed should erase from public consciousness the presence of the other illegal passenger, the humble stowaway, and stretching behind him, the memory of a whole history of dispossession. The sad truth is that the stowaway is not alone. Hidden behind that figure are the untold millions in countries like India or Pakistan who dream of a different future. Often, these young men and women have been turned into migrants in their own land because of poverty, or famines, or wars waged by others in the fields where their families have toiled for generations. How removed is the pathos of the stowaway from the rage of the hijacker?

The body falling out of the sky is the other and silent half of the story of international travel and tourism. We are reminded that not everyone crosses borders alive, despite the cheerful acceptance of globalization by many governments of the world. Standing near his son's unmarked grave, a mound of brown earth ringed by stones and covered with a plastic sheet, Mohammed Ayaz's father said, 'My son was as strong as four men but he died in search of bread.'

I can try to imagine the dreams that come to the stowaway when he begins to drift into sleep despite the cold and the noise in his shuddering cage. But these would be speculations. The stowaway will not share his secrets with the writer. It is impossible for me to know if the stowaway is nostalgic for the fields in his village and the familiar sunshine on the wall of his house. He had wanted to leave them behind. The plane is carrying him into the future. He tells himself that he can bear hunger for a long time. He is a quick learner. Once he has his feet on the ground he will find a way to earn money soon. These are the thoughts that I surround the stowaway with, as if he were, in reality, trapped inside the darkness in my head. It is because I am telling myself over and over that he does not feel any pain. He feels light-headed. He is not fleeing anything anymore. He is flying.

EPILOGUE

PANKAJ MISHRA

There's No Place Like Home

I spent much of my twenties in a little Himachali village north of
Shimla called Mashobra. It was a serene and fulfilling time; and like
most good things in life it came about with a minimum of fuss, with
no anticipation or planning.

I had gone to Shimla in the spring of 1992 in order to find a cottage
I could rent cheaply for a few summers. For the first couple of days,
a lethargic estate agent showed me around a few sunless houses with
damp cement walls, and it became clear that the silence and seclusion
I associated with living in the mountains weren't to be found in the
city's aggressive favela-like squalor. I had given up on Shimla; and that
morning, when I took the bus to what had been described as a 'nice
picnic spot' in my guidebook, I was hoping only to kill some time
before taking the train back to Delhi.

The half-empty Himachal Roadways bus never stopped groaning,
as it travelled through the broad open valley that slumbered peacefully
in the pale sunshine. After about half an hour, we were surrounded by
damp pine trees, and didn't regain our freedom for some time.
Miniature mountain ranges of snow sat muddied beside the rutted
road; at tea shacks in dark little clearings, men in woollen rags hunched
over pine cone fires.

The bus left the highway, stuttered down a steep road cramped by
tottering houses of wood and tin, and then abruptly stopped. The
driver killed the ailing engine, and everyone got out.

I was the last to leave. After the warm pungent smells of the bus,
the cold came as a little shock. I saw that I was on a long ridge, facing

a vast abyss filled with the purest blue air. The overall view, extending far to the east, was clear and quite spectacular: a craggy row of white mountain peaks, watching over, along with its minor underlings, the layers and layers of hills and ridges, a deep wooded valley.

The cliché fantasy broke with renewed force into my mind: wouldn't it be wonderful, I thought, to live here? I wondered if I should ask someone about places to rent. But the bus had emptied fast—I had been the only tourist on it—and there was no one around. It was then that I noticed the red tin roof of a largish house, and the steep spiralling dirt path that seemed to lead towards it.

The house was indeed big and handsome, if in an old-fashioned, unostentatious way—it had been built, I later learnt, in the early seventies, when wood was plentiful and cheap. Flower pots with peonies hung from the eaves; on the wide sunny porch, some red chillies lay quietly drying on a bright yellow sheet.

A window on the second floor was open; so was the main door that opened, I could see, on to a wooden staircase. I knocked and then heard the thump of bare feet on the floor. Someone appeared in the second floor window: a boy. I tried to explain what I was looking for. He disappeared and then a little later Mr Sharma came down the stairs.

He was a tall man, and seemed even taller in his Fez cap, which I didn't see much as the years passed, and the air of sombre dignity it gave Mr Sharma deepened by itself, became an air of mourning.

I told Mr Sharma, a bit awkwardly, that I was a student from Delhi, had spent two summers in Mussoorie and was now looking for a place in the mountains where I could read and write for a few years.

Mr Sharma gazed uncertainly at me for a moment, and then said that he would show me a cottage he had just built.

We walked through an orchard—I didn't know then that these were apple and cherry and peach trees—and came to a narrow spur at the corner of the hill. It was here that a small cottage stood, directly above a cowshed and what looked like storage rooms for fodder.

It was just about functional: there were altogether three rooms, built in no particular order or design, but plonked next to each other; a bathroom and kitchen had been tacked on to them almost as an afterthought. The rooms were still full of the aroma of wood shavings—

it stayed for many months until pushed out in October that year by the fragrance of freshly plucked apples stored underneath.

It was the balcony, however, that held me. It had the same view I had seen as I came out of the bus—the valley and the sky locked in a trance so private that you could only watch and be still yourself. In my mind's eye, I could already see myself sitting there on long evenings and gazing at the darkening world.

To my surprise, Mr Sharma asked for only Rs 1000 per month. He said that he too had come to Mashobra many years ago, wanting to read and write. His father had set up the first Sanskrit college in Shimla; he himself published a magazine in Sanskrit. He said he hadn't built the cottage to make money; it was meant to host needy scholars like myself.

I felt uncomfortable with being called a 'scholar': I had two mediocre degrees in Commerce and English; I hadn't written anything more than a few ill-considered reviews; I had barely any idea of what I could write about. But I didn't correct Mr Sharma; I did not wish to disappoint him. I had lived far more precariously in Mussoorie, at boarding houses run by Christian missionaries who saw me as a potential convert, who accosted me on my evening walks and wished to know the state of my soul. As I saw it, I was closer to being a scholar than a Christian.

And then it didn't really matter after I moved to Mashobra—just a few days after my first visit—and began to look like, with all my books and my steady absorption in them, a scholar of sorts.

I was awakened very early in the morning, the sun bullying its way even through the thick coarse-textured blue curtains of my window. The day stretched long and somewhat emptily, even though I went to bed babyishly early, at around 9 p.m., by which time the whole village was already asleep. I read all morning and then walked up the hill for lunch at a dhaba called Montu. It was run by a hospitable Punjabi couple from the Kangra valley who lived in two low-roofed rooms at the back, curtained off from the dhaba with a torn cotton sari. I seemed to be their only customer at lunch: I sat alone on the wooden bench, under the outdated calendar with pictures of Shiva's exploits, and read the censorious articles in *Punjab Kesari* about masturbation (bad for eyesight) and blue jeans (bad for blood circulation), while

Neeraj, the couple's young son, kept bringing in warm chapattis on a small aluminium plate.

The food was unremarkable; the menu, unchanging. There was frequently a lot of something called 'mixed dal', which was all people could afford by way of dal in those days of post-liberalization inflation. But Neeraj asked hopefully each time if I had found the food satisfactory, and I had to lie.

On the way back I stopped at the post office, a large dusty room with a disused telephone booth and an old damaged clock. There usually wasn't much mail for me; but the ageing postman was always grateful to give some for my landlords and save himself the steep walk to and from the house. I, in turn, would hand the mail to Mr Sharma's mother who sat knitting at the open second floor window. She would sit there from late morning, all through the long drowsy afternoons until the sun disappeared behind the hills to the west, when the shadows glided swiftly across the orchard and the valley, and the soft golden peaks in the distance seemed to hold, briefly, all the light in the world.

The days acquired a rhythm; began to pass. The Sharmas sensed my mood and left me undisturbed, except on early mornings when Mr Sharma's mother would send around a plate of aloo parathas and a steel tumbler with steaming chai.

The Sharmas themselves lived quiet if disciplined lives, except when a special occasion—a festival, a shradh, or a yagna—brought the scattered family together in a happy whirl of silk chunnis, crying babies, and sizzling puris (some of which came my way). Much of their time went into tending the fruit trees and the cows. Mr Sharma's father, Panditji, a sprightly octogenerian, was also known as an astrologer; people from places as far off as Chandigarh came to consult him. And each month, Mr Sharma brought out a Sanskrit magazine, *Divyajyoti*, from an antique printing press kept in one of the dark rooms just below my cottage.

Mr Sharma told me that it had a circulation of 500 copies, and it went out to Sanskrit colleges and institutions. He wrote most of the magazine himself during the first half of the month—articles on social and political issues—and brought the loose pages to the press, smiling awkwardly when I passed him on the narrow path through the orchard.

For the second half of the month, Daulatram, the big round-faced jovial printer and handyman, would laboriously hand-typeset the longhand version, a lonely figure in a corner of the dark room messy with wooden galley trays and metal sticks: the tips of his fingers were stained black when he came up to my cottage to replace a fuse, or to offer some peaches. A week before the fifteenth of each month, the issue would be printed. The press would begin to hum loudly as Daulatram turned on the power, and then after an uncertain staccato start, ease into a regular beat, its rhythms as peculiarly soothing as that of a train at night. Then, on the morning of the fifteenth, Daulatram would jauntily walk up the hill to the post office, holding the finished copies in a small bundle under his giant arm.

My association with the Sharmas gave me a certain status in the village. Strangers said 'namaste' as they passed me on the road; the dukaandaars, idle behind open sackfuls of rajma and channa and rice, were attentive, eager to talk, and offer me gossip about panchayat politics. But I was shy with them. I did not want to get too involved in the life of the village, or with anything that took me away for too long from reading and writing and the silence of the valley.

I was grateful for the lack of middle-class people in the village; it would have been more difficult to avoid them. The owner of the small fruit juice factory, a certain Mrs Jain, rarely left Delhi, and left most of the management to an old Gurkha. I did see once or twice the retired colonel who lived in a strange looking house which I subsequently realized had been modelled on the semi-detached houses of England. He made mushroom pickles, and sold them in jars of Kisan jam that were placed in neat rows on a rickety table underneath a fading beach umbrella in his front lawn.

There were other old houses, built during British times, and never properly possessed by their later owners. One of these, I heard, belonged to Waheeda Rahman, although I never saw her in Mashobra, never saw the chains taken off the iron gates to her house. One summer, the gates were painted over with black. I thought then that she might be on her way. But weeks went past; the monsoons came; the paint began to peel off and reveal the rust underneath; and the tufts of wild grass covered the cobbled driveway to the house.

The bells on the old church that loomed over the village were silent on Sunday mornings, until the time the local diocese set up a drug-rehabilitation programme there, when trendy-looking young men from Assam and Meghalaya appeared in the kiraana dukaan with unusual demands for Maggi soup; and you heard, passing below the church, the soft guitar chords of songs by John Denver and Simon and Garfunkel.

The summer months saw a few bored-looking tourists in the village. They didn't stay for more than an hour or two; there was little to hold them: most people, I had heard, came to Shimla for the promenades on the Mall, idlis and softies at Baljis, and the video games parlours.

When I came to live in Mashobra, its first big hotel called 'The Gables' had just come up. I went there occasionally, when wearied by Montu's unchanging fare. The vast panelled lobby and giant paintings of durbars and banquets could be unsettling after the dusty shabbiness of the village. The menial staff consisted of villagers who were always embarrassed to be found out in their Raj-style cummerbunds and tunics. Conversation with them was always strained in that setting, the stylish young manager from Sector 17, Chandigarh, watching us warily from behind the reception counter. I was always relieved when the time came to pay the bill and get out of there.

Another tourism venture began to come up towards the east of the village, in a hamlet called Daojidhar, where fluoroscent-bright tents appeared one day on a grassy spur. I often went walking there; the views of the snows and the valleys were more extensive from that side of the hill, beyond which lay Kufri and Wildflower Hall, the house Kitchener, the C-in-C of the British Indian army, had lived in. One evening, I met the entrepreneur. He was from Shimla, and restless with plans. Shimla was dead, he declared; it had been killed by tourism. Mashobra could be a wonderful alternative to those who loved quiet places in the hills.

He had had partial success, I think, with backpacking students. On cool summer nights, I saw bonfires on his property, and heard sounds of singing: once again, college-festival favourites. But the summer remained serene for the rest of the village. The afternoons were particularly still, for the inhabitants found the thirty degree centigrade heat excessive. Maruti vans loaded with tourists and blaring Hindi songs would arrive at the spot where I had my first glimpse of the valley and then hurtle off to Craignano, two miles north, where an Italian adventurer had built a house in the mid-nineteenth century. Meanwhile, the kiraana dukaans remained closed, the men retired for siestas behind wooden multi-hinged shutters covered over with faded photos of Hema Malini endorsing Lux beauty soap, and Dara Singh weighing in for Milkfood ghee.

The village looked even more withdrawn during the monsoons, when some shops didn't open at all for days on end, the empty road offered a hundred small and big muddy mirrors, and the damp drew the map of the former Soviet Union on the white walls of The Gables. It rained heavily and almost constantly, but you got used to it quite fast—so much so that on nights when the drumming on the tin roof finally ceased and the thousand nameless creatures in the forest took up an eerie chant, I would wake up, feeling a bit desolate, and only renewed rain could then send me back to sleep.

The day was a grey blur; stray clouds kept sneaking into the house; you couldn't see more than a feet or two ahead. The sun would timidly break through occasionally, and then the rain-battered roof hurriedly tried to dry itself and cracked its joints in short sharp impatient bursts.

The rain abruptly ceased in mid-September. It was rarely overcast again before the first snow of the winter; and it was the best time of the year, the present, as well as the future, brimful of bright clear days. The apples were lazily picked; the corn cobs laid out on the roofs; and the long grass cut and patiently stacked into little igloos which were sunburnt blonde in a few weeks.

On autumn afternoons, it was chilly inside the house, and I lay on the grassy platform above my cottage. I smelt the dew-damp earth, gazed into the deep blue endless sky, which faded just above the snow-capped peaks, and felt the blankness that I was beginning to recognize as part of being happy and content.

Such luck! I felt blessed, but also anxious. I hadn't signed a lease with the Sharmas. I depended on their goodwill, but it could run out any moment. Even after many years in Mashobra I couldn't quite believe in my good fortune; never ceased feeling the fragility of my claim upon the place; and I returned to Mashobra at the end of each winter burdened with a grim sense of foreboding, my imagination hectic with scenarios of rejection and disappointment.

There were other, related insecurities. Mr Sharma had seen in me a needy scholar; he wasn't entirely wrong. I wasn't really a scholar but I was certainly needy—not so much for money, the lack of which didn't preoccupy me as much as my desire to write, a desire that I felt I had no choice but to fulfil, but which seemed impossible to realize until I knew what writing was all about.

I thought I would find out by reading more books in Mashobra; but it didn't work that way. I felt dwarfed by many of the books I read; whatever skill and intelligence I managed to see in them seemed beyond my capabilities; and it didn't help that I was trying to assess them in print. Reviewing is and should feel like a fraudulent activity until you have done at least some good writing of your own; and I was troubled by the ease with which my callow glib judgements travelled into the world. I felt I could go on churning out these 800 word reviews and remain as clueless as before. I tried my hand at a couple of novels; but I quickly lost momentum after the energetic starts.

Then, one afternoon, when I hadn't gone out for lunch, the postman brought a letter from a publisher in Delhi. He had seen my reviews and he now wanted to know if I was interested in writing a travel book. I wrote back, proposing a book on small towns—somewhat rashly, since I disliked even the trip I had to make to Shimla once a month.

But the book was an opportunity to redeem at least partially all the promises I had made to myself; and for five months I travelled across small-town India. During that long absence, I never really stopped missing my life in Mashobra, never stopped wishing that I was in my cottage instead of the grim dhaba-hotel full of echoing TV noises where I usually found myself at the end of a day's journey.

It accounted for the impatient, frequently intolerant tone of the book I wrote, working flat out in Mashobra for three months. I barely looked at it again after I sent it off to the publishers. I went out of my way to avoid reading the reviews.

As it turned out, the book was noticed. The postman suddenly had more mail for me. One of the letters asked me if I was interested in a job in publishing. I should have said no. I had spent too much time by myself; I could no longer work in an office. But I was seduced by publishing's glamorous image.

And the decision exposed me to many more worlds and people than I had known in Mashobra. I travelled to England and America. My desires began to change, to become more complicated, until the point where I couldn't quite recognize them as mine. They involved me with more and more people; kept me out of Mashobra for long stretches, and took me back there only for very brief periods.

On one of these short trips I learnt that Mr Sharma's mother had died the previous week. Mr Sharma and his father had just returned from immersing her ashes in the Ganges at Hardwar. The next issue of *Divyajyoti* was dedicated to her memory. The cover had a photograph of her, taken one bright summer afternoon from my camera. Inside, there were tributes from her son, daughters, sons-in-law and other people whose lives she had touched, even altered, in small but significant ways. It made you see how much solid endeavour and achievement even a restricted life as hers could contain.

There were other losses. The entrepreneur at Daojidhar died suddenly. The brightly-hued tents disappeared; tall wild grass grew in their place; no excited singing voices drifted in from the east anymore. Wildflower Hall was burned down in one of the mysterious fires that had claimed many old buildings in Shimla. I went to see the charred ruins. The flower beds still bloomed in the blackened lawns and tourists in Himachali folk-dress posed for pictures amidst them.

The Sharmas' big house now felt oddly empty. The second floor window, where Mr Sharma's mother had sat on sunny afternoons, lay open as before, but the new void there came as a pang each time I walked past it. I noticed grief beginning to work upon Mr Sharma's face; deepening the melancholy in his eyes; lining his mouth.

It was a difficult time for me. The publishing job had ended badly; and I hadn't known what to do for some time. I saw myself drifting, and felt powerless before the fact. It was really out of boredom and confusion that one day a stray memory of an earlier time in Benares came to me.

I started to write about it. The piece went through a couple of drafts before being published. It found appreciative readers; and then grew, in my mind, into a novel. I went back one summer to Mashobra to write it, and had new reasons to feel grateful for the silence and the solitude that I had come almost to take for granted.

It has been two and a half years since then. My life has changed even more. I feel much less insecure as a writer. I travel a lot, mostly for work. It has become harder to spend time in Mashobra. I once thought of it as home; I am no longer so sure what or where home is. The cottage is still there, with my books and music. But I really can't go back for too long, and I can't be too sentimental about it. The longings and aspirations that gave point and urgency to my time in Mashobra have been partly realized; they now take me further away from it, and into the larger world.

In any case, time hasn't quite stood still for Mashobra. Places as much as people can be unfaithful. My slow betrayal of Mashobra has been accompanied by its own keen embrace of the modern world. You can buy Maggi soup as well as Tropicana orange juice in the jazzed-up kiraana dukaans. The Gables has a new wing. New buildings, some of them hotels, have come up in the vicinity of my cottage; the seclusion I so cherished, that made possible all my reading and writing, is gone.

This at least is what I tell myself—if not always convincingly. On days when I am far away from Mashobra, in very different landscapes, I only have to see a patch of mellow light on a lawn, only have to feel a fresh bracing quality in the air, or hear the rain being fierce with a roof, to know that I want to be back, and never leave; and it's no use reminding myself then that the senses—those semi-magical faculties of sight, smell, hearing—hold not only your most truthful memories but also your most hopeless desires.

NOTES ON CONTRIBUTORS

NIRAD C. CHAUDHURI's first book, *The Autobiography of an Unknown Indian* was followed by many others, including *The Continent of Circe*, for which he won the Duff Cooper Memorial Prize, *Thy Hand Great Anarch*, and *Three Horsemen of the New Apocalypse*.

SALMAN RUSHDIE is the author of the novels *Grimus*, *Midnight's Children* (winner of the 'Booker of Bookers'), *Shame*, *The Satanic Verses*, *Haroun and the Sea of Stories, East, West*, *The Moor's Last Sigh*, *The Ground Beneath Her Feet* and *Fury*. He also wrote *The Jaguar Smile: A Nicaraguan Journey* and *Imaginary Homelands*, a collection of his essays and criticism. His most recent collection of essays is titled *Step Across This Line*.

AMITAV GHOSH has been a journalist and is the author of *The Circle of Reason*, *The Shadow Lines* (Sahitya Akademi Award, 1990), *In an Antique Land*, *The Calcutta Chromosome*, *Dancing in Cambodia, At Large in Burma* and *The Glass Palace*. A selection of his prose pieces has been published in *The Imam and the Indian*. He currently holds the post of Distinguished Professor in the Department of Comparative Literature, Queens College, City University of New York.

NISSIM EZEKIEL has been an editor of the journal 'PEN' for several years and a guiding force of the Poetry Circle in Bombay. He has published several collections of poetry including *A Time to Change*, *Sixty Poems, The Third, The Unfinished Man, The Exact Name, Three Plays* and *Snakeskin and Other Poems*, translations from the Marathi of Indira Sant, and *Hymns in Darkness*.

DEAN MAHOMED was the author of the first book ever written and published by an Indian in English. He served in the East India Company's Bengal Army for fifteen years. In 1784, Mahomed emigrated to Ireland and married an Anglo-Irish woman. He also became a Protestant. Later, in Brighton, he established 'Mahomed's Baths' where he himself served as 'Shampooing Surgeon'. (The word 'shampoo' comes from the Hindustani *champi* for 'pressing the head'.) His book, *The Travels of Dean Mahomet* (1794) was based on his experiences in the colonial army.

SUNITY DEVEE was the daughter of Keshub Chunder Sen, leader of the Brahmo Samaj in the nineteenth century. In 1878 she married the English-educated Maharaja Nripendra Narayan, of Cooch Behar, both eventually becoming favourites of the courts of Victoria and later of Edward. Sunity Devee was influential in women's reform movements during both her husband's and their son's reigns. She died in 1932 at the age of 68.

RABINDRANATH TAGORE, Nobel Laureate for Literature (1913), wrote successfully in all literary genres. Among his fifty odd volumes of poetry are *Manasi*, *Sonar Tari*, *Gitanjali: Song Offerings*, *Gitimalya* and *Balaka*. Tagore's major plays are *Raja*, *Dakghar*, *Achalayatan*, *Muktadhara* and *Raktakarabi*. He is the author of several volumes of short stories and a number of novels, among them *Gora*, *Ghare-Baire* and *Yogayog*. Besides these, he wrote musical dramas, dance dramas, essays of all types, travel diaries and two autobiographies. Tagore also left numerous drawings and paintings, and songs for which he wrote the music himself.

MOHANDAS KARAMCHAND GANDHI, known as the Mahatma, was an Indian nationalist leader. He advocated a policy of non-violent non-cooperation to achieve independence from colonial rule. His writings include *An Autobiography or The Stories of My Experiments with Truth*, *Key to Health*, *Hind Swaraj, or Indian Home Rule* and *Satyagraha in South Africa*.

SAROJINI NAIDU was the first Indian woman to be elected president of the Indian National Congress and to be appointed a state governor. She published several books of poetry—*The Golden Threshhold*, *The Bird of Time* and *The Broken Wing*—all in English, and was elected to the Royal Society of Literature.

SUBHAS CHANDRA BOSE was born in Cuttack and educated at the universities of Calcutta and Cambridge. He left a career in the Indian civil service to fight for India's independence. Under his leadership the Indian National Army fought against the British on the Burma-India frontier until 1945. He was killed in a plane crash while fleeing to Japan in August of that year.

JAWAHARLAL NEHRU was Indian nationalist leader and statesman and the first prime minister (1947–64) of independent India. His writings include his letters to his daughter Indira Gandhi published under the title *Glimpses of World History*, *Letters to Chief Ministers* (five volumes), and an autobiography published in the US titled *Toward Freedom*. His addresses and articles have been published under the titles *The Unity of India* and *Independence and After*.

MULK RAJ ANAND was a pioneer of Indian writing in English and a founding member of the Progressive Writers' Association, a national level organization that wielded considerable influence during India's freedom struggle and beyond. In England, Anand interacted with the likes of E.M. Forster, Herbert Read, George Orwell and members of the Bloomsbury group and wrote short reviews in T.S. Eliot's *Criterion* magazine. During World War II, he worked for the BBC's films division as a broadcaster and scriptwriter. He is the author of *Untouchable, Coolie, Two Leaves and a Bud, The Village, Across the Black Waters, The Sword and the Sickle, Private Life of an Indian Prince, Confessions of a Lover* and *The Bubble*. He was also the recipient of the Sahitya Akademi Award (1972) and the title of Padma Bhushan by the Government of India (1974).

QURRATULAIN HYDER is one of the leading writers of Urdu fiction in India and a Fellow of the Sahitya Akademi. A prolific writer, she has so far written some twelve novels and novellas, including *Aag Ka Darya* (*River of Fire*) and *Aakhir-e-Shab ke Hamsafar* (*Travellers Unto the Night*), for which she received the Jnanpith Award in 1989. She has also published four collections of short stories and has translated a number of classics. A recipient of the Sahitya Akademi Award (1967) and the Ghalib Award (1985), she was conferred the honorific title of Padma Shri by the Government of India for her outstanding contribution to Urdu literature.

R. K. NARAYAN's first novel, *Swami and Friends*, was published in 1935. His other novels include *The Bachelor of Arts, The Dark Room, The English*

Teacher, Waiting for the Mahatma, The Guide (winner of the Sahitya Akademi Award, 1958), *The Man-eater of Malgudi, The Painter of Signs, Talkative Man* and *The World of Nagaraj.* He has also published six collections of short stories including *A Horse and Two Goats, An Astrologer's Day and Other Stories, Malgudi Days* and *Under the Banyan Tree,* two travel books (*My Dateless Diary* and *The Emerald Route*), and five collections of essays (*Next Sunday, Reluctant Guru, A Writer's Nightmare, A Story-teller's World* and *Salt and Sawdust*), and a memoir, *My Days.* His translations of Indian epics and myths (*The Ramayana, The Mahabharata* and *Gods, Demons and Others*) are well-known. R.K. Narayan was awarded the A.C. Benson medal by the Royal Society of Literature in 1980 and was made an Honorary Member of the American Academy and Institute of Arts and Letters. In 2000 the Government of India conferred on him the title of Padma Vibhushan. He died in May 2001.

DOM MORAES published his first book of poems, *A Beginning,* in London in 1957 and won the Hawthornden Prize, at that time the most coveted literary award in England, for it the very next year. His other books of poetry include *Poems* (Autumn Choice of the Poetry Book Society, 1960), *John Nobody, Absences* and *Serendip.* He has also written twenty-three prose books including *Answered by Flutes, Out of God's Oven,* and a biography, *Mrs Gandhi.* He became the editor of the *Asia Magazine* in 1971 and joined the UN in 1976.

FARRUKH DHONDY is a writer and columnist living in England. He is the author of *East End at Your Feet* and *Come to Mecca* (both winners of the Other Award), *Poona Company, Bombay Duck* (shortlisted for the Whitbread Award, 1990), *C.L.R. James: A Life,* and his collection of short stories *Trip Trap.* He has written widely for television and stage including the comedies *No Problem* and *Tandoori Nights* for Channel Four and was a recipient of the Samuel Beckett Award for a series of six plays for BBC TV.

VED MEHTA has had a distinguished career as a staff writer for the *New Yorker* during which he received two Guggenheim Fellowships and a MacArthur Prize Fellowship. He is the author of *Face to Face,* an autobiography, *Walking the Indian Streets, Portrait of India, Fly and the Fly Bottle, John is Easy to Please: Encounter with the Written and Spoken Word, Rajiv Gandhi and Rama's Kingdom* and *Remembering Mr Shawn's New Yorker.* His other autobiographical writings include *The Ledge between the Streams*, *Sound Shadows of the New World* and *The Stolen Light*, now collectively titled *Continents of Exile*.

A.K. RAMANUJAN, poet, translator and folklorist, wrote four volumes of verse in English—*The Striders, Relations, Second Sight* and *The Black Hen*. He was awarded the honorific title Padma Shri by the Government of India in 1976 and received the MacArthur Prize Fellowship in 1983. His pioneering translations of ancient Tamil and Kannada poetry into modern English are well known. His translations include *Interior Landscapes: Love Poems from a Classical Tamil Anthology*, *Speaking of Siva*, *Hymns for the Drowning* and *A Flowering Tree and Other Oral Tales from India*. A. K. Ramanujan died in 1993.

SIR V.S. NAIPAUL is the author of a number of novels including *The Mystic Masseur* (John Llewelyn Rhys Memorial Prize, 1957), *The Suffrage of Elvira*, *Miguel Street* (Somerset Maugham Award, 1959), *A House for Mr Biswas*, *Mr Stone and the Knight's Companion* (Hawthornden Award, 1963), *The Mimic Men* (W.H. Smith Award, 1968), *In a Free State* (Booker Prize, 1971), *The Enigma of Arrival*, *Reading and Writing: A Personal Account* and *Half a Life*. He has also written several travel books—*The Return of Eva Peron*, *An Area of Darkness*, *Among the Believers: An Islamic Journey*, *A Turn in the South* and *India: A Million Mutinies Now*. He was awarded the Nobel Prize for Literature in 2001.

BHARATI MUKHERJEE is a winner of the National Book Critics Award for fiction. She is the author of *The Tiger's Daughter*, *Wife*, *An Invisible Woman*, *Darkness*, *The Middleman and Other Stories*, *Jasmine*, *The Holder of the World* and *Leave It to Me*. She is currently a professor of English at the University of California, Berkeley.

HANIF KUREISHI is the author of *The Buddha of Suburbia*, which won the Whitbread Book of the Year Award for the 'first novel' category, *The Black Album*, *Intimacy*, *Gabriel's Gift* and two collections of short stories, *Love in a Blue Time* and *Midnight All Day*. He wrote the screenplays for *My Beautiful Laundrette*, which was awarded Best Screenplay award from the New York Film Critics Circle, and *Sammy and Rosie Get Laid*.

ABRAHAM VERGHESE is an acclaimed non-fiction writer and a physician. He is the author of *My Own Country* and *The Tennis Partner*. His writing has appeared in *The New Yorker, Granta, The North American Review*, and many medical journals including the *Annals of Internal Medicine* and *American Journal of Medicine*. He lives in the US.

AMIT CHAUDHURI's novels include *A Strange and Sublime Address, Afternoon Raag, Freedom Song* and *A New World*. He has also edited *The Picador Book of Modern Indian Literature*. He won first prize in the Betty Trask Awards, the Commonwealth Writers Prize for Best First Book (Eurasia), the Encore Prize for Best Second Novel, the Southern Arts Literature Prize and the *LA Times* Book Prize for Fiction (2000).

MEERA SYAL is the author of *Anita and Me* (which won the Betty Trask Awards and was shortlisted for the 1996 Guardian Fiction Award) and *Life Isn't All Ha Ha Hee Hee*. She has written the screenplays for *My Sister Wife* and *Bhaji on the Beach*. She co-writes and is a cast member of the popular BBC TV comedy series *Goodness Gracious Me*.

ANURAG MATHUR is a journalist in the electronic and print media. He is the author of *The Inscrutable Americans, Scenes from an Executive Life* and *Making the Minister Smile*.

ANITA DESAI is the author of eight novels, including the internationally acclaimed *Clear Light of Day, In Custody, Fasting, Feasting*, all three finalists for the Booker Prize, and *Journey to Ithaca*. She won the Winifred Holtby Prize from the Royal Society of Literature for her novel *Fire on the Mountain* and the Guardian Award for Children's Literature for *Village by the Sea*. She currently teaches creative writing at MIT, Boston.

AGHA SHAHID ALI's volumes of poetry include *Bone Sculpture, In Memory of Begum Akhtar and Other Poems, The Half-Inch Himalayas, A Walk Through the Yellow Pages, A Nostalgist's Map of America, The Beloved Witness: Selected Poems, The Country Without a Post Office, Rooms Are Never Finished* and *Call Me Ishmael Tonight: A Book of Ghazals*. He is also the author of *T.S. Eliot as Editor*, translator of *The Rebel's Silhouette: Selected Poems by Faiz Ahmed Faiz*, and editor of *Ravishing Disunities: Real Ghazals in English*. He died in April 2001.

ROHINTON MISTRY is the author of *Swimming Lessons and Other Stories from Firozsha Baag, Such a Long Journey* (Commonwealth Writers Prize for Best Book of the Year, 1991), *A Fine Balance* (Commonwealth Writers Prize,

Royal Society of Literature's Winifred Holtby Prize and a Booker Prize finalist). His most recent novel is entitled *Family Matters* and was shortlisted for the Booker Prize in 2002.

PANKAJ MISHRA is the author of a travel book, *Butter Chicken in Ludhiana*, and a novel, *The Romantics* (*LA Times* award for the Best First Novel). He is a regular contributor to the *New York Review of Books*, the *Times Literary Supplement*, the *New Statesman*, and other publications.

COPYRIGHT ACKNOWLEDGEMENTS

The editor and the publishers gratefully acknowledge the following for permission to reprint copyright material:

Prithvi N. Chaudhuri and Jaico Publishing House for the extract from *The Autobiography of an Unknown Indian* by Nirad C. Chaudhuri;

Wylie Agency, Inc. and Pantheon Books, a division of Random House, Inc. for the extract from *East, West: Stories* by Salman Rushdie, copyright © 1994 by Salman Rushdie;

Ravi Dayal Publisher for the extract from *The Shadow Lines* by Amitav Ghosh;

Oxford University Press India, New Delhi, for 'Goodbye Party for Miss Pushpa T.S.' by Nissim Ezekiel from *Ten Twentieth Century Indian Poets*, edited by R. Parthasarathy, 'Some Indian Uses of History on a Rainy Day' from *Selected Poems* by A. K. Ramanujan, and the extracts from *The First Indian Author in English* by Michael H. Fisher and *Conversations in Bloomsbury* by Mulk Raj Anand;

Bloomsbury Publishing PLC, London, for the extract from *Rabindranath Tagore, An Anthology*, edited by Krishna Dutta and Andrew Robinson;

Navajivan Trust, Ahmedabad, for the extract from *An Autobiography or The Story of my Experiments with Truth* by M.K. Gandhi;

Kali for Women, New Delhi, for the extracts from *Sarojini Naidu: Selected Letters 1890s to 1940s*, edited by Makarand Paranjape, and *River of Fire* by Qurratulain Hyder;

Netaji Research Bureau, Kolkata, for special permission to reprint Subhas Chandra Bose's letters from *Subhas Chandra Bose, An Indian Pilgrim*, edited by Sisir K. Bose and Sugata Bose;

HarperCollins Publishers India, New Delhi, for the extract from *Before Freedom: Nehru's Letters to his Sister*, edited by Nayantara Sahgal;

C. S. Chandrasekharan, Sreenivas Chandrasekharan and Bhuvaneshwari Srinivasamurthy for 'My America' by R.K. Narayan;

Serpent's Tail, London, for 'Changes of Scenery' by Dom Moraes and 'Speaking in Tongues' by Farrukh Dhondy from *Voices of the Crossing*, edited by Ferdinand Dennis and Naseem Khan;

Georges Borchardt, Inc. for 'Naturalized Citizen No. 984-5165' from *A Ved Mehta Reader*, copyright © 1998 by Ved Mehta;

Gillon Aitken Associates and the author for the extract from *The Enigma of Arrival* by V.S. Naipaul, copyright © 1987 by V.S. Naipaul;

Wylie Agency, Inc. for the extract from *The Jaguar Smile* by Salman Rushdie;

The New York Times Syndicate for 'Two Ways to Belong in America' by Bharati Mukherjee;

Rogers, Coleridge and White Ltd., 20 Powis Mews, London W11 1JN, for the extracts from *Anita and Me* by Meera Syal, copyright © by Chestwig and Flares Productions Ltd, 1996; *Life Isn't All Ha Ha Hee Hee* by Meera Syal, copyright © by Chestwig and Flares Productions Ltd, 1999; and 'Wild Women, Wild Men' by Hanif Qureishi, copyright © Hanif Kureishi, 1992, first published by *Granta 39* in Spring 1992;

Mary Evans Inc. and the author for 'The Cowpath to America' by Abraham Verghese, copyright © 1997 by Abraham Verghese, originally appeared in the *New Yorker*, all rights reserved;

A.P. Watt Ltd. on behalf of Amit Chaudhuri for the extract from *Freedom Song: Three Novels* by Amit Chaudhuri;

Rupa & Co., New Delhi, for the extract from *Inscrutable Americans* by Anurag Mathur;

Houghton Mifflin Company, New York, and Rogers, Coleridge and White Ltd., 20 Powis Mews, London W11 1JN, for the extract from *Fasting, Feasting* by Anita Desai, copyright © 1999 by Anita Desai, reproduced by permission of the author c/o Rogers, Coleridge and White Ltd., 20 Powis Mews, London W11 1JN, and Houghton Mifflin Company, all rights reserved;